GATEWAY TO YELLOWSTONE

GATEWAY TO YELLOWSTONE

The Raucous Town of Cinnabar on the Montana Frontier

Lee H. Whittlesey

TWODOT®

GUILFORD, CONNECTICUT
HELENA, MONTANA

A · TWODOT® · BOOK
An imprint of Rowman & Littlefield
Distributed by NATIONAL BOOK NETWORK

Copyright © 2015 by Lee H. Whittlesey

British Library Cataloguing in Publication Information Available

Library of Congress Cataloging-in-Publication Data Available
ISBN 978-1-4930-1066-0 (paperback)
ISBN 978-1-4930-1666-2 (e-book)

♾ ™ The paper used in this publication meets the minimum requirements of American National Standard for Information Sciences Permanence of Paper for Printed Library Materials, ANSI/NISO Z39.48-1992.

To Hugo J. Hoppe, who deserves his place in Montana history, and to his descendants Robert Moore and Darnell Jean Wills, who have long wanted to give it to him.

They're going to build a railroad,
And they're going to build it soon.

—Poem by Sarah Gassert about Cinnabar, Montana, established
1883

CONTENTS

ACKNOWLEDGMENTS

Where the creation of this book is concerned, I am as usual in debt to a fair number of people. My National Park Service supervisor at Yellowstone—Tobin Roop, who is our busy branch chief of cultural resources—is the person responsible for this book's publication because he made the enlightened decision to allow me to dust off the 1995 NPS manuscript, bring it up to date, and submit it to a publisher. It has turned out to be even more fascinating than I anticipated. My thanks also go to Bob Moore of Livingston, Montana, and Patrick Hoppe of Gardiner (the great-great grandson of Hugo J. Hoppe), both of whom are experts on the Hoppe family and who helped to identify the people in the family's 1885 "porch photo." (Bob comes to his interest in the family through his wife, Darnell Jean Hoppe Wills, whose mother was Jean Elrose Hoppe, daughter of Paul Hoppe.) Bob gave me much additional information in 2001 and 2013 about various family members who are characters in this book, and I have thoroughly enjoyed our conversations. Patrick and his mother, Patricia Ann Crossen Hoppe (1931–2014), wife of Wayne Hoppe, showed me important family materials that are in their custody, as passed down from Patrick's great-great-grandfather Hugo Hoppe.

Paul Schullery of Bozeman, Montana; Jeremy Johnston of the Buffalo Bill Historical Center in Cody, Wyoming; and Steve Mishkin of Olympia, Washington, are historians (Steve is also a lawyer) with whom I often consult about various phases of Western history and the history of Yellowstone. In this book, Paul has helped with numerous points, Jeremy was especially helpful with information about Buffalo Bill's show tryouts at Cinnabar, and Steve has given me continuing additional information about Carroll Hobart, Joseph Keeney, and other historical persons who appear here. In addition, Steve is an expert editor whose suggestions made the book markedly better, and Paul has provided a couple of historic maps that I did not have. I am grateful to all three of these men for our always stimulating discussions of Yellowstone's and regional history that keep me sharp.

Librarians, archivists, and museum professionals have been invaluable to me in producing a book that hopefully extends the accessible record. These include Colleen Curry, Anne Foster, Shawn Bawden, Bridgette Guild, Jackie Jerla, and Jessica Gerdes at the Yellowstone Heritage and Research Center of Gardiner, Montana; Kim Allen Scott at Montana State University, Bozeman; Elizabeth Watry, formerly of the Museum of the Rockies, Montana State University, and now curator of the Museum of the Mountain Man, Pinedale, Wyoming; Paul Shea and Karen Reinhart at Yellowstone Gateway Museum of Park County, Livingston, Montana; and Tamsen Hert at the University of Wyoming, Laramie.

Independent researchers have aided me as well. Dr. Judith Meyer at Missouri State University translated portions of Dr. G. M. Von Rath's 1883 Yellowstone trip from its original German. Randy Ingersoll of Gardiner, Montana, constantly keeps me on track by finding new tidbits in the massive Yellowstone bibliography, by finding rare photos and documents on the Internet, and by field checking local geographic sites for precise data. Bob Berry of Cody, Wyoming, and Paul Rubinstein of Charlottesville, Virginia, both continue to find obscure, historical photographs that open new windows to the past and are always generous in sharing their discoveries, some of which appear in this book. Long ago, my friend Donna McGiehan Stahl of Reston, Virginia, helped me research land records at Livingston and Bozeman, Montana, which have proven twenty years later to be invaluable for this project.

My reviewers are all experts in the history of the Yellowstone region: Tamsen Hert, Randy Ingersoll, Steve Mishkin, Bob Moore, Leslie Quinn, Karen Reinhart, Paul Schullery, Paul Shea, and Elizabeth "Betsy" Watry. Betsy in particular has an amazing talent for creating chapter titles and for performing editing in a way that maximizes emotional impacts in the text. Thanks to them all. Any errors that have crept into the book are my own, but these folks have saved me from making both key errors and smaller ones.

Finally, I wrote the original version of this book for the National Park Service on government time, and all present revisions were also written on government time as a function of the park's need for information about Cinnabar and of my official position of park historian at Yellowstone National Park. Hence, all proceeds from this book have been donated to the National Park Service. The book contains no internal NPS information that is otherwise not available to all members of the general public.

May you enjoy this Montana adventure!

INTRODUCTION

THE SETTING FOR UNDERSTANDING THIS BOOK

This book is about Cinnabar, Montana—a town that no longer exists—and the manner in which it served as the immediate railroad gateway for a generation of visitors to Yellowstone National Park from September 1, 1883, through June 15, 1903, and then how that land was inexorably added to Yellowstone National Park. It is also about a Montana pioneer named Hugo J. Hoppe (pronounced *hoppy*), the town's greatest believer and promoter, who was patriarch of one family trying to "make it" in the American West. As many Western towns were, Cinnabar was a raucous place, to be sure, and it was also a place whose story and legend I fell in love with shortly after I came to work in Yellowstone way back in 1969, even though I never saw the town in existence.

Cinnabar was not the first gateway to Yellowstone. That was Livingston, Montana, one year earlier. When the Northern Pacific Railroad's surveyors and land speculators arrived there in late 1882, the event not only established Livingston as a town, but it also pointed the way south for the future rails to Yellowstone National Park—rails that everyone knew would soon be built. Officials at the Northern Pacific Railroad (NPRR), based in St. Paul, Minnesota, had believed as early as 1871 that they would someday be building a line to the new park or preserve (or whatever it was to be called), which would soon be established in that remote region where Montana, Wyoming, and Idaho territories all came together.[1] None of those places was yet a state; all three were raw territories and would remain so until 1889 and 1890.

When the tracks of the NPRR actually arrived at Livingston on November 30, 1882 (the surveyors, graders, and speculators arrived earlier), the new national park was only nine years old, and there were essentially no other towns in the immediate region. To the north, Bozeman, Montana, existed, but Cinnabar and West Yellowstone did not. To the south, Jackson, Wyoming, did not exist, nor did Cody, Wyoming, to the east. Livingston had essentially existed for only a year in the form of the two hamlets of Benson's Landing and Clark City, and its new iteration was similarly small. Gardiner, Montana, existed as a tent city of less than fifty rough inhabitants, and the railroad would not reach it for almost twenty years.

Cooke City, Montana—just outside the new park's northeast corner—was barely in existence as a seasonal mining town of four to twenty-five people that would nearly vanish each winter. Thus if one wants to be technical, Cooke City was and is the only entity in the upper Yellowstone region that is older than Yellowstone National Park (and then only if you call four men with picks and shovels a "town"). To reach it, one had to go *through* the new national park. So by the time those early visitors reached Cooke City, they had already been traveling through Yellowstone Park for more than fifty miles. For sixty-five years, there was no reason to even have an official park entrance at Cooke City, because there was no effective way to reach the town except through the park. Thus Cooke City would not serve as a true gateway to the national park until the 1930s (when the road from Red Lodge, Montana, was built to it), because it was effectively cut off from the outside world.[2]

Even with no gateway towns and regardless of the fact that it was difficult to reach prior to its branch railroad, Yellowstone National Park became famous quite early. The Grand Old Park was established by Congress in 1872 and because its wonders were world class, the newspapers of the United States and Europe began publishing articles about it quickly. The *New York Times*, *New York Tribune*, *New York Herald*, *The Times* of London, and many others made the new park well known for eleven years before anyone could travel there by train. To get there in the 1870s, travelers from the east faced a long train ride to Utah Territory on the Transcontinental Railroad before they rode horses (or drove wagons) four hundred miles north through Idaho to Montana and from there turned south to reach the national park on horseback (there were as yet no wagon roads in the park). Or they could ride a steamboat up the Missouri River to Montana, where they would still face a long horseback ride across wild country to Yellowstone Park. Regardless of which route these travelers selected, they effectively had to travel north to get south, that is, they had to go through Montana Territory to ride horses south into Wyoming Territory, because mountain ranges blocked the way into Yellowstone from Wyoming and Idaho. Therefore, Yellowstone's first two entrances were its north entrance and its west entrance, both in Montana Territory. The south and east entrances to the park did not yet exist, and as mentioned, the northeast entrance at Cooke City would not be reachable directly from Montana until 1936. By 1883, when the Northern Pacific's rails reached Cinnabar, more than thirteen hundred US newspaper articles had been written about Yellowstone National Park. Those, combined with many more that were written and published in Europe, had already made Yellowstone famous the world over.[3]

Even though Yellowstone's story has been well told elsewhere, the Cinnabar story is separate but integrally related. When the national park was established, poachers, railroads, and mining interests viewed it greedily. The nineteenth-century way of seeing wilderness as empty land upon which to capitalize would need to change before these threats could be removed forever. Some of that story is told here, because through time, that philosophical change did occur in the minds of Americans. This change was one of the abstract elements that ultimately prevented our viewpoint character Hugo Hoppe's dream for Cinnabar from occurring and one which he had no way of anticipating. But it was only one such element, and the story of Cinnabar is much more complicated. The most direct factor in the town's life was the Northern Pacific Railroad.

After more than a decade of media coverage, the world was poised to actually see the magic of Yellowstone, and when the railroad arrived, that trip suddenly became possible and exciting. It seemed like everyone who could afford the ticket—from middle-class people in New York City to army generals William Tecumseh Sherman and Philip Sheridan to President Chester A. Arthur—wanted to ride the train to see Yellowstone during the first year that it was reachable by train. And when they stepped off the train in 1883, they stepped into the small town of Cinnabar, Montana Territory.[4]

1

BEFORE CINNABAR
Puzzling Out the Parcels

Bart Henderson has been working with his [labor] force on the Point of Rocks. And . . . he now has his wagon road completed up to the [Yankee Jim] canyon, where his camp is located.
—Bozeman *Avant Courier*, November 2, 1871

The trail [at Yankee Jim Canyon] led us on up the valley, *past two ranches*, from which supplies were obtained, to within a few miles of Gardiner's River.
—Captain William Ludlow, 1875

Along the north boundary of today's Yellowstone National Park, just west of present-day Gardiner, Montana, is a prolongation of that boundary that extends north of the otherwise straight, east-west park line. This seventy-six hundred acre area,[1] roughly bounded by Electric Creek and Reese Creek on its northwest and the Yellowstone River on its northeast, was not part of the original (1872) Yellowstone Park but instead was gradually added to the park during the period 1925–1941. Variously called the "Game Ranch," the "Gardiner Addition (to Yellowstone)," or the "Cinnabar triangle," this land was originally owned by private ranchers and the Northern Pacific Railroad. (A few pieces never left federal ownership.) The Cinnabar triangle also contained the small town of Cinnabar, Montana, during the period 1883–1903.

The history of this parcel is complex and convoluted, but it is also a fascinating part of the evolution of Yellowstone National Park, and it is tied irrevocably and unwaveringly to Montana. Much of its story revolves around the establishment and use of the Northern Pacific Railroad's railhead there and the town that grew up when the rails arrived. But the land history of this area began earlier with the establishment of James Henderson's ranch probably in 1871, Yellowstone National Park in 1872, and George Reese's ranch (about two miles southeast of the mouth of Reese Creek) in 1875.

THE FIRST TWO RANCHES IN THE CINNABAR TRIANGLE

James Henderson settled sometime in 1871 at the base of Sepulcher Mountain on what would become the Stephens–Keeney–Hoppe ranch in the Cinnabar triangle, and he and his brother, prospector A. Bart Henderson, used it as headquarters that fall while they were building their "Bozeman toll road." Certainly Henderson was the first settler on the Game Ranch parcel. His cabin was located southwest of the point where the Stephens Creek dirt road leaves the main "Cinnabar road" (Old Yellowstone Trail) today and probably about where the National Park Service buildings are today located at "Stephens Creek Ranch."[2]

Here we momentarily jump ahead of our settlement history to examine the Hendersons' role in an Indian battle. Little known was Stokeley Henderson, apparently another brother of James and A. Bart Henderson, who per the US Census of 1880, was living in the upper Yellowstone River country then and apparently also in 1877, because his son Stirling Henderson (age about fifteen) became a character in the battle.[3] The James Henderson ranch was the site of an Indian skirmish that occurred during the Nez Perce War of 1877. On the morning of August 31, 1877, a party of Nez Perce Indians appeared near the ranch. Young Stirling Henderson and John Werks were at the ranch house while "Uncle" Joe Brown, George Reese, and William Davis were down at the river fishing. Werks spotted the Indians, so he and Stirling took rifles and ammunition down to the others. As the Indians dismounted at the house, the five defenders ran south to some large boulders nearby. They fired on the Indians as the Nez Perce tried to drive the horses out of the corral, and that began the battle of Henderson's ranch.

When the firing began, the Indian horses stampeded, so the Indians ran behind the house and barn. The defenders stayed in position for about two hours, firing occasionally to keep the Indians from getting to their horses. Ten other Indians sat on their horses watching from a bench east of the ranch. When the whites finally quit firing and crawled back to the river, the mounted Indians followed them to fire parting shots as the ranchers crossed to the north bank of the Yellowstone in a boat. The Indians then set fire to the Henderson house, collected their horses, and started south for Mammoth Hot Springs.

Lt. Gustavus Doane and his men from Fort Ellis at Bozeman, who were southbound and just then passing Cinnabar Mountain, saw smoke from the burning ranch, spurred their mounts, and recovered nineteen horses from the fleeing Nez Perce. There were no casualties from that two-hour skirmish, but the house burned down.[4]

The Henderson ranch (we may assume the ranch house was rebuilt) continued in Henderson family hands until sometime between 1879 and 1882, when park assistant superintendent Clarence Stephens purchased it.[5] Stephens left the park and went to the ranch to live in May of 1882, after his boss, Superintendent P. W. Norris, was ousted and when it became apparent that Stephens would be replaced by a new assistant named G. L. Henderson (no relation to James and A. Bart Henderson). Stephens sold the ranch (or divided it) to area loiterers George Huston and Elias Joseph Keeney in early 1883,[6] and they in turn conveyed it to Carroll T. Hobart of the Yellowstone National Park Improvement Company in late 1883.[7]

After James Henderson, the next to settle in the Cinnabar triangle was George W. Reese (1837–1913) in April of 1875.[8] Captain William Ludlow, who passed the spot on August 13, 1875, with a military party, stated that there were only two ranches in the vicinity then (the Henderson and Reese ranches) and that from their occupants he obtained supplies.[9] George Reese was in the Yellowstone country as early as 1867, prospecting as one of the "Bear Gulch stampeders," but he appears to have wanted a more permanent homestead, because 1870s land records placed him on present Reese Creek. A water rights case, *Pisor et al. v. Reese*, was settled in his favor in 1878, and it gave him water rights to eighty inches of Reese Creek.[10] A government surveyor named Rolling Reeves who passed Reese's ranch in 1879 described it as having "a store and ferry,"[11] so it appears that Reese had no trouble getting back and forth across the

Yellowstone River. Apparently not seeing the Henderson ranch, surveyor Reeves noted that above Reese's ranch were no other cabins, except one about a mile below the mouth of Gardner River (occupant unidentified by Reeves and unknown today). George Reese's "Declaration of Ranche," made November 20, 1882, gave his initial year of settlement there as 1875 and described his homestead property as extending south from the mouth of Reese Creek for about half a mile. He would later enlarge that to the 160 acres, allowed under the Homestead Act.[12]

Reese stated in his Homestead Testimony that his house in April of 1875 was fourteen by sixteen feet in size but that he "now" (1883) had another house sixteen by thirty-two and a third one sixteen by eighteen. He stated that his land was one hundred acres fenced, with a stable, a corral, and a root house, and that he had an irrigating ditch and water rights. He stated that he had two acres of garden each year and that "last year" he had raised two acres of oats and vegetables, one acre of "tame grass," and "stock" on the land.[13]

During their long years on that land, George Reese and his sons appear to have had at least three different houses there. The first one, probably the one shown on the 1881 map of General Philip Sheridan, seems to have been farther south than the others and was probably located in present Section 17, T9S, R8E. A cabin on lower Reese Creek, probably in present Section 8, was described later by Helen Reese and existed from about 1890 to about 1950. A third house was located higher up on Reese Creek, probably in present Section 7.[14] George's sons Thomas and John J. Reese stated that fall wheat was good at Reese Creek in July of 1881 and that they had one hundred acres of oats in September.[15]

In June of 1883, George Reese sold to the "Rocky Mountain Railroad Company" (the Northern Pacific Railroad) "a piece of ground" for one hundred fifty dollars. Essentially he sold them a right of way so that their tracks could come through his property. Had Reese not done this, the town of Cinnabar would probably have risen just to the north on the site of the later town of Horr. Because of Reese's sale to them, the Northern Pacific Railroad was able to finish its tracks into Sections 16 and 17, on present national parkland.[16]

Although the ranches of James Henderson and George Reese[17] were in place early, Cinnabar really began with the mining claims of men like George Huston, E. J. Keeney, and Hugo Hoppe and then embraced a railroad. In the autumn of 1881, at the time George Reese and his sons were harvesting their oat crop, Hugo Hoppe was just arriving on the Cinnabar flats and already dreaming of starting a town at the end of the rails.

2

CINNABAR

The Name and the Founding

The fools are going to work the mines, and the wise men are going to work the fools.
—*Livingston* (MT) *Enterprise*, March 5, 1898, quoting an unnamed Seattle newspaper editorial about men heading for Alaska

Mining figures into nearly every aspect of Montana's general history, and that of Cinnabar is no exception. Montana's mining history is deep, wide, and fascinating but so complicated that historians both avocational and professional have struggled with its complexity and have failed to produce an overarching study. To summarize it for now, the history of mining is a story of boom, bust, danger, destruction, disappointment, and pollution, not only in Montana but throughout world history. For every person who got rich, there were hundreds who remained poor and discouraged. A miner's wife in Cooke City summarized twenty-four years of that frustration in an 1895 poem.

> Tired and worn, long years ago,
> Two men went plodding, sad and slow;
> With pack on back, and pick in hand
> They were searching for the Promised Land—
> A land where silver in streams should flow;
> For there they intended to make their home
> And wait for the boom that would surely come. [1]

But in so many cases in Montana and elsewhere, that boom never came. Instead, miners spent fruitless years searching and hoping. The mining booms in the American West began in California in the 1840s, jumped to Nevada and Idaho in the 1850s, and then moved to Montana in the 1860s, with many of the same miners traveling to several or all of those places. Many unsuccessful Montana miners then migrated to Alaska in the 1890s when those strikes were publicized, only to become poorer and more disillusioned up there. Newspaper editorials and letters written home warned potential prospectors about horrendous difficulties in Alaska, but like those who came before them, truly determined seekers of gold and other minerals could not be swayed. The quotation that begins this chapter makes it clear that at least one contemporary observer thought that many miners were fools and that the real money was in selling supplies to miners.[2]

Mining was the reason for the name Cinnabar. According to the fiftieth anniversary issue of the *Livingston Enterprise* (1933), the name Cinnabar Mountain "perpetuates the discovery of a quicksilver mine [there] by the Soule [*sic*: Sowl] brothers on one of their trips to Yellowstone City [Emigrant, Montana] in 1866."[3] The brothers probably gave the name Cinnabar to the mountain.

David B. Weaver says the year was more likely to have been 1865, but both sources were correct because they were referring to the winter of 1865–1866. Weaver, a prospector who claimed in 1922 to have been the last living discoverer of the Emigrant Gulch gold (1863–1866), stated that Charles H. and James Soule (or more likely Sowl) were the two brothers in question. He says they discovered Cinnabar Mountain in late summer or fall 1865 (with its characteristic red streak between two prominent geologic sills), believed that they had made a great quartz strike, and thought that the red streak was caused by the presence of cinnabar (mercuric sulphide). Weaver says that about November 1, 1865, the two men rode into Emigrant Gulch with their news. Their story caused a little excitement, but the other miners in general did not believe it. None of them accepted the Sowl offers to let them stake claims. The brothers went back to Cinnabar Mountain, and Weaver says they "worked away at the tunnel till the spring of 1866, ate their grub, burned their powder and failed to reach the place where they could find quicksilver. Finally they packed their outfits and started for the diggings at Last Chance [Helena]."[4]

In 1871, Dr. F. V. Hayden surveyed the Yellowstone Park area. He found the remnants of the Sowl brothers' mining activities and pronounced their red "ore" to be simple iron oxide. But to acknowledge the "strike" of the Sowl brothers, Hayden officially recognized the name Cinnabar Mountain, which he said was "sometimes" applied to the place. As early as 1874, the Earl of Dunraven affirmed that Cinnabar Mountain was "apparently so called because there is no cinnabar there."[5]

One wonders how the Sowl brothers pronounced their last name and whether it rhymed with "owl" rather than having the long "o" as in "sole." Charley Sowl (as the *Livingston Enterprise* spelled it on at least three occasions) lived and prospected at Emigrant Gulch for many years, and he was still there in 1887, trying vainly like so many others to make the big strike. Sowl died in 1889 without heirs, for the newspaper reported the selling of his land and noted the fact that he had "located Devil's Slide as a cinnabar claim." Traveler W. H. Dudley in 1885 hiked partway up the slide and found "a prospect hole and a claim stake" (probably placed there by the Sowl brothers), but "what the prospector claims," he wrote, "I am at a loss to conjecture, for the vein is oxide of iron and one doesn't need to dig a hole into it in order to discover that."[6]

By late in the century, the origins of the name Cinnabar were already obscure. Traveler T. S. Kenderdine noticed in 1897 that local Cinnabar residents were arguing about where the name came from:

> Now there is a difference between drivers and cooks as to the origin of this town's name. Some say, from the back-woods pronunciation of bear, that it comes from *skin-a-b'ar*; others, as well posted, say *seen-a-b'ar*; while others still derive it from a contraction of Cinnamon bear. The name really comes from some streaks of reddish mineral on the side of a near-by mountain resembling Cinnabar; whence comes mercury.[7]

While Mr. Kenderdine had somehow figured it out, the town itself seemed to have few locals who remembered its history. Perhaps they simply did not know the definition of the word *cinnabar*, although one would think that some of the miners would have known it.

That some of this distorting of the name Cinnabar was occurring as early as 1886 is evident from the account that year of a "Pilgrim" who stated:

At Cinnabar we left our palace railway coaches for those drawn by six horses. This little village has sprung into existence as the terminus of the park branch. It nestles at the base of the somewhat isolated Cinnabar mountains, down the side of which are immense, perfectly smooth tracks, called the "Devil's Slide." They look like two mammoth toboggan slides except for the lack of snow and ice upon them. I judge that down these dikes his Satanic Majesty made his entrée into the Park region. The bright red grooves indicate by their position and general appearance that when the "Old Boy" fell from the world above, he struck on top of *Sinner-bar* mountain so suddenly that he could not get a foothold and therefore slid over into Wonderland and started up business on his own hook.[8]

Notwithstanding the fact that the town of Cinnabar was located more than two miles southeast of Devil's Slide rather than at its base, this writer's story or others in circulation then may have been the inspiration for William Tod Helmuth's ridiculous but well-loved 1892 poem about the devil titled "Yellowstone Park and How It Was Named," which was reproduced and sold to park tourists for many years.[9]

THE RAILROAD ARRIVES

The Northern Pacific Railroad (later officially renamed the "Northern Pacific Railway") surveyed the route for its Yellowstone branch line in 1882 and then laid its track south along the Yellowstone River from Livingston, Montana, to Cinnabar in the winter, spring, and summer of 1883.[10] Railroad officials intended to lay tracks all the way to Gardiner, but a mining claim blocked the route, and citizens of that town were angry about it. A newspaper picked up the story:

The people of Gardiner on the National Park branch of the Northern Pacific are beginning to fear that no depot will be located there on account of a dispute between the railroad company and one Buckskin Jim [Robert E. Cutler], who jumped a claim, the squatter's right to which had been purchased by Ed. Stone, for the railroad. The residents of Gardiner and vicinity are now trying to purchase Buckskin Jim's claim, with a view to presenting it to the railroad company.[11]

What happened was complicated but much of it was later sorted out by historian Aubrey Haines. Ed Stone was the NPRR's man in charge of obtaining lands for the railroad's right-of-way. When he arrived at Gardiner in October of 1882, he discovered that Gardiner's founder, James McCartney, owned the relevant land between Gardiner and what would become Cinnabar, so Ed arranged to purchase it for the railroad for fifteen hundred dollars. But this deal became more complex when Ed learned that McCartney had previously leased most of this (his) desert land claim to Robert Eugene "Buckskin Jim" Cutler (1860–1921) who refused to give up his lease (a lease, like full ownership, carries hard legal rights). Worse yet, Cutler "sublet parcels of land" to various people "in a manner that was construed as a sale," and that bollixed up everything for the Northern Pacific. Although Ed was later able to "legally dispose of . . . Buckskin Jim," he was "unable to similarly dispose of the host of people who claimed to have purchased" from Cutler. As a final complicating matter, Cutler threw a mining claim across the right-of-way. All of these factors prevented the railroad from reaching Gardiner for nineteen years. [12]

The NPRR thus stopped its rails and placed its terminus at what was soon to become the town of Cinnabar. The *Livingston Enterprise* announced on July 2 that "a case involving the right of possession of the townsite of Gardiner will be heard before Judge Seward on Tuesday, James McCartney being the plaintiff and Robert E. Cutler the defendant." But McCartney failed to show up for court, so the judge dismissed the case. On August 20, the newspaper regretfully announced that "arrangements could not be made by which Buckskin Jim's claim upon the Gardiner townsite could be transferred to the Northern Pacific and hence the new location"—at Cinnabar. [13]

Our central character in the history of Cinnabar, Hugo J. Hoppe, was initially a prospector, a saloon owner, and a brewmaster, and he eventually became a freighter. A freighter was a person who made money by hauling other people's stuff in heavy wagons pulled by many animals. Modern observers became familiar with freighters through Kevin Costner's motion picture *Dances with Wolves* (1990). In that movie, a bearded freighter named Timmons shouted "Gee!" and "Haw" to his mules before a Pawnee Indian shot him full of arrows. Turning Cinnabar, Montana, into a thriving town was freighter Hugo Hoppe's dream. What he wanted was to own a hotel there, along with a store, a saloon, and a share of the tourist business entering Yellowstone National Park. He also entertained thoughts of purchasing land early in what he believed would be this booming town's history and making money from selling those lots as the land values increased.

Cinnabar consisted only of Hoppe's freighting warehouse until the railroad, which reached Livingston on November 30, 1882, arrived at Cinnabar nine months later. As already described, the NPRR purchased a right-of-way through George Reese's property, and the company's track-layers reached, on August 30, 1883, the flat that would become the town of Cinnabar, "using easy curves and moderate grades" to "permit a safe speed of forty-five miles per hour." Actual (if unofficial) rail service to the park began earlier that summer, as tourists exited the train at various temporary termini whose existence depended on the spot to which the rails had been completed. Traveling to Yellowstone, visitor Margaret Andrews Cruikshank rode the train to what was probably its terminus at today's "Trestle Ranch" on August 22. Upon her return from the park on August 30, she reported that because of "the lack of the last siding," her party had to ride horseback north of Mammoth for fifteen miles to board the train somewhere beyond what would become Cinnabar.[14] That loca-tion—probably the final temporary terminus before the rails were ex-tended to Cinnabar—was on the north bank of, and at the mouth of, what was soon to be called Mulherin Creek (then called "Cinnabar Creek"), because the railroad was briefly stymied there in order to build a substan-tial trestle.[15] This spot today accords nicely with Margaret Cruikshank's stated distance of fifteen miles—five miles from Mammoth to Gardiner, three miles to Cinnabar, five miles to the present Corwin Springs Bridge, and two more miles to Mulherin Creek.

Officially, train service to Cinnabar began on Saturday, September 1, 1883. On that day NPRR conductor A. J. Bent and engineer T. J. Erwin brought up a train from Livingston pulled by engine no. 163. It included the special car "Montana," with the chief engineer of the railroad and the engineer in charge of the Park Branch, along with the cars intended for the use of President Chester A. Arthur, who was then touring the park. The president's party had entered the park from the south on horseback and was leaving via the newly completed Park Branch to Livingston. If they could not be the new line's first literal passengers, the NPRR no doubt wished it to be ceremonially so. But things worked out for the

NPRR, because those VIPs were indeed the first official passengers out of the park heading north, as the *Enterprise* reported.[16]

Reading Hugo Hoppe's account, one gets the impression that half of the world was there on the day the first official train arrived at Cinnabar on September 1:

> Freighters were there to get freight; guides were there for hunting trips; men were there who ran pack outfits through the Park for parties they had booked and stage coaches were there for the tourists who were to tour the Park by way of the hotel system. Gamblers in broadcloth, [with] black, broad-brimmed hats and wearing diamonds that would make a bull's eye blink; trappers in fringed buckskin jackets, buckskin trousers and beaver caps; cowboys in Stetsons, chaps and spurs riding ponies that bucked in celebration of the event when spurred to action; prospectors, unshaven and unkempt; miners from Cooke City with buckskin bags full of gold dust; ranchmen and farmers with their families in buckboards and democrats were [all] there the day the first train pulled into Cinnabar.[17]

After more than two decades of "looking for a strike," said Hoppe, he was sure that he had struck it rich! The above quote may have been the way he remembered it, but the local newspaper—which was admittedly busy reporting completion of the railroad, President Arthur's party, and Rufus Hatch's large group of VIPs—did not mention any such gala festivities at Cinnabar. Attributing its information to a "correspondent" writing from Cinnabar "last Saturday" (September 1), the *Enterprise* stated only that

> [t]he presidential party with their escort arrived here today at 9 a.m., and left by special train. Passengers were landed here today at the terminus of the National Park branch, and everything looks prosperous for our town. Bullion is coming down daily from Cooke City for shipment east.[18]

Additionally, neither the Bozeman *Avant Courier* nor the *Bozeman Weekly Chronicle* mentioned any such celebration at Cinnabar as Hoppe claimed. While it makes sense that at least some people would have been waiting there to see President Arthur, there was nothing present in the way of facilities at Cinnabar to host such onlookers. If the event occurred, the only buildings present were Hoppe's single warehouse, some scattered cabins, and the railroad's wooden platform, probably joined for that celebratory moment—if it happened—by a few tents for the onlookers.

As the Livingston newspaper saw it,[19] Cinnabar was intended to be temporary as a railhead, but the small town lasted for almost twenty years because "Buckskin Jim" refused to sell his land. Then as now, "nothing was as sacrosanct as a mining claim!" Although NPRR installed the tracks three-fifths of a mile beyond Cinnabar, they were removed in 1885 when it became apparent that Cutler would not budge.[20] That stymied the railroad at Cinnabar until 1902, when the dispute over the land rights was settled and tracks were primitively completed to Gardiner.[21]

While other factors also impeded it, there is no question that the ever-present anticipation of railroad extension to Gardiner prevented big growth of Cinnabar, and even twenty years later newspaper editors mentioned that fact.[22]

3

DREAMS OF STRIKING IT RICH

Hugo J. Hoppe's Life before Cinnabar (1848–1881)

Do you think there's any chance of anyone striking it rich like they did in forty-nine?
—Hugo Hoppe in California to another German miner, 1851, per Ida McPherren

Not everyone agreed that Cinnabar was to be temporary. With the possibility of extensive coal mining operations looming at what would become the nearby towns of Horr and Aldridge, the promise of gold and silver mining in the adjacent districts of Cooke City and Bear Gulch (part of which would become present Jardine, Montana, in 1898), and the strength of railroad travel to Yellowstone Park, some people expected that Cinnabar would grow into a great town. Foremost among those speculators was Hugo John Hoppe (1835–1895). Getting rich in his new country was on his mind early, as it was for many of his fellow westerners. His quotation above might have been strictly anecdotal. But he probably said those words in one form or another. And he continued to think about making a big mineral strike and to search for one when he reached Montana.

By the time he founded Cinnabar, Hoppe had been in Montana Territory for twenty years. To understand him, we must look at his earlier life, and it truly was that of a Montana territorial pioneer thoroughly engaged in what he and many others called "border life." Born on February 4, 1835[1] in Grenzhausen Nassau, Germany, as Hans Hugo Friedrich Emil

Hoppe, Hugo Hoppe emigrated to the United States at age thirteen in 1848 and traveled west on the Oregon Trail at age sixteen. The German name that he personally preferred and that he wanted to live under should he ever return to Germany was Hugo Von der Gabelenz. His parents, Justus Jacob Balthasar Hoppe and Wilhelmine, were fleeing the Revolution of 1848 just in time for their son to head for the California gold fields.[2] Hugo followed the Oregon Trail beginning on April 15, 1851, with ninety-four other people including a lot of German immigrants. He lived in California for nearly five years and then went to Utah in 1856 for one winter and then back to California. He joined the Nevada mining stampede in 1859 and, when the Civil War broke out, enlisted in the Second California Cavalry. After serving as a private and mustering out in 1863,[3] he returned to Salt Lake City to marry Mary Gee James and adopt (spiritually if not legally) her six-year-old daughter, Maggie Ann James, before continuing "the turbulent life of a rough frontiersman."[4] Hoppe was thin and of medium height with reddish brown hair (little Ida Miller would later call it "auburn") and gray-blue eyes that were probably quite striking. From at least the 1870s, he sported the classic nineteenth-century chin beard and mustache, and at times his sideburns connected completely into his beard. Mary was a short brunette with thin lips, who parted her hair in the center. Hugo and Mary settled in Montana in 1863, where they lived for twenty years before Mary helped Hugo plow his hopes into Cinnabar.

Ida McPherren's book *Imprints on Pioneer Trails* is a book of oral history about Hugo Hoppe's life and adventures, and he had *many* adventures in the American West before he founded Cinnabar. Hoppe kept a memorandum book of his life (lost today) and also told the stories of his adventures to his five sons and stepdaughter. Son Albert Hoppe produced a long manuscript (also lost today) about his father's life based upon that memorandum book and what Hugo and other relatives told him through the years. In 1894, Hugo Hoppe purchased train fare for his niece (Geneva Miller) and her daughter Ida to come to Cinnabar, and the two of them spent the rest of their lives in the area. His grandniece—Ida Geneva Miller McPherren—used Hoppe's diary, Albert's manuscript, and her own interviews to write the story of Hugo Hoppe and their related families. Because her book is largely composed of oral history, it must be used cautiously by historians with a vigilant eye for inaccuracies. But it recorded many events for us that otherwise would be lost to history.[5]

Through Ida McPherren, Hoppe stated that he rode into Virginia City, Montana Territory on November 17, 1863. That was nine months before the first newspaper was published in the Territory, the *Montana Post*, which began there on August 27 of the following year. "The first man I met was Henry Plummer," said Hoppe who described Sheriff Plummer "as dapper looking as when I first saw him in California." Hoppe soon learned that Plummer was a murderer and robber, so Hugo became a member of the vigilante committee that hanged him less than two months later on January 10, 1864. And Hoppe was in or near Virginia City when Calamity Jane's parents abandoned her and her siblings there in December of that year, and thirty years later he met and talked to her at Cinnabar.[6]

Only 20,595 people lived in Montana Territory in 1870 (a decrease from 1866, when mining increased the population to 28,000) and only 39,159 in 1880. That was not very many people to inhabit such a vast landscape, which still contained roaming Indian tribes. The 1860s and 1870s were the years, as newspaperman George Wright later proclaimed, "when men carried their lives in their hands," and Hugo Hoppe was one of those. There was precious little law and not much order on the plains and in the mountain valleys of territorial Montana. It was easy for a person to get killed in that huge, unsettled country, whether on the plains or in the mountains, and for no one to even know it, as his or her corpse was devoured by animals that left the bones bleaching on the ground. Occasional mysterious and unidentified bones turned up fairly often, such as in 1883 when visitors returning to Virginia City from Yellowstone found a "civilized woman's skeleton" on Madison River, and again in 1900 when a sheepherder discovered a skull with a bullet hole in it at Dillon, Montana.[7]

In Virginia City, Hugo Hoppe began experimenting with making a living in the unpopulated, sprawling territory—not easy to do when one considers that he still could not speak English well. He sold whiskey, prospected, and may have even considered freighting but probably was not doing it yet. Pregnant and escorting her seven-year-old daughter, Maggie, Mary Gee James Hoppe met her husband there in May and their son, Walter Monroe Hoppe, was born at Virginia City on August 6, 1864. Ever after, Hugo Hoppe claimed that Walter was the "first white child born in Montana Territory."[8] And indeed, Walter could have been that first such child born in the territory (created by President Abraham Lincoln on May 26, 1864), because his parents were in Virginia City early enough and some baby somewhere had to fill that role.

Of course many of those settlers at Virginia City and at Montana's only other sizable town of Helena were itinerant prospectors—men ultimately responsible for the region's nickname "The Treasure State"—and Hugo Hoppe was no exception. Except for his mere name in a list of postals to be claimed at Virginia City in 1864, the earliest known original documentation of him in Montana appeared in the *Montana Post* in 1866 when he was prospecting at Blackfoot City, Montana, about twenty miles west of Helena. A writer known only as "Items," who saw him there on July 4, 1866, stated in the Virginia City newspaper:

> The glorious fourth passed off quietly. Salutes were fired in the morning and at noon by the anvil battery. I must not pass over the actions of one patriotic and truly loyal man—Hugh Hoppy—who not seeing any flag flying, went round to ascertain the cause, and found that there was not a flag in the town, although it was nearly noon. He went and bought the material, and in an hour had the Stars and Stripes floating in the breeze. Not satisfied with this, he procured a spring-wagon, had four horses attached to it, got the brass-band accompanying the California Minstrels into it, and then mounting the seat with the driver, with his banner (which was about fifteen feet in length), he paraded the streets, while the band played national and patriotic airs. From here, he went to Carpenter's Bar where the same programme was repeated.[9]

In territorial Montana with its many Southern sympathizers, such Fourth of July celebrations meant a great deal to supporters of the Union, like Hugo Hoppe, at a time when the Civil War—only over for fifteen months—was still a fresh wound of memory.

But another observer in Blackfoot City a few days later made it clear that Hoppe was almost as interested in getting his brewery business going as he was in prospecting. "Through the enterprise of Judge Johnson and friend Hoppy of the brewery," proclaimed the observer, "the town is supplied with clear sparkling water conducted through pipes and hydrants."[10] Brewing beer, after all, required plenty of water. It is also worth noting that Hugo Hoppe established a couple of Montana's earliest breweries, even if they did not survive continuously.[11]

From Virginia City and Blackfoot City, Hugo and Mary kept their eyes on Last Chance Gulch and Confederate Gulch in Helena and the supply point for those towns—Fort Benton on the Missouri River. At this time in Montana, it seemed like everyone was itinerant, constantly traveling from small towns to mining camps to distant railroads and steamships. Hoppe was not yet a full-time freighter—an occupation commonly called "bullwhacker" or "mule skinner"—but he was proximate to so many men who were doing it that the idea was already forming in his head. A bullwhacker whom Hoppe probably knew (and who may have influenced him) recalled fondly those "days of '66 when [I was] plying the vocation of freighting between Fort Benton and the various mining camps of Montana."[12] He was one of many such freighters that Hugo and Mary Hoppe watched and imitated. They ran among all those places, experimenting with freighting as they also looked for other ways to make a living. The couple probably lived at Fort Benton during some periods, because their second son, "Hughie," was born there[13] on September 25, 1865. His happy parents named him Hugh Benton Hoppe, for that celebrated inland port that had seen its first two steamboats, named the *Chippewa* and the *Key West*, arrive on July 2, 1860.[14]

Hugo Hoppe was already learning that freighting might be more profitable than gold mining. As a British traveler noted only a few years later, freighting was priced so very high in Montana because of the territory's nonexistent communication and primitive transportation that

> working any but the very richest ores cannot possibly be remunerative. When it is considered that freights have to be hauled over almost impassable roads, from Corinne on the Union Pacific Railway, or have to ascend the Missouri in boats to the mouth of the Mussel Shell, whence they must be transported by mule or ox-trains, it is not to be wondered at that quartz mining does not pay.[15]

It was a problem that Virginia City, Cooke City, and numerous other isolated Montana towns would face for many years.

From 1866 to late 1869, Hugo Hoppe and his family lived mostly in Helena, where he gushed later that he was one of the earliest subscribers to the *Helena Weekly Herald*. Building a cabin, he prospected, "salooned," hunted, farmed, and freighted to Fort Benton like many others, but he also ran the Springfield Hotel at "Lincoln Gulch." In Helena, he met Frank Grouard and others of future western fame. At this time the Bozeman Trail for gold seekers, which ran from Casper, Wyoming (on the Oregon Trail), to Fort Smith to Bozeman, was opening, and the Utah and Northern Railroad was trying to build north from Utah Territory into Montana. Helena was able to grow because its citizens had gold dust money and because it had freighters who ran supplies from the railroad in Utah through Idaho to Montana. It was probably in Helena in 1868 that Hoppe refined his skills in making beer by learning from a fellow German, and it was a continuing skill that would later serve him well in Glendale, Butte, and Bozeman. By way of personal jubilation, he and Mary were at Anaconda (Deer Lodge County) in late 1868 when their third son, George Lincoln Hoppe, was born. But tragedy struck in late July or early August of 1869 when they lost an infant daughter at Helena's Lincoln Gulch, an all too common wrenching misfortune for families on the western frontier.[16]

When it looked like the gold at Helena was playing out, Hugo Hoppe sold his claim there for ten thousand dollars to Eastern capitalists (who intended to mine it with heavy machinery) and moved his family to Bozeman. It was there that fourth son, Leander Black Hoppe, was born on February 19, 1870, and where the family was present for the territory's first census.[17] The sale gave Hugo the money to dabble in various businesses in Montana for the next decade. As he watched the freighters who ran the Diamond R Company at Helena, he wondered: "if a man went to a new town where there were no freighters yet and bought a good outfit [whether] he couldn't strike it rich freighting at ten cents a pound . . . like [the] owners of the Diamond R had." Having four biological children now plus a stepdaughter and armed with his new money, Hoppe bought "several farms" in Bozeman during the period 1870–1872, ran a saloon, and kept the freighting idea in mind. Hoppe family member Bob Moore says Hugo accumulated about four thousand acres in Gallatin County through land swaps and purchases. Hoppe also decided to look for coal and gold while running a new freight outfit to Cooke City (although it was not named yet), through what would soon become Yellowstone Park. A. Bart Henderson and three other men had struck gold at Cooke in 1870, and that seemed to Hoppe like an opportunity. In his spare time, he dabbled in horse racing, where some easy money could be made when local racers put their monies together. One of the horses that was advertised to run against someone else's "Conover Mare" was Hoppe's "Bozeman Chief."[18] And his fifth son, Albert Vincent Hoppe, was born on February 4, 1872, thus becoming—with his father Hugo, his brother Lee, and his sister Maggie—the fourth person in the family to have a birthday in February.

Congress established Yellowstone National Park on March 1, 1872, and Hugo Hoppe must have immediately seen that as another down-the-road moneymaker. Meanwhile he was offered the position of post trader at Benson's Landing—the first permanent settlement in what became Park County—so in 1873 he moved to that barely begun spot. It and sites close to it would become Clark City and then Livingston nine years later. Benson's Landing (also called Benson's Crossing) was only a ferry and store run by Amos Benson, but there Hoppe could dabble in freighting from Benson's to Cooke City and from Bozeman to Cooke City (there was no real traffic east yet, because the town of Billings did not exist). And he could sell whiskey, always profitable for men on the frontier. Historian Mark Brown has called Benson's Landing "an unsavory sort of place" whose merchants "were regarded with disfavor" by the government agent at the nearby Crow Agency. That opinion would soon pertain directly to Hugo Hoppe. [19]

Then in December of 1873, Hugo Hoppe's new friend Oliver P. Hanna offered him a gold-hunting trip for three months, and Hoppe could not resist taking it. Newspaper announcements stated that "Professor" J. L. Vernon had made gold discoveries and was asking for citizens to join the gold hunt. This "Yellowstone Wagon-Road Expedition of 1874" was funded by citizens of Bozeman, supposedly to open a better wagon road east to the head of steamboat navigation on the Bighorn and Yellowstone Rivers. Those citizens in Bozeman also wanted to build a fort on the river to protect their own and other settlers from Indians, and indeed they would soon need it. [20] But according to three historians, one of whom wrote an entire book on the affair, the real reason for the expedition was "to go down and stir up a ruckus" among the Indians in the Yellowstone Valley. That way, said historian Mark Brown, the government could "take the tribes in hand and thereby open the Yellowstone and Big Horn [areas] for trade and provide a market for the agricultural surplus of the valley." [21] With 146 men and 269 stock, that was certainly likely. The four-month trip introduced Hugo Hoppe to important men in Montana—like J. V. Bogert, Frank Grounds, William T. Hamilton, J. Muggins Taylor, Jack Bean, and photographer H. B. Calfee—but also revealed Hoppe to be a bit headstrong and almost cost him his life in fights with Indians even though he collected a "prized scalp." During the trip, Hoppe carved his name on Pompey's Pillar and probably set the stage for the naming of a Bighorn River steamboat the "Maggie Hoppe" for his adopted daughter.[22] Little is known about it except that it was a smaller-than-normal steamboat that Hugo Hoppe built at his own expense.[23]

It was just after this trip (if not during it) that Hoppe caused himself to be labeled a whiner when he wrote a minority report for the *Helena Weekly Herald* classifying the 1874 expedition as a failure. After fighting Indians and being subjected for months to many hardships, the leaders and the majority of the expedition—fearing a lack of supplies that would leave them vulnerable to Indians—voted to return to Bozeman while Hoppe and a minority of the men wanted to remain in that country prospecting. As usual, Hoppe was not about to let even eight hundred Indians and a few missing supplies get in the way of his gold hunting. "So fully are we convinced of the existence of . . . rich deposits of gold in that country," he wrote, "that nearly one hundred men" have signed their names and pledged to return to that country.[24] But Indians, lack of supplies, and the remoteness of the country kept that from ever happening, although Hoppe's memory of the affair remained emotional to him for the rest of his life.[25] The Earl of Dunraven, who visited Montana that same year, confirmed that the territory had not yet fulfilled expectations as a gold-producing country, but attributed this not so much to the absence of minerals "as to the fact that communication is difficult and transportation laborious."[26] Hugo Hoppe was one of those men who was planning to improve transportation if he could not discover gold.

With Hoppe complaining about it, the expedition returned to Bozeman in May of 1874 and in June, he and O. P. Hanna went back to Benson's Landing. While he was there in late July, Hoppe was again attacked by Indians, but this time it was more serious. As E. S. Topping told it in his 1883 book, two settlers named Olson were fired upon by Indians just above the mouth of Shields River. Seeking safety in numbers, they rode south to Benson's Landing just in time to get into a fight with a group of Sioux Indians who were trying to steal horses there. Several men rushed out of the buildings and began to shoot at them. "Hugo Hoppy was hit in the shoulder and fell," said Topping.

> As he dropped, the Indians gave a shout of triumph. Hoppy jumped up, and not to be outdone yelled back, and then walked in and told the boys that he was shot through the breast. There was no bullet hole in his skin or clothes, but his left breast was bruised and discolored, and

the conclusion arrived at was that he had been hit by a spent bullet. The Indians turned back and disappeared in the bluffs, without capturing any of the stock.[27]

The version of this story that found its way to Helena stated that Jim Odair was killed in the fracas and described Hoppe's breast injury. A man named Jim Magee saw Odair's body when it was brought into Bozeman and told the newspaper that

> [w]hen found, he had been shot in several places with arrows and also with bullets, had been scalped, and presented a most horrid spectacle. The Indians, in their retreat, shot at H.J. Hoppy several times, one of the bullets hitting him, but he was at such a distance that it merely bruised his breast. This was a close call. The soldiers [from Fort Parker] followed the Indians down to the Yellowstone, but finding they had scattered, and not overtaking them, returned.[28]

Notwithstanding his injury, Hoppe was attempting at this point to improve affairs at tiny Benson's Landing (as the newspapers called it), where he and Amos Benson kept a trading post. The Helena *Independent* called him "indefatigable," noting that he was circulating a petition to establish a post office there, and a secondary source says that he served as postmaster at "Yellowstone Crossing" from November 30, 1874, until it was discontinued on July 28, 1875.[29] Hoppe described Benson's Landing at this time as "comprised of a log house as a dwelling place for the post trader; a store for trading with the Indians or selling goods to the whites; a shed to hold cord wood" for any steamboat that happened to make it up the Yellowstone River, "and a squat, log stable for horses." It was a place that irritated the nearby superintendent of Indian Affairs in Montana, James Wright at Fort Parker. Wright called it "a whiskey shop kept by one Benson." "Men pass by this shop and obtain whiskey," fumed Wright, "get drunk, come here [to Fort Parker] on business and annoy us very much."[30]

Meanwhile, Hugo Hoppe's "Mormon friend" named Bob told him that while Hoppe and Hanna were out fighting Indians and hunting for gold, some eastern capitalists came through and told Bob that they were planning to put up a smelter in Cooke City. According to Hoppe, Bob thus gave him the idea to start a freighting business through Yellowstone Park to Cooke City. "A man could freight," said Bob, "and look-around [for gold and coal] at the same time." Bob did not have the money for such a venture, but Hoppe did. "Six months later," said Hoppe, "I owned three freight outfits of three main wagons and six trailers and fifty mules using twelve mules to a wagon and the extras for emergencies." Hoppe still had some of his "nest egg" left over from the Helena sale. He says he drove one wagon himself and hired two Mormons (one was named Hi Jehnsen) to help him in the new enterprise. On an early trip to Cooke City, he staked out thirty claims and recorded them all at Bozeman.[31]

But as usual, Hoppe was also selling whiskey and looking for another adventure, so he temporarily left his two hirees in charge of the freighting. He did not want to get "crosswise" with the army for selling whiskey to Indians or otherwise mess up his position as post trader, but he also needed to make a living. And anyway, the location of the Crow Agency was about to be moved in the summer of 1875 from Fort Parker on Mission Creek to Rosebud Creek near the mouth of Stillwater River, a point about sixty miles east of Benson's Landing. Losing his post-trader status but seeing a moneymaking opportunity near the new agency to the east, Hoppe and another man named Horace Countryman loaded up their whiskey kegs. They packed downriver and set up a saloon on the north bank of Yellowstone River exactly opposite the mouth of the Stillwater— "as close to the new agency as the law would allow," says historian Brown. Hoppe also helped in the fields that summer at the new Crow Agency with a surveyor named O. F. Mason.[32] But this whiskey venture with Horace Countryman, which was sometimes called "Countryman's Ranch," was short-lived because it "was too close to the Sioux danger and too far away from the agency headquarters to ever become more than a frontier outpost."[33] Hoppe resumed his habit of running back and forth between Benson's Landing and Bozeman, probably in the autumn of 1875.

Benson's had been busy during the spring and summer of that year. Bozeman businessman Walter Cooper told the newspaper in May that "times are lively at the crossing." "The trade in robes and furs this season," he stated, "has been almost double that of any former season." Cooper believed that "as soon as it is generally known among trappers and hunters that a good market is open for them at the Crossing . . . that the fur trade on the Yellowstone will exceed any point in the Territory."[34] Hugo Hoppe's traveling back and forth between Benson's Landing and Bozeman put him in constant touch with the territory's robust animal populations, and he soon saw them as another way to make money. Probably before he made the trip with Horace Countryman, he was involved in the game-and-hide business, as was his friend Morgan T. Williams. The *Bozeman Times* reported on June 1 that James Anderson's large "train" of freight carried 19,621 pounds of hides and furs to the railhead at Corinne, Utah, for eight consignees in Bozeman, including M. T. Williams. "Large quantities of robes and hides," said the editor, "are coming in from the Yellowstone . . . Hoppy and Daniels have made large collections, and are still trading."[35]

After his brief adventure of trying to sell whiskey to Indians, Hoppe dabbled in hides and ran the trading post at Benson's, because a land sale that he made to a friend so stated. The sale reported in December of 1875 was plotted in the recordation as being from a "point situate[d] on the north bank of the Yellowstone River about midway between [the] Benson place and the house or dwelling lately occupied by the said Hoppy as a trading post." The man to whom Hoppe sold this land was Morgan T. "Bud" Williams, and Hoppe could not have known then that Williams would marry his daughter, Maggie, at Bozeman before October 30, 1876, and eventually follow her family upriver to Cinnabar. At Benson's in 1875 and early 1876, Hoppe also must have encountered the well-known "Yankee Jim" George—already proprietor of the Yellowstone toll road—because Jim was a "conspicuous character" when he visited there who was resplendent in a "rainbow" Indian-blanket coat.[36]

As 1876 approached, Hugo Hoppe was among all the settlers in this part of Montana who were affected by the upcoming Great Sioux War. His friend Mason was killed by Indians near Fort Pease on December 17, 1875, and that angered Hoppe enough for him to make plans to lead a group of citizens east to help the army protect that small settlement at the mouth of the Bighorn River in early 1876. "Mr. Hoppy," said the *Bozeman Times*, "is among the first to pledge himself to the cause of his friends on the Yellowstone." Meanwhile, Mrs. Hoppe was running a hotel in Bozeman, and Hugo undoubtedly joined her there for at least some of the period between his trip to Fort Pease and summer. In April, Hugo and Mary purchased "Quinn's ranch on the Yellowstone" near present-day Livingston, intending to "move to it, erect good buildings, and open a good station for the traveling custom."[37]

The Custer battle on June 25, 1876, made everyone in Montana fearful. We know that Hoppe was in Bozeman for at least part of that summer because he again made the local newspapers. They proclaimed him "Captain Hugh Hoppy" who watched the hills for the signal fires of hostile Indians and ran about warning other settlers at a time that everyone was on edge. His family's safety was no doubt high in his mind at this point because he now had five sons plus his stepdaughter. A group photo of the five little boys, taken about this time, must have swelled his and Mary's hearts with pride whenever they looked at it. Apparently wanting to be nearer to them, he sold his "Half-Way Ranch" between Bozeman and the Yellowstone River in March of 1877.[38]

Hugo Hoppe continued to run his freighting business at Bozeman and Benson's Landing until the summer of 1877, when Governor Benjamin Potts appointed him the first sheriff of the new Custer County at Miles City, Montana. While in Bozeman one day, Hoppe recognized a Mr. Potts as being the Lt. Col. Potts he had met during the Civil War at Camp Douglas, Utah Territory. They renewed their friendship, and it became the basis two years later for Potts's appointment of Hoppe to that position. Sworn in on June 14, 1877, he worked there as sheriff for about two years. During this period Hoppe, like other Montanans, found himself hearing about the Nez Perce Indians' desperate flight from the US Army through Yellowstone National Park. No doubt reading about it in the *Bozeman Times* and the *Avant Courier* and wanting to be near the excitement, Sheriff Hoppe traveled that fall to Reese Creek. There he says he stood on the very site that would later become his own town of Cinnabar and thought deeply about his friend Richard Dietrich, a German school teacher whom the Nez Perce had just killed at Mammoth Hot Springs. Hoppe was naturally saddened by the death because he had met Dietrich in 1851, when Dietrich and his sister were members of the very wagon train in which Hoppe traveled across the Oregon Trail.[39]

One story has emerged from Hoppe's time at Miles City that shows his incurable desire to search for gold even when he was working as a sheriff. In July of 1878, Hoppe was escorting a prisoner back to town on Yellowstone River below Miles City when he heard of a gold discovery at Hart Mountain. He immediately turned his prisoner over to his assistant Pat Gray and started south with some others to the new gold field. Sheriff Hoppe must have had other adventures at Miles City but so far we do not know about them. Tom Irvine succeeded him as sheriff in 1879, and Hoppe moved his family back to Bozeman.[40]

And as always, he continued to look for any excuse to travel to the strange wonderland on the upper Yellowstone. For example, when his health acted up in September of 1879, he considered going to Mammoth Hot Springs to bathe in the hot waters at the resort of James McCartney.[41] Whether he went or not is unrecorded, but it shows that every so often his thoughts were on that upper Yellowstone country.

Using Bozeman as his base, Hugo Hoppe spent much of the next two years freighting with Bob and Hi Jehnsen to Cooke City and Gardiner (which Hoppe must have visited just as it was being founded in 1880) and also in bartending and prospecting. Like other Montanans, he traveled widely to search for gold—to Glendale, Butte, the Judith Basin, and even east to White Sulphur Springs. The Diamond City newspaper reported in early October that

> [a] party of Bozemanites—Messrs. Cline, Hoppy and others—were at ·
> the [White Sulphur] springs on Monday last on their return from the
> Judith diggings. They bring very encouraging news. There is no longer
> a doubt but that a permanent camp has been struck.[42]

That permanent mining camp was never established, but the optimistic boosterism of Montana newspapers with regard to mining was unending.

It was probably during this period (1877–1880) that the following event or something like it occurred. What the story may lack in truthfulness, because it appeared as reminiscence twenty years later, is made up for by the fact that it illustrated Hugo Hoppe's frontier outlook in whatever saloon he managed or owned. A Lt. Lovell Jerome stationed at Fort Ellis, whose family otherwise had a great deal of money, acquired the reputation in Bozeman for drunkenness, for not paying his bills, and for attempting to gamble without money in saloons—like any "tin horn" gambler. After Col. R. F. May sent some of Jerome's bills to the Department of War for collection, pressure on the lieutenant increased and everyone in Bozeman to whom he owed money also started pressing him to pay his bills. When Jerome entered Hugo Hoppe's "gambling house" and "made a lucky run at faro," Hoppe demanded to see Jerome's money that would have backed him up if the lieutenant had lost the betting. Jerome put him off, and then Hoppe personally "searched him to find him penniless." "I'll pay you this way," Hoppe is reported to have said, "and this, and this!" as he dished out a swift kick and a stinging slap with his every word. "The lieutenant," stated the chronicler, "did not gamble there again when he had no money."[43]

In 1881, word reached Hoppe and Montanans that the Northern Pacific Railroad was coming toward Yellowstone National Park and what would soon become Livingston. Everyone wanted to be in place for the financial windfalls that that event seemed to promise, especially Hugo Hoppe, but he still needed to make a living while he waited for the railroad to arrive. So he took a sojourn to Glendale and Butte, Montana, to continue with the saloon and brewery business. He was dabbling in it in Bozeman anyway and the Northern Pacific Hotel and bar that he and Mary managed there was closing. He was present in Glendale in 1880 for the US Census, and also in July and August of 1881 when he ran a brewery with John Petritz, because two newspapers reported it.[44] During 1882, the *Butte Daily Miner* was loaded with references to Hoppe's "Butte Brewery" and its saloon. Being there also allowed him to run back and forth to Glendale to go prospecting.[45] While in Butte in early 1882, Hoppe nurtured his German roots by affiliating with the Liederkranz Society and helping them stage a town-wide "Mardi Gras Masked Ball" on February 22.

For whatever reasons (his family must have been a consideration), Hoppe returned to Bozeman in late 1882 and resumed freighting to wherever he was hired. But he also could not resist the excitement of the approaching railroad, the promise of gold at Cooke City and Bear Gulch, and his dreams of somehow making money from all those tourists who were sure to ride the new trains to Yellowstone Park. The Northern Pacific Railroad's graders and surveyors reached Livingston in the autumn of 1882, and that event started the town. With the railroad beginning its construction southward toward the park in early 1883, Hoppe must have been chafing at the bit to go to that country. But suddenly he was busy defending himself in Bozeman against charges of manslaughter. The incident occurred "at John Smith's Bar" on February 22, 1883, because of a $6.25 bet in a poker game the night before, and the story sounds to us today like the Wild West of Hollywood movies. The Butte newspaper described what happened:

> On the night of the affray the parties met in a gaming hall and renewed their quarrel. When Hoppe pulled his revolver, Walters follow[ed] immediately. Before Hoppe could shoot[,] Walters had reached his side and pressing the muzzle to his [Hoppe's] breast pulled the trigger,

but the pistol missed fire [misfired], undoubtedly saving Hoppe's life. Walters thereupon jumped aside[,] receiving the deadly ball from Hoppy's gun. The men then clinched and a desperate struggle . . . ensued lasting several minutes in which Hoppe was severely punished. Friends interfered and separated them, and Walters, unassisted, walked to his room two blocks away. He lived twenty-six hours after being shot, and was conscious to the last. Hoppe was arrested and jailed immediately after the death of his victim. Both men exhibited wonderful nerve and desperation. The fatal ball entered Walters' side[,] emerging from his stomach.[46]

The man whom Hoppe shot was Patrick H. Walters, previously from the Black Hills of South Dakota. It was not uncommon in that day for someone named Patrick to receive the nickname Patsey. The story in the Bozeman *Avant Courier* is illegible in places, but from it we can discern that witnesses to the poker game on the twenty-first were unable to determine who won the money and that no bystander could attest to either man having made a threat against the other. On February 22, said the *Courier*, the following action occurred:

A gentleman who heard the conversation between the men reports Hoppy asking Walters if he "[felt] as much like fighting as he did last night." Walters replied he did not want to fight. Hoppy then asked him to go [outside] but Walters replied if he had to fight he would fight right there. Then the fight began. It is not known, or if known cannot be ascertained, who first drew his pistol. The first shot fired by Hoppy struck the trigger-guard of Walters' pistol, rendering it impossible for him to shoot. Hoppy fired five shots, only one of which took effect, the ball entering Walters' side above the pelvic bone and coming out above the umbilicus. After receiving the shot Walters used his pistol as a club and struck Hoppy over the head, [inflicting] a wound half an inch in depth. He was continuing his warfare when an excited bystander knocked Hoppy down with a chair, and the men were separated. Walters walked home, undressed himself and went to bed. A physician was called, but his services were of no avail, and Walters died about twenty-four hours after receiving the shot.[47]

Hugo Hoppe was immediately jailed at Bozeman and apparently held for weeks if not several months. The *Butte Daily Miner* noted on June 26, 1883: "H. J. Hoppe, formerly of Butte, who killed Patsey Walters in

Bozeman last winter, has been indicted by the grand jury and held in $5000 bail" in "Gallatin District Court." The reduced charge was manslaughter but the new court docket did not begin until October, so it was no wonder that the story disappeared from summer newspapers.[48] While one researcher believes that Bozeman officials held Hoppe in jail there all summer, the Bozeman *Avant Courier* referred to him on October 4 as "H. J. Hoppe *of Cinnibar*" [*sic*] and stated that *"during the past few months* Mr. Hoppe has been doing a rushing business" at Cinnabar.[49]

Hoppe family historian Bob Moore believes that Hoppe was ultimately set free because he was an old Montana resident who carried influence while Patsey Walters was a powerless newcomer from South Dakota. What probably happened is that Hoppe was released from jail for the summer because officials knew that Hoppe's long residence in the area and his family home in Bozeman meant that he could not escape, and it is likely that he was then rearrested or voluntarily submitted himself in October.[50] In early November, District Attorney Thomas R. Edwards decided not to prosecute Hugo Hoppe under the doctrine of nolle prosequi. We do not know the reasons, and Edwards was under no legal obligation to give them. Perhaps the evidence was not strong enough against Hoppe, although that is hard to imagine. More likely Edwards decided that Patsey Walters was at fault for attempting the first shot and Hoppe acted in self-defense. Whatever the reasons, the judge released Hugo Hoppe.[51]

Like the *Avant Courier*, the *Butte Miner* ran the story that Hoppe had spent the summer at Cinnabar, referring to the new townsite at the terminus that many people believed was only temporary because the railroad would soon be extended to Gardiner.[52] This belief received further support when the *Bozeman Weekly Chronicle* reported "Gold Galore" discovered at Gardiner in October and referred to that town as "the terminus of the Park branch." This terminal claim was nothing but boosterish optimism, as was the alleged gold strike itself. Although the *Chronicle* reported that placer miners at Gardiner were making from one hundred dollars to one hundred thirty dollars per man per week and that the "outlook is fine" with every gravel deposit "rich in gold," the gold strike there failed to pan out.[53]

If he had not been in jail awaiting his trial in Bozeman, Hugo Hoppe would have been ecstatic at this news! It would have given him one more reason to be confident about the prospects and fortunes that surely augured well for his new town of Cinnabar.

4

"WHAT A BONANZA FOR A FREIGHTER!"

Hugo Hoppe Moves to the Upper Yellowstone River
(1881–1882)

What a bonanza for a freighter!
—Hugo J. Hoppe, 1881, per Ida McPherren

As previously noted, not everyone agreed that Cinnabar was temporary. Hugo Hoppe—arguably the most important person in the establishment and life of that town—was convinced that it would endure as Yellowstone Park's permanent railhead and would someday become the biggest town in Montana. Reflecting on the late 1870s, he stated that while living at Miles City he saw the need for coal to run steamboats on the Yellowstone and Bighorn Rivers and thus spent most of his time prospecting for coal and gold, "but I never found a big strike of either." Hoppe says he first arrived on the Cinnabar flat in 1881, and land records show that he declared a coal claim near Cinnabar Mountain on May 6, 1882 (he must have returned to Butte and then Bozeman after that). On March 7, 1883 (while freshly in trouble for the shooting of Patsey Walters), Hoppe recorded water rights for "Wilson Springs" in present Yellowstone National Park at the head of Spring Creek, and on August 4, 1883, he recorded (at Bozeman) his ranch at the base of Sepulcher Mountain.[1] Also in 1883, he appropriated five hundred inches of Stephens Creek to irrigate his ranch but did not record that claim until late 1885. Except for the first two, all these recordations for his lands were likely made *after* he was occupying the lands. Accompanying Hoppe to the upper Yellowstone at this time or slightly later was Hoppe's friend Washington "Wash" Y. Northrup, who would work for the Hoppe family for the entire lifetime of Cinnabar.[2]

Hoppe's initial reasons for coming to Cinnabar were freighting, ranching, and coal, but he was also interested in the gold at Cooke City and Bear Gulch (later Jardine) and in tourism if that should ever come to pass. As already chronicled, he like almost everyone else in Montana scratched about doing nearly everything to make a living, including prospecting; operating a trading post and ferry; farming and ranching; fur trading; running hotels, saloons, and breweries; freighting; and hoping for tourist transportation to and in the new Yellowstone National Park. From land records, which often spelled his name the old way, "Hoppy,"[3] it is apparent that ranch and coal claims were important to him, and he registered them at various times in several places other than Cinnabar—near Cinnabar Mountain, near the mouth of Gardner River, on the head of what would become Electric Creek in the park, and on Turkey Pen Creek in the park near the old structure known to prospectors as "Turkey Pen Cabin."[4]

Through Ida McPherren, Hugo Hoppe told us how he formulated the plans to move to Cinnabar from Bozeman. He says the initial idea occurred to him in 1881 in connection with his freighting:

> When I heard the Northern Pacific was on its way up the Yellowstone valley to the Park I went down to Benson's Landing and learned there that the railroad would reach a point about three miles west of Benson's Landing the next year, and would run a spur up to five miles this side of Gardiner, which was as near to the Park as a railroad was allowed to go. What a bonanza for a freighter! [The new railhead would be located] [o]nly five miles from Gardiner and then over the mountain to Cooke City. I was all worked up; I went up to the [James] Henderson ranch to negotiate a deal for the purchase of the ranch for I had heard that Henderson wanted to sell out because the railroad would run too close to his cattle ranch for safety for the herds he ran on the open range. I made a deal with him whereby I traded him sections of land I owned in Gallatin Valley and a cash bonus for his holdings at the foot of Cinnabar Mountain and running north [sic: south] toward the Park. I planned at that time on operating from the terminus of the railroad to Gardiner and Cooke City and [believed that I could] [a]mass a fortune like the Diamond R that ran from Ft. Benton to Helena, when I lived at Helena.[5]

As mentioned, Hoppe recorded his claim at Cinnabar Mountain in 1882 and his ranch in 1883, but he also continued to maintain a family home at Bozeman.[6] In March, he moved his family and freight business from Bozeman to the new ranch, finding there James Henderson's two frame bungalows, a commodious barn, a ranch house, and a bunkhouse. He planned to run freight and supplies from the railhead to Cooke City on the backs of twelve mules and several horses with the help of his teenage sons, Walter and Hughie. His land testimonial stated, "I settled [at Cinnabar] March 26, 1883 and continued actual residence to May 25, when I began [construction of a] permanent house." Hoppe added that he purchased the land and fencing from E. J. "Joe" Keeney and erected a 16 × 20 house, with a corral, an outhouse, and an irrigating ditch. His statement says that he cut the wild hay on the land, "cultivated 30 acres to oats and potatoes," and raised forty tons of oat hay and about two hundred bushels of potatoes.[7] The fact that Hoppe could make these statements in late 1883 so soon after his shooting of Patsey Walters in Bozeman is another factor that augurs against his having been kept in jail for all summer while awaiting trial in that affray.

Hoppe's scheme to make a good living at the end of the tracks continued to expand. He applied to the Department of the Interior for permission to run a dairy in the park to serve visitors, a proposal that was ultimately rejected. As for Cinnabar itself, he said that one day an idea occurred to him, "like the sudden inspirations that move empires." His idea was to build a town at the end of the rails. It was not a completely original idea in the American West, where end-of-the-tracks towns routinely sprang up on their own, but he was entrepreneurial enough to get in on the ground floor or at least to have been thinking about it. He said he had the railroad bring up a bar and fixtures, liquors and gambling devices, and two hotel-size stoves, and he, his sons, and his friend Hi Jehnsen all set to work. He also built a hotel with a false front on it. (As he explained, "Every business house of any importance of that time had a false front that made the building look like it had one more story than it did.")

The best evidence is that all of this happened much later than Hoppe remembered. It appears that Hoppe had the initial idea for Cinnabar but that Carroll Hobart, with the railroad supporting him, platted the town in late 1883 and, according to the local newspaper and land records, purchased and promoted it in 1884. Regardless, Hoppe and his sons owned their ranches near Cinnabar as well as some of the townsite, and his early activities were forefront in the town's establishment. He also said he purchased the entire town in 1890, but if this is true there is no indication of it in either the local newspaper or the land records' "grantee indexes" of land conveyed to Hoppe that year. Hoppe stated that "the officials who came on the train" named the town Cinnabar after nearby Cinnabar Mountain. He implied that this happened on the first day the railroad arrived, which was September 1, 1883.[8]

THE RAILROAD AND LOCALS JOIN FORCES AND HUGO HOPPE BECOMES ALLIED WITH CARROLL T. HOBART

Of course, the moment the railroad arrived, it needed a terminus site of some sort. The Northern Pacific was able to purchase a piece of land from George Huston and E. J. Keeney, whose ranch had been sold to them by the park's assistant superintendent Clarence Stephens (Stephens had purchased part of the James Henderson ranch before Hugo Hoppe did). Keeney made his "Declaration of Ranche" on April 21, 1883, so the NPRR must have purchased its terminus site from him just after that time and at about the same time that the company obtained its right-of-way through George Reese's land. On land that the NPRR purchased from Keeney and Huston in Sections 16 and 17, the town of Cinnabar began to rise, albeit slowly.[9] As will be seen, Carroll T. Hobart soon purchased some of the Keeney–Huston land, and Hugo J. Hoppe was its self-appointed superintendent for years, although at times that position was more of a superintendent-want-to-be.[10]

On August 17, the *Enterprise* reported that a party of surveyors was "at work laying out a townsite about two miles this side of Gardiner as the terminus of the Park branch." On August 20, the newspaper reported that the "new town" (still unnamed) was being "surveyed and staked out," and only a few weeks later a German geologist named G. M. Von Rath saw a surveyor working at the town and apparently spoke to him. Von Rath observed while waiting for his train that "Cinnabar City stands as [only] two tent residences, and yet Mr. Hallidge [Hollidge] busied himself laying out streets and avenues."[11] Carroll Hobart's comment to the local editor about the new town generated this boosterish announcement calculated to produce excitement:

> Since the town was platted and advertised great numbers of applica-
> tions have been received for property and it looks as though the 1,200
> lots the company have [*sic*] placed on the market will be sold very
> readily. The saw mills in the Park are to be moved down to Cinnabar to
> manufacture lumber for building purposes.[12]

But so far, the lots were not selling and the construction was not happening, at least partly because most people still thought that Gardiner would
become the railroad's ultimate terminus.

That summer and fall and during the winter of 1883–1884, the NPRR
ran newspaper advertising attempting to sell the lots, as Carroll Hobart's
campaign of boosterism continued:

> CINNABAR! Gallatin County, M.T., is situated at the terminus of the
> National Park Branch of the NPRR seven miles north of the Mammoth
> Hot Springs, one mile from the National Park line on the west bank of
> the Yellowstone River. A Warrantee [*sic*: warranty] [of] Title has been
> obtained in favor of the Northern Pacific Railroad and other capitalists,
> who will spare no pains in opening it to speedy settlement. On and
> after December 15th books will be open to those wishing to obtain title
> to lots. No one wishing to invest in town property can afford to loose
> [*sic*: lose] the present opportunity, owing to the liberal policy of the
> Company relative to price and terms of payment.
>
> The surrounding country abounds in COAL equal to the bitumuous
> [*sic*] coal of Pennsylvania, making this an excellent point for smelting
> works, for the Bear Gulch and Clark's Fork Mines, where smelting ore
> is inexhaustible. East of CINNABAR is a vast grazing country, afford-
> ing excellent facilities for stock raising. The lands lying north and
> south along the Yellowstone Valley are exceedingly fertile, mountain
> streams affording ample water for all irrigating purposes, making it a
> desirable country for those wishing to engage in agricultural pursuits.
> Full particulars, price and terms of payment furnished upon application
> to Park Improvement Co.[13]

This reference to the Yellowstone National Park Improvement Company
(YNPIC) within a boosterish advertisement pointed up the connection
between those new concessioners in the park and their parent company,
the Northern Pacific Railroad.

Who was this Carroll Hobart? He was a key player in both companies,
and because of that fact he became an important character in both the

history of Cinnabar and Yellowstone National Park. Mr. Hobart (1837–1915) hailed originally from Vermont and started with railroads there at the very bottom. He was a mere conductor on the Vermont Central Railroad on April 18, 1865, when he witnessed John H. Surratt, one of the Abraham Lincoln assassination conspirators who was fleeing to Canada, riding the train between Essex Junction and St. Albans, Vermont, and testified to that flight in Surratt's conspiracy trial. Hobart appears to have turned that momentary burst of fame into upward mobility within the railroad. Then he moved west to make money, and by 1869, he was one of the chiefs of construction for the Central Pacific Railroad. In the 1870s he became general superintendent of the Northern Pacific Railroad when Jay Cooke was ascending. That put him in position in 1882 to join Rufus Hatch, a New York financier, in a scheme involving the new Yellowstone National Park that they were sure would make them both rich.[14] It did not work out that way.

Carroll Hobart, with Rufus Hatch and Henry F. Douglas, obtained a lease from the Department of Interior in 1882 to put up the Mammoth Hot Springs Hotel. A tourist who saw him at Mammoth Hotel in 1883 called him "a bright, alert, hazel-eyed man, the picture of good health and energy and the real motor in the company's enterprise." Hobart would ultimately remain in the area, managing it and his company's Old Faithful Shack Hotel until autumn of 1885, before being forced out by the collapse of his Yellowstone National Park Improvement Company. But in late 1883, he had just finished his first summer in the park, and on November 22, he and a surveyor drew a plat for the new town of Cinnabar, to be partly owned by his company. In December, he contracted with O. W. Bennett of Bismarck, Dakota Territory, to officially obtain his company's portion of the new town of Cinnabar that he had purchased from Huston and Keeney.[15] Although the town, excluding Hugo Hoppe's and E. J. Keeney's ranches, was to be officially owned by YNPIC, Hobart eventually held the receiver's lease for the entire company, and this gave him future speculative rights in the town of Cinnabar with Hugo Hoppe. Joe Keeney was a player too, at least in the opinion of the Bozeman *Avant Courier*, which would soon refer to Keeney as "the owner of the park branch terminal town site—Cinnabar."[16] That reference must have irritated Hugo Hoppe, but dealing with his rough neighbor Joe Keeney was something to which he was quickly becoming accustomed.

Hobart's "Plat of the Town of Cinnabar," dated November 22, 1883, was surveyed by H. H. Hollidge of Bozeman and witnessed by A. L. Love, a public notary. An oversized map, it laid out and named the avenues in Cinnabar that ran north and south as follows: Sage, Cascade, Montana, Cinnabar, York, Yellowstone, Terrace, Electric, Gallatin, Shoshone, and Tacoma. Hobart named the east–west running streets (as they were laid out south of Main Street) as follows: Norman Hatch, Cavanaugh, Villard, Huston, Hugo, and Dawson. Norman Hatch Street was named for one of Rufus Hatch's relatives; Dawson Street was named for Edward Dawson, Hobart's "spy" friend in the Department of Interior; Huston for area old-timer George Huston, who had owned land there previously; Villard for Henry Villard to curry favor with that head of the Northern Pacific Railroad; and Hugo Street for Hugo J. Hoppe. [17]

From this it is apparent that Carroll Hobart was already friends with Hugo Hoppe, for Hoppe owned the land just west of YNPIC's new property at Cinnabar, and numerous letters from Hoppe to Hobart in the Carroll Hobart Papers at Yale University make their relationship clear. Each man needed the other one—Hoppe needed Hobart's money and influence in the park and in Washington, and Hobart needed Hoppe's Montana connections and his continuing physical presence on site. This connection between Hoppe and Hobart was to become important for both of their interests and at least initially for the new town of Cinnabar. The two men cultivated another moneymaking scheme together, namely the organizing of the "Cinnabar & Cooke Transportation Company." That plan looked forward to a time when and if the US Congress ever passed the bill segregating the Montana strip away from Yellowstone so that a railroad could be built through that part of the park (if not Lamar Valley!) to Cooke City. When that did not happen, Hugo Hoppe sold pieces of his ranch to his Bozeman friend Matthias Mounts to raise money, and he and his sons continued to run his freighting company back and forth to Cooke City. Another of his and Hobart's moneymaking schemes was the proposed railroad itself, which was to be called the "Cinnabar & Yellowstone Park Railway" and which they thought would bring direct profit to Hobart's company and perhaps employment for Hoppe himself. [18] In late 1884, when Hobart's company began financially failing, Hobart took actions that would benefit Hugo Hoppe, and we will return to those actions shortly.

During Hobart's attempts to sell lots at Cinnabar and all through 1884, townsmen at Gardiner were continuing to seethe that the railroad's inability to secure the right-of-way to their town threatened to obstruct their prosperity. These citizens believed that only one of the two towns would ultimately survive, and they desperately wanted it to be Gardiner. The *Enterprise* noticed this continuing conflict on August 12. Headlining its story "The Next Yellowstone City," the newspaper must have angered Gardiner townsfolk even more when it gave the advantage to Cinnabar:

> There are many rumors at Gardiner, Cinnabar and Mammoth Hot Springs about the great town that is to be made of one of the first two named hamlets—probably Cinnabar. Overtures have been made to the people of Gardiner to pay certain sums of money to have upon their town conferred the advantages that are to produce metropolitan fruit. The weight of favor rests at present with Cinnabar which, according to report, is to be resurveyed (probably with the object obtaining more front and corner lots) and is to be endowed with a fine depot, two or three smelters and incidental institutions calculated to promote its greatness. The townsite rests under attachments to the amount of ten to twenty thousand dollars, but trifles like that will probably not stand greatly in the way of its prosperity. Just who is to start the boom is not stated, but it is supposed to be C.T. Hobart. To the good sense of the upper Yellowstone people is due the fact that they are not yet taking any great stock in these reports. There will be a good town in that vicinity, but not just yet.[19]

Indeed, anyone who looked at F. Jay Haynes's 1884 photograph could clearly see that Cinnabar comprised little more than Hoppe's warehouse, two tents, a wooden platform, and a couple of box cars serving as a depot. Regardless, Hugo Hoppe must have loved reading this report in the newspaper.

Meanwhile, Hoppe still had a house (perhaps more than one), a big family, and loose ends to tie up, all in Bozeman. Ida Miller says that High Jehnsen "bought out" Hugo's freighting outfit that year[20] in a time when all that it consisted of was animals and wagons with no "rights" of any kind. Thus Hoppe was free to purchase more animals and wagons and go right back into the business whenever he wanted after regrouping for a while in Bozeman.

Just before Christmas of 1884, Hugo and Mary Hoppe suffered a stunning personal loss at their residence on the corner of Main and First

Streets in Bozeman. The *Chronicle* reported that their "elegant residence" was "burned to the ground" on Tuesday morning, December 9, 1884. "Elegant" might have been stretching it. The *Chronicle* put the loss at five thousand dollars but the *Courier* gave it as only fifteen hundred to two thousand dollars. Hoppe had rented part of the brick-veneer house to boarders named Owen Matthews and a Mr. Cummings, and the cause of the fire was the usual "stove pipe protruding through the roof."[21] To make matters worse, the weather was abysmally cold right then, with the mercury plunging to "below zero every night for the past two weeks." It was a bad Christmas for Hugo, Mary, and their sons—even with firefighters managing to save their adjoining livery stable—and the loss probably hastened the family's complete move to Cinnabar. The fire also changed the plans of Mary Hoppe's family members—the Gees plus daughter Maggie who was married to Bud Williams—all of whom were living in Bozeman. These folks began making plans for, or at least considering the idea of, moving to the upper Yellowstone River.[22] In particular, Bud, forty-two, and Maggie, twenty-seven, would soon rejoin the family and begin playing important if chaos-inducing roles as allies.

Hugo Hoppe's longtime acquaintance and now son-in-law, Morgan T. "Bud" Williams, must have been an unexpected ally. Born in Hamburg (Erie County), New York, in or about 1842, Bud served in the Civil War in Company K of New York's First Cavalry. He was captured by confederates and paroled; then he deserted and reenlisted, being promoted to sergeant. Wounded, he stayed in the service until he mustered out on June 27, 1865—so late that one suspects he loved the action. Described as having gray eyes, brown hair, and fair complexion, Williams was also tall and had stunning good looks that he used to his advantage, as anyone would have done. As early as 1870, he was a frontier hanger-on working as a "barkeeper" who married Hugo's daughter by late 1876 and lived with her in Bozeman. But he was also a bit of a "rustler" in a time when that word meant *go-getter*, and he may have had some money from selling his piece of land at Benson's Landing. By 1884, Morgan was respected enough in Bozeman for the *Courier* to refer to him more than once as "Governor," another of those nineteenth-century appellations that attempted to respect or flatter ordinary folks rather than to refer to any real title.[23] When Bud and Maggie moved to Cinnabar and obtained a homestead at what became Horr, they represented increased family power for Hugo Hoppe and extra labor for his burgeoning enterprises.

Meanwhile Carroll Hobart's YNPIC was in serious financial difficulties, so Carroll Hobart stored many of his personal belongings at Hoppe's ranch at Cinnabar and stored some of his company's property there too (something he had probably done the previous winter and a move that would later get him into legal trouble). Most critically, Hobart made arrangements for Hoppe and his wife to manage for the winter of 1884–1885 the huge, barnlike National Hotel (also called the Mammoth Hot Springs Hotel). Hobart was no doubt hoping that by trying to keep his hotel at least partly open for the winter, some much needed money might be made for his floundering company. On October 1, before he traveled east to argue with Rufus Hatch about company finances, he hired Hugo Hoppe at the rate of fifty dollars per month for the fall and winter. That was a good salary for the founder, freighter, and ranchman of Cinnabar.

Hoppe's appointment to manage the Mammoth Hotel was a perfect way for him not only to support himself through the destruction of his house at Bozeman but also to insert himself into the civic affairs of the Mammoth–Gardiner–Cinnabar communities. And it fit in with his plans to make Cinnabar a thriving community. For New Year's Eve, he and his wife "gave a free entertainment and a splendid supper, or an early New Year's Breakfast" at Yellowstone's Mammoth Hotel complete with "luxuriant" food. That story appeared on the front page of the *Livingston Enterprise*, which also noted that the Hoppes would sponsor a grand ball at the hotel on January 8, 1885. This was a time when these early proprietors and owners of Mammoth Hotel had still not discovered that their huge, barnlike structure—even with its giant woodstove in the lobby— would prove difficult to heat and thus to keep open in winter. The existence of Hobart's new fifty-two-hundred-dollar steam-heating system in the hotel, installed in the summer of 1884, probably delayed their discovery that the hotel would continue to be hard to heat. Hoppe's festivities must have been chilly, but apparently the New Year's Eve and January 8 activities were somewhat successful, for the newspaper announced on February 14 that the Hoppes would sponsor a dance "at the National Hotel" on the evening of February 20.[24] It was a date that would soon figure into the demise of Yellowstone Park superintendent Robert Carpenter.

That was yet to come. Aided by another project that winter, Hoppe ingratiated himself into the tricommunity while simultaneously guaranteeing that his social galas at Mammoth Hotel would be well attended. He did these things by personally building (in the winter) a road bridge across Gardner River and just below Boiling River at a spot that Lt. Dan Kingman's road crews had been unable to complete that fall. "Hugo Hoppe has taken the matter in hand," proclaimed the *Enterprise*, "and by the assistance of E. Lamartine [Kingman's immediate assistant], Alexander Young and some others, a temporary bridge forty feet in length and twelve in width has been constructed." According to the newspaper, this construction "would insure the safety of all visitors to the Springs and all the guests who may see fit to share Mr. Hoppe's hospitality at the National Hotel."[25]

Hoppe was obviously no fool at public relations or at keeping money in his own pocket, for such well-attended activities at Mammoth Hotel would keep his boss and friend, Carroll Hobart, happy, too. The local newspaper noted approvingly that "the people of Gardiner, Mammoth Hot Springs, and the extreme Upper Yellowstone generally, in spite of the fact of their comparative isolation during this season, are whiling away the winter months with a series of frequent dances and social gatherings that are very largely attended and are conspicuous for their enjoyability . . . at the National Hotel."[26]

That winter, as Hugo Hoppe drove his wagon or rode his horse back and forth from his ranch at Cinnabar to Mammoth Hotel over Lt. Kingman's just-completed road through Gardner Canyon, he became embroiled in an ethically crooked scheme to claim park land in the event that Congress privatized some of it by segregating away its Montana strip. Technology chose that moment to rear its head in the area, when a telephone was installed at R. A. Bell's store in Gardiner (soon to become W. T. Hall's store[27]) that was connected to Livingston's Western Union office—an office that received many telegraph messages for this part of Montana. By suddenly having telephones available, someone's "father" in Washington, DC, could get a message to his "son" in Livingston (described as "a prominent citizen") that Congress had acted to separate the Montana strip from Yellowstone National Park. Or at least this was the story put forth by the editors at the *Livingston Enterprise*, who seemed to have all the other pieces of the puzzle in hand. The agreed-upon signal would be to "secure that horse at once," which was an order for riders on horseback to head for Soda Butte and other nearby locations to stake off "certain coal lands" and "other valuable properties" abutting the new railroad's proposed right-of-way within Congress's newly privatized section of the park. An alternative code to signal passage of the bill was "no wind in Livingston."[28]

The "father" in this affair was probably either park superintendent Robert Carpenter or YNPIC general manager Carroll T. Hobart, both of whom were spending the winter in Washington, DC, to lobby Congress for the passage of that railroad bill. Historian Aubrey Haines believed that Carpenter was the party who sent the telegram. Regardless, on February 20, when it appeared that both houses of Congress had passed the bill, the "father" in Washington sent a telegram to his "son" in Livingston, so the "son" dutifully picked up the telephone and called Gardiner.[29] No doubt present at the Gardiner end of the telephone line was Hugo J. Hoppe.

But the phone at Gardiner represented new technology and did not work very well. "The order to secure that horse was indistinct and mixed," said the *Enterprise*, and the "no wind in Livingston" did not work either. That phrase was, as the editor stated, "so manifestly mysterious and [simultaneously] doubtful in its probability"—because the wind was *always* blowing in Livingston—"that it aroused suspicion outside the circle for those whose benefit it was particularly intended."[30]

"The ensuing shouting" at the Gardiner end of the line, as historian Aubrey Haines has stated, "soon put all the loafers in Hall's store[31] on the qui vive." Many there who did not know the plan were immediately suspicious. Meanwhile the conspirators-in-the-know began making plans for an early horseback trip the next morning, and when they rode east before sunrise, some forty or fifty extra riders followed them to Soda Butte and points beyond to "secure" a "horse." The result was that a lot of names of Gardiner locals appeared the next day on claim stakes for land, among them George Huston, Joe Keeney, Adam Deem, George Haldorn, A. L. Love, and three men who were suspiciously absent from Gardiner: Dave Roberts, Carroll Hobart, and most brazenly Robert Carpenter, the park superintendent.[32]

But the segregation bill had *not* really cleared the Senate. After both houses seemingly passed the bill, Senators Vest, Harrison, and Manderson added an amendment that tabled the bill into conference, and then they refused to act further on it and adjourned the Senate. Thus the conspirators' entire plan had been hatched prematurely, and this affair merely made their awkward scheme public.[33]

We now know that Hugo Hoppe was the person who rode out to the Soda Butte country and erected stakes bearing the three names of the absent men. He also put his own name on a stake and that of one of his sons, probably his eldest son, Walter. Hugo Hoppe was thus one of Hobart's conspirators. He was friends with Carroll Hobart, and he may also have been acting at the instigation of Superintendent Carpenter, although Carpenter later denied that direct connection. "The use of my name in locating those coal lands was without my knowledge, consent, or expectation," claimed Carpenter unconvincingly. "When I heard that Mr. Hoppe had done so, I was very sorry, as I knew it was not in accordance with my official position and might lead to a false inference, which has been the case."[34] Queen Gertrude in "Hamlet" would probably have said of Carpenter's comments: "He doth protest too much, methinks." Carpenter was sorry, alright—sorry that he got caught. Two months later, the Secretary of Interior fired him from the Yellowstone National Park superintendency.

A humorous postscript to this story is that Hugo Hoppe's friend Dave Roberts had been assigned by someone to wait at Livingston in case the telephone did not work. So at 5:00 p.m., when the telegrapher received the message and the "son" picked up the telephone to call Gardiner, Roberts mounted his horse and rode all night long through snow and cold at breakneck speed for sixty miles through Paradise Valley. He arrived at 8:00 a.m. the next morning at Gardiner to find everyone already gone. In the subsequent jokes made about the affair, Roberts was nicknamed "fly-by-night" Dave or "the Lightning Courier."[35]

The remaining question in this affair is who was the "son" at Livingston who called Gardiner on the telephone? Historian Steve Mishkin and this author do not believe that it was any of Robert Carpenter's or Carroll Hobart's children, mainly because all those children were too young to have been involved in this affair.[36] So who was the tipster in Livingston? It might have been Dave Roberts who made the aforementioned horseback ride, but Roberts was arguably not positioned with important friends or even particularly politically aware.

A letter to Carroll Hobart—saved by Hobart himself in his papers at Yale—makes it clear that its writer could have been, and probably was, the tipster at Livingston. John N. Shoolbred—treasurer of the Wills Smelting and Mining Company and a Cooke City resident—wrote a letter to Carroll Hobart from that place on January 10, 1885. From the letter, it was clear that he was interested in the passage of the railroad segregation bill and sympathetic to Superintendent Carpenter's trip to Washington to lobby for its passage. The relevant portion of the letter made Shoolbred the likely tipster, and it read as follows:

> And now sir about these lands[,] to secure them we shall have to be alive [alert?] when the time comes. The line you speak of cuts off all the coal lands by Gardiner—have you made any arrangements to se-cure them—or do you wish me to do so—excuse me suggesting but I know that there will be a suit when the time comes from—would it not be better if the bill is certain[,] to at [have?] me get one or two men who can be trusted to go on the ground & wait there till we get the news. Also if you want me to do anything let me know as soon as possible when I had better be in Livingston, for it takes a considerable time to get out of here now [that] the snow is deep and I know others are on the watch all the time.[37]

So if Shoolbred was the tipster, what was his exact connection to Hobart? That is unknown; however Shoolbred's use of the term "sir" in the letter plus his addressing it to "T.C." Hobart (Hobart's original initials but ones that he had long ago quit using in favor of "C.T.") suggest that he was not a close friend of Hobart but rather someone who was hired by him for (or at least who had more than a passing interest in) such an assignment. Nevertheless, his status as an "attorney-in-fact," a Cooke City resident, and an officer in a mining company located there no doubt made him valuable to Carroll Hobart.

For Hugo Hoppe, there must have been some soul searching after this whole affair. Was he an actual friend of Robert Carpenter and directly in cahoots with him? Or was he merely asked to ride to Soda Butte by his friend Carroll Hobart, who had been with Carpenter lobbying Congress all winter in Washington? We do not know, but regardless, Hoppe must ever after have regretted his role in the fly-by-night-secure-that-horse affair, or at least pondered it introspectively as he lived on his ranch at Cinnabar for the next decade.

As 1885 progressed, things got worse for Carroll Hobart and the Yel-lowstone National Park Improvement Company. In late January, Hobart put his portion of the townsite of Cinnabar up for sale,[38] which must have disturbed his friend Hugo Hoppe at Mammoth Hotel. Rufus Hatch's com-pany had fallen into receivership in April of 1884 and again failed to make money that summer, so in May of 1885 Receiver George B. Hulme leased the entire company to Hobart for one dollar to give him a final summer to fix it. Hugo Hoppe continued to manage Mammoth Hotel for Hobart until June 16, nearly a month after Hobart returned to the park. Two weeks later, on June 30, Hoppe bought back from Matthias Mounts the three pieces of his ranch that he had sold to Mounts in late 1883. He probably used money he had received all winter from managing the Mammoth Hotel. At that point, Hoppe was also out of a job but fortunately E. J. Keeney was very busy with his new wife and with being a constable at Lower Geyser Basin, so he either leased his hotel to the Hoppes for the summer or simply hired them to manage it. They were thus in place to have been the couple that Ms. O. S. T. Drake encountered that summer. Traveler W. H. Dudley stated that there was a hotel at Cinnabar in 1885 and Keeney could not have been present, so Hoppe must have run it. By doing this, Keeney established the procedure of allowing Hoppe to sometimes run his hotel while he did other things. Meanwhile Carroll Hobart was vainly trying to save his company in the park. Although he personally made money during that summer of 1885, he plowed much of his $4,250 salary back into the company and ultimately failed to keep it afloat.[39]

That autumn, as he rode back and forth between Mammoth Hotel and his friend Hoppe's ranch, Carroll Hobart knew that his days in the park were numbered. Thus he also knew that he would soon have to travel from the East Coast to Cinnabar for business matters, perhaps several times. He must have wondered where he would stay once his hotel was turned over to new owners. Hoppe probably put him up at the hotel at Cinnabar, for Hugo did not have room for guests at his ranch cabin, which housed a wife, at least four sons, and probably some ranch staff. Regardless, Hugo Hoppe's fascinating family photo taken on his porch on October 8, 1885, shows a gentleman standing at the rear who can be none other than Carroll Hobart. As one might expect, he did not look happy at this moment. On October 31, the local newspaper reported the new syndicate's takeover of Hobart's company. On November 14, it reported the departure of Carroll Hobart and his wife on the train heading east.[40]

But where he now had to stay when visiting Cinnabar was only a side issue for Carroll Hobart. For more than a year Rufus Hatch had been blaming Hobart for his own overextensions, and in the late fall of 1885, the company's creditors were getting impatient. On November 25, two of

Hobart's creditors (doing business as the Dabney Brothers) sued Hobart and YNPIC in a Wyoming district court for monies owed. Alleging that YNPIC's assets were worth one hundred fifty-five thousand dollars, their attorney, D. H. Budlong, went after everything that the company had in order to satisfy his clients' owed debts.[41]

Suddenly having no funds, Hobart turned to his friend Hugo Hoppe at Cinnabar, and it became Hoppe's turn to grant a favor. He loaned Hobart five hundred dollars and of course continued to let Hobart store his company and personal possessions at the Cinnabar ranch. He also wrote a letter to the railroad on behalf of Carroll Hobart, asking it to "stand by him and do him justice." But nothing was working for Carroll Hobart. "Hatch is abusing me shamefully . . . he is turning heaven and earth to ruin me," wailed Hobart to his wife, Alice, in late December. "God knows I have stood so much trial in this park matter that I am nearly ready to return [to the East] penniless and start new in a more genial drive."[42] Two days later, Hobart told her that "[Attorney] Budlong is an unmitigated scoundrel [who has] vilified me in every Conceivable way." This "vilification" referred to Hobart's loaning of some company furniture to a woman at Bear Gulch who was destitute and dying of consumption (the furniture was subsequently returned), for storing other company furniture with Hoppe, and for everything else involved in the lawsuit against YNPIC.[43]

When the Wyoming court set the date for sale of the company's assets as May 1, 1886, Hobart panicked that he would not be able to pay back his loan from Hoppe. "I am nearly distracted at this delay as it leaves me so long until a deal," wrote Hobart, who then denounced his entire adventure in Yellowstone: "My property will simply be sold so that we have ended our miserable career in the Park. Thank God for that." He told Alice to tell "our good friend Hoppie . . . that I cannot get my money from NPRR until May then every cent will be returned to him." He also instructed her through Hoppe to "sell my horses, desk, everything to get me $1,000." "That is all I need," he cried, so that "we can get on" with our lives.[44]

Meanwhile, in the autumn of 1885, Hugo Hoppe's summer job at Keeney's hotel seemed to be running out—the bane or jubilance of all Yellowstone summer workers that continues for them today. Fortunately Keeney was still busy with other matters, so he leased his hotel to Hugo and Mary for the winter of 1885–1886. Hugo Hoppe was obviously excited about this opportunity, because from late December through mid-June of 1886, he ran the following advertisement in the *Livingston Enterprise* newspaper:

> Cinnabar Hotel! Stable and Blacksmith Shop in Connection. Hay, Grain, and General Supplies Always on Hand. Also Headquarters of the Cinnabar and Cooke Transportation and Forwarding Co., W.M. Hoppe and Co., Proprietors . . . H.J. Hoppe, Manager, Cinnabar, Montana.[45]

Knowing full well that the hotel business was slight during this off-season, Hoppe also continued freighting all winter, breaking open the road to Cooke City in January with no difficulty even after a severe snowstorm. The *Enterprise* credited him with demonstrating "that freighting by teams from Cinnabar to Cooke the year round is practical beyond a doubt."[46] That was easy to say during a winter of relatively light snow.

Carroll Hobart's legal problems dragged on, but he continued his relationship with Hugo Hoppe. In February of 1886, Hobart was writing to Robert Harris, president of the Northern Pacific Railroad, to assure him that Hoppe had safely kept YNPIC property at his ranch and assuring him that Hoppe was trustworthy. On February 15, he wrote a personal thank-you letter to Hugo Hoppe.[47]

In March, Mr. Hoppe got into some kind of fracas with Joe Keeney, and again it looked like today's "Wild West" of Hollywood. Probably it was a disagreement inside Keeney's saloon that Hoppe was leasing for the winter. The district attorney at Bozeman prosecuted both men in April for "drawing and exhibiting a deadly weapon." Hoppe's trial found him not guilty of the weapons charge, but a jury convicted Keeney and fined him twenty dollars plus court costs for a total of three hundred dollars! That result was a commentary on the way things seemed generally to go in both men's lives—well for Hoppe and not so well for Keeney. Hoppe's assault charge remained briefly pending, but eventually it was either dropped or deemed "small potatoes," for nothing more of it appeared in the newspaper.[48] One can bet that Joe Keeney carried a grudge against Hoppe for this incident.

In June of 1886, Hoppe's lease of Keeney's hotel expired, so he decided to concentrate on his ranch and temporarily shelved his "Cinnabar and Cooke Transportation Company." Hoppe stated to the newspaper that barring the small amount of freighting he had been doing for the Yellow-stone Park Association (successor to his friend Hobart's company within the park) since late April, operation of his business had ceased. "For the present," said the *Enterprise*, "he will devote his attention to his ranch at Cinnabar."[49]

That announcement was premature and completely temporary with regard to freighting. Keeney wanted his hotel back for the summer in 1886, and he was no doubt still mad at Hoppe over the bar incident. Hugo still had to make a living, and hay ranching alone would not suffice. Hence by July 24, Hoppe was announcing that merchants in Cooke City had engaged him to carry their freight back and forth to Cinnabar, and in August he began advertising the transportation company again as well as running it part-time.[50] Puzzlingly, by September 1, Hoppe was also writing to Hobart that visitation to his hotel had been "great," so apparently he was again running the hotel for Keeney but also freighting to Cooke City. At the end of the season he suddenly suffered some health problems. On September 1, he wrote to Hobart in the East telling him that his "nerves are bad" but that he was optimistic about conditions at Cooke City. "Both smelters are running successfully & buying all [the] ores they can get," he gushed, adding that "we all" are wishing for the railroad to be approved. His stationery, which proclaimed "Cinnabar and Cooke Trans-portation Company," made it apparent that he and son Walter, now aged twenty-two, were running his transportation business together.[51] As ever, the freighting business—like the hotel business—was sporadic and sea-sonal.

Hoppe continued to keep Hobart updated, because he nourished hopes that Cinnabar would someday become important and he hoped that Ho-bart would return as a potential partner. In September, he mailed Hobart a newsy letter, claiming that new Yellowstone Park Association president Charles Gibson was the "most unpopular man in the park." Hoppe's health had improved enough that he could attend the Montana Territorial political convention, where he helped nominate W. F. Sanders (1834–1905) as delegate to the US House of Representatives (territories were then allowed one nonvoting delegate to Congress). And Hoppe indi-cated that he was still running a hotel at Cinnabar (apparently Keeney's), for he stated that business was good: "45 [persons] last night and 27 night before." In October, Hoppe assured Hobart that his sons had "shipped all your goods" except for the "bureau" from the furniture set that Jack

"Baronett bought." (Clearly, Hobart was trying to convert as much personal property as possible into cash.) By way of parting, Hoppe assured Hobart that he would continue to consider him "in with me should Cinnabar amount to anything."[52]

That did not happen, but Hoppe would never give up on it. During the next two years, Carroll Hobart failed to get any money or sympathy from his former friends at the NPRR but somehow got the money to travel to South America in 1887 on a venture that was similar to his Yellowstone one. In 1892, nearly six years after he left the park, Hobart must have been surprised when Hugo Hoppe sued him for money damages in some kind of civil matter. It may well have been for the storage and/or removal of supplies that Hobart left in Hoppe's barn. Whatever the reason, the district court awarded plaintiff Hugo Hoppe $1,138.97 plus court costs.[53] By 1898, Mr. Hobart was engaged in "location and construction of a government road in the Argentine republic."After that he largely vanished from the historical record and died at his home in Norfolk, Virginia, in late November of 1915.[54]

Carroll Hobart was a strong influence upon Hugo Hoppe, who stimulated and added to Hoppe's already existing excitement about Cinnabar's potential but who ultimately failed both in Yellowstone and at Cinnabar. The failure was rooted largely in Rufus Hatch's lies to Hobart about his own financial stability, but it was also partly attributable to Hobart's arrogance and poor treatment of people around him. Hobart's inability to get Cinnabar going left Hoppe depressed. "I have lost all faith in almost everything," he wrote to Hobart, "and [so] let things go as they may and make the best of it."[55]

But as the next few years went by, Hoppe's old optimism returned, and he renewed his efforts to make Cinnabar into something special. Already aware that he preferred being a hotelier to the dirtier and harder job of transporting freight and knowing that aging was already hindering him in mining and prospecting, Hugo Hoppe began saving money toward the goal of purchasing Cinnabar and its hotel for himself and his family. Along the way he would enlist the aid of all his offspring and his son-in-law to help him obtain the real estate, knowing that if he succeeded he could leave it to his children.

Hugo Hoppe was anxious for his dreams to come true. But he still had a long time to wait.

5

FREIGHTING, FARMING, AND POLITICS

Hugo Hoppe Fancies Owning Cinnabar (1883–1892)

Dare to live the life you have dreamed for yourself.
—Ralph Waldo Emerson, 1803–1882

The year 1887 saw Hugo J. Hoppe return to freighting while braving one of the coldest winters in Montana's history. It also ushered in that factor that many aging Americans eventually encounter, namely the increasing importance of politics in one's life, as Hugo began to take an interest in both the workings of Congress and the workings of the Montana Legislature to improve his own life. E. J. Keeney had taken back his Cinnabar hotel for the winter, but Hoppe knew that its business in winter was limited anyway. Much worse was the increasing likelihood that Keeney would keep his hotel for the following summer, so Hoppe resigned himself to freighting and ranching. In addition to looking after the hotel, he freighted all autumn of 1886 but was forced by bad weather to take his teams off the Cooke City road in early December.[1]

The winter of 1886–1887 became known in the history of the American West as the "legendary harsh winter." Blizzards swept through the Dakotas, Minnesota, Wyoming, and other states. As temperatures dropped to sometimes fifty below zero, cattle froze by the thousands across the West. Snow accumulated to legendary depths. By January 15, old-timers in Livingston were saying that the snow was the deepest they could remember for many years, and at Mammoth, G. L. Henderson was stating that the snow was the deepest in the five years of his life there. At

Mammoth, it was minus twenty-five on February 2, while simultaneously snowing too hard to see—an unusual phenomenon. In Gardiner, the lethal cold killed Alexander "Mormon" Brown. In Cooke City, a mile-long avalanche swept Anthony Wise and Clarence Martin to their deaths. Out in the park, Frederick Schwatka's "first winter trip" became a disaster for Schwatka but successful for photographer F. Jay Haynes, who took the first wintertime photos of Yellowstone.[2] At Firehole Hotel in Lower Geyser Basin, where James Dean was serving as winter keeper, gale-force winds blew all through February, causing intense drifting of more than ten feet of snow. "I have never witnessed such storms," wrote Dean, "nor have I ever read of any to equal what we have had here."[3]

In February, Hugo Hoppe was forced to ride a frigid stagecoach to Livingston because trains could not run in the deep snow for at least six weeks. He did this to purchase feed for his horses—feed that had to await shipment south by train from Livingston to Cinnabar. The cold made it so difficult to work that he decided to take time off and visit the state legislature in Helena, hoping to learn tactics to improve his businesses. On the way there and back, he noticed the increasing coal-mining activity at Cokedale, west of Livingston, so in March when the weather improved a bit, Hoppe began freighting loads of coal for the Livingston Coal and Coke Company to the coking ovens at nearby Coalspur, west of Livingston. Similar such operations at Horr, Montana, were not yet occurring.[4]

By the end of April, the terrible winter had lessened, and Hoppe was on his ranch superintending spring seeding and planting. He knew that his freighting for the coal company was paying off, so with the help of his sons he headed north with wagons and teams and within a few weeks requested three extra teams to be sent north.[5] In May, his son Walter was badly injured at Coalspur when heavy timbers fell on him during freighting.[6] At some point, probably in January, Hoppe or someone else in his family acquired a saloon at Cinnabar, but the family would sell it in September. Apparently this short-lived saloon was merely a moneymaking step to the Hoppes' bigger dreams of owning a hotel, store, saloon, and a share of the tourist business entering Yellowstone National Park.[7]

In June, Hoppe succumbed to the lure of Cinnabar and Yellowstone's burgeoning summer activity and moved all of his teams and wagons from Cokedale back to Cinnabar. Working at Cinnabar would save him money on lodging as well as the hassles of living away from home. He bid on a contract running from Cinnabar to Mammoth and later obtained it.[8]

Meanwhile, Joe Keeney announced that he would indeed be running his hotel for the summer of 1887 at Cinnabar, along with a saloon and a livery stable. Perhaps Keeney had finally gotten serious about running a business at Cinnabar. Keeney soon needed more horses, and Hugo and his sons were in place to sell them to him and continue freighting for the summer.[9]

But with all of Hoppe's efforts, he was still not acquiring the money quickly enough that he needed for his heart's desire, namely purchasing Keeney's hotel at Cinnabar. He hit upon an idea. Even though his homesteaded ranch that the United States had approved in 1886 would not ripen into full ownership until 1890,[10] he could still legally sell or lease it. Thus on September 23, 1887, he tried doing again what he had done earlier, namely selling it. This time he and his family sold their ranch to their neighbors Harry Gassert and Jacob Reding by warranty deed for $5,742.15.[11] The Hoppes apparently received a down payment, but they definitely carried the note for the new owners and agreed to let Gassert and Reding pay it off in three years. The down payment represented a windfall of money for the family's dreams, but it also meant that Hugo and Mary Hoppe and their three minor sons suddenly had to find housing elsewhere. To remedy this, the adults in the family—Hugo, Mary, Walter, and Hughie—executed two additional contracts: 1) to sell the family's freighting business[12] and 2) to immediately lease back the ranch from the new owners with a clause allowing the Hoppes to assign the land if they desired.[13] Meanwhile, Gassert and Reding decided to spend the winter of 1887–1888 in California,[14] so the Hoppes remained on the new owners' ranch, which was now leased back to them for an annual fee. In those days, sale of a business such as freighting did not automatically carry a side agreement that the sellers would not engage in such business in competition with the new owners. Hence Walter and Hughie Hoppe— ages twenty-three and twenty-two, respectively—were free to start (again) their own freighting business, which Hugo also soon joined, at least in theory.

Hugo Hoppe now made ready to open a new business of sawmilling while his sons ran their new freight operation. The background for his sawmill involved the town of Horr, and the sawmill resulted in the naming of Hoppe Creek in 1888. That stream was located northwest of Cinnabar and over Electric Peak's northerly ridge, and it ran north and northwesterly from near Little Joe Lake into Mulherin Creek. Mr. Hoppe needed lumber as early as 1882 to erect his house and barn at the base of Sepulcher Mountain. It was an easy matter at that time to simply climb the hill back of his ranch until he reached timber. As long as he did not go too far up Stephens Creek or up the stream to its west, called Spring Creek, he was outside the national park and could take the timber he needed. Or he could ride his horse up Reese Creek and take whatever timber he needed from the public land there that was not yet inside of Yellowstone National Park. Continually needing lumber for building materials, Hoppe established a steam-powered sawmill on Reese Creek in 1887, but Acting Park Superintendent Moses Harris did not like it because the enterprise required "constant watching" to make sure that its timber was not being cut from the park. Hoppe wanted to use water power rather than steam anyway, so in April of 1888, as the newspaper intoned, "The wide awake and rustling Hugo J. Hoppe" moved his saw-mill from Reese Creek over the long northerly ridge of Electric Peak and onto the next stream west. It was a new source of timber. There he set up a water-powered sawmill and the stream became—and remains today—Hoppe Creek. A bonus for working there was that Hugo Hoppe could sell extra wood to residents of nearby Horr, Montana, whose coal mines were just being opened by the enterprising Harry Horr. [15]

It was this steady gearing up of the new town of Horr that factored into Hoppe's decision to sell his ranch and freighting operation and instead concentrate on making what he thought was quicker money in that burgeoning town. So Hoppe's financial prospects were improving if his dreams were not. In an era when many persons did not live past forty, that must have disturbed Hoppe because he was fifty-three years old, but what could he do other than be optimistic? After all, he had five sons, a son-in-law, and a daughter helping him. As he listened to the noise of his saw-mill or helped his sons run freight that spring and summer, he must have been envious of E. J. Keeney, especially whenever he read the *Livingston Enterprise*'s continuing references to "Joe Keeney, the irrepressible proprietor of the Tourists' Pleasure Resort at Cinnabar." [16] That description of Keeney's hotel was a ridiculous stretch, but the statement intruded directly into Hoppe's dreams and thus must have exasperated him.

There was another big item that swirled around in Hugo Hoppe's head. He was still hoping that his other ranch (declared at the mouth of Gardner River) would someday amount to something. Having sold his main ranch to Gassert and Reding in late 1887, Hoppe was nurturing that nest egg and banking further money from sawmilling and his sons' freighting (and other activities) to purchase the hotel at Cinnabar. He was fervently hoping for the ranch that he had declared in 1885 on the east side of Gardner River to become truly available, for even if the government would not let him "prove up" on this second homestead, he could always transfer it to one or both of his sons—now of legal age—and let them secure title to the land. But there was the nagging question as to whether that ranch was technically inside Yellowstone National Park. Many men were now waiting to stake coal claims on the flats west of Rattlesnake Butte should surveying show otherwise, or should Congress segregate that portion of the park away from the rest of Yellowstone through legislation. If either of those things happened, these waiting men, including Hugo Hoppe, envisioned a future extension of Gardiner spilling east onto those flats, or perhaps a separate town would grow up there altogether. In the spring of 1888, the local newspaper was discussing the flats as being part of the strip of land that might soon return to the public domain.[17] All of these prospects boded as possible moneymakers for Hugo Hoppe, and he saw them as figuring into his dreams of Cinnabar.

Late in 1888, Hoppe also realized—if he hadn't already—that entering politics might not only make him some more money toward his dream but also might introduce him to important people (they, too, might make him money). In September, he attended a local Republican convention and wrangled himself a nomination for one of the three seats on the Park County Commission in Livingston. In early November, after his endorsement by the *Livingston Enterprise*, voters indeed chose him to be a Park County Commissioner.[18] When Joe Keeney sold his Cinnabar hotel and saloon to another freighter, A. T. French, only a month after Hugo was elected, Hoppe must have had momentary regrets about his choice of working in Livingston.[19]

If so, he swallowed them and looked forward to his new adventure. This election to office would change Hoppe's life. It would result in his having a "real" job that would add to his personal finances, because the salary was sometimes as high as $590.50 per year.[20] Additionally, in those days there were no ethical prohibitions on public officials simultaneously running their own businesses and delving into side deals to make extra money, even if those deals presented conflicts of interest. But it would also mean that he would soon have to move fifty-two miles north to Livingston, at least for part of the time.

Livingston, Montana—the town that Hugo Hoppe would help to govern for the next four years—had its own raucousness, but unlike Cinnabar it had an on-site sheriff and deputies to keep order. It was a small but fascinating place, a brawling sort of a burg that seemed to exhibit the very elements responsible for today's stereotyped images of the "wild west." It had been named in 1882–1883 by townsite owner Crawford Livingston for his uncle—Johnston Livingston—who was a Northern Pacific Railroad director. In 1891, the town held only 2,850 people, while the entire county contained a mere 6,881 people.[21] Although not as mean of a place as Butte or Miles City, it was nevertheless a town where three murder trials proceeded simultaneously on more than one occasion, although the county's first death penalty and hanging were late in arriving (1894) compared to other towns in Montana.[22] It was a place where black prostitutes legally sold their wares on B Street and where Chinese laundries and restaurants were also tolerated, at least until it came time to raid opium dens (also on B Street).[23] From 1883 through 1917, Livingston had twelve different newspapers,[24] which existed only by one to three at a time but which were often loaded with gossipy stories. In that era before libel lawsuits, editors did not hesitate to write judgmentally, as when they referred to two black women as "colored Cyprians." ("Cyprians" referred to ancient Cyprus, alleged birthplace of Aphrodite, and thus the word had come to mean "lewd persons or prostitutes.") Lula St. Clair and Daisy Peckham were convicted of "selling liquor without a license," and one has to believe that their real crime was merely being suspected of prostitution.[25] Likewise, the editor of the *Enterprise* reported that Mary Mason, "a colored woman who is an old offender against the peace and dignity of Montana," was convicted for drunkenness and disturbing the peace when her real crime was probably unprovable prostitution.[26] In early 1896, the editor announced the arrest of "Alice Fairfax, the dusky member of the demi-monde" for alleged robbery, a charge that was subsequently dismissed.[27] Again one suspects that her real crime was the harder-to-prove prostitution.

Reading Livingston's newspapers, one is hard-pressed to believe that it was a small town, because so much was happening there. In 1891, W. O. Hart—night watchman and so-called detective for the Northern Pacific Railway—was "set upon by two masked men" in the railroad yards who spirited him east of town, stripped off his clothes, bound his hands, horsewhipped him, and then covered him with tar and feathers from his "neck to his lower extremities." (Hart was apparently not well liked, because a fellow railroad employee was soon arrested for the crime but found not guilty. [28]) Livingston and Park Counties warred with cattle rustlers at the same time that Johnson County, Wyoming, was similarly involved (1892), and more than one Montana rustler—including William Corker, who was "generally regarded as a hard character"—was shot to death in Montana at the same time that Wyoming was dealing with its rustlers. [29] Thomas Leforge, a renowned local rancher who would later write the famous book *Memoirs of a White Crow Indian*, criminally prosecuted his wife and her lover for adultery in local court in 1893, even though his truant spouse and her "gay Lothario" had run off to Butte. [30] A few months later, sixteen-year-old Bertha Blazer accidentally shot her gambler boyfriend between the eyes in McDonnell's saloon while demonstrating her "unloaded" gun. [31] When the Livingston post office was robbed in 1894, a local mob "lynched" the black man who had allegedly done it by lifting him with a neck rope four or five times before he confessed and was let down alive. (The newspaper was moved to call it "a sickening story of cruelty" that should "never again be chronicled as happening in this city." [32]) In reporting on an unfortunate ten-year-old black resident of Livingston who had run away to become the "Smallest Tramp on Earth," the *Enterprise* felt sorry for him and called him "a bright little fellow [who] accepts the vicissitudes which fortune has thrust on him with the greatest complacency." [33] Even though its newspapers seemed to enjoy needling black residents in print, Livingston seems to have treated those minorities a lot better than did many other Western (and especially Southern) towns during the same period. That Livingston was in the West and not the South was also evidenced by the fact that a Sunday closing law was apparently not even thought of until 1900, when a petition to require saloons to close on Sunday failed in the city council. [34] In short, the town of Livingston was constantly home to interesting events, whether they were related to minorities, Yellowstone National Park, drownings, murders, prostitutes, gambling, mining, big game hunting, or the railroad.

Livingston also had culture in the form of live theaters—as it still does today—and at times there were more than one of these. During the 1890s, many issues of the *Enterprise* carried articles and snippets about opera house productions at Fowlie's Hall and the Hefferlin Hall. Whether these musicals and plays were performed by traveling troupes of professionals who arrived on the train or by local performers who rehearsed in town, Livingston was perfectly situated to perpetuate a long-term history of local theater. Traveling circuses also occasionally passed through to offer temporary excitement to residents starved for entertainment. [35]

This was the community to which Hugo and Mary Hoppe were moving. Initially, they stayed at the Albemarle Hotel and then they house-sat for their friend J. H. Elder, who let them stay there all winter. [36] In April of 1889, the federal government hired George Hoppe as clerk for the railroad mail service, a job that would last a little less than a year. He suddenly needed housing at Livingston too, so Hugo Hoppe began thinking about building a house there. [37] (The house he built that autumn would soon allow him and his family members to easily move back and forth.) But as spring arrived, Hoppe again got "Yellowstone Fever," an itching that today still infects hundreds of ex-park employees each spring, whenever it comes time to return to Yellowstone National Park for the summer. So Hugo and Mary returned to their leased ranch at Cinnabar. The move corresponded to Hoppe's having figured out a way to make still more money from his ranch, namely by running an advertisement putting it up "for sale or rent." [38] That ad was somewhat misleading because he had already sold the ranch, but legally he could assign his own lease to someone else and let that person live there, thus effectively getting that person to pay his not insubstantial rent of $689 per year. If he worried about such pretenses, it did not really matter because it took a year for anyone to respond to the advertisement.

What Hoppe did at Cinnabar during the summer of 1889 is uncertain, but seeing A. T. French running the hotel there must have irked him. Hoppe probably worked in agriculture on his ranch and helped his sons with their freighting business, although he probably also spent time at Cooke City with a mining claim that he had purchased as an investment for his dreams. [39] He still owned the sawmill at Horr, so he probably worked there too, along with his hired help. Sometime during this year, he and Mary moved to Horr, perhaps leaving sons Lee and Albert on their pieces of what was left of the Cinnabar ranch (they were now ages nineteen and seventeen, respectively). Or perhaps he left them on a (another) ranch that the family owned at Horr, a residence whose story will soon be hypothesized. Maggie and Bud Williams, who also were living at Horr, were likely having domestic trouble by this time, so Maggie may have spent some nights with Lee and Albert at one or the other of those places too.

How Hugo and Mary moved to Horr and where they lived there is something of a mystery. As mentioned, Hoppe owned the sawmill at Horr, but he also had two coal claims—one near the sawmill located at the head of Hoppe Creek in today's Cinnabar Basin and the other near Cinnabar Mountain.[40] It is also likely that one or more of his sons (and definitely his daughter and son-in-law) owned land at Horr. That town was developing into a substantial place more quickly than was Cinnabar and so there was housing available there, which Hugo and Mary needed. Additionally, any real estate that family members owned played instantly into Hugo Hoppe's dreams of making money to obtain Cinnabar, because all family members were involved in saving and contributing money for the family's eventual purchase. Perhaps Hugo and Mary lived at the sawmill or on the ranch of a relative, or perhaps they lived on Hugo's coal claim. Most likely they lived on their own piece of land, for a newspaper snippet in November mentioned Hoppe's "ranch at Horr." Regardless, they were living in Horr by August, and Hoppe was telling the newspaper that he would again run for commissioner in Livingston. This would require that he once again move to Livingston, so in September he did so and began building a house on Third Avenue, a site located north of the railroad tracks.[41] Hoppe was confident that he would be reelected in November to a four-year term. It was a new election that was suddenly made compulsory by the admission of Montana to statehood on November 8, 1889, and he was indeed reelected.[42]

In the midst of all this, Hoppe's son-in-law, Morgan T. "Bud" Williams of Horr—now facing the possibility that Maggie would soon divorce him—somehow got the money to purchase the Cinnabar hotel from A. T. French and did so in November.[43] Probably hoping that his ascent into responsibility would impress Maggie, he began work on getting the building "thoroughly renovated" and putting it "in first class condition for the accommodation of guests."[44] But then Bud made the mistake of threatening to kill Maggie. When the local prosecutor took him to court, Maggie dropped her charges but her mind was made up. Another court granted her a divorce in mid-January,[45] and she probably moved to one of her family's cabins while her dad and oldest brothers were traveling back and forth to Livingston. In the next several weeks, Bud Williams was arrested and convicted twice for public drunkenness and disorderly conduct, and he also suffered through a lawsuit of some kind with Gardiner's James McCartney.[46]

Exhibiting all the signs of being an alcoholic, Morgan T. Williams was to have one more go-round with the Hoppes and bad publicity, and it came a year later. In April of 1891, the *Livingston Post* published a derisive poem that could have referred to no one else but Bud Williams. Titled "An Enterprising Skunk," it went like this:

> A smart young Aleck
> Who lived by his wits,
> And drank Bourbon whiskey
> Until he had fits,
> Secured a big contract
> From Hoppe the chief,
> But had to disgorge
> Like the commonest thief.
> When he saw he was foiled
> In his grab for the pelf,
> He brayed like an ass
> When he kicks at himself;
> He ripped, and he swore
> By the devilish host,
> That he'd pour out his spleen
> On the Livingston Post.
> So he ran to the sewer,
> Got on a big drunk,
> Till he looked and he smelled
> Like an Iowa skunk;
> The air was redolent
> With Enterprise roses,
> But his patrons insisted
> On holding their noses.[47]

It is not known what "contract," as the poem stated, was "secured" by Bud Williams. Perhaps it merely referred to his marriage contract for the hand of Maggie Hoppe Williams. Perhaps it referred somehow to the Cinnabar hotel owned by the two of them. Or perhaps it referred to other agreements that Bud had with the Hoppes through the years involving money for the family's dreams. Regardless, even before this public denouncing in the newspaper, his divorce and arrests were too much for Morgan T. "Bud" Williams. So in late April of 1890, he sold the Cinnabar hotel to John Work, a Bozeman pioneer, and made plans to move to Horr to be a coal miner.[48] Bud Williams was headed for obscurity; never again would he enjoy the excitement and renown that he had known with the Hoppes. John Work must have been looking forward to owning the hotel at Cinnabar for the upcoming summer of 1890.

Hugo Hoppe was probably a little envious of John Work, but he was also relishing his new public job, his part-of-the-year life in Livingston, and the fact that two if not three of his five sons were working for or with him in family businesses. By March, his house in Livingston was almost finished (both he and son George would eventually occupy it), while George Hoppe—having finished his clerking job—made plans to open a confectionery store on the west side of Main Street.[49] In the midst of working with Hughie in their father's freighting business, Walter Hoppe was also planning to open a butcher shop at Horr, which his brother Hughie would eventually operate.[50] Hugo and Mary were getting used to riding the train back and forth from Cinnabar to Livingston and staying in the family house there when it was necessary. From what Hugo told Ida McPherren later, it is apparent that he had convinced all of his sons to pour their combined resources into attempting to obtain businesses at Cinnabar.

In May of 1890, Hugo's advertising to lease his ranch finally paid off, and the person who responded to the ad became very important in the history of Cinnabar and Gardiner. William A. Hall, a store owner for several years at Fridley (later Emigrant), Montana, expressed an interest in moving to the Gardiner–Cinnabar area, so Hoppe leased the ranch to him on a one-year trial basis.[51] Hoppe thus was the key player in how W. A. Hall came to Cinnabar. Even more good news came Hoppe's way when Yellowstone Park awarded him and a partner named Paul McCormick—previously a steamboat pilot whom Hoppe knew from his Fort Pease days—a freighting contract to carry hay and other supplies to Fort Yellowstone. Hugo apparently either assigned this contract to Walter Hoppe or else ran it with Walter, so that is probably what he did at least part-time during the summer in his "downtime" for county commissioners. His son Lee Hoppe was definitely working for the freighting company this summer, although he probably started earlier. Hugo Hoppe also sold some coal lands at Mulherin Creek to a developer named C. E. Llewellyn, thus adding money to the family's dreams.[52] And he most likely continued to run his sawmill, although when he sold it or abandoned it is not known.

In November of 1890, after owning the Cinnabar hotel for less than seven months, John Work, while retaining some lots in Cinnabar, sold the hotel to a Gardiner businessman named E. J. Fairfax for five hundred dollars. Fairfax had previously suffered mightily when on August 31, 1889, much of the nearby town of Gardiner caught fire from a dropped cigar and burned to the ground. Hotel owner Fairfax lost his entire business, but fourteen months later he purchased the Cinnabar hotel from Mr. Work.[53] Watching this, Hugo Hoppe must have (again) felt pangs of envy, but he could not yet afford to purchase the hotel himself. Thus Fairfax must have looked forward to owning the hotel during the summer tourist season of 1891. As we shall see, that would not happen.

Hugo Hoppe spent the following year getting paid as county commissioner while also freighting, and these activities plus those of his family brought him still closer to being a hotel owner at Cinnabar. The newspaper reported in March that "Commissioner Hoppe" had gone to Bozeman "on business connected with his transportation contracts." Today that might be an ethical conflict but in 1891, it was perfectly legal. Hoppe also geared up to work (or to oversee) the government's renewal of his freighting contract of moving one million pounds of supplies to Camp Sheridan (soon to be renamed "Fort Yellowstone") in Yellowstone Park.[54] In February, George Hoppe sold his Livingston confectionery and cigar store to his brother Lee and sister Maggie.[55] Hugo and Mary were probably happy to have more family members ensconced in Livingston. And in May, the newspaper reported that Lee Hoppe had resigned his new job with an Eastern cigar company to go to Cinnabar to help the family manage the government freighting contract. He did that for a short time and then became proprietor of the Cinnabar store. Beginning in July, he ran advertisements in the newspaper for "The Cinnabar Store, L.B. Hoppe & Co., Props.—Only Store in Cinnabar."[56] Also that summer in July, Hughie Hoppe's wife, Millicent, decided to buy out Maggie's interest in the store at Livingston. Millicent did not last long in this, and Maggie took it back over later that summer. That too was short-lived, and Maggie soon turned the store's stock over to Lee Hoppe, who moved it to his new store at Cinnabar.[57] As usual, the Hoppes were doing everything they could to make and save money for the family's visions of success.

   Meanwhile, Cinnabar hotel owner E. J. Fairfax got himself into trouble in late January, during another cold winter. Old-time park scout Jack Baronett—who had been in Montana since 1864—told the newspaper that February (and presumably most or all of the winter of 1890–1891) was the coldest he could ever remember. Cooped up in his hotel with friends and customers and trying to stay warm, Mr. Fairfax ran his saloon as a gambling house without a license, and the sheriff came up to arrest him for it in late January.[58] Hugo Hoppe must have smiled at this as he read it in the *Livingston Post*.

   The fact that Lee Hoppe now owned or at least managed a store at Cinnabar was big news for his father. Just as important was the fact that Hugo Hoppe's friend W. A. Hall was suddenly thinking about purchasing the Cinnabar hotel. These two developments boded well for Mr. Hoppe's—and his entire family's—dreams of making the terminus town into a meal ticket and a lifelong business. Thus, in early 1891, Hugo Hoppe was no doubt feeling moments of satisfaction if not genuine excitement!

6

A DREAM REALIZED

Hugo Hoppe Finally Owns the Cinnabar Hotel (1892–1895)

Go confidently in the direction of your dreams.
—Henry David Thoreau, 1817–1862

It was probably in February of 1891 that E. J. Fairfax sold his hotel and saloon at Cinnabar to W. A. Hall. Licenses reflected it by April,[1] and that seemed to portend a great future for the Hoppe family. Before Hugo Hoppe headed south from Livingston for the summer of 1892, he finished a large freighting job at Manhattan, Montana.[2] Then Hugo and Mary went to Cinnabar to superintend the family's government freighting contract (back and forth to Mammoth). But when other opportunities beckoned, the couple was forced to let their sons take over the freighting.

The years 1891 and 1892 were benchmark years for Hugo Hoppe, because they ushered in the first concrete pieces of his several dreams involving Cinnabar. One can argue that in some ways, 1891 was the beginning of the best five years of his life. One can also argue that those last five years were bittersweet. Whichever they were—and probably they were both—those years were eventful in both his life and the life of Cinnabar. With his friend W. A. Hall now operating the hotel, saloon, and a livery at Cinnabar and his son Lee running a store there,[3] Hugo Hoppe probably enjoyed the summer of 1891 more than usual. Things got even better when he purchased or otherwise obtained a saloon of his own at

Cinnabar in June of 1892.[4] Billie Hall may have simply leased his own saloon to Hoppe or hired him to manage it. Whatever the arrangement, Hoppe kept running freight and also retained his seat as a county commissioner, thus continuing for a while longer his lifestyle of running back and forth on the train between Cinnabar and Livingston. More good news came later in June, when postal officials appointed Lee Hoppe as Cinnabar's first postmaster and he installed the new post office in his store.[5] With this development, Hugo Hoppe must have been ecstatic in believing that his dreams were coming to pass! In July, he and his sons were confident enough of Cinnabar's future to begin constructing a ferry across the Yellowstone River. They stretched the cable and were building the boat by July 20.[6] A plan in their heads was to construct a more direct road northeast from the ferry (later a bridge) to the Bear Gulch and Crevasse mines in hopes that increased traffic on that road would add to their business.

The best news of all came sometime before September 1, and it was that Hugo and Mary Hoppe were finally able to purchase W. A. Hall's hotel at Cinnabar![7] A reasonable guess is that eventually they sold or traded Lee Hoppe's store to Mr. Hall in the deal, with Lee Hoppe remaining postmaster. W. A. Hall would keep his own saloon and his livery business so that effectively the two families could eventually trade businesses, Hall being the store and livery owner and Hoppe the hotel owner, with both parties owning saloons. But for the moment, the store remained with Lee Hoppe.

Looking at affairs inside Yellowstone National Park, Hugo Hoppe must have been both encouraged and a little apprehensive at what was happening there. The opening of large hotels at Canyon in 1890 and at Fountain and Yellowstone Lake in 1891 probably encouraged him to believe that Cinnabar would soon be inundated with park visitors. But the expulsion of George Wakefield's stage company and its replacement by the reorganized Yellowstone National Park Transportation Company— with the park's accompanying harassment of small stagecoach operators—must have discouraged him. Still during this summer of 1892, he had to have been excited by seeing Silas Huntley's new six-horse tally-ho stagecoaches loaded with gaily dressed park visitors. For example, traveler Carrie Belle Spencer saw several of the new coaches heading for the park between Cinnabar and Gardiner on August 17.[8]

Hugo Hoppe still needed to complete the thirteen months left in his term as county commissioner, so he continued to travel to Livingston but leased his house at Livingston that winter to a new sheriff.[9] The family probably wanted to add its rental fees to their bank account, and anyway they now had a hotel at Cinnabar that was large enough for the entire family to inhabit. Hugo and Mary moved completely to Cinnabar as soon as they could. The voting registration logbook—which listed Cinnabar independently for the first time in county voting records—showed that Hugo and family were all living in "Hoppe's Hotell [sic] at Cinnabar," and these notations indicated that the family had not yet decided upon a formal name for the establishment. Those voting records also recorded that at least ten other Cinnabar residents were living in the hotel as boarders, as they had done with earlier hotel owners. Some of these people were the Hoppes' very first hotel patrons.[10]

Things looked even better for the Hoppes in 1893, at least initially. In April, Hugo Hoppe began enlarging and remodeling his hotel at Cinnabar, anticipating a good tourist season, and indeed the upcoming World's Fair at Chicago offered the likelihood of travel being stimulated to Yellowstone. "The hotel," noted the newspaper approvingly, "will be a building 20x50 feet."[11] Hoppe must also have been encouraged when his fellow Cinnabar businessman, A. W. Chadbourn, purchased two thousand dollars' worth of new Concord stagecoaches. Meanwhile Lewis Van Dyck, who was Hughie B. Hoppe's partner in the butcher shop at Horr, showed his optimism for Cinnabar by purchasing land on Reese Creek from longtime Hoppe employee W. Y. "Wash" Northrup.[12] Hoppe's sons—all putting money into the family's dreams—were optimistic about their large freighting contract and became more so as the summer's supplies began to arrive at Cinnabar. By way of a nice decoration for his new hotel, Hugo Hoppe paid Livingston's Wittich brothers to wall mount a huge trout that "Specimen" Schmidt caught from the Yellowstone River, and he told the *Enterprise* about it. The fish was twenty-six inches long and weighed eight pounds, nine ounces, and the newspaper stated that it was the largest fish "ever caught" from the Yellowstone River "so far as we are aware." A week later the paper poked fun at "Yankee Jim" George—a self-declared champion fisherman—by stating that Schmidt's fish shamed Jim, who was usually "the champion liar, [or] fisherman we mean."[13] A bit of a negative appeared when a newspaper article reminded the Hoppes that Joe Keeney purchased (or still owned) two lots on Cinnabar's main street as well as nearby ranching land.[14] One wonders whether Keeney had really gotten serious about business at Cinnabar or whether this was no more than a galling reminder that he was still there. Perhaps it was both. Regardless the Hoppes would, as usual, have to deal again with Joe Keeney.

And then, after months of threatening, the Panic of 1893 struck the nation in summer! It and its accompanying economic depression would last for four years and would effectively keep Hugo Hoppe from making the money from Cinnabar of which he so dreamed. It would reduce income across the nation as banks closed, workers of all kinds were laid off, and at least fifteen thousand businesses went "belly up." Nationally it was an incredible disaster, but for Hugo Hoppe the disaster was personal and local. It stifled travel to Yellowstone for four summers, and that directly affected him.[15] One wonders whether it hastened his death. Regardless, it made his last two years harder.

Historian Doris Kearns Goodwin has described what happened nationally. She observed that

> [w]ithin twelve months, more than four million jobs had been lost. At the nadir of this collapse, nearly one in four workers was unemployed. Jobless men begged for food; homeless families slept on streets; farmers burned their crops rather than send them to market at a loss. Millions feared that in the wreckage of the Gilded Age, democracy itself would crumble.[16]

It was no better in Montana. Hugo Hoppe watched nervously as the Northern Pacific Railroad shut down in June, and it must have truly alarmed him when he read that at least five banks had closed nearly simultaneously during the week of July 29. The Gallatin Valley Bank of Bozeman, the Merchants' Bank of Livingston, the Merchants' National Bank of Great Falls, and two banks in Helena all barricaded their doors. The *Livingston Enterprise* exhorted its readers to "think it over" before withdrawing funds from banks, but that pleading was largely unsuccessful.[17] A week later the National Park Bank of Livingston ceased business, the Chicago Board of Trade crashed, and the Chicago and Milwaukee Railroad cut the salaries of its employees.[18] A coal miners' strike and the Pullman Strike the following year made everything worse for the nation. Eventually, the Northern Pacific Railway, the Union Pacific Railroad, and at least one hundred other railroads went into receivership. The NPR ordered a 10 to 20 percent reduction in salaries of anyone making over twelve hundred dollars per year and began studying the possibility of doing it to all employees. In November, the railroad extended those pay cuts all the way to the bottom. [19]

Hugo Hoppe must have swallowed hard more than a few times in worrying about the country's deepening depression, but he also resigned himself to optimism. We know this from his boosterish note to the *Enterprise* some months later. For the moment, Hoppe contented himself with finishing the season at his hotel while also doing all of the following—welcoming the renewal of his freighting contract back and forth to Fort Yellowstone; worrying about his wayward son Lee, who had quit his job as Cinnabar postmaster to follow his homesick wife back to her parents in Bozeman; being a little apprehensive when his oldest children, Walter and Maggie, decided they simply would not miss the Chicago World's Fair; and being truly startled by Acting Park Superintendent George Anderson's sudden expulsions of a number of private transportation operators in favor of Silas Huntley's new stage coach operation. Hoppe's friend W. A. Hall was one of these operators, so Hugo no doubt feared that those expulsions would hurt his own business. [20]

Affairs in southwestern Montana got worse, and that must have increased Hoppe's fears. The deepening depression caused his county commissioner job to rear its head in an unusual, off-season way. Park County suddenly called upon him to distribute three hundred dollars in public provisions to laid-off coal miners at Horr, while forty or fifty more of the unmarried miners left town to seek other work. Hoppe's son Hughie ended his partnership in the butcher shop at Horr with Lewis Van Dyck, probably because he wanted to be a rancher but perhaps also because he was influenced by the financial panic. Horr was soon hit again hard when the "company store" run by J. H. Conrad's coal company closed and was sold in a sheriff's auction. County officials then began attachment proceedings against all Horr residents who had creditor problems. The Northern Pacific announced that it would again cut all employees' salaries by 5 to 10 percent or perhaps more in some cases. A bittersweet moment for Hugo Hoppe was his last day as county commissioner on November 7, when his four-year term at Livingston expired. In the midst of all this "perplexity"—a word of that time—there were two good things that happened: Albert Hoppe began classes at what would soon become Montana State University, and Hugo Hoppe welcomed his first grandson on November 16, when Lee's wife, Jessie, presented Wilbur Saunders Hoppe to the world.[21]

Hugo Hoppe was surely hoping that 1894 would be a better year. Instead, it got worse, because Mary Hoppe—his wife of more than thirty years—got sick.

We do not know when her illness became clear to Hugo, but it might have been as early as January of 1894, at the time he ran a long advertisement in the *Enterprise* putting all his land and personal property up for sale because of "sickness which interfered with his business."[22] It might have been later in the winter, when he asked his relatives Geneva Miller and her daughter "Little Ida" to come to Cinnabar from St. Louis to help him take care of Mary (a story that will soon be told). Or it might have been as late as May 5, when the newspaper reported that Mary Hoppe and her daughter, Maggie, traveled together to Livingston—perhaps merely to visit Lee Hoppe and his wife but more likely to see a doctor.[23]

Unable to do anything about it, Hugo Hoppe busied himself with making plans for summer. In late March, he boosterishly told the newspaper that "prospects for an early and lively season" were good at Cinnabar. He noted that the Yellowstone Park Association was already shipping supplies from Cinnabar to Mammoth, that the snow had disappeared, and that spring plowing would begin on March 27.[24]

But as Mary Hoppe got sicker in 1894, the nation's and the park's affairs worsened, too. Opponents of railroads and the Pullman Company burned train bridges and threatened to wreck trains around the country, and they burned two bridges near Livingston. Soldiers were brought in to keep order around the nation, and that included the NPRR yards at Livingston, where a June 27 walkout by trainmen "was nearly total." "The only men willing to work," says historian Richard White, "were some conductors and a very few brakemen," and most Livingston residents (and Montanans in general) supported the strikers.[25] At President Cleveland's order, Fort Keogh sent US troops to Livingston on July 10, and at Fort Yellowstone Captain George Anderson sent soldiers to Muir City just west of Livingston to protect the railroad's tunnel there. When the Park Branch trains quit running to Cinnabar, tourists hired private stages to take them to Yellowstone. With no trains running, the Yellowstone Park Transportation Company sent stage drivers and their coaches to Livingston to drive the stage route between there and Helena. Hotel managers in the park discharged about fifty "girls" due to lack of park business and sent them to Livingston by stagecoach.[26] Meanwhile, 151 members of the "Distressed and Stranded Tourist Association," who were marooned in the park from June 26 to July 12, submitted their formal thanks to General Manager J. H. Dean of the park's hotel company, his assistant C. A. Lindsley, the soldiers at Fort Yellowstone, and even the beleaguered Northern Pacific for kindnesses extended to them.[27]

As the national Pullman strike was paralyzing the Park Branch railroad, Hugo Hoppe was making plans to begin threshing the oat crop that he had grown on one hundred sixty acres. When trains began running again he told the newspaper that things were suddenly "quite lively" at Cinnabar because of "the large number of Park tourists, many of whom are making the journey by private conveyance from points adjacent to the Park." This was merely more optimism and boosterism, because 1894's final visitation of only 3,105 tourists turned out to be Yellowstone's lowest since 1882. Acting Superintendent George Anderson stated in December that 1894 would "probably stand as the most disastrous to business interests of any in the history of the park."[28]

In the midst of his worries about Mary's illness, Hugo Hoppe must have become even more agitated with regard to business affairs when federal troops got into a violent confrontation with strikers at Livingston on July 10. As they stepped off the train there, soldiers under Captain B. C. Lockwood confronted a crowd of one thousand people including old men, women, and children. Lockwood—probably drunk and definitely pumped up by threats received during his train ride from Billings—overreacted to what he saw as "a threatening mob." Mayor Frank Beley begged the hysterical Lockwood to calm down, but Lockwood called him a son of a bitch and announced that "I [Lockwood] am running this place just now." He struck one man in the head with the flat of his saber and threatened to "run him through" if he did not move farther back. He then struck another man. That night over one thousand people convened in the opera house to hear anti-Lockwood, anti-railroad, and pro-striker speeches by Livingston officials.[29]

Trouble seemed to be surrounding him, but even in the midst of his turmoil, Hugo Hoppe saw considerable brightness in Cinnabar's future. Before we continue his story and chronicle the details of Ida Miller's summer of 1894, we must pause to flesh out the colorful details of Cinnabar itself.

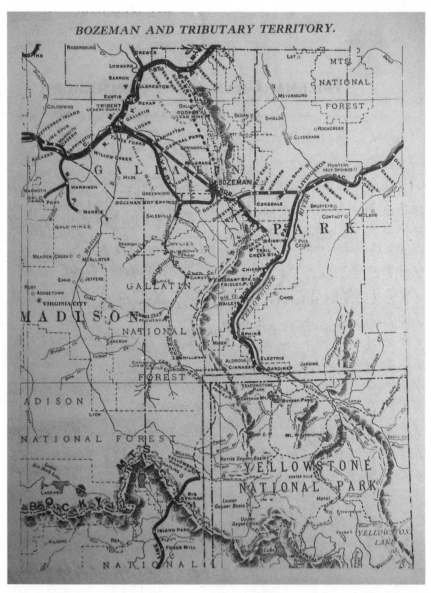

Bozeman Chamber of Commerce map showing Cinnabar, circa 1910. Paul Schullery collection

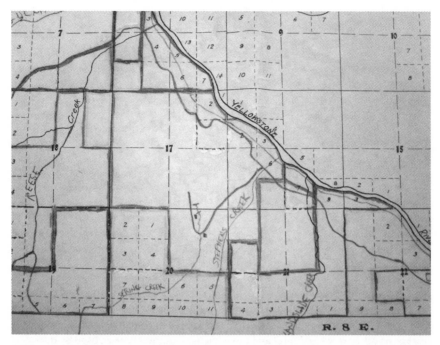

Cinnabar lands map, drawn by Lee Whittlesey, 1995, showing the Hoppe Ranch in sections 17, 20, and 21 YNP Museum Collection

Photo of man sitting in front of tent (foreground) who is probably Hugo John Hoppe in 1874, taken by photographer Henry "Bird" Calfee. Calfee took the photo during the "Yellowstone Wagon-Road Expedition of 1874." Photo by Henry "Bird" Calfee

In this photo of Cinnabar, Montana Territory, taken in late summer or fall of 1884, we see Hugo Hoppe's large building—a combination warehouse and livery stable—standing at left center. The two small buildings to its left are probably his blacksmith shop and outhouse. The tent complex was probably the Yellowstone Park Association's primitive hotel and kitchen. Two small buildings at right (probably storage or other work building) and the passenger car at left were used by the NPRR for a temporary depot and also sleeping and eating quarters for visitors, including teamsters and freighters, to the area. Horses lined up at the wooden loading dock were probably for visitor rental and transport into the Park, as operated by YPA. Photo H-1544, F. Jay Haynes, "Cinnabar City, M.T., 1884," Montana Historical Society

The Hoppe "porch photo" was taken by F. Jay Haynes on October 8, 1885, at Hoppe's Ranch, Cinnabar, Montana. Left to right in the top row are Morgan T. "Bud" Williams, Maggie Hoppe Williams, Mary Gee Hoppe, Hugo J. Hoppe, Walter M. Hoppe (standing in doorway), unknown woman, Carroll T. Hobart (standing in doorway), unknown man, Dan Tripp (arm on chair), four unknown men. Left to right in bottom row are Albert V. Hoppe, Hughie B. Hoppe, Leander B. Hoppe, and George L. Hoppe. In addition to the mystery of who the unidentified four men at right are (probably Hoppe hired hands or merely friends), two even more intriguing mysteries are the identities of the man and woman at center who are looking at each other so suspiciously or perhaps angrily. Dan Tripp, originally from Maine, drove stagecoaches in the park and also owned a bar in Gardiner for many years after this photo was taken. F. Jay Haynes, photo H-1573, Montana Historical Society

Activity on the Hoppe Ranch, Cinnabar, Montana, looking northeast, taken October 1885. F. Jay Haynes. Photo H-1572, Montana Historical Society

A panoramic view of Cinnabar, probably taken by one of the Hoppes and published in Bill and Doris Whithorn's Photo History of Aldridge. The date of this photo is a bit of a mystery. Family lore says that it was taken in 1903 to show what was left of the town after it began moving to Gardiner. However, comparison of this photo with three others reproduced in this book (August 18, 1889; August 17, 1896; and September 16, 1896) casts doubt on that dating. A ramshackle building that appears at far right in the photo of August 18, 1889, also appears in this panoramic as the last building at far right. But this building, probably used as the town's second depot as well as for the depot operator's housing, does not show in either of the 1896 photos (August 17 or September 16). Note also that the town's third and final depot, moved to the site just before June 29, 1895, is not present here, so this panoramic photo must date from the period 1889–1895. A blowup of this panoramic reveals interesting activity in the town—a dark horse pulling a cart, two men sitting on the porch of the third white building, a white horse in front of the fourth white building, and a hay wagon in the field at far left. Collection of Patricia Crossen (Mrs. Wayne) Hoppe

Cinnabar on August 18, 1889, unknown photographer. Yellowstone National Park Museum Collection

"Company D, Minnesota National Guard Arrival at Cinnabar, Montana, [1892]." This photo shows Cinnabar from the east looking west. The Hoppe buildings are the ones facing Main Street. Unfortunately, we cannot see many of the buildings to the left (south). This trip by the Minnesota National Guard in 1892 was reported in numerous newspapers and the scrapbook of L. H. Tubbesing of that trip reposes at the Minnesota Historical Society. See "Marching Through Wonderland," *Livingston Post*, Aug. 18, 1892, p. 1; and "Bold Soldier Boys," *St. Paul Daily Globe*, September 22, 1893, p. 8, which talks of the trip through Yellowstone "in August, last year." Photo H-3005, F. Jay Haynes, Montana Historical Society

Portrait of Hugo J. Hoppe, no date, probably 1890–1895. Photo 20060442411, Yellowstone Gateway Museum, Livingston, Montana

Photo of six-horse stagecoach driving from Cinnabar, Montana, to Gardiner, Montana, 1900. Photo YELL 129376, 1900, in album #129375, YNP Museum Collection

Cinnabar Hotel, no date, probably 1900, with members of the Hoppe family probably standing in front of it, as it was published in *Livingston Enterprise Souvenir*, March 1900, reprinted 1976. Photo 2006.0449306, Yellowstone Gateway Museum, Livingston, Montana

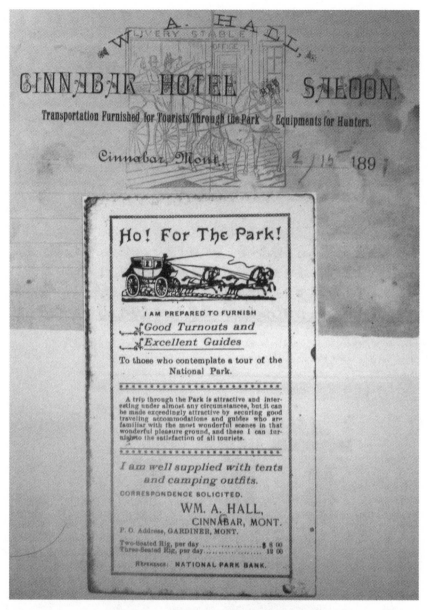

Here are the business cards for "W.A. Hall, Cinnabar Hotel and Saloon" and his livery operation. The hotel card was hand-dated February 15, 1891, likely the date that Hall purchased the hotel and saloon from E. J. Fairfax. Hall sold the hotel to Hugo Hoppe in 1892, but kept a saloon until he moved all of his businesses to Gardiner. He ran his livery operation from April of 1891 through at least 1898 and probably all the way through. And he obtained the Cinnabar store in the summer of 1893 and his Gardiner store in 1895. Yellowstone National Park Museum Collection.

Portrait of Albert V. Hoppe, no date, about 1900. Originally published in *Livingston Enterprise Souvenir*, March, 1900, and reprinted 1976.

Portrait of Walter Hoppe, no date, about 1885. Originally published in *Livingston Enterprise Souvenir*, March, 1900, and reprinted 1976.

"Specimen Bill" Lindstrom, who sold souvenirs at Cinnabar, was shown here circa 1885. Photo by T.W. Ingersoll, photo 1151-B, Bob Berry collection.

Washington Y. Northrup standing in front of Cinnabar Hotel, 1895. Always called "Wash," he came to Cinnabar in 1883 with Hugo J. Hoppe and worked for the family continuously until he died in 1903. Voting records dated Oct. 12, 1892, show that he was then livng at "Hoppes Hotell, Cinnabar." By Oct. 12, 1894, he lived at "Hotel St. (Cinnabar)." From Whithorn, *Sixty Miles of Photo History*, p. 43.

This is the group portrait allegedly taken at Cinnabar, Montana Territory, on July 4, 1887, at "tryouts for Buffalo Bill Cody's Wild West," with caption listing all men. Hoppe expert Bob Moore says his mother-in-law Jean Hoppe Foster swore to her dying day that she had loaned this photo to historian Doris Whithorn but the photograph was lost until recent years when Moore and others at the Gateway Museum encountered it among Whithorn's pictures. Yellowstone Gateway Museum of Livingston, 2006.0450589.

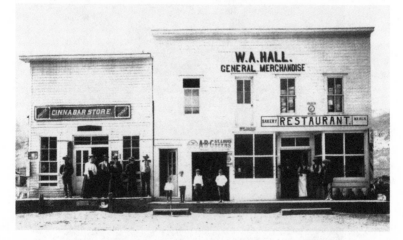

The W.A. Hall store at Cinnabar (right) with the Hall family standing in front of it, no date, but probably 1895 or 1896, because of the ages of Warren, Earl, and Arthur Hall. Warren (8) was born in 1893 and here appears to be about two or three years old, while Earl was born in 1889 and Arthur in 1888. At this time, Mr. Hall owned the hotel and a saloon and no longer had the hotel and livery. As shown at the top of the photo, the family identified a number of people in the photo such as Lulu Hall (6), W. A. Hall (7), and Gilbert Smith (10), who was probably a son of liveryman Charley Smith. Yellowstone Gateway Museum of Park County.

"Arrival at Cinnabar" of the Burton Holmes party and other travelers as shown in Burton Holmes Travelogues (p. 11). The *Livingston Post* for August 19, 1896 ("Local Matters," p. 3), recorded that E. Burton Holmes and his party of seven "went up to the park on a private car Monday morning [August 17]." Thus the date of this photograph is August 17, 1896. Burton Holmes Travelogues.

A little more of Cinnabar on August 17, 1896, with the vantage point simply moved to the left, as shown in Burton Holmes Travelogues, and labeled "Cinnabar Station" (p. 12). The train and its conductor are at right while a stagecoach driver loads passengers at left. Burton Holmes Travelogues.

NP Locomotive 418 at Cinnabar Depot, 1895 F. Jay Haynes photo, Montana Historical Society.

"Train at Cinnabar, Montana (W.S. Webb Excursion), September 16, 1896." Cinnabar was much larger when this photo was taken and its growth occurred in 1895–1896 as a result of increased (or at least anticipated) visitation. The *Livingston Post* for September 16, 1896 ("Local Matters," p. 3), announced the arrival of Dr. Webb's group in a private car containing him and a party of nine people plus attendants and stock. They were headed for Jackson Hole on a hunting trip. The train made a brief stop in Livingston that day and then proceeded on to the Park. "Their special train contained five cars, a baggage car and a day coach belonging to the St. Lawrence and Adirondack Railway, a dining car and two Wagner cars." Wagner cars were sleeping cars and parlor cars, invented by Webster Wagner. When the train arrived in Livingston it had five cars but several more were added for the trip to Cinnabar. F. Jay Haynes, photo H-3621, Montana Historical Society.

Photo of six-horse stagecoach driving from Gardiner, Montana, into Yellowstone National Park, 1913, with driver named "Happy Jack." E Happy Jack album, YELL 118239, YNP Museum Collection.

Site of the Hoppe family's former bridge at Cinnabar, taken nearly fifty-six years after the bridge washed out, on March 26, 1962. Aubrey Haines photo, YELL 33370, Yellowstone National Park photo archives.

7

THE TOWN ITSELF

Life at Cinnabar (1883–1903)

It is amazing how soon the picture of a particular time disappears.
—Aubrey L. Haines, historian, to Lee Whittlesey and history class,
1996

Cinnabar was eventful and picturesque during its twenty years. Hugo
Hoppe has described the town's early arrangement for us. He says he
initially put up a livery stable, blacksmith shop, sawmill, and icehouse,
although as will be seen, his sawmill was first located at his ranch (nearer
to timber) and the icehouse was probably underground.[1] He says the
hotel, bar, and store (all in one building)

> had false fronts and board walks in front of them to make up a Main
> street; the other buildings were back [south] of Main street, the whole
> making a town similar to the many towns that had mushroomed up at
> the end of the rails and pockmarked the wild, open prairies. . . .The
> well-defined road [east–west through Cinnabar and north–south to the
> ferry] had been made by the [James] Henderson cowboys driving cat-
> tle across the river to graze.[2]

This was a great description, but Hugo Hoppe did not put up these buildings until much later. Notwithstanding what Ida McPherren wrote or what
Hoppe thought he remembered, Cinnabar grew very slowly, and the
wooden hotel, store, and saloon south of Main Street were not present

initially, as an 1884 Haynes photo and descriptions from visitors make clear. At first the town could not even boast that it had a train station. Historian Whithorn says that instead in 1883 there were two train cars placed at Cinnabar: "one for a sleeper for ladies and the other a dining room where meals were served at seventy-five cents each."[3] A. M. Ingersoll, who passed through in August of 1884, stated that the town consisted of only "four houses and a depot in a box car." Traveler "F.B.," who passed through on September 13, called it "a dull, unprepossessing place, [which] consists of a limited hotel, a store, and few log houses." Writer "F.F.F." and another man who stopped there the same day saw even less, noting that there was "nothing there but a few tents and a saloon on the wagon road."[4] Visitors who arrived at Cinnabar on the 5:15 p.m. train that year remained there overnight, and if they were lucky they could find lodging in a tent or train car. The "limited" hotel was no doubt Joe Keeney's ranch house slightly improved, and the saloon was his as well.

Haynes's 1884 photo of Cinnabar shows no depot yet; instead it shows only the following: one substantial building, a large tent with two attached rooms, two other small buildings (one with an outhouse and the other attached to the tents), two buildings (at the west, replacing the earlier mentioned two train cars) that were located immediately south of the main track, and a sidetracked train car (at the east) that was probably used as either the depot or the ladies sleeping car or both. The new buildings were likely the "two, new third-class sleepers" mentioned by the *St. Paul Globe*. The nearby tent in the photo was probably the kitchen. Unless the previously mentioned "saloon" was housed in the tent complex, it was added after Haynes took his photo, and the "limited hotel" was Keeney's ranch house outside the photo. It is also likely that this early Cinnabar contained a few other dwellings and barns outside the photo to the north, which would explain the "four houses" and "a few log houses" descriptions from tourists.[5]

The largest building shown in the 1884 photo was Hugo Hoppe's combination warehouse and livery stable—the first building that he says he built—and the smaller building to the west was probably his blacksmith shop with outhouse. Also prominent in the photo was the unloading platform that Hoppe said was made of rough pine boards and was "the size of an ordinary town lot—fifty feet by one hundred fifty feet," with men and horses lined up to receive passengers from the train.[6] Hoppe's personal dwelling and his sawmill were already established at the base of Sepulcher Mountain, and those were not in the photo. As mentioned, his icehouse (probably the same as his root cellar) was not in the photo either. And the Cinnabar hotel, store, and saloon (all in one sprawling building), which would become the signal structures in the history and identity of Cinnabar, were not yet present.

Ms. O. S. T. Drake passed through Cinnabar on her way into the park in the summer of 1885. Like others, she noted that the town consisted of only "a wayside saloon and a few huts." But on her way out of the park, Drake had more to say about the town's main building and the unidentified couple who ran it, who probably were Hugo Hoppe and his wife, Mary:

> The hotel at Cinnabar turned out to be a little timber house, consisting of a bar and back parlour, and two or three bed-rooms above. A married couple kept the house; the wife said she had never had a lady under her roof before [until I arrived]. They gave me a very clean bedroom, provided with the only jug and basin in the house. There was no door, but she nailed a sheet over the door-way and unnailed it in the morning; the food was excellent, and the good woman waxed quite pathetic in her regrets over the fact that we were hardly likely again to meet in this world.[7]

Her description of a "little timber house" with "bed-rooms above" sounds like a primitive cabin, which means that Joe Keeney had apparently remodeled it a bit.

Like Drake, traveler W. H. Dudley mentioned a "hotel" at Cinnabar that summer. He described the town in August as "a few ranches, a hotel, two or three stores, twice as many saloons, a few private houses, and the railroad depot."[8] His and Drake's descriptions make it clear that the Cinnabar hotel, with Drake's second story "above," was in place by July or August of 1885. Someone built it but who and when are not known, and the *Enterprise* did not mention any construction. Hugo Hoppe had run the Mammoth hotel all winter for Carroll Hobart, but he was out of that job in June. Perhaps Joe Keeney built the hotel or renovated it during the winter, but how could he—a simple good old boy and a bit of a ne're-do-well at that—get the money for such a project? The *Butte Daily Miner* gave us a possible answer. In January, Keeney and his partners at Cooke City had sold their Morning Star mine to men who were soon to be his neighbors at

Cinnabar—Jacob Reding and Harry Gassert.[9] Keeney sold his mining interest just as the townsite of Cinnabar again came up for sale but before he got into a shooting affray with Cal Swift, which will soon be told. In late spring he got busy with his new, young wife, and in summer with being a constable at Upper Geyser Basin. Because of these factors, Keeney needed a summer manager for the new hotel. Hugo and Mary Hoppe were available, and it appears that he leased the place to them. Or perhaps he merely hired them to manage it for him, with or without a share of the profits.

JOE KEENEY'S STORY

Elias Joseph Keeney (1847–1938) has been mentioned as an initial landowner at Cinnabar who was associated with (and who prospected with) the more famous early Yellowstone guide George Huston. As early as August of 1883, Keeney was running a primitive "hotel" at his ranch house and a saloon. Even before the railroad was completed to town, Keeney was putting up tourists at his ranch, because an unnamed stage traveler in August of 1883 stated that his driver—properly fearful of a steep, muddy road—insisted upon stopping there for the night in a torrential thunderstorm. Discussing this with the stage driver, the traveler made up his mind "that he and Keeney had an understanding." Thus Keeney drifted into the hotel business and was apparently the proprietor of the "limited hotel" that 1884 visitor "F.B." mentioned.[10]

Writer Owen Wister's fortunate diary entry for 1887 is our only source for a look at the inside of Keeney's Cinnabar "hotel," and it makes it clear that Keeney was indeed using his own residence as such. Wister and a companion were traveling toward Cinnabar from Gardiner when they encountered a man on foot chasing after a prodigal, on-the-run daughter. The man

> turned out to be the landlord, Joe Keeney, who became our friend, gave us drinks, and turned his family out of their room and made us sleep in it, and generally saw us through. The room was papered with one circus poster that amply covered wall and ceiling. It was furnished comfortably, and for methods of diversion contained a parlor organ, a guitar (to which someone sang during the early evening), a violin, a late number of the Police Gazette, and the poems of William Cullen

Bryant. We did not intrude there till bed time, for it was the family sitting room. But when they departed we entered, and slept well. Joe Keeney has a taste for fire arms and wanted to buy my rifle, after having discussed its fatal defects very thoroughly. [11]

Joe Keeney was a colorful if somewhat disreputable character who hailed originally from Albany, Oregon, and came to Montana in 1875 with his brother Eli. Eli's name was far too similar to Joe's own first name of Elias, so it was no wonder that Joe went by "Joe." Like Hugo Hoppe and everyone else in this primitive region, Joe Keeney dabbled in many activities to make a living, but he was also a raucous rounder who could not seem to stay out of trouble. Typically, he met numerous early Montanans at Virginia City including legendary vigilante John X. Beidler. In 1879, he watched his brother Eli exchange shots with Bill Roberts in a Bozeman bar fight that killed both shooters. [12] At the time that he and his friend George Huston were mining in Cooke City and selling pieces of their Cinnabar land to Hugo Hoppe and Carroll Hobart, a newspaper referred to them as "paragons of enterprise, if not of virtue." This was a hint that both men were a bit rough. In the fall of 1884, Keeney attempted to collect a disputed account in Gardiner in the restaurant of a hotel owned by Mrs. "Jumbo" Ahart—a woman whose nickname probably referenced her weight. When she refused to pay him, he screamed vile epithets at her, upset a table, and grabbed a plate to throw at her. She grabbed a .44, aimed it at him, and yelled, "You get out of this house and take that, you son of a bitch!" Then she shot him twice in the groin. Watching him bleed, she quietly resumed her duties in the dining room. The sheriff came up from Livingston and decided that Keeney was more to blame than Mrs. Ahart and did not charge her with any offense. Nor did he charge Keeney for starting the fracas, probably figuring that being shot was enough punishment. [13]

Joe Keeney convalesced, but it seemed that trouble either followed him or else he caused it. Only a few months later near Cinnabar, he was hosting Cal Swift and Box Miller and listening to Swift growl that "his heart was bad" at Joe Keeney. All were probably drinking or perhaps Cal drank a bit later. Regardless, they split up for a while, and soon Swift and Joe happened to be riding horses in opposite directions and passed each other. When very close to Swift, Keeney made a comment of some kind and Swift drew his gun. The two men were so close that Keeney "struck Swift's gun" and knocked it up into the air as Swift fired two shots. Both bullets missed Keeney, whose gun was probably already out. Keeney fired four shots at Swift, one of which "struck Swift in the fleshy part of the right leg above the knee," making a painful but not dangerous wound. Deputy Sheriff O. P. Templeton, who happened to be present in Gardiner, arrested Swift and took him to Livingston, where Judge McNaughton fined him twenty dollars plus costs. Keeney apparently greased out of the affair after reporting to the sheriff in Bozeman. [14]

An aside about Cal Swift and Box E. Miller—they were typical of drunken, violent troublemakers everywhere. Swift hung around Cinnabar for a while and then moved north of Horr, where he actually registered to vote in 1894. Eventually he joined the mining stampede to Alaska and was allegedly murdered there in 1899 by one Tommy Dolan. [15] Box Miller was far worse. He and his brother Frank lived on a ranch at Tom Miner Basin, and a few years later the two of them got into it. Box got drunk, stormed into the barn with an ax where his brother was saddling a horse and tried to brain him with it. Instead, Frank took the ax away from Box and gave him a lethal ax blow to the head. Box continued to scream "I'll kill you!" even as he lay bleeding and dying on the ground. His last words, uttered from the ground, were "I'll kill you yet." When neighbors at W. A. Hall's adjoining ranch arrived to find out what was going on, they heard Frank Miller claiming self-defense. A week later, a grand jury at Livingston exonerated Frank for having defended himself against his drunken brother. [16]

Joe Keeney's trouble with Cal Swift had happened over a woman, and one wonders whether it was Keeney's wife or another woman, perhaps one that Cal Swift fancied as his own. Predictably, Keeney was not yet finished with trouble involving women. A few years earlier, he had married Clara Parker of Massachusetts, who one day took their two children and traveled to the East. At about the same time that Keeney shot Swift, Clara returned to Cinnabar. When she stepped off the train, the locals noticed that she had brought along her younger sister, Mary, age sixteen, to live with them. One thing led to another, and by summer Joe Keeney had run off to Cooke City with the little sister and married her. Clara Keeney saw "red" and went to Bozeman to seek a divorce, but what she did not know was that Keeney had already outwitted her by getting the divorce while she was in the East. Of course Mr. Keeney's friends claimed that Mrs. Keeney got violent with her sister and that the first wife had full notice of his philandering with the second wife. Meanwhile a fair number of folks were mistaking Mary Keeney for Joe Keeney's daughter, and Joe probably liked that. In the style of the day, the *Enterprise* ran the long, gossipy story on its front page under the headline "Joe Keeney furnishes another interesting news item."[17]

From all of this, we must wonder how Keeney found time that year to serve as a hotel operator and a government constable, but the only historian who has noticed him says correctly that he was "the kind of cat who always lands on his feet." In the summer of 1885, he was working as a government constable in the park at Lower Geyser Basin, so his limited hotel at Cinnabar was probably being run by either Clara or Mary, and most likely Mary. Later in the summer, Hugo Hoppe was either working for Keeney or leasing Keeney's hotel so that he and his wife could be in place to be the unknown couple that O. S. T. Drake encountered (Keeney was then probably not its proprietor because he was elsewhere and not part of a stable marriage that summer). According to the Bozeman newspaper, Keeney returned to Cinnabar in the summer of 1886 and ran a sort of hotel at his house along with a livery and feed stable, and both Owen Wister and the newspapers say Keeney was also there in 1887.[18] An 1891 newspaper article made it clear that the second Mrs. Keeney was running their saloon (if not their primitive "hotel" in the same building) that year when she was arrested for allowing gambling on the premises. Her husband had been arrested two years earlier for gambling without a license in his own saloon.[19] As we have already seen, properties at Cinnabar seemed to move fluidly and constantly among various owners.

E. J. Keeney's connections with Cinnabar were long, interesting, and important, and he was at Cinnabar until 1891 when he decided to go prospecting on Boulder River. As already described, he leased his "lodging and eating house" at times to Hugo Hoppe or hired him to manage it. For example, after Keeney's busy summer of 1885 at Cooke City and Upper Basin, he returned to Cinnabar in 1886. The *Enterprise* stated in June:

> E.J. Keeney has assumed proprietorship of the hotel and bar at Cinnabar [implying that there was only one such hotel], in connection with which he has fitted up and will conduct a feed stable and keep saddle animals for hire. Until the first of the present month the hotel accommodations at Cinnabar were managed by H.J. Hoppe whose lease of the house expired on that date.[20]

The word "house" confuses the issue of whether this was the formal hotel or merely Hoppe's having leased Keeney's ranch house hotel, but probably it was the latter. This quote and an article on June 19[21] together tell us that Hoppe was temporarily out of the hotel business and turning his attention to only his ranch, at least for the summer of 1886.

Keeney operated his ranch hotel in 1883, 1884, 1886 (until Hoppe got it back), 1887, 1888, and finally 1892, after Hoppe purchased the larger hotel.[22] Beginning in 1891, Keeney prospected on Boulder River for several summers, returning to Cinnabar each fall, winter, and spring. This became a habit. Eventually he took his entire family with him, founded the small town of Independence, Montana, and was still there in 1897. But in 1898, he went to Alaska to go mining, thus ending his connection to Cinnabar.[23]

THE DEPOT AND STAGECOACHES: ALWAYS THE CENTERPIECES OF CINNABAR

By the summer of 1885, Cinnabar had grown a little, and the railroad had indeed erected a "depot." Hugo Hoppe says the train station was erected in the summer of 1883, but it actually did not happen until 1885. He says it was

> the same style [of] little red depot that dotted the plains [all over the West] with the coming of the rails; it was a small station with a waiting room that had long, wooden benches along three walls, a pot-bellied stove that ate up huge rounds of pine trees and a window between it and the baggage room next to it where the ticket agent-telegraph operator-baggage man-express man and janitor sold tickets for a ride on the runt train. There was a telegraph instrument in the baggage room besides an iron safe. Above this combination station-depot were the living quarters of the five-men-in-one and his family. In front of the station-depot there was a platform made of rough pine boards that was the size of an ordinary town lot—a[t] fifty feet by one hundred fifty feet.[24]

As mentioned, W. H. Dudley noted the presence of a depot in 1885. Traveler Catharine Bates described it in 1886 as "only a wooden shed," so apparently she thought less of it than did Hugo, but later photos confirm it to have had a miniature gothic look, as Hoppe implied in his "same style" comment. Edward Marston did not mention it, instead characterizing the town in 1885 as consisting of "about twelve shanties [and] several of these are drinking saloons," while 1887 traveler Owen Wister stated that the town consisted of "a railroad depot, one saloon, a hotel, and some sheds." W. J. Van Patten that same year stated that the town had only "a small hotel, several saloons, and a few houses." An 1889 traveler known only as "Mrs. Paris" found Cinnabar to be "really no more than a depot and a small collection of horse sheds," but that did not include dwellings, for an anonymous fisherman who left a journal from that same year said the town consisted of "about twenty houses or shacks, made roughly by the miners of pine logs."[25] As late as 1894, Ida Miller mentioned tourists being horrified by Cinnabar's "two-building Main Street."[26] This shanty-town look of Cinnabar is confirmed by the descriptions of all these travelers and the few photos that exist of the place before 1896. Ida Miller's comment makes it clear that Cinnabar's increase in size did not happen until after Hugo Hoppe's death, and the newspapers backed that up. So did the party of F. E. Stratton, who got off the train there in June of 1895. He noted that "Cinnabar is just a little supply station" and that his party stopped only long enough to board a six-horse tally-ho stagecoach.[27]

Part of the town's increase in size actually happened in 1895, just after the Strattons disembarked. When the depot at Gallatin City, Montana (opposite the mouth of the Gallatin River at present-day Three Forks, Montana), was abandoned, the Northern Pacific moved the building to Cinnabar "to be used as the terminal depot for the Park Branch."[28] This was the depot that subsequently appeared in 1896 photos and served to the end of Cinnabar's life.

Small and shantylike or not, Cinnabar was very busy with transportation managers and stagecoach operators and their wagons from the moment the railroad got there, for those coarse men saw it as an opportunity to earn money carrying tourists through Yellowstone National Park. Traveler T. H. Thomas encountered this chaotic scene in 1884:

> The carriages, with their horses, were called 'rigs.' The drivers, 'carters.' It was for us to select. A fellow passenger who took an interest in our proceedings, waving his hand, so as to indicate the whole assembly, said, 'There is not one of these gentlemen as can't be fully recommended in every way.' Heavens! What an assemblage of sun-baked, frost-dried, grisly faces! Brown, hollow-cheeked, dark-bearded, with

the skin tightly drawn over the foreheads and ropy veins meandering about their thin temples and necks. Every mouth clinging tightly round a long black cigar, and with a brown smear at the corners. Yet [they were] young men, almost all of them, in full health and energy, as the bright eyes rolling in their sunken orbits fully testified. . . . All seemed to be trustworthy in essentials, and under a very rough and swaggering exterior there was plenty of shrewdness and good temper.[29]

An 1885 visitor known only as "J.H.H." stepped off the train to see an array of vehicles: "buckboards, mud wagons, farm wagons, omnibuses, spring carts, and saddle horses," and his party rushed for the saddle horses.[30] Visitor Charles Stoddard in 1886 found a similarly excited situation on the platform near the Cinnabar "depot":

[Our] excursion party naturally monopolized the attention of the drivers, who for the most part owned their teams, and were in hope to strike a bargain on the spot for a five or six day tour in the valley. Imagine the hubbub. Heaps of luggage lay upon the platform; everyone was in a wild state of excitement. To get a good team was the first thought; at a reasonable price, the second; and one with a driver who was likely to be intelligent and obliging, the third. But each must have a conveyance of some sort; and a first choice was of great importance, for the last one might result in misery and a series of misfortunes. Tourists and drivers rushed madly into each other's arms and bargained briskly.[31]

The fare to Mammoth Hot Springs that year was two dollars, and one dollar extra for each trunk.

By 1890, the scene at the Cinnabar train station was more organized, with less of the chaos that characterized earlier years, although a certain wild excitement always prevailed at the depot. "The weather-beaten stagecoach drivers in their soft slouch hats and dust-colored clothes," exulted a woman traveler, personified "the incarnate history and romance of the wild West." Traveler Fred Slocum also captured the scene well that year:

The train slows up—we have reached Cinnabar, and everybody is bustling about their baggage and getting off. I grasp my shawl strap in one hand and umbrella in the other, and step down on[to] the platform as a large stage coach dashes up, drawn by six fine dapple grays. This is but the first of a line of some dozen stages, drawn by from two to six horses that are ready to take the party to the Mammoth Hot Springs Hotel, some eight miles distant. The inside[s] of these coaches are rapidly filled with ladies, and I clamber, with some other gentlemen, and with some difficulty, to the top of the first coach. We count and find there are twenty-one passengers aboard our coach—about one-half being on top. Then there is a flourish and crack of whips, and yo-ho! And we are off for the Park![32]

In the six-horse tally-ho coaches, as Slocum explained, there were seats on the top of the coach that improved both the view and the passenger count, and historic photographs back this up. The excited situation following the disgorging of train tourists at Cinnabar was the rule for the town's entire life. And it was the same at the end of the trip, when visitors boarded the train outbound to Livingston. George H. Bockoven, an 1895 tourist, certainly saw it that way. As he left Mammoth hotel on his tally-ho, he opined:

Our coach is an immense affair, carrying some eighteen or twenty passengers with their baggage and is drawn by six white horses. On arriving at Cinnabar, all is confusion, asking questions, claiming baggage, and sleeping and chair-car accommodations, etc., making a perfect bedlam.[33]

These tourists' descriptions of the scene on the depot platform summarized what Cinnabar was really all about during its twenty summers of existence on the sagebrush flats north of Yellowstone Park.

COMFORT, A GOOD TABLE, AND "THE GAIETY OF THE DANCE"

In many accounts, travelers mentioned only that they reached Cinnabar and did not describe the place. Unfortunately for historians, most travelers were more interested in writing about their upcoming Yellowstone tour than they were in recording their impressions of the small town at the terminus of the railroad. To make matters worse, they also seem to have saved their camera film until they got into the park, thus depriving us of complete photographs of the town. One rare account by traveler Amelia

Lyle is atypical in that respect, because she actually wrote a bit about Cinnabar in 1900, even if she got some of it wrong. She joked about its small size, noted that its Chinese cook was still present, and misunderstood that Walter Hoppe was in charge of the hotel and not the deceased Hugo J. Hoppe:

> Cinnabar does not compete with Greater New York or Chicago in point of population. In fact the census man may have missed it altogether. "Where is Cinnabar?" we asked upon leaving the train. "The second house, Madam," was the reply. It boasts of one hotel, and it does not rival the Continental of the Quaker City, nor the Palmer House of Chicago; but cleanliness and comfort with a good table are its characteristic features. It is a story and a half structure, kept by H.J. Hoppe [*sic*: Walter Hoppe], the first white child born in Montana. Mrs. Hoppe's father [Selleck M. Fitzgerald] was a classmate of Montana's multi-millionaire Senator Clarke, and a warm supporter of his cause. Tourists find this a comfortable place to rest after the fatigue of travel.[34]

Traveler Lyle thought Hugo was Montana's first native white child instead of his son Walter and was completely wrong about the census taker not finding Cinnabar, for we have the 1900 US Census of the town.

Hotels were relatively stable businesses throughout the Yellowstone region, but probably there were no more than two at Cinnabar at any one time ever—Joe Keeney's ranch house and a larger one. We have seen that the larger hotel varied in its ownership through time. Keeney may have owned it too at some point, but other owners definitely included A. T. French, John Work, E. J. Fairfax, Morgan Williams, and W. A. Hall.

This larger hotel at Cinnabar was run by the Hoppe family from 1892 until the town died. According to Hugo Hoppe's grandniece Ida Miller, the inside of her uncle's hotel looked like this in 1894:

> The sitting-room was a handsome, Victorian parlor with a dark, velvet-napped Wilton carpet; a dark, somber Phyle sofa and a dozen matching chairs; a bureau-book-case-writing desk; a large heavily shaded hanging lamp that could be adjusted to the right height by a chain and pulley contrivance and dark tapestries of the fox and hunt nearly covered the walls. There was no stove or fireplace for this room was a waiting room for the tourists who stayed at the hotel for some reason and it was not in use except during Park travel.

The hotel's interior seems to have impressed Hoppe's young relative for she recalled it in some detail:

> The dining-room was as Western as the sitting-room was Eastern. . . . It was a large room, one hundred feet long and half as wide, and extended from the front wall to the kitchen wall. The table ran from within a few yards of the kitchen door to a high Gothic archway between the dining-room and the barroom. This nine-feet-wide archway made the two rooms suitable for dancing or banquets. The dining-room had nothing in it but the table and the chairs that bordered on its sides. Enlarged photographs of Park scenes, neatly framed, hung on the walls.

Ida Miller also recalled the hotel's kitchen, probably because her mother worked there with the Hoppes' Chinese cook Tung Loo:

> The kitchen of the Cinnabar hotel was a sixteen by twenty room with two, large Majestic ranges on one side with tin sauce pans, tin kettles and iron skillets hanging on nails around it. Half a dozen stove-size Dutch ovens were standing on the ranges with foodstuffs in them for dinner. . . . Close to the ranges was a long table which was the cooks' work table; close to this table was a tier of shelves for the chinaware. Not far from the stoves and partially partitioned off was a pantry and pastry room; at one end of it was a small compartment with ice, where perishable food was kept. The Hoppes put up their own ice as soon as it was cold enough for the Yellowstone [River] to freeze and packed it in sawdust from their own sawmill.[35]

One man from Livingston liked the food in 1898, or did he? At that time Walter Hoppe was the owner of the hotel. "Do you ever call at the Cinnabar Hoppe hotel to refresh the outer man?" he asked his readers. "Well, I did yesterday and found . . . the dining room, crowded with happy, cheerful guests." Referring to himself, he stated, "This scribe had a sharp, keen, voracious appetite when he went in and, strange to say, lost it all."[36] From this, we cannot be certain whether he lost his appetite by being satisfied or had it killed by bad food. But his "happy, cheerful guests" comment augurs well for his having liked the fare at Hoppe's hotel.

Dances were an activity at Cinnabar that went hand in hand (pun intended) with hotel facilities, and the hotel at Cinnabar held them often.

Officials of the Northern Pacific Railroad, army officers on their way to tour the park or to inspect the post, local cowboys and other residents, soldiers from Fort Yellowstone, and of course tourists all stopped to eat or purchase a drink at the hotel. Many stayed for the occasional "shin-digs," as the cowboys called the dances, wherein any of those folks might stay late to "step it off" with ladies in calico and high-buttoned shoes.[37]

In those days, the various small towns in the region took turns holding the annual Independence Day celebration, and in 1894 and 1899, it was Cinnabar's turn. In 1894, little Ida Miller watched a three-day celebration there that she said was a large rodeo to celebrate the open-range cattle industry of earlier days. Townsfolk ate, drank, danced, and watched the rodeos. Ida was amazed to see every one of the twenty-five seats at the hotel's dining room filled for all three days. "The band from Fort Yellow-stone played the three nights of the celebration," she recalled, and she remembered that "in the gaiety of the dance," there was no caste system. "Cowboys, soldiers, farmers, ranchers, gamblers, bartenders, miners, freighters, and tourists mingled together on a common footing, happy in the moment's pleasure, all real or imaginary grievances forgotten." In 1895, the big celebration was at Gardiner, where, if one believes the newspaper, more than one thousand people gathered for horse racing. In 1896, it was at Fort Yellowstone, up the hill at Mammoth Hot Springs.[38]

Notwithstanding grand preparations by George and Albert Hoppe, the 1899 celebration at Cinnabar was a complete failure. The *Livingston Post*'s front-page story on the festivities was headlined "Glorious Fourth—Cinnabar Celebrates Independence Day in Style." But the story gave no interesting details about the town's activities, instead publishing the text of attorney M. R. Wilson's dry speech—an excruciatingly boring rehash of patriotism and ancient history. Meanwhile that year, Livingston held races, and Fridley presented fireworks and a dance. In Jardine, a drunken Henry Rockinger shot Mark Terrell to death and was later sent to prison for it.[39] Cinnabar sometimes had excitement on Independence Day, but in that year the excitement was elsewhere.

Regardless of that, the planning for dances continued at Cinnabar. One example happened in late July of 1899, perhaps a reaction to the failed Fourth of July celebration. "A very pleasant evening was spent in dancing on the splendid open air platform at Cinnabar Saturday evening July 29th," enthused the *Enterprise*. "Most elegant music was secured for the occasion and an elaborate lunch was served at Hoppe hotel." Perhaps encouraged by this success, the town planned a winter party. A grand ball was slated to be held at "Holem's new hall" at Cinnabar for New Year's Eve 1900 with music by Brundage and North, and the newspaper confirmed that it was indeed held. [40]

SALOONS

Saloons arrived with hotels, and Cinnabar had more saloons than we have available history on them. In fact, not including Gardiner's affairs, the earliest known bit of saloon raucousness in the area occurred in the summer of 1883, probably after Hugo Hoppe erected his first building but just before the railroad arrived. It actually happened at what could be called Cinnabar's immediate predecessor—a saloon at the mouth of "Cinnabar Creek," which became today's Mulherin Creek. In August of that year, the railroad was temporarily stranded there for a couple of weeks while its laborers constructed a trestle bridge over the substantial canyon at the mouth of the stream. Because it was the railroad's terminus, a saloon was already in place. It was the "Cinnabar Saloon" or "C.B. Saloon" being run by J. H. "Frisky John" Mulherin (1836–1904), who we know was a settler on the upper Yellowstone as early as 1876. [41]

A traveler named John Cumberland wrote an entertaining account of this event titled "A Night at Cinnabar," but in mid-1883, "Cinnabar" still referred to Cinnabar Mountain and the creek on its north side. The likely identities of the people he encountered, whom the US Census tells us were present in that sparsely settled country, are some of the reasons that his story is fascinating to us today. Cumberland says he toured the park and then returned to Gardiner on a Friday looking for a ride back to Livingston, only to learn that the local stage "would not start north again until the following Monday." He spoke to the postmaster, who was none other than Gardiner's first resident, James McCartney, operating out of a tent. According to Cumberland, McCartney's speech made it clear how colorful the region already was. Cumberland says he walked up to the postal tent and heard McCartney speaking:

> "Nothin' fer you," said he as I came up, thinking, no doubt, that I was about to inquire for a letter. "Only three letters in the shebang. One's for Dan Hull. He'll never call fer it, yer bet; deader 'n a post—filled full o' holes last night at the den over thar. Tother tew are fer a feller in

jail for hoss stealin'. He'll swing tew 'fore mornin'. Jest let the boys
get a little steamed up, pard. He'll never read his sweetheart's letters,
poor cuss."[42]

That speech was purely Western, and we wonder of course whether
McCartney—originally from Shelby, New York, but who had been in
Montana for many years—really talked that way, but he certainly could
have. As for the Dan Hull story, Cumberland might have made it up
because no story of such a shooting has been found in the Livingston
newspaper or in either of the two Bozeman newspapers.[43]

However, the horse thieves are completely possible—in fact likely. If
Gardiner had any kind of jail in 1883, it was no doubt a thick, wooden,
and probably windowless cabin, and unless several local men threw the
horse thieves into that secure cabin, the sheriff had already taken them to
Bozeman and/or Billings. The horse thieves could have been any of sev-
eral arrested that summer, but the most likely were John "Black Jack"
Miller and "Horse Thief" Scotty Crawford, who were captured in late
August at Cooke City and brought through the park by Sheriff James
Ferguson of Billings.[44]

According to Cumberland, a store clerk in Gardiner's "Blue Front
Store" told him that Nels Olson's wagon was headed north but would
stop for the night and advised him to start hiking in order to catch Olson.
Mr. Cumberland began walking north, strolling inadvertently past Olson's wagon in the dark. On the way, he stopped for information and
water at a "ranchman's hut" near the road, which must have been the
home of George W. Reese. He saw the new railroad bed that laborers had
worked on earlier that day and hiked on to a lone saloon and boarding
house at "Cinnabar creek," arriving about midnight.

Walking into the saloon, Cumberland saw two men and a bartender
that he called "mine host," a congenial reference of that era, which usually applied to innkeepers. To appear friendly, he bought drinks for all three
of them and himself. The host was almost certainly John H. Mulherin.
One of the other men, Cumberland learned, "had once been a sailor" and,
although he could have been Robert McCune, it is more likely that he was
C. J. "Jack" Baronett. Baronett was a longtime resident in the region—in
fact, one of the few who had been such a seafaring man. The third character was named "Bill," and he was probably William Bassett, who lived

across the river on Bassett Creek and later married one of John Mulherin's daughters. Cumberland described the men and what happened:

> Mine host was what one would call, in Western language, a tough customer. He was large, burly; his eyes were bleared and his face red. His two companions were in keeping with him. One of them carried a large revolver in his hip-pocket; the other, whom I had learned from the conversation, had once been a sailor, wore the mariner's usual weapon, a large knife in a leathern sheath. All were dressed in the mountain costume, large boots with pantaloons tucked in[to] them; slouch hats, blue shirts, and a belt to hold things in proper place. All this preliminary would be useless if not for the fact that I was in a "hard country." Everything had the new appearance except the men: they looked old, weather-beaten, reckless, and determined. . . . I tried to act like a mountaineer myself, or I should never have taken the whisky, as my newspaper companions very well know. . . . It was nearly 1 o'clock before [our] little company about the comfortable fire broke up. The old sailor was first to go. Hitching up his pantaloons and buying a large glass of rum, he departed in silence, slamming the heavy door behind him. Just here, mine host interrupted the proceedings. "Wall, boys," he said, addressing the other individual and myself, "the beds be all let." This I supposed was a gentle hint to leave for other quarters. As I was pretending to be asleep in my chair, but really thinking what to do, my companion settled the affair. "Yer wouldn't turn a feller out to-night, would yer, pard? Jest let us sleep on the floor; give us that air hoss blanket 'n we'll roll up an' snooze—hic—like babes." Although I did not fancy rolling up with such a fellow, I could not object under the circumstances. . . . The host grumbled assent to the request of "Bill," and threw down the blanket from the shelf.[45]

Mr. Cumberland was apprehensive but decided to play along. The host locked the outside door and left them alone, barring his inner door before he walked down the hall. "Might's well make the best on it," remarked Cumberland casually, but Bill did not answer. He had crept silently behind the bar and was now drinking straight whiskey in large amounts to his heart's content. Cumberland stayed awake until Bill fell onto the floor beside him. "Putting my hand on my forty-two caliber Smith & Wesson," he noted, "I waited." Poetically, he added, "Outside, the wind moaned dismally and the noisy Cinnabar creek sang a monotonous treble to the stately bass of the Yellowstone [River]."

Cumberland fell asleep but awoke with a start as he "saw a figure crouching like a panther, knife upraised over me." He commenced struggling mightily with his assailant, throwing him off balance into a beer keg and jumping onto him, while crying out, "Murder! Fire!" He suddenly heard people jumping from their beds and rushing down the hall. "Ten or twelve men in undress crowded eagerly about us," said he, "and it was then that I awoke from my nightmare." Everyone laughed loudly at Cumberland, including Bill, and all went back to bed. Using a well-known slang expression, Bill chuckled, "Pard, you're a daisy! Gimme your card!" Clearly Cumberland had been deathly afraid of these Western men, but he was smart enough to pretend that he was one of them. "One was obliged," he wrote, "to keep his eyes open and be a member of the common brotherhood or endanger his life."[46]

The town of Cinnabar and its saloons were every bit as colorful as John Cumberland's story. An 1885 traveler named Dudley stated that of the dozen or so buildings in town, four to six were drinking saloons, and Edward Marston agreed that year that the town had "several" saloons. If that was the case, these were operated out of private houses (probably crude cabins), and we do not know who owned them. Mrs. Harriette Cutler, Buckskin Jim's second wife, who arrived in Cinnabar in 1901, remembered that there was a saloon "every other step," but she was remembering only that year and perhaps 1902. In 1887, traveler Van Patten reported "several saloons," and we know that Hugo Hoppe had a saloon that year from January to October that he finally sold for extra money. We also know that Mary Keeney was claiming that the Keeney saloon, hotel, and livery were solely owned by her and not her husband.[47]

While it is harder to document these earliest saloons, we can document many saloons during the period from 1889 to 1895 at Cinnabar from the quarterly list of licenses issued by Park County and published in the *Enterprise*. At least three are known for 1889—A. T. French's saloon (he also owned the main hotel that summer), Mary Keeney's saloon with gambling, and Christy & Link's saloon, which eventually would become Larry Link's sole establishment. Morgan and Maggie Williams owned the main Cinnabar hotel and saloon for the off-season of November 1889 to April 1890, and then they sold it to John Work, who owned it until the autumn of 1890, when he sold it to E. J. Fairfax.[48] During those two years, Mary Keeney and Christy & Link each owned a saloon in Cinnabar. Meanwhile E. J. Keeney left his saloon at Cinnabar in Mary's custody in December of 1890, purchased the Bank Saloon in Livingston, and essentially moved there. Apparently he and Mary were either not getting along well or else were living apart to make and save more money. It was probably the latter, for the newspaper indicates that they stayed married for many years.

W. A. Hall, who purchased Cinnabar's main hotel in April of 1891 from E. J. Fairfax, may have taken his cue from Joe Keeney's arrest for gambling without a license and paid the county's fees so that his saloon could legally have both general gambling and the game known as "faro." Mary Keeney still had her saloon and so did Christy & Link, and Mary soon got into the same trouble as her husband had done earlier. County officials arrested Mary Keeney in 1891 for "permitting gambling upon the premises without a license." After arguing with court officials, she found a way out of her trouble, but Joe was convicted and thereafter carried grudges against W. A. Hall and the Hoppes. The lesson here was to simply pay the license fee, for gambling was otherwise legal in Montana.[49]

Once Hugo Hoppe became the owner of the Cinnabar hotel in 1892, he and his offspring also found themselves in the saloon business there for more than a decade. This year there were at least four saloons in Cinnabar—those of Hoppe, W. A. Hall, Link & Christy, and Mary Keeney. Larry Link also opened his second saloon, this one in nearby Gardiner. Meanwhile Joe Keeney injected chaos into the winter business scene by trying to frame W. A. Hall for gambling. Keeney complained of an illegal faro game at Hall's saloon. County officials issued a warrant for Hall's arrest, but the warrant was not served because Keeney's claim could not be proven and in fact Keeney had malicious intent. From 1893 through 1895, issued licenses suggest that the saloons were Hoppe's, Hall's, and one owned by Link & George (Link also maintained his separate saloon in Gardiner). In late 1895, commissioners began referring to these licenses as "retail liquor" rather than "saloon." The Hoppes and W. A. Hall seem to have run saloons in Cinnabar until the end of its days.

Although they were not the entire story, saloons were related to raucousness. The soon-to-be-famous John Muir visited Yellowstone Park in 1885 and found Cinnabar to be an uncivilized place. His description tells us that the town's rowdy atmosphere, which began almost as soon as the rails arrived as it did in so many other hell-on-wheels towns in the American West, was in place that year. Muir proclaimed:

This Cinnabar 'city,' so named from the cinnabar seams and bars and stripes that make American flags of the mountains that environ it, is a terrible place. It is the nearest approach that the Government allows to the Park, and the result is the lodgment against the limits of the Park of a singularly motley crowd of old hunters, trappers, traders and grizzled old pioneers, to say nothing of gamblers, roughs, and desperadoes.[50]

So Cinnabar was already raucous in 1885, and it was so stated by none other than John Muir! Saloons of course led the way for raucousness, and some of them were housed in the crude cabins in which these lowbred men lived.

A description of the interior of the saloon at Hugo Hoppe's hotel—managed from 1892 to 1897 by George L. Hoppe—has survived:

The Barroom had a walnut bar with high, swivel stools lined up in front of it and on the back wall a four by twelve mirror reflected the expensive glassware on a shelf below it. Under the bar was a place to rinse the glasses and to keep the often-needed revolver. Windsor-back, all wooden chairs stood along the wall beyond the archway and brass cuspidors, spittoons they were called in those days, were half concealed between the chairs. Huge, wood burning stoves were set up in the rooms in the winter time. A large chandelier was suspended from the ceiling in the barroom that lit it up like day; this was a necessity in those days. Two kerosene lamps hung from the ceiling in the dining-room. Stuffed animal heads were fastened on the walls of the barroom.[51]

As mentioned, Larry Link, later a store owner in Gardiner, had a saloon in Cinnabar beginning as early as 1889. In 1892, he and his son Mike also lived in the building, which the local newspaper called "an oasis in the sagebrush." His saloon—co-owned by A. R. Christie—had a combination pool and billiard table, upon which local residents practiced "until they are almost able to 'ramps' a game on any sucker who thinks he has struck a pin pool snap in the town of Cinnabar." This cryptic message, written in the jargon of the day, apparently meant that the local pool "sharks" thought they could best all comers.[52]

Cinnabar saloons were typical, raucous Montana bars that regularly played host to fights such as the one in 1896, when a drunk nearly killed Adam Gassert with a knife. The row started when a soused laborer from the railroad tried to beat up stage driver George Marvin. Adam Gassert intervened and punched out the drunk, who left the bar and returned with a knife. He slashed at Gassert and narrowly missed severing Gassert's jugular vein. Marvin ran away. The *Enterprise* not surprisingly called it a "disgraceful affair." But no one seems to have been killed in Cinnabar saloons, unlike in Gardiner where a couple of deaths were recorded. [53]

Cinnabar was even the site of a highway robbery on a cold Saturday night in January of 1900. William Mitchell, a discharged soldier from Fort Yellowstone at Mammoth, chose that night to point a gun at two men riding in a wagon between Gardiner and Cinnabar and to demand their money. He relieved George Fadder and a companion of fifty-three dollars and then proceeded to Gardiner, where he "blew the money," probably drinking. Deputy Sheriff Frank Bellar transported Mr. Mitchell to jail at Livingston, where he was soon convicted in court. [54]

Cinnabar's reputation for raucousness was deserved, as evidenced by these enumerated accounts and at least two others. In 1900, park traveler Robert McGonnigle rejoined his cook and guide at Cinnabar, a man named Bill Jones, who was visiting Montana from Medora, North Dakota. By way of polite conversation, McGonnigle asked Jones how he had been getting along while he was waiting for them at Cinnabar and was told: "Fine, sir; I was drunk twice and had one fight." [55] In late summer of that same year, a group of rowdy drunks who worked on park road crews got into an argument at J. H. Pisor's ranch, and John Jackson Jr. shot Charles Fisher. Jackson intended only to scare Fisher but drunkenly wounded him in the abdomen and thus wisely decided to surrender to authorities. [56]

Finally with regard to saloons, an Eastern writer used Cinnabar in 1896 as his setting for a piece of Western fiction. William H. Walsh used the town as inspiration for his imaginary tale that took his viewpoint character to "C___, Montana" near "Bear Gulch" and then to the "Miner's Rest" hotel and saloon, where a proprietor was "clerk, waiter, and porter all in one," much like Hugo Hoppe had been and like his sons became later. After witnessing "an everyday scrap" between two Irish miners named Tim and Tom, others carried the drunken, passed-out Tim to the back room and wrapped him in a sheet. Then they woke him and convinced him that he had "killed" his friend Tim in the fight. They then carried him to a jail cell, left him there for the rest of the night, and took him in the morning to a trial that he thought was real. Terrified, Tom heard the words "guilty in the first degree" pronounced upon him and then heard laughter and Tim's Irish voice saying, "Phere's the divil who says oim dead? Sho him ter me, the bloody omadon; and phere's poor old Tom?" A good laugh was then had by all.[57]

One wonders how author Bill Walsh learned of Cinnabar to write about it. Probably he had simply been another one of the thousands of visitors who stepped off the train there on his way into Yellowstone National Park.

GENERAL STORES

General stores were also in evidence at Cinnabar. W. A. Hall came to Cinnabar "without a dime," according to one ex-resident, and erected his large store there first. Both Hugo Hoppe and valley old-timer Joe George have claimed that Hall had a store at Cinnabar in 1883,[58] but people sometimes misremember things when looking back on them. Hoppe's memory of constructing Hall's building at Cinnabar (in 1883 and 1884) appears not to have actually happened until 1891. Two obituaries in Livingston newspapers have stated that Mr. Hall arrived in 1883 in what became Park County,[59] but he located in Paradise Valley, not Cinnabar. The *Enterprise* mentioned him as owning (or at least running) a store "on [B. P.] Van Horne's ranch" at Fridley, Montana, in 1887 and 1888, and also mentioned that his first son was born there at that time. By 1893, he owned his own ranch at Tom Miner Basin and formally received the homestead rights on it in 1894.[60]

How W. A. Hall got started in the store business at Cinnabar was (and is) complex and incomplete. Born in Humansville (or Hermitage), Missouri, on April 30, 1861, Hall was eventually adopted by the O. D. Fisher family and—"cowboying his way out of Missouri" according to his sons—he found his way to Montana.[61] Two obituaries have stated that he "came to Montana when he was 20 years old" and punched cattle for George R. "Two Dot" Wilson in the country around what is now Two Dot, Montana. Somehow he moved to a ranch in Paradise Valley in or about 1883.[62] Marrying Lulu (or Lula) F. Brown on December 30, 1886, Hall ran the Fridley store in 1887, fathered sons Arthur and Earl in 1888 and 1889 there, and moved to Cinnabar in 1890 by answering Hugo Hoppe's advertisement to lease and live on Hoppe's ranch at Cinnabar.[63] This last statement squares with Hall's own memory, for he told Jack

Haynes in 1953 that he first came to Cinnabar in 1890, at which time he bought Hoppe's store there. Whatever that small building was, Hall says he later moved it to Gardiner, where it served for many years as the barbershop, owned by George and Otho Mack.[64]

Initially, Mr. Hall did not have a store at Cinnabar. Instead, he ran Hoppe's ranch in 1890 and then purchased a livery, saloon, and hotel in 1891 and 1892, for the newspapers and a hand-dated business card made this clear. In April of 1891, the *Livingston Post* reported that Hall was opening a livery in Cinnabar. He "is perfecting arrangements to take tourists through the national park during the present season," said the *Post*, which added that "he has already purchased the horses and vehicles necessary to perform all that he proposes to do in the way of transportation of passengers." By late May, Hall was also "proprietor of the Cinnabar hotel," having purchased it from E. J. Fairfax. The county commissioners, including Hugo Hoppe, issued a formal license to Hall for this hotel at Cinnabar.[65] Meanwhile, Lee Hoppe opened "the only store in Cinnabar" in the summer of 1891 and would be named the town's first postmaster in June of 1892.[66] W. A. Hall continued to manage his several businesses and in December, County Commissioner Hugo Hoppe issued him a license for the hotel and its saloon but with new permits for general gambling and "faro." As noted earlier, this sudden competition for gambling made Joe Keeney mad, so he tried to frame Mr. Hall by reporting that Hall was running an illegal faro game. When Keeney's ruse of "malicious intent" was discovered, the sheriff refused to serve the warrant on Hall. That was poetic justice because Keeney and his wife, Mary, had both been arrested and Joe convicted in October for illegal gambling. In March of 1892, the Keeneys were again in trouble, this time for doing business without a license.[67]

The upshot of all this for W. A. Hall's store at Cinnabar is that he and the Hoppe family appear to have essentially traded businesses (although Hall continued to run a saloon at Cinnabar through at least 1902). The trading was caused, or at least made more likely by, Lee Hoppe's resigning as postmaster. When Lee and his sister, Maggie, closed their mutual confectionery store at Livingston, Lee took the stock to Cinnabar to reopen his store there in the spring of 1892, and in June, federal officials chose him as first postmaster of Cinnabar. He continued running this store with its post office until midsummer of the succeeding year (1893) when he resigned, apparently trying to save his marriage by following his flighty wife, Jessie—who had a tendency to suddenly take off—north to Bozeman.[68] W. A. Hall became Lee Hoppe's replacement as postmaster in July, and when the Panic of 1893 struck shortly after that—along with park superintendent George Anderson's order suspending Hall's transportation privileges in the park—Mr. Hall must have panicked a bit. By August 19, W. A. Hall owned the Hoppes' store in Cinnabar, from which he could also operate as postmaster. Thus he began his lifelong career as a store owner in Cinnabar and Gardiner.[69] In early 1895, Hall opened his store in Gardiner, for the newspaper shows him suddenly holding two "merchant" licenses at that time.[70] That he added to his property at Cinnabar in late 1898 is evidenced by the newspaper's reporting of Hall's purchase of seven town lots from the Cinnabar Townsite Company for $779.15.[71]

In summary, Hall was in the region early, but he did not live at Cinnabar until 1890 and ran a livery/saloon/hotel for two years before establishing his own store there in 1893. His Cinnabar store had groceries, hardware, dry goods, and the post office. Hall also had stores in Fridley (until October 1, 1894, when he turned it over to his partner D. S. Terry), Gardiner (1895), and Aldridge (where his initial store burned in 1901, and he rebuilt it in 1902), and his advertisements touted himself as "Dealer in everything." He built his largest and most famous store in Gardiner in 1903 (probably the store Mrs. Cutler was remembering), and today this historic building has been remodeled into the Yellowstone Association's bookstore and a continuing visitor center for the town of Gardiner.[72]

Of course the Hoppe family had their own store that operated in connection with their hotel. In 1892, it was described as "a combination confectionery, dry goods, grocery, drugs and millinery store conducted by Leander B. Hoppe." W. A. Hall had his saloon-and-livery business nearby (probably less than a block away) that year, from which he rented "teams, vehicles, and camping outfits with or without drivers," but it was not yet a store because Lee had "the only" store in Cinnabar. By 1898, Hall was advertising this part of business in the *Anaconda Standard*: "Guides familiar with the Park furnished."[73]

Another later Cinnabar store was a small notions shop that was attached to Frank Holem's blacksmith shop and run by Frank's wife, Maggie A. (Hoppe) (Williams) Holem, who by that time preferred her name rendered as "M. A." to escape a bit from her own raucous past. Her store—which she ran simultaneously while serving as the town's postmistress in the same building—began in 1897 and grew much larger so that by 1900 the local newspaper could report the following:

> This general store, conducted by M.A. Holem, has had a successful business career, first starting in August, 1897, with a small stock in a room at the corner of Main street and South avenue. By trying to please the public in honest prices and just dealings, M.A. Holem was forced to establish herself in larger quarters, now occupying the post office building near the Park line depot. The stock is now complete in its line as to the present demands of its patronage, carrying a neat line of gloves, stationery, patent medicines, cigars and tobaccos, fruits, confectionery and toilet articles. M.A. Holem is also postmistress, and besides waiting on the public in a pleasant and congenial way, she is numbered as one of the promoters in any enterprise that has a tendency to develop the town.[74]

The O. M. Hefferlin Mercantile Company of Livingston opened a branch store in Cinnabar in 1901, calling it "O.K. Stores." A newspaper noted in May of 1901 that "they carry everything and are among the heaviest dealers in Park County." The Hefferlin O.K. Store, like many other businesses, moved to Gardiner in the late fall of 1902, when Cinnabar died.[75] By 1901, the *Enterprise* declared that there were three stores in Cinnabar, and Mrs. Harriette Cutler remembered some details about them, because she arrived that year. She says that W. A. Hall ran one store and "had a house across the street" from his store, while Frank Holem ran a blacksmith shop with a "notion store attached" that was run by Frank's wife. Thus the third store must have been the Hefferlin O.K. Store.[76]

Frances Lynn Turpin, an 1895 traveler, found the shopping in one of Cinnabar's stores entertaining:

> Stopped at Cinnabar to mail letters and do a little shopping; Martha and I bought hat pins, Mr. Kenyon a pair of shoes. How odd it seemed to shop in that funny little town. The clerk looked at me with an amused smile when I asked for Pond's Extract. I suppose he thought I was preparing for bruises.[77]

If that clerk was not merely a hired hand for the summer, he might well have been W. A. Hall.

STREET VENDORS, ZOOS, TAXIDERMY, AND RODEOS

In addition to a depot, a hotel, stores, saloons, a livery, a post office, a sawmill, an icehouse, a rodeo ground, and a blacksmith shop, Cinnabar had local hangers-on who set up temporary street businesses, all of them attempting to interest tourists disembarking from trains. William Davis was one of these. Called the "poet laureate of the Yellowstone" by one newspaper writer, Davis entertained visitors on the depot platform in 1887 by telling them stories about the items he offered for sale on an old discarded poker table. Those items ranged from crystalline specimens to petrifactions to brass grapeshot that he claimed was found in the mines at Bear Gulch after having been "fired by the Hudson Bay Company at hostile Indians years and years ago."[78] One wonders whether he was the same William Davis who, seven years later, drowned in Paradise Valley while trying to force his reluctant horse to swim across the Yellowstone River.[79] The horse knew better than to swim the Yellowstone, especially in June. It survived, but Davis did not—indicating that the horse was smarter than he was or at least a stronger swimmer.

Another Cinnabar street vendor was "Specimen Schmidt," whose sign reading "For Sale—Specimens from Out of the Park" caused park superintendent George Anderson to drive to Cinnabar "in a cloud of dust." Confronting Schmidt angrily, the superintendent heard Schmidt say in his thick German accent, "Captain, I vas careful mid dot sign; you see it says 'specimens from OUT of the Park, nod from IN the Park.'"[80] Cinnabar voting records revealed that he was August Schmidt, age fifty-seven in 1894. It is not known when Schmidt came to the Cinnabar area, but it may have been as early as 1879, for an 1894 newspaper article stated that he had been there fifteen years then.[81] According to historian Doris Whithorn, Schmidt served as babysitter for Walter Hoppe's new son, Paul, in 1898–1899, and he was then sometimes in the company of Martha "Calamity Jane" Canary. (Jane peddled the little pink booklet with her life story in it and photos of her dressed in fringed buckskin while Schmidt sold his petrified wood at Cinnabar.)[82] Selling souvenirs at Cinnabar made Schmidt quite the reputation, for when he traveled on the train to Livingston in 1892 to apply for a pension, the event made the newspapers and the townsfolk—including a "juvenile drum corps"—turned out to see him in large numbers. The editors stated that he "crossed the plains 35

years ago with a team of burros" and that his trip to Livingston was his
first time ever on a train and his first time ever to visit Livingston.[83]

While Schmidt was perhaps the best known of Cinnabar's street ven-
dors, another one was "Specimen Bill" Lindstrom. The local newspaper
stated that he had been at Cinnabar since 1883, selling "specimens and
other curios to Park tourists." Photographer T. W. Ingersoll encountered
him at Mammoth Hot Springs in the 1880s and took a photograph of him
coating specimens on the terraces there. Traveler Albert F. Zahm met him
in 1888 and stated that he "has made this a business for nearly six years."
If correct, that put Lindstrom at Mammoth in late 1882, before the better-
known Ole Anderson arrived to sell coated specimens to park tourists.
William Lindstrom came down with dropsy (edema) in 1891 and, having
no means to treat it, died about a year later at age forty in June of 1892.[84]

Still another street vendor at Cinnabar was "Geyser Jim," who sold
specimens coated in the waters of Mammoth Hot Springs and bottles of
colored sand, much like Ole Anderson and Andy Wald were making at
Mammoth. Little Ida Miller talked to Jim on several occasions at Cinnabar in 1894, and he regaled her with stories. One wonders whether he was
the same "Geyser Jim" (Jim Nelson) who had been arrested a few years
earlier for both petty larceny and aiming a revolver at the front-desk clerk
in Livingston's Riepen Hotel.[85]

Hotel owner Joe Keeney originated the idea at Cinnabar of exhibiting
captured animals for tourists, much like happens today in small roadside
zoos all over the country. Writer Owen Wister stayed at Keeney's primitive hotel in 1887 and discovered that its proprietor was "fond of animals,
and has by the hotel a tame elk, a coyote, two of her half-breed sons, and
a black bear cub of this year, who stands on his hind legs with his paws
not quite to your waist and receives caramels with placid human sounds
of content." Also in 1887, the street vendor named William Davis
charged a fee to show off the live rattlesnakes he had gathered into a box.
Visitor J. E. Williams, who saw the animals at Cinnabar in 1888, offered
testimony that this idea was continuing that summer:

> Here is a yard [fenced enclosure] of live natural history specimens,
> illustrating the wild animals of this region, including a little kiota
> [coyote], which looks something like a wolf, some elk, deer, antelope,
> and a black [bear?] cub, three months old, which [the street vendor]
> wished to sell me for $25, and owing to its cheapness and playfulness,

I enquired about its habits for the purpose of purchasing it for my memorabilia of the trip. [86]

In November, Joe Keeney was referred to by the newspaper as the "all around rustler and proprietor of the menagerie," and he was busily bringing animals to Cinnabar when he could not simply capture them there. In December, he sold a number of them to a New York City banker and accompanied them on the train to that place. There Keeney and local New Yorkers must have exchanged fascinated stares at each other. He was not through with this enterprise. In early 1891, the *Enterprise* reported that Keeney held a bighorn sheep on his ranch that he had captured and domesticated, presumably to show to visitors who stepped off the train. [87]

Visitor F. B. Nash testified to the existence of a small "zoo" in 1891, including a captive bear and a "wolf" (perhaps a coyote):

> At Cinnabar we were treated to a little zoological entertainment. In a box with a glass top was a hideous rattlesnake of very large size. One look at this diabolical reptile was enough to convince one that he would have been a proper recipient of the satanic nomenclature. A big awkward bear sat in a latticed enclosure, chained to a tall post. At the command of his keeper, emphasized by the flourishing of a pole large enough to serve for a carriage tongue, the big beast scrambled up the post, and lolled over a board set there for the purpose. An amiable wolf wagged his tail joyfully, and fawned on his master with as genial a smile as any house dog could have mustered. Two fine horned owls stared at us in solemn protest. And a tiny antelope fawn, meek and gentle, patiently accepted the miscellaneous caresses bestowed upon it with a generous prodigality. [88]

These kinds of zoos were typical in small towns of Montana during a time when game laws were less strict; in fact by 1893, Harry Gassert was raising elk, deer, moose, and even a few buffalo on his ranch at Cinnabar:

> He reports his band of elk and deer doing splendidly. He has five experienced hunters hunting the calves of moose, elk, and buffalo. They are taken when but a few days old, and then raised by hand until old enough to feed themselves. [89]

During that same year former hotel operator Joe Keeney raised a couple of bears at his Cinnabar ranch. In June of 1893, when he decided to go mining on Boulder River, he took the bears to Big Timber, Montana, to exhibit them, and the local newspaper mentioned it:

> Two bears—one a cinnamon and one a black bear—were brought down from Cinnabar on Thursday by Joe Keeney, who caught them when they were cubs and raised them on his ranch. The animals are now chained in an enclosure near the N.P. depot and attract a crowd of visitors daily. [90]

Speaking of bears, the Cinnabar depot was the site of a circuslike event involving a bear one day in the summer of 1900, when the famous Elwood "Uncle Billy" Hofer attempted to load one of his captured black bears into a train car. Mr. Hofer, one of the Yellowstone area's best-known guides since the 1870s, brought a bear to Cinnabar in a wagon for transport. William E. Curtis, a reporter for the *Chicago Record*, happened to be there during his trip to the West to visit Indian sites and Theodore Roosevelt's ranch. Curtis, whom one writer called "the most reliable newspaper writer in America," penned a colorful account of the complicated story that cannot be improved upon, so we quote it here:

> Elwood Hofer, the official hunter and trapper of the United States Government out in the Yellowstone country, not long ago caught a big black bear in one of his patent traps, which also answers as a transportation cage. It is made of iron rods and oak timber—the trap, I mean, not the bear—has a drop at either end, and is baited with honey. When the bear enters and commences to paw the honey the drops fall and lock him in as tight as if he were in an exhibition cage at a menagerie. The cage can then be shipped anywhere the bear is wanted, and Billy Hofer supplies bears and other wild beasts to the Central Park Commissioners of New York and several zoos throughout the country, as well as to the Smithsonian Institution at Washington. Well, Billy hauled the bear down to the railroad terminus at Cinnabar, backed the wagon up against the door of a freight car, ran out a couple of planks for skids, and then hitched a chain to the cage so as to draw it into the car. A pair of mules on the other side of the car [were] attached to the other end of the chain and the driver was instructed to be very careful in starting with them. He obeyed orders to the best of his ability, and everything went right until the cage was drawn into the car. The bear, being without experience in modern transportation facilities, did not quite comprehend the situation, and expressed his anxiety in a pro-

longed "Woo-o-o-o-o!" which alarmed the mules and caused them to start across the railroad yards at a 240 gait. They snatched the bear cage through the other door of the car and dragged it over the ground as they ran, first on one side and then on the other. One minute the bear would be standing on his head and the next on his feet. The cage bounded along as if it were light as a chicken coop, and the louder the bear said "Woo-o-o-o-o!" the faster the mules ran, and their fright was not in any measure allayed by having six or seven men yelling after them. It was an excellent test of the strength of Billy Hofer's cage, for when a field of stumps was reached on the other side of the road, it bounded from one to another until finally it dropped into a place between two stumps that was not wide enough for the cage to pass through. This checked the team with a jerk, and caused them to stop so suddenly that they turned somersaults. But they were on their feet in a moment, and when the bear said "Woo-o-o-o-o!" again, they made a desperate jump. The mules being stronger than the chain, they were released, and did not stop running until they were several miles away. Ever since then, those mules have shied at freight cars. The team of sober-minded horses, which had hauled the cage down from the mountain, was brought up to the stump field and dragged it back to the car. The cage suffered no damage, and the bear got an extra ride for nothing.[91]

The opposite end of the fascination with the Yellowstone region's wildlife centered on trophies for one's walls, and still another business run by Hugo Hoppe in Cinnabar was a taxidermy service. Ida McPherren mentioned that Hoppe had a small building constructed for that purpose in 1892, and she stated that men from all around brought their kills to him to be stuffed because Livingston was a train ride away. Sometimes a tourist would purchase an especially attractive head, said McPherren. Certainly the US Army was suspicious of this part of Hoppe's business, for an 1893 article in *Harper's Weekly* stated that "the settlement [of Cinnabar] is a frontier hamlet, whose inhabitants are of the kind that the military men of the park suspect whenever a new bison's head is found on exhibition at the shop of a taxidermist in Livingston."[92]

A later addition to Cinnabar was a rodeo ground of sorts. Hugo Hoppe says that in 1890 he erected a grandstand about a quarter mile from town and back from (probably south of) the stage road half a mile. This distance sounds like he built the structure on or near his own ranch, against the hill. According to him it had seating capacity for a thousand specta-

tors (probably an exaggeration) and a wide-open area "for bronco busting, horse racing and calf roping." He says celebrations were held here
"every Sunday and on holidays" for tourists who wanted to see a horse
buck. Ida McPherren says that it was the site of tryouts for Buffalo Bill's
Wild West show, held when she was there in 1894.[93] The best evidence
for this having happened earlier (in 1887) is a photograph that the Yellowstone Gateway Museum possesses. It is a group picture of twenty-
nine cowboys taken on July 4, 1887, and it lists all of their names. The
event, whatever its nature, was probably the origin of Hugo Hoppe's
statement that Cinnabar was "often selected as the place for the tryouts,"
which were conducted by Buffalo Bill Cody's assistant Sherman Canfield.[94]

Hoppe stated that William F. Cody's man Sherman Canfield was assigned to recruit and hire skilled cowboys into the show. He said that
Canfield would travel to Cinnabar and then telephone from Gardiner all
of the surrounding small towns to give notice that tryouts would be held
for the show. He claimed that Canfield also sent riders to area cattle
ranches to notify them of the tryouts.[95]

Ida Miller McPherren was a nine-year-old girl at Cinnabar in 1894,
and she remembered Sherman Canfield getting off the train that summer
there to stage another such "bucking contest." She stated that it was held
in the arena in front of Cinnabar's grandstand "as soon as the last stage
had rolled Parkward." Sherman Canfield was the sole judge, and McPherren says Hugo Hoppe called it "one of the greatest exhibitions of bronco
busting I have ever witnessed." According to McPherren, Hoppe told the
story this way:

> A young man, about twenty-three years of age, came riding up the road
> leading a wild horse. The man was wearing cowboy boots and spurs
> but no chaps, sombrero or the customary vest. He asked to ride in the
> tryouts. Stares, sneers and sniggers were openly directed in his direc-
> tion but Sherman said to let him ride. A cowboy held the wild horse
> while the stranger uncinched his flimsy old saddle, transferred it to the
> bronc, and climbed aboard. With that the fun was on. With his head to
> the ground and back arched like an angry cat's the wild cayuse bucked
> and pitched, sun fished, jumped straight up and came down a twisting,
> and then shook himself in an effort to get rid of the man on his back.
> But the man on his back stayed on. He fanned the animal and raked
> him from neck to tail with his spurs. The crowd caught the spirit of the

game and yelled, 'Ride 'im, cowboy. Thata boy." Then the rider gave
the yell of triumph, 'Ya-hoo-yip-yee-ee-hee-ee!' as he waved his left
arm. Unable to unseat his rider the horse broke into a run down the
road and out onto the wide expanse of wild prairie with the pickup men
in close pursuit. The horse ran until exhausted and then the stranger
turned him, and, with the pickup men flanking him, the stranger
brought his horse back to the arena and stood in front of the grandstand
where Sherman stood waving his hat and cheering one of the finest
rides he had ever seen. The cowboy who had practiced every spare
moment for a year for the event but who did not have enough money to
purchase a cowboy outfit got the job. [96]

Hoppe also mentioned Johnny Davis and Jimmy Parker, two local Cinnabar residents, who he said rode for Buffalo Bill in the Wild West show
after having "won their spurs" at the Cinnabar grandstand. [97]

Also by 1894, William Wallace Wylie, who ran stage tours through
Yellowstone Park, had erected a barn for his horses past Hoppe's grandstand and "half a mile from Cinnabar's Main Street." It was the place
where little Ida Miller stowed away in a stagecoach one morning. Both
the grandstand and the Wylie barn seem to have been located west or
south of Cinnabar rather than north or east of it, but the true locations are
unknown. [98]

CINNABAR'S IMPERFECT BUSINESS SPHERE

In 1892, a newspaper writer visited Cinnabar and described its business
scene, a status that must have frustrated Hugo Hoppe and which lasted—
because of the nation's financial depression—until the park's sudden increase in tourism in 1897. The writer stated that Cinnabar

is the same Cinnabar of old and will probably continue to be the same
as long as there is a national park. It has been demonstrated that just
about so many people visit Cinnabar each year; that it takes just about
a certain amount of provisions to appease their hunger; just about a
certain amount of liquid refreshments to keep the cobwebs out of their
throats between there and the [Mammoth] Springs; just about a certain
number of horses to accommodate those who wish to make the trip by
private conveyance. Knowing all these things, the residents of Cinna-

bar have established a certain number of business houses which will
probably neither increase [n]or diminish for several years to come. [99]

The writer of this passage could not have anticipated the Panic of 1893
soon to come, but he was generally correct, because visitation to Yellowstone remained stable at only three thousand to seven thousand people
from 1883 through 1896. In 1897, stimulated by the "Christian Endeavor-
ers," Yellowstone Park's visitation jumped to more than ten thousand. At
that point, the "business houses" in Cinnabar began to increase a little. [100]

A BIT OF CIVILITY IN A FRONTIER TOWN

Telegraph and postal services to Cinnabar seem to have been reasonably
good. Summer mail ran on the train to the park every day. Winter postal
arrivals were increased to six times per week in December of 1896,
whereas before that deliveries had been only three times per week in
winter. The first telegraph in Cinnabar apparently arrived in 1883, in
connection with the rails, for the Bozeman paper stated that President
Chester A. Arthur "was the first person to send a message over the Western Union line to Yellowstone Park." [101] An 1884 photograph shows telegraph poles at Cinnabar. The telegraph line was extended to Mammoth by
October of 1886, per Moses Harris. [102] As already mentioned, a telephone
was in place in Gardiner in R. A. Bell's store in February of 1885 and in
the hotel at Mammoth by the summer of 1886. In Cinnabar, a government
telephone that connected the town with Mammoth Hot Springs was in
place by March of 1896, and telephones for private parties were looming
at that same time, when Livingston businessman A. W. Miles helped out
by investing in that business. [103]

SCHOOLS

Cinnabar did not always have a school. Historian Doris Whithorn found
evidence that a school was funded there in 1884 from the contributions of
Hugo Hoppe and others, but nothing else is known of it. The *Enterprise*
stated that an attempt was made in 1901 to separate the school district of
Cinnabar from that of Horr, so it is likely that Cinnabar students traveled

to school at Horr for many years before a school was reestablished. [104] A remnant of another school has survived in the scrapbook of Chet and Irene Allen of Paradise Valley. Chet's father, Clarence Bradley Allen (1886–1962), attended the school at Cinnabar in 1901–1902. The teacher then was Pearl Fitzgerald, perhaps a granddaughter of Assistant Park Superintendent S. M. Fitzgerald, whose young and pretty picture stares out at us today from the pages of the Allen scrapbook. Trustees for the Cinnabar school in 1901–1902 were M. A. Holem, W. A. Hall, and Charles Smith. Other students known to have been present in that session were Gilbert Smith, Bertha Cleveland, Arthur Hall, Earl Hall, Warren Hall, Bert Reese, Ira Reese, and Eddy Green. In December of 1902, Park County school apportionment statistics indicated that there were a total of only eleven students in school at Cinnabar. By February of 1903, there were only three students, and the *Enterprise* called it "probably the smallest school in the county." Miss Nellie Mahoney was the teacher that year, which was the last year that Cinnabar had a school. [105]

WEDDINGS AND FUNERALS

Like anywhere else, Cinnabar was sometimes the scene of weddings and funerals, although because it had no church these seem to have been few and held at either the hotel there or at private residences. A noteworthy one was the wedding of Frank Buttrey, store owner at Aldridge, to Jane Boucher, which occurred at Cinnabar with Justice of the Peace E. C. Culver officiating in June of 1896. [106] Another, according to park columnist G. L. Henderson, occurred on January 24, 1888, when Henry Ruckelshausen and Lillian Hope Pickering exchanged vows in front of Justice of the Peace M. Metcalf. Probably unique in the history of Cinnabar if not the region was the fact that the groom was in California while the bride was in Cinnabar. The groom had already said his vows in the presence of witnesses and a notary public in California while the bride said hers at Cinnabar in front of Metcalf, Henderson, and (apparently her friend) Mrs. Mary Keeney. Henderson called the wedding the victory "of love over all mere ordinary obstacles." [107]

THE EMERGENCE AND INFLUENCE OF NEARBY HORR, MONTANA

If tours of the park caused Cinnabar to be the "busy little place" that one occupant recalled, the emerging town of Horr would soon make Cinnabar even busier and more colorful. Resident Harry R. Horr (1842–1912) was preparing to open the "Cinnabar coal mines," as they were initially called. Mr. Horr,[108] who had earlier homesteaded at the Mammoth Hot Springs, and his brother Joseph, with their agent Horace F. Brown (who represented capitalists in Helena and Butte), were making arrangements to develop and open coal mines at what would become Horr, Montana. Harry Horr declared his homestead there in 1884, and he also had one at Cinnabar the following year. The men negotiated with the railroad for a sidetrack at Horr, and buildings were "going up rapidly" in October 1887, with the first shipment of coal reaching Livingston soon after that. Coke ovens were slated to be built in the spring of 1888.[109] As mentioned, the new town's sudden emergence caused Hugo Hoppe to abandon freighting and open a sawmill on what became known as Hoppe Creek, and he probably had some hired hands as well.

The opening of coal and coking operations at Horr (only a mile north of Cinnabar) and at Aldridge (just west of Cinnabar Mountain beginning in September of 1892) stimulated activity at Cinnabar and would continue to do so for all of Cinnabar's life.[110] When Aldridge geared up in 1893, citizens of it and Horr immediately began donating money for the construction of a mountain road to connect them, a road that would eventually be used by Cinnabarites as well.[111] Hughie B. Hoppe, who by that time lived at Tom Miner Basin to the north, was involved in the initial planning for this road but ultimately got pushed aside when Park County asked for bids to build the road in 1896.[112] Harry Horr established a post office at Horr in 1888,[113] and that must have depressed Hugo Hoppe, who well knew that Cinnabar did not yet have one.

FARMING AND RANCHING

Of course a major business at Cinnabar was agriculture. Numerous landowners farmed, and almost everyone ranched—raising horses and cattle, growing hay for the animals' sustenance, and selling hay to others. A. W.

Chadbourn, Charles Stoll, Hugo Hoppe, and many others made full or partial livings in this fashion. In 1896, the *Livingston Post* praised the ranch of Sarah Gassert, whose husband, Harry, had just died and left the place to her and their sons Adam and Henry. Calling it the "best farm on the upper Yellowstone," the editor described it as "280 acres of excellent farming land, mostly under a high state of cultivation." Noting that there were hundreds of acres of good grazing lands in connection with this farm, the writer placed Gassert's buildings at the base of the mountains, with the farming lands stretching north toward Cinnabar. "Large fields of wheat, oats, and meadows of timothy and clover as well as alfalfa meet the eye in every direction," gushed the reporter, who affirmed that they would soon be ready for the reaper and binder. The article also stated that Jacob Reding, "the life-time mining associate and bosom friend of the late Mr. Gassert, still has his home on this farm" and that he helped every day with farm labor. At Reding's death the following year, heirs pressed a long, messy lawsuit to probate an alleged will, which ultimately failed. [114]

TRAINS: SCHEDULES AND WRECKS ADD COLOR AND EXCITEMENT TO THE CINNABAR REGION

In a small town like Cinnabar where the railroad was such a commanding presence, train schedules were naturally important. Trains generally did not run year-round to Cinnabar, especially in the winter; instead operations ceased for several months, generally from January to March. Park superintendent Captain Moses Harris complained in February of 1887 (during the famous "hard" winter of 1886–1887) that the NPRR had not run a train for a month. The wagon road from Mammoth to Livingston was closed on account of snow, so team freighting "is difficult," complained Harris, and the "comfort of the troops is at stake." After October of 1887, trains ran only weekly until January 20, 1888, when they were discontinued until March. But during the winter of 1888–1889, train service began three times per week sometime after January's discontinuance because of the new coal mines opening at Horr. [115]

Times of train arrivals and departures at Cinnabar varied with the year. For example, the park superintendent noted in 1888 that trains left Livingston at 8:30 a.m. and arrived at Cinnabar at 11:00 a.m., thus putting travelers to Mammoth at the hotel at 1:00 p.m. This was "a much better arrangement than that of last year," wrote Captain Harris, who noted that those earlier travelers did not reach their hotel until evening. Likewise, the evening train back to Livingston varied in its departure time according to the year. Departure was 8:30 p.m. in 1895 and seems to have been no earlier than 5:00 p.m. most years.[116] No attempt has been made here to produce a year-by-year timetable for trains to and from Cinnabar, but the daily schedule was usually posted on page two in the *Livingston Enterprise* newspaper.

As happened in many towns, the railroad attracted men wanting work, and when they could not find it there, they looked elsewhere locally. Often these men would hear that Yellowstone National Park would be hiring road workers come spring. Park superintendent George Anderson noted in 1891 that great numbers of laboring men gathered at Mammoth Hot Springs, claiming to be waiting for work. When they ran out of money and provisions, many of them wandered to Gardiner and Cinnabar and continued to hang around those towns. Anderson called them a "tramp nuisance."[117] That scene repeated itself year after year.

As they did all over the American West, trains added much color to the upper Yellowstone River country. Almost immediately after its completion, the Northern Pacific Railroad experienced a spectacular train wreck a mile north of Mulherin Creek. It occurred on September 5, 1883. The tracks at that point were laid across the center of a tall embankment between the Yellowstone River (seventy-five feet below) and very steep cliffs above that reached fifty feet higher than the tracks. The northbound engine and five cars included a boxcar loaded with bullion, a baggage car, second-class car, first-class car, and the private car "Railway Age" occupied by the wealthy E. H. Talbott and his friends. All cars except the bullion car contained passengers. It was raining hard when Engineer J. W. Moore suddenly noticed that the railroad bed was washed out, causing the tracks to be unsupported for about ten feet. Too late to avert the calamity, he pulled the reverse lever as the locomotive crossed the washout with a terrible lurch. The heavy bullion car then struck and snapped the bent rail and plunged down the embankment, pulling the baggage car and the second-class coach with it while derailing the first-class coach. Halfway down the bank, the bullion car became so buried in the wet soil that it stopped abruptly, and the two other cars stacked up against it. Meanwhile, the engine had reached a trestle, and when the boxcar left the tracks, it jerked the engine from the rails. The engine fell through the trestle, top downward, and crashed fearfully into the ravine below.

Three men on the engine—Engineer Moore, Fireman James Meadows, and George Munro (brother of the master mechanic)—had no time for escape, but somehow all three picked themselves out of the water at the foot of the bank, alive but bearing injuries. The passengers were shaken but uninjured. "It seems like a miracle that there are no fatalities to record," stated the *Enterprise*, the editor marveling at how a train could fall from that kind of embankment without great loss of life. Had Mr. Talbott not insisted earlier upon suddenly placing his private car at the rear of the train, that car would have been in front and would have piled up in the wreck at the foot of the bank instead of being stopped by the bullion car, likely causing deaths. All the cars remained mostly upright except the locomotive, which was totally crushed, so that recovering it later involved "vast labor and expense."[118] Welsh traveler Jules LeClercq passed the spot outbound the day after the wreck, confirming that a rainstorm had caused the tracks to subside and calling what he saw a "heart-rending sight":

> The locomotive was submerged in the river upside down, its smoke-stack mired in the mud and its wheels in the air. The baggage car had suffered the same fate as the engine; as for the passenger car, it was hanging above the precipice, on the verge of completing the parabolic trajectory it had begun. It seemed that a providential hand had held it back from the brink of the abyss.[119]

So deep into wilderness America was this part of Montana that activities aboard trains to and from Yellowstone National Park became colorful in accordance with the Northern Pacific's tendency to run its Western affairs informally. Henry Finck, a passenger to the park in 1887, noted that as the train passed through Paradise Valley it stopped for ten minutes for two reasons. The first was to leave a box of merchandise in a field, probably for W. A. Hall's store at Fridley, Montana, later known as Emigrant. The second reason was "to dispose of a bucketful of buttermilk which a nut-brown maiden had brought there for the trainmen and passengers." Shortly after that, Mr. Finck noted that the train again stopped because the engineer saw a couple of prairie chickens on the hillside. "He pursued them with his revolver," reported Mr. Finck, "bagged one of them, and the train stubbornly proceeded to its destination, notwithstanding the polite request of one of the passengers to the conductor to wait until he had caught a string of trout in the adjacent Yellowstone River." A week later, on his way out of the park, Mr. Finck noted that the train stopped for fifteen minutes while conductor, engineer, and brakeman "amused themselves with a game of baseball."[120] At this early day, the motto of the Park Branch seemed to be "Why hurry?" Historian Aubrey Haines has pointed out that only later did the Northern Pacific adopt the motto "That's the Way to Run a Railroad!"

The combination of railroad color and unusual people at Horr was responsible for "Dago Joe"—last name unknown and obviously the recipient of an anti-immigrant nickname—jumping from the train at George Reese's water tank one day in August of 1891. The train had just left Cinnabar and was proceeding at a lively speed when Conductor Winston received word that one of the passengers had jumped. He stopped the train and backed it up to that location to find "Dago Joe" lying insensible at the side of the track. Restored to consciousness by the cries of bystanders, he stood up and displayed only surficial injuries. It seemed that his hat had blown out the window and he did not want to part with it, so he tossed his blankets out and jumped from the car. He told the conductor that he did not want to reboard the train and, shouldering his blankets, set off walking to Horr.[121]

A winter crash occurred just south of Livingston. The twelve-car train left Cinnabar on January 21, 1892, in the afternoon and ran normally until it struck a broken rail at Brisbin. The engine and many cars passed over it safely, but the passenger coach wrenched the track loose and carried it away. However, the coupling pin held the coach in place, and it made another half mile before being thrown onto its side and dragged some distance. Fortunately no one was killed and only James McCartney, the so-called mayor of Gardiner, was injured. He sustained two severe cuts on his left hand and painful bruises.[122]

Only a few months later, on June 13, 1892, another train wreck occurred, this time in the canyon near "Yankee Jim's" place. At a point one mile west of Sphinx, several large boulders rolled onto the track. Rounding a curve, Fireman Wilson saw them too late, yelled for Engineer William Vaupel to jump, and then jumped himself. Vaupel applied the air brakes, pulled the reverse lever, and then vaulted just in time to save his own life. The engine crashed into the boulders, left the track, and rolled down a forty-foot embankment into the river. Three coal cars followed, piling up at the foot of the embankment. Wilson and Vaupel sustained only minor injuries, but W. B. Sleeper of the Park Coal and Coke Company was less fortunate. Thrown from the boxcar into the river, he suffered a badly disfigured face but was able to swim ashore. All traffic was blocked until 6:00 a.m. the following morning. [123]

The difficult topography at Yankee Jim Canyon seemed to lend itself to train wrecks. One of the worst ones occurred two miles north of Sphinx on May 8, 1893, when Engineer George Eldridge, who was southbound in locomotive 586 and pulling twenty cars of railroad ties, hit a bad spot in the track. The location was just west and a little north of "Yankee Jim's" place and fortunately at river level. There was a tie crew of twelve or fourteen laborers on board along with Fireman Frank Straub, Brakeman James Morrison, and Conductor Ed Winston. Eldridge suddenly saw a "sun-kink"—a place where the rail was warped due to overheating—in the left track. Before he could slow down, the engine struck the warped rail, breaking it and causing the locomotive to careen off the track toward the river followed by eight of the loaded cars. Dropping down a three-foot embankment, the engine toppled into the river on its side and then continued to be pushed along by cascading and jackknifing cars behind it, each car splintering as it struck. Eldridge was thrown through the cab window, landing on his shoulder. He rose to his feet, walked fifty feet, and passed out unconscious. Brakeman Morrison picked himself out of a barbed-wire fence, badly bruised and somehow fifty feet ahead of the train. Making a quick search, he and others found the mangled and lifeless body of Fireman Straub, age thirty-five, crushed beneath the coal car and pinned down by brake rods and splintered cars. Conductor Winston borrowed a horse from the nearest ranch and rode pell-mell toward the nearest telegraph—at Cinnabar, fifteen miles away. After messaging for help, he pumped a handcar to Horr, where he picked up Dr. W. H. Allen and took him back to the wreck scene so that emergency aid could be rendered until another train could arrive from Livingston. [124]

Only a few months earlier those very railroad workers had probably read the article "How It Feels to Be in a Railway Wreck," as it circulated around the nation from the *Chicago News-Record*. Any man who has not been in such a wreck, said the writer, "would not believe how long it takes for cars to get through piling up." He described it as follows:

After the first crash there is a rebound clear to the back of the train, and then the whole thing takes another lunge, something gives way, and maybe three or four more cars telescope. Then there's another jerk backward and another lunge, and it seems as if the cracking and groaning and tumbling keep on for five minutes. When a man is mixed up with the trucks under the whole stack it seems like an hour. "Make it an hour and a half," said an ex-brakeman as he scratched his nose with the only claw-like finger remaining at the end of [his] twisted and shriveled stump of a hand. [125]

The onlookers and listeners to this story laughed heartily because they were observing that the ex-brakeman knew personally of what he spoke, having lost his hand in a genuine train wreck.

It was one of these two train wrecks, either the 1892 or the 1893 one, that apparently generated a place name within Yankee Jim Canyon. Today's raft guides who take float trips on the river through the canyon have referred for some years to the last and most westerly rapids in the canyon as "Boxcar." The river is very deep (about eighty feet) at this point, and one or more of the boxcars may still be in the river, thus influencing the rapids and remaining the likely reason for that place name. Regardless, the rapids appear to have been named from a train wreck.

With this background completed on the town of Cinnabar, we now return to Hugo Hoppe's story and that of his grandniece, Ida Miller. She left us detailed and vibrant memories about "Uncle Hugo" and his terminus town during her unforgettable summer of 1894.

8

"THE ONLY LITTLE GIRL IN CINNABAR"

Hoppe's Niece and Her Daughter Arrive (1894)

Cinnabar, where the aristocratic East met the democratic West.
—Ida Miller McPherren, in *Imprints on Pioneer Trails*

Notwithstanding a Pullman strike and a great depression that were both paralyzing much of the nation, Ida Miller, age nine, and her mother (Geneva Miller) stepped off the train at Cinnabar, Montana, on June 9, 1894. The two were Hugo Hoppe's grandniece and niece from St. Louis, and he had paid for their transportation to the West, ostensibly to help care for his ailing wife, Mary. Little Ida was smitten almost instantly with Cinnabar, and she remembered it all her life. "It lingers in the memory," she wrote, "like the first kiss of a true love, or the smile of a first born, or the scent of the first rose of spring."[1]

Whatever those feelings were, they imprinted strongly upon her young mind. Ida remembered the runt train that they had ridden from Livingston, comprising only four cars and an engine, pulling up to Cinnabar's "little toy station." "White attired, colored porters, with grins like politicians," she wrote, "opened the doors of both Pullmans; hopped down the steps with stools in their hands; set the stools at the foot of the steps, and helped to alight the ladies whose hands were occupied in holding several bolts of billowing petticoats and skirts in a way not to reveal their ankles."[2] Many of these people were tourists heading into Yellowstone National Park, but Ida and her mother were staying at Cinnabar.

Ida spotted her Uncle Hugo immediately, whom she knew from the previous year when he had visited them in St. Louis. Distraught about Mary and probably a bit sick himself, he was much thinner than she remembered. His shoulders sagged, she recalled, and his eyes looked as though some of the "zest for life" had gone out of them. "But he was still a fine looking man," she said later, "with the aquiline nose and classic features of the high-born German; light complexioned with auburn hair and grey-blue eyes." Ida was struck by how much he looked like her mother and by how much both of them resembled the likeness she had seen of her own great-great-grandmother (Hugo's grandmother), Henriette Johanne Baumbach. Suddenly she noticed four stagecoaches lined up alongside the board platform and decided that her party was going in one of them to Cinnabar. "Uncle Hugo," she said, "aren't we going to Cinnabar?" Hugo Hoppe smiled quietly and answered, "Isn't this big enough for Cinnabar?"

Then it struck Ida that she was already in Cinnabar. She looked around at the "motley crowd of people milling around on the platform," and this is what she remembered:

> Guides for pack outfits or private camping parties; farmers after freight; folks waiting to go to Livingston when the train went back; porters dancing attention at five dollars a jig; men loading the stages with tourists and their luggage; freighters after their freight; spectators watching the frontier drama and the tourists[,] comedians of the drama, for the tourist of that day came to go through the Park dressed to attend a Grand Ball, and they acted for all the world like they had sailed across the sea to a land of wild people. [3]

Ida's perception was on track, because the residents of Cinnabar and Yellowstone thought that those visitors were wild people too. "That was the way the East and the West clashed at Cinnabar," recalled Ida. "The Easterner came west to treat the cowboys like wild animals in a zoo, and the cowboys resented their peanut-throwing overtures." [4]

And she loved the platform at the Cinnabar depot, where exotic tourists alighted from the daily train. Many of the women, she noted, seemed fearful of everything around them in this new environment. Some wore tiny bottles of smelling salts chained to their necks, she observed, and others became downright frantic when they saw the swaying-and-rocking stagecoaches that they would soon be riding through very tall mountains.

Many of them, Ida concluded, "seemed to have the impression that it took a lot of courage" to travel in Yellowstone. Her description today places us vividly in Cinnabar among tourists heading into Yellowstone:

> Some of them were horrified when they saw the little, red, combination depot and station, the two-building Main Street of Cinnabar, the acres and acres of rolling prairie hemmed in by snow-capped mountains, and stages with six horses and only one man to drive them. They all carried Guide Books and some would thumb through them to make sure that they hadn't been side-tracked to some rendezvous of some highly organized band of professional robbers. . . . A surprisingly large percentage of the tourists who visited the Park before the turn of the century regarded it as an alien land whose origin of strange phenomena was enveloped in mystery and its wonders clouded by weird and distorted tales told by men who were awed by the spectacle. No wonder that some of the tourists brought vials of smelling salts to buoy them up or lorgnettes to make certain they saw all the dangers in the road ahead, or wore bustles to bounce back on when they were blown up, or wore crescent-shaped, diamond breastpins to light the way of the robbers.

"While they looked askance at the stages," laughed Ida, "they kept sniffing the smells to bolster their nerve to take a chance on being dumped for the coyotes to feed on."[5]

Ida, Geneva, and Uncle Hugo walked to Hoppe's hotel, and Hugo Hoppe led the way into the dining room. He pulled the chairs out for the tourists at the near end of the table and then "led mama and me to the other end, near the kitchen, where the family always sat to eat." Joining them at the table were Ida's other relatives: Hugo's wife, Mary (soon to be bedfast from cancer); Hugo's sons, Walter, Hughie, George, and Albert; and his stepdaughter, Maggie Hoppe Williams. His son Lee was not present at that moment (he was the only one married), but Ida would meet him soon. According to the town's 1892 and 1894 voter registration, Hugo and four of his sons were then living in "Hoppe's Hotell [sic] at Cinnabar." Their homesteads had been sold to raise money for the hotel venture. It was Ida's first exposure to Maggie's meanness and Walter's crankiness, but she loved everyone else in this big family affair.[6]

Cinnabar was entertaining, and it changed Ida's life for the better and her mother's for the worse. Maggie Williams—a short brunette who resembled her mother, Mary—immediately ordered Geneva into the kitchen to work with the Hoppes' Chinese cook Tung Loo. Most Cinnabarites were cordial to Ida, who believed she was "the only little girl in Cinnabar," but Mary Hoppe and Maggie persecuted Ida's mother thoroughly. Ida said later that she would never forget the "trapped look" on her mother's face "when she realized that she was not to be treated as one of the family." "Don't go away, Ida," said Geneva to the little girl through tears, "because mama has to work and can't look for you if you get out of sight."[7]

Ida was certain that Aunt Mary and Cousin Maggie were jealous of her mother, but regardless she loved her first summer in Cinnabar. She met its residents along with those of Gardiner, Horr, Aldridge, Cooke City, and Mammoth that season and continued meeting them for eleven summers afterward. Even when Ida later attended high school in Livingston, she still spent summers in Cinnabar or in the nearby towns of Gardiner, Horr, or Aldridge. Ida met Montana's famous Marcus Daly that first summer, and she says he was handing out twenty-dollar gold pieces and gave her one. (Montana's strange election to decide where the state capitol was to repose was being held that year, and Daly was campaigning for Anaconda.) She encountered "Geyser Jim," one of the souvenir sellers at Cinnabar, who advised her that "you won't never get lost if you stay in sight of the river." She rode the Cinnabar ferry across the river to meet and have lunch with the striking "Mrs. Schreiber," who would marry George Hoppe three years later. She met the black man, Bill Price, who claimed his father was General Price, a white man from Missouri, and who claimed that he saw the Doolan gang hide fifteen thousand dollars in bank money and then stole it from the robbers and drove it in his wagon to Montana. She reveled in Cinnabar's Fourth of July rodeo and festivities that summer, saw Calamity Jane in person, was photographed by F. Jay Haynes, and learned the idiosyncrasies of the Hoppe family. But most important, Ida described Cinnabar for us—both its people and its buildings—and we share her impressions throughout this book.[8]

When Ida arrived in 1894, the youngest of Hugo Hoppe's five sons was twenty-two years old, Ida's Aunt Mary was dying of cancer, and her Uncle Hugo was in the final fifteen months of his life. Hugo's five boys had grown up during the family's eleven years (to date) at Cinnabar, Horr, and Livingston. Walter, the oldest, had been nearly nineteen in the summer of 1883, old enough to go into his father's freighting and transportation business and to help run Keeney's hotel at Cinnabar when he was needed. He helped his father transport lumber into the park for the new Mammoth hotel that year, and fifty-seven years later his obituary credited him with that piece of history. Hughie, seventeen; George, fourteen; Lee, thirteen; and Albert, eleven, did what they could to help their father run his freighting operation and get Cinnabar going but also began trying to make their own way. Because the eldest son's legal rights (known as primogeniture) still prevailed in those days, Hugo's younger sons would likely not be able to inherit much of anything.[9] When Ida arrived, each of Hugo Hoppe's sons was eleven years older than they were at the time Cinnabar began. Ida was getting to know all of them, and Maggie too.

Uncle Hugo's stepdaughter, Maggie Hoppe Williams—who was twenty-six in 1883 and thirty-seven when Ida arrived—had married Morgan T. "Bud" Williams by late 1876 and was always a difficult and challenging person for everyone else in the family. Her husband's uncultured tendency to drink and fight and to argue with her did not help the situation, for either the family or her own marriage. Because Maggie was older than her brother Walter by seven years, Hugo Hoppe gave her what was essentially the assistant manager's job at their Cinnabar hotel, and at times she ran its affairs like a tyrant. Ida Miller told stories of Maggie's meanness and remembered that in 1894, "Maggie Williams had a husband Bud Williams, but she did not know where he was and she was not looking for him because she wanted to marry the village smithy."[10] Therein lies a fascinating tale that we shall tell shortly. Little Ida immediately despised Maggie, but she liked the five brothers, even Walter.

Leander Hoppe, known as "Lee" to the family and "Leo" to his father, helped Cy Mounts manage the Laclede hotel in Bozeman when he was only twenty. Two years later, he became the first of the Hoppe sons to wed when he married Jessie (or Jesse) S. Boomer of Bozeman on December 22, 1892. He and Maggie briefly ran George's store in Livingston before he moved back to serve as Cinnabar's postmaster in 1892 and early 1893, while also running the family's store there. His father Hugo says that at some point he built the couple a frame bungalow at Cinnabar, where they lived until they split up. Jessie, who was only sixteen years old when they married, missed her parents so began running back and forth to Bozeman. Lee resigned as postmaster and followed her to Bozeman in 1893 and again in late 1894, before both of them returned to

Cinnabar in 1895. He had turned twenty-four when little Ida met him, and she quickly became very fond of him.[11]

Hughie Hoppe was twenty-eight and unmarried when Ida met him (he married Millicent Iverson in late 1895) and, like his brothers, had been working in the family's freighting business. Beginning in 1892, he worked in the family's hotel business but lasted there only a couple of years, while also running a butcher shop at Horr with L. H. Van Dyck. That partnership dissolved in 1893, and in May of 1894, Hughie filed his homestead claim and began living and working on his ranch at Tom Miner Basin.[12] Thus he was not around much to visit with little Ida, so she did not know him well until later in their lives.

Eldest son Walter was the third to marry, but it would not happen until after his father's death. When little Ida arrived, he was close to thirty years old and had spent years working for and then running both his father's and his own freighting operation. He had long been caught up in his father's dreams and had done whatever he could to help obtain the hotel, store, and saloon at Cinnabar. Now that the family owned them, he was second in command—essentially an overworked, assistant manager whose dying mother and anxious father put a lot of extra stress upon him and who knew that the family's business would soon fall directly onto him. Little Ida thought Walter was cranky, but he had many reasons to be so.[13]

George L. Hoppe was the last of the sons to marry, and he would marry three times. Like his brothers, he worked for his father's freighting operation and then briefly labored as a clerk for the railroad mail service in Livingston before opening a news and confectionery store there in 1890. In 1891, he began managing the store next to what became the family's hotel at Cinnabar, while also dabbling in mining for the next two years at Bear Gulch and Crevasse and spending what must have been a life-changing winter in the East in early 1893. In 1894, little Ida saw him dating Georgetta Schreiber on the sly. She witnessed the two of them riding horses together and pretending not to see her, even though she had just had lunch with "Mrs. Schreiber" the day before. Georgetta was more than four years older than George and must have utterly swept him off his feet, for Ida described her as "a very young woman with peroxide-blond hair; deep-blue eyes; a buttermilk complexion, and a slim figure correctly corseted to the wasp waist and the billowy bosom of the era." She made a huge impression on little Ida. "I can see her standing in the doorway with the morning breeze gently whipping the yards and yards of light-blue organdie," recalled Ida, "and showing the laces on the stiffly starched ruffles of many petticoats." Mrs. Georgetta Schreiber looked "crisp and fresh" to the nine-year-old girl.[14] When little Ida arrived, George was twenty-five and dabbling in mining while secretly visiting Georgetta, who must have looked much younger than her thirty years.

Albert Hoppe never married and—except for a brief education at Bozeman and adventures in Butte and Spokane—lived in Cinnabar, Jardine, Tom Miner Basin, and Gardiner for the rest of his life. That he too was involved in making money for the family's dreams is apparent from his purchase in 1893 of town lots and other land at Cinnabar, which he conveyed to his father, Hugo, two years later.[15] Albert was living and mining at Jardine from at least 1898 to 1900. Family lore and the newspapers indicate that he also lived for a time in Tom Miner Basin, where he helped his brother Hughie raise cattle, and he was doing it in late 1900 and again from 1902–1904.[16] His story involving his father's town land at Cinnabar did not really begin until long after the town had died, and that story became complicated in the 1920s. It is a tale that we shall tell later. At the time that little Ida came to Cinnabar, Albert was twenty-two and a student at Montana State University who worked for his family's businesses only in summer.

These were Ida Miller's relatives, the people who were showing Cinnabar to her and telling her about the country adjacent to Yellowstone National Park. They had no idea that the small, nine-year-old girl would later write much about each of them, thus saving many of their stories for posterity. Ida liked Lee Hoppe the most, probably because he talked to her more often and more earnestly than did the other adults. "I don't know what we did for amusement," chuckled Lee, "before little Ida came."[17]

Lee Hoppe's comment was predicated on Ida's big adventure with the Wylie Camping Company in which she got a taste of what the stagecoach drivers did in Yellowstone National Park. William Wallace Wylie, who ran a movable touring-and-camping business in the park, had erected a livery and barn at Cinnabar to be his north-entrance facility. Walking toward buildings one day on the road, Ida discovered it. "I could hear horses munching hay inside the barn," she recalled, "but the stage coaches were standing around on the outside." Ida climbed into a stagecoach, sat on a seat, and pretended that she was holding a lorgnette, carrying a vial of smelling salts, and playing with her fan—just like the fancy lady tourists she had seen. She climbed onto the driver's box and pretended to "rein" the horses. But suddenly hearing voices, she ran to the back of the coach and climbed into the "boot" (the leather or canvas storage at rear) only to feel a saddle tossed into the compartment, which landed right on her. Surprised and trapped in there, she remained quiet.[18]

Now Ida was fearful but also fully committed to her misadventure. She felt horses being hooked up to the coach and heard the Wylie drivers talking trash and making jokes about sexual matters that she did not understand. The coach rolled over to Cinnabar with her in it, and she felt "satchels, carpet-bags, parasols, and umbrellas" all thrown into the boot beside her. Then she and the coach went "bouncing along" up Chadbourn Hill, on their way to Gardiner and Mammoth. When a lady fell out of the coach, Ida heard screeching and yelling, and the coach stopped to reclaim the lady. Then Ida felt the clattering vehicle resume its journey, and she laughed quietly at the passengers' ongoing comments about the incident.[19]

At Mammoth, the driver and his friend sitting beside him became tour guides. They "pointed out the different phenomena to the tourists," said Ida, "and answered any questions they could answer and to those they could not answer, they would say 'Only God knows that.'" Then the stage went on to what was probably the Wylie Company's temporary facility there, an apparent restroom-and-stopping place used by the company before it proceeded on south to its overnight camp at Apollinaris Spring. There at Mammoth, the man riding with the driver "climbed down and assisted the tourists to get out of the stage coach." Then he started to unload the boot, and when he did that, he grabbed something that moved. It was Ida![20]

Ida recalled that half a century later she could still visualize the look of surprise and apprehension on his face. According to her he exclaimed, "Rolled bull's tails if it ain't that Hoppe kid that's been in more runkus [ruckus] than a cattle rustler since she come!" The tourists gathered around and scrutinized her, one "old hen" cackling, "Where did she come from?" Ida immediately answered, "St. Louis!" and that tickled the driver's assistant, who lifted her up onto the box saying, "Like to ride up on top with me and the driver? You'll see more of the country and won't be alone!" Ida instantly thought she was in heaven, feeling, she wrote, "as big as any grandchild of Queen Victoria." They reached Cinnabar before the kitchen help was ready to eat lunch, and Ida was apparently never missed. It was an adventure that she never forgot!

Cinnabar and its fair region never departed from little Ida's head and heart. In fact, they etched an ineradicable message upon her being. After Mrs. Georgetta Schreiber fed her lunch that day on the Yellowstone River, Ida and Georgetta picked wildflowers on its north bank—bitterroot, phlox, wild rose, bluebells, and Solomon's seal, which Ida called "Lily of the Valley." On that day, remembered Ida many years later, "there was born deep down inside me a love for the West, and never again, even in any of the years of disillusionment and heartache that followed, did I wish to leave it."[21]

9

HOPPE PLATS THE TOWNSITE, REORGANIZES HIS COMPANY, AND DIES, BUT CINNABAR LIVES ON (1895–1903)

And in the end, it's not the years in your life that count. It's the life in your years.
—Abraham Lincoln

Go for it now. The future is promised to no one.
—Wayne Dyer, author

Hugo J. Hoppe was central to affairs at Cinnabar from 1892 almost to the day he died in September of 1895. For years he was busy trying to acquire Cinnabar but got busier during the years 1888–1893, when he served as one of the Park County commissioners, and busiest of all during his last two years of life. According to his own statement (through Ida McPherren), the Northern Pacific Railroad sold him much of the land in the townsite of Cinnabar in 1890. The newspapers for 1890 and 1891 say nothing about any such transfer nor can this author find it in land records, but something like that must have happened because he platted the townsite and incorporated. In early 1894, he advertised for sale all of his real estate and personal property—at Livingston an "elegant" residence and at Cinnabar his residence, hotel, ranch-related buildings, stock, and various chattels. His reason for selling was "sickness which interfered with business," undoubtedly that of his wife, Mary. But he had no buyers. On June 4, 1895, with the Montana Coal and Coke Company scaring him by arriving at nearby Horr to develop Aldridge, he made a last desperate attempt to get attention for his town of Cinnabar by incorporating with J. D. Finn and A. J. Campbell. The three men capitalized their stock at thirty thousand dollars. Hoppe traded 45.4 acres of land at Cinnabar to his new company in return for 2,991 shares of its stock. His partners purchased eight shares of stock.[1]

The purpose of the new company, called the Cinnabar Townsite Company, was to hold, improve, and sell real estate at Cinnabar; to build a new bridge across the Yellowstone River to replace Cinnabar's ferry; and to construct and operate an electric light plant (this last effort would fail because of the emerging town of Horr that later became known as Electric, Montana). Another part of Hoppe's plan was to build a new road directly to Bear Gulch, which he believed would soon produce tons of gold. On June 20, 1895, Hoppe as president and Campbell as secretary issued a plat of the townsite, mapping the lots for two blocks north from the railroad to the Yellowstone River and also depicting the lots for three blocks south of the railroad. It was reminiscent of what Carroll Hobart and H. H. Hollidge had done in 1883, but interestingly Hoppe and his partners did not use any of the names that Hobart and Hollidge had given to the streets twelve years earlier. Instead they gave ordinary names to many fewer Cinnabar streets: Front Street, Park Street, and First through Fifth Streets, with a Bridge Street located as the most easterly north–south thoroughfare, where Hoppe intended to build the river bridge.[2] His sons would construct it after his death. Finally, Hoppe advertised a total of one hundred ninety acres of agricultural land for sale at his Cinnabar townsite and also advertised Mary Hoppe's eight lots for sale at Livingston. The *Enterprise* heartily approved of all this, noting way too optimistically that "Cinnabar has a bright future" because "she is now the distributing point for one of the richest sections in Montana."[3]

Notwithstanding that prediction, personal health problems and the two rapidly expanding towns to the northwest proved too much for Hugo Hoppe. As the land he advertised failed to sell, his health worsened during 1894 and 1895, and did not get better even with his big plans for incorporation looming. Seeing the town of Horr expanding phenomenally and the town of Aldridge also gearing up, both at the expense of Cinnabar, had to have hurt him during that summer—the summer that his grandniece "Little Ida" enjoyed so much. Little Ida represented a key difference between old people and young people. The old torment themselves by worrying about their financial and family problems. The young dance, drink, and chirp. It is a story as ancient as humans.

By August of 1894, Hugo's wife, Mary, was seriously ill with cancer, and on October 30, she died at Cinnabar.[4] Hugo Hoppe was devastated.

With Mary gone at the relatively young age of fifty-seven, Hugo's mind must have wandered back over the thirty years of their "Enoch Arden" romance. That famous poem authored by Alfred Lord Tennyson and published on July 30, 1864—only one week before their eldest son was born—had been a foundation of the Hoppes' marriage, and they talked of it to their children. In the poem, Enoch Arden left his wife, Annie, to go to sea to support her. When he was stranded for ten years on a desert island, Annie gave him up for dead and married his childhood rival. Enoch returned to learn that she was happily married with a child but elected not to interfere with her happiness and instead pined away and died of a broken heart. Like Annie in the poem, Mary Jane Gee from Ohio was twice wed and had a child with her first husband. She married Richard William James from Kentucky in her hometown of Salem, Ohio, on June 2, 1854. They moved to Utah Territory, where their daughter Margaret "Maggie" Ann James was born in 1857. In 1860, they were probably the family shown in the US Census as living at Spanish Fork City, where Richard James was an "Indian interpreter." Like so many of that era, Richard James went to the Civil War (to Quantrill's guerrillas in Kansas, according to Hugo Hoppe), and Mary soon "had word that her husband had been killed in battle." "As he did not return and she could learn nothing more," said her daughter-in-law Ella many years later, "she concluded the report of his death authentic and married Hugo J. Hoppe." They moved to Montana Territory, apparently living for a time at Fort Benton. "It was at Fort Benton," recalled Hugo, "that the most poignant experience of my life took shape," for there he encountered Richard William James unexpectedly alive. Mr. James, recalled Hugo, "saw Mrs. Hoppe and told a saloon full of men that she was his wife." That was merely "Dame Gossip," declared the citizens of Helena, but like Enoch Arden in the poem, Richard James fortunately did not pursue Mary Gee Hoppe.[5] Regardless, Hugo Hoppe from that moment on must have always kept an eye over both his and Mary's shoulders.

Mary's death was an emotional blow for Hugo Hoppe, and it affected his health. "He did not know what was the matter with him," wrote Ida later, "nor did he consult a physician because he believed he was run down from overwork and worry." Instead he went to Chico Hot Springs in November, where he hoped to be benefited by bathing in the hot water there. "I noticed how thin and tired he looked," she remembered.[6]

The vengeful Maggie Williams wasted no time in ejecting Ida and her mother from the Cinnabar hotel as soon as Hugo left for Chico. Maggie "told Mama that she would have to find work somewhere else," said Ida, "because she was not needed at Cinnabar any longer." Devastated, Ida and her mother rode to Gardiner in a "livery rig" driven by George Hoppe. Mr. and Mrs. John Spiker, hotel owners there, gave Ida's mother temporary work, and she sent little Ida to Livingston to live with friends while attending school. At Christmas, Ida's mother had a minor heart attack, and Ida went back to Gardiner to take care of her. Hugo Hoppe came to see them and Ida eavesdropped on the conversation at her mother's bedside. "Both broke into soulful weeping," says Ida, "and I cried with them."

> Between sobs mama cried out, "Oh, Uncle Hugo, why did you have me come out here when you knew how mean Maggie is—you couldn't help but know it. Uncle Hugo sat on the edge of the bed and answered, "Yes, I know how mean Maggie can be when she wants to but that has not been my only cross—one of my boys [is] too. But I had no idea that Maggie would treat you like she did and I was worried [about Mary] and did not know. She told me that you wanted to come to Gardiner. Leo told me when you took sick that Maggie asked you to leave. It was a terrible thing for her to do without consulting me. But it is too late now to do anything because I found out I have quick consumption and—"

At that, Ida says, her mother gasped! She turned ashen gray and cried out, "My God, Uncle Hugo!"[7]

It was true. Hugo Hoppe had tuberculosis—an untreatable death sentence in those days, called "consumption" because it seemed to consume the body. While Ida's mother cried her eyes out, Hugo told her that he wished he could do more for her but that he was a broke man who had pooled his holdings with others (including his boys and Bud) and put most of it into Cinnabar. The rest he had spent on Mary's medical bills. "My family has been a family of bickering," he lamented to Geneva, "and I did most anything to keep trouble down." But he remained adamant that Cinnabar would someday "be the largest town in Montana," that the railroad would never extend its tracks to Gardiner, that Cooke City and Bear Gulch would someday be great mining centers, and that the park's northern strip would someday be removed from the park for a railroad.[8] Alas, none of those things would ever happen.

Hoping a change of climate could make him well, Hoppe and his daughter, Maggie Williams, made plans to go to California. Before they left, Hoppe spoke to Walter. The *Enterprise* reported on December 29 that "H. J. Hoppe has disposed of his business at Cinnabar to his son Walter," but perhaps that was only unofficial, inheritance talk.[9] Then he and Maggie entrained to San Diego, California, on January 12. They returned in July but left almost immediately for Portland and then went south to California again. In the midst of these health problems and trips to California, Hugo platted Cinnabar and incorporated his company but died in San Diego on September 12, 1895.[10]

One instinctively wonders whether any of the furniture (or blankets!) or other items borrowed by the woman who had tuberculosis at Bear Gulch years earlier were stored by Carroll Hobart at Hugo Hoppe's ranch and whether Hugo Hoppe had contact—perhaps sometime later—with those items in his barn. Getting the ultra-contagious tuberculosis in this way is something of a long shot, of course, but the thought does occur. If that happened, there is irony in it, in that Hugo's kindness to his friend Hobart and his desire to use Hobart to make Cinnabar work resulted in his contraction of the fatal disease that shortened his life.

Hugo Hoppe would have been heartbroken to learn that seven years later his dream town of Cinnabar would die when the railroad extended its tracks to Gardiner. He overestimated the abundance of the area's gold and coal, overestimated the influence of terminal towns along the railroad, underestimated the existence of Gardiner, and underestimated the power of Yellowstone National Park and its burgeoning tourism. But in all of that he cannot be faulted. The powers of minerals, railroads, and terminal towns were proven powers while the power of a new park's tourism was not. No one knew whether Yellowstone would ever receive many visitors or whether tourism would even work in the American West, let alone that this park would become a worldwide touristic phenomenon.

Almost symbolically, two events transpired that eerily echoed Hugo Hoppe's death and presaged the death of Cinnabar itself. In October the body of an unknown man, age about forty-five, was found "wedged among some rocks in the river near Cinnabar." He was identified as W. R. Popejoy, a man who had lately been acting "somewhat demented" at Horr. In early June of 1896 the new bridge over Yellowstone River at Cinnabar, on which Hugo Hoppe and his two oldest sons had worked so hard to erect to replace his ferry, was swept away in high spring water. The bridge had been completed and in place for only a few weeks. [11]

With Hugo Hoppe gone, all five of his sons tried to fill his shoes. Initially, they enlisted the aid of their friend W. A. Hall, and all pulled together that spring by making Cinnabar larger. "H. B. Hoppe will soon begin the erection of a substantial building," said the *Enterprise*, "and when completed will establish therein a feed and sale stable." At the same time, W. A. Hall was constructing a two-story frame "business block" that adjoined his existing store. Whenever he finished it, his plan was to turn the old store into a saloon. John Ennis leased Hugo Hoppe's original transportation barn to open a new "general livery and feed stable." The *Livingston Post* recognized the men's united efforts in the summer of 1896, noting that "the Hoppe boys at Cinnabar are doing a rushing business in that thriving burg." But sadly, that proclamation was nothing more than gushing boosterism, for 1896 was a year still caught in the economic depression of the previous three years, so travel to the park remained relatively low that summer. [12]

Walter Hoppe's story becomes longer here than those of his brothers', because he was the eldest son—the person who was "assigned" to continue his father's dreams. Walter inherited Hugo and Mary's hotel and land and some of their personal property at Cinnabar and through time bought out the interests of the rest from his siblings. [13] He married Ella E. Fitzgerald (1875–1968), daughter of the former assistant superintendent of the park, Selleck M. Fitzgerald, on May 4, 1896, and must have tearfully regretted the fact that his dead father had just missed attending the wedding. [14] Walter and Ella's first child, whom they named Walter Paul Hoppe but whom they always called Paul, was born February 1, 1898. Walter and Ella eventually had four children—Walter Paul, Marjorie Pearl, Mildred M., and Harold. Walter continued to run the family's freighting company, acquiring the lucrative contract with Harry Bush's new Bear Gulch Mining Company at Jardine in late 1898, just as that town began to boom. This required that he use fifteen four-horse teams, and so he busily purchased more horses and wagons and became important in the early (and short-term) bustle of that mining camp in the mountains above Gardiner, which was trying so fervently (and fruitlessly) to become a town.[15]

Seeing the sudden increasing population and activity of Jardine, Walter branched out to take over the Bear Gulch Hotel there in 1899 and also continued managing his father's dreams at Cinnabar. The Jardine hotel and the freighting operation quickly took more of his time than he could give, so he turned the management of the Cinnabar hotel over to his brother George Hoppe on April 1, 1899, and traveled back and forth to oversee both places.[16] The US Census of 1900 showed that he and Ella had ten boarders at their hotel at Cinnabar and two servants who all worked in jobs described as bartender, cook, bookkeeper, day laborer, and teamster. In 1902, Walter purchased from his in-laws and began running the Fitzgerald hotel in Gardiner, and in 1903 he purchased additional buildings at Jardine.[17] In late 1903, Walter and his brother-in-law Frank Holem together repurchased Hugo Hoppe's old ranch from Sarah Gassert, and eventually Walter bought out Holem's half interest.[18]

From his home on his father's land at Cinnabar, Walter became known for shipping the first Yellowstone elk to zoos beginning in 1910. In 1914, he served as a hired elk trapper for the state of Montana. He must have simultaneously loved and hated the ever-present elk—loathing them for eating his hay and invading his land but loving the meat, money, and adventure that they furnished. Amidst much disagreement from his brothers and with a triple mortgage weighing upon it, Walter sold his father's land to the park in late 1925 and moved to Gardiner. His son Paul grew up to be a bison keeper in Yellowstone National Park. Because parents are not supposed to bury children, the deaths of his son Harold in 1929 and his daughter Marjorie Pearl in 1939 had to have been exceptionally painful tragedies in Walter's later life. He died in 1940.[19]

Albert Hoppe attended school first at Helena Business College and later at what became Montana State University (founded in 1893 just as he became interested in attending it) and was known in the family as the "scholar," even though his brother George also obtained education. As mentioned, Albert finished writing his father's life story in 1917 but could not find a publisher and so gave the manuscript to Ida Miller McPherren. More interesting was the trouble he got into in 1900 and 1901 over a married girlfriend, with whom a family member says "he had an affair."[20] In 1898, when Harry Bush purchased the Bear Gulch mines at what would soon become Jardine, Montana, Albert became friends with

Harry, and Harry eventually hired Albert to be his personal secretary and "assayer." All was well until Albert took a shine to Harry's wife, Ada, whom historian Doris Whithorn has called "The Party Girl of 1900." That little problem may have caused Albert to travel back and forth to mining jobs in Butte and Spokane, Washington, or perhaps he was only visiting his brother George in both places as an excuse to see Mrs. Bush. In April of 1901, the *Park County Republican* reported that Albert moved to Spokane on the heels of Harry and Ada's having *also* moved to Spokane. It is not known how long the affair went on, but in October Albert and Harry got into a brawl at Livingston, where the Bushes still maintained a residence. Harry Bush claimed that Hoppe threatened to kill him, and Hoppe claimed that he only slapped Bush's face for accusing him of misappropriating company money. The argument moved back to Spokane when Albert Hoppe followed the Bushes there and was arrested at the Pacific Hotel. Bush again claimed that Hoppe threatened to kill him and his wife, while Hoppe claimed that Bush fabricated the entire affair due to jealousy involving Bush's wife. Bush's criminal claim fizzled, but two years later Albert Hoppe went after Bush again, this time suing him civilly to allege that Bush owed him one hundred thousand dollars in shares of the Jardine mine. That claim also fizzled (mining pun intended), Bush's company having gone into receivership in 1901 from lack of capital. [21]

Of course any tale is always more complex than a simple summary, and this one was no exception. The *Livingston Post* called the case "racy" and splashed it across its front page in a story that must have embarrassed Albert Hoppe locally for years, as it remained in the minds of residents. Harry Bush's letter to Hoppe in the affair was called a "gem," and attorneys read it aloud in open court. In it, "Bush called Albert Hoppe everything from a fiend incarnate to a thief, including a few cognomens, such as snake, slimy, with the instincts of a murderer, a traitor, and a fit subject for a rope with a noose which might be hung over a particular limb of a tree." [22] This last was metaphorical and apparently referred—in the crude way men sometimes talk about their enemies—to Albert Hoppe's anatomy rather than a real tree. Nevertheless, the judge dismissed the case against Hoppe and charged the court costs to Harry Bush.

Albert never married, and naturally one wonders whether the affair involving Mrs. Harry Bush had any bearing on Harry Bush's misfortunes and whether it influenced Albert's hesitancy to marry. Walter Hoppe's wife, Ella, believed in this hesitancy theory. She told her grandson Jack

Hoppe that Albert and Mrs. Bush developed an intimate relationship during the time Harry Bush was away looking for investors. Ella believed that Mrs. Bush broke Albert's heart and stated that "she was the reason he turned to the bottle."[23]

There is a final piece to this story of Albert Hoppe's affair with Ada Bush, and it probably was the reason for his unsuccessful 1904 lawsuit. It may have also been the impetus for Albert's arrest in Spokane and his bar fight in Livingston. In July of 1901, Harry and Ada Bush conveyed, at least on paper, what appeared to be a great deal of property to Albert Hoppe. Ada conveyed personal property and "improvements in Jardine" as well as "all shares of the stock of Robinson General Mining Corporation," ten cottages in Park County, and a "house in Spokane." Harry Bush conveyed "personal property" along with all of his company's real property, contracts, notes, causes of action, and options to purchase "anywhere in the U.S." that they might exist. Harry and Ada Bush together conveyed "personal property and real estate in Spokane, Washington."[24] The Bushes conveyed (or seemed to convey) so much property that one cannot help thinking that all of it was simply a scam to get rid of Albert Hoppe with items that were worth nothing. Couched in legal language that Albert probably did not understand, the three conveyance instruments must have confused and fooled him completely. It was small wonder then that he physically followed the Bushes to both Livingston and Spokane and sued them later to no avail. That he received virtually nothing of value from Harry and Ada is apparent from the fact that he remained a poor man to the end of his days. But Albert Hoppe must have taken some consolation in early 1902 from a front-page article in the *Livingston Post* proclaiming that Ada was suing Harry Bush for divorce and restoration of her maiden name.[25]

Albert Hoppe continued to live on his father's, then Walter's, then Yellowstone Park's land for the rest of his life, always a farm laborer. He occupied a small cabin just north of the Cinnabar townsite and on the bank of Yellowstone River until he died in 1936. His death came about in a strange fashion. On May 9, he was taking a bath and discovered an embedded tick that he had picked up in the field at old Cinnabar. He ripped the tick out but left its head in and gave the matter no more thought. The following morning he fainted at breakfast and then had two more attacks in the next few days before family members took him to the hospital. He died on May 24 at age sixty-four of Rocky Mountain spotted fever, succumbing at that time to Montana's third ever recorded case of that disease.[26]

As already noted, George L. Hoppe was social and a romancer of women. He had three wives and probably many girlfriends. While running his family's Cinnabar saloon and dabbling in mining, he married Georgetta Schreiber on March 1, 1897, and the Aldridge cornet band traveled by sleigh to Cinnabar to serenade the newlyweds. In a small place like Cinnabar, this wedding to a woman who had supposedly been happily married caused a bit of a scandal, especially when her ex-husband, W. H. Schreiber, was still in the area mining and running a store at Bear Gulch, today's Jardine. That was probably a factor in why George and Georgetta Hoppe relocated to Cooke City for the summer of 1897. After W. H. Schreiber moved to Livingston to open a beer hall and eventually to Billings, George moved back to Gardiner, where he leased a building from James McCartney for his mining office and also leased the Park Hotel from S. M. Fitzgerald. Later that year, he "called" the Christmas Eve dance ("one of the grandest events of the kind that ever took place on the upper Yellowstone") at "Fitzgerald's hall" in Gardiner.[27] The person who "called" a dance in those days had to be verbally skilled, and this was often a person like George, who was popular and sociable. George Hoppe again leased the Park Hotel in March of 1898 (his brother Walter would eventually purchase it). On April 1, 1899, he began managing the Cinnabar Hotel (with that name finally capitalized and with his own name on its official stationery), because his brother Walter was needed to manage the family's new Bear Gulch Hotel at Jardine. The US Census of July 1, 1900, stated that George and Georgetta were then living at Cinnabar, where he was a "saloon keeper." In late 1900, the newspapers announced that he moved to Butte, and only a few weeks later reported that he was moving to Spokane, Washington. By autumn of 1901, the *Enterprise* stated that he had moved to Seattle.[28] George never lived in Montana again.

George Hoppe started in Seattle as a bar owner and eventually parlayed his Cinnabar experience into a lifelong, comfortable meal ticket as a hotelier (e.g., he is known to have sold his Leopold Hotel in Seattle in 1922). At some point, he obtained formal education and became a podiatrist (foot doctor). George and Georgetta divorced before 1907, for George married Anna (maiden name unknown) Hoppe in 1907 and

Agnes L. Hoppe by 1920. George—the third oldest of the five Hoppe brothers—lived the longest, dying in 1951 at age eighty-three.[29]

Leander B. Hoppe—whom the family called "Lee" and his father called "Leo"—moved away to other Montana towns to run stores and sell merchandise. He relocated to Livingston with his wife, Jessie, in 1896, where he again ran a confectionery store. In 1897, he opened a short-lived store in Aldridge, and then the couple moved to Bozeman, where Lee took a traveling salesman job with an Eastern company. They had two sons named Wilbur and Lester. Sadly, Jessie died of appendicitis on August 6, 1900, in Bozeman just before her twenty-fourth birthday. Probably devastated by her death, Lee floundered about. He worked a brief stint as a bartender at Livingston's Albemarle Hotel, defeated a light case of smallpox, and then returned in late 1901 to being a traveling salesman—the occupation in which he would remain for the rest of his life. He left Cinnabar and Livingston in about 1903 and almost died from typhoid fever in 1905, but recovered and lived for thirty-seven more years.[30] His son Wilbur worked for the railroad in Livingston and later in Missoula. Lee Hoppe somehow became connected to Wyoming, for in 1907, he married Mrs. Coda Belle Lyle in (what became) Bighorn County. He was in Helena at the Windsor House during at least the period 1904–1909 and then in Miles City in 1916 to run stores and be listed as a salesman of dry goods. The US Census of 1930 recorded that at age sixty, he was back at Cinnabar living with his brother Albert and was still called a "traveling salesman." That census showed him as "married," and an obituary stated that he outlived his wife. It appears that Lee and Albert lived on the family's old Cinnabar land until Albert died in 1936. Albert's death ended the life estate on the land, and the reversion owner—the National Park Service—destroyed Albert's cabin, a story to be told later.[31] Because of the land reversion, Lee Hoppe was forced to move to Gardiner, where he lived out his life. As the United States entered World War II, he became ill and went to Missoula to stay with his son Wilbur Hoppe. He died in a hospital there on February 27, 1942.

Hugh B. Hoppe, who Ida says "was always called Hughie to distinguish him from his father," never really wanted to be anything except a farmer and rancher. Indeed the US Census for 1880 at Glendale listed him at age fourteen as "herding cattle," while it merely recorded "at home" and "attending school" for his brothers Walter and George. He seems to have had one brief life adventure before returning to Cinnabar, that being

a short residence in Hot Springs, Arkansas, in 1893. He homesteaded a
ranch at Tom Miner Basin in 1894, worked in the family freighting business until he got married to Millicent Iverson in 1895,[32] faithfully ran the
hotel/saloon/store while his father was sick, tried his hand at transporting
tourists in the park in 1897, and finally moved back to his ranch at Tom
Miner—sixteen miles to the north. He dutifully helped build the big additions to Cinnabar in early 1896 and was peripherally involved in construction of the Horr/Aldridge road that same year. Hughie and his wife
had a brief fracas with the law for assaulting a washerwoman at Cinnabar
for which they paid a one hundred thirty dollar fine plus costs. Then they
settled into the quiet life at Tom Miner, where Millicent bore their first
child, Mary Lucille, in 1901. In the next sixteen years, they had five more
children. As it loomed for so many people during the teens, the 1918 flu
epidemic became the monster tragedy of Hughie's life because it killed
both his wife, Millicent, and his sister, Maggie. That left him with six
children, ranging in age from toddlers to teenagers, to rear on his own.[33]
He died in 1931, at the age of sixty-six, the day after his youngest daughter, Dorothy, got married. It was a wedding that was announced in the
same issue of the *Park County News* as his own death, and from this story
one gets the impression that he was either devastated by the approaching
departure of his last child or too sick to attend.[34]

Maggie Williams's (Hugo Hoppe's stepdaughter) story became temporarily stranger after her father died and she heartlessly fired Ida Miller's mother from the Hoppes' Cinnabar hotel. Maggie and her husband,
Bud, divorced in mid-January of 1890, and Bud began a spiral into drunkenness, getting convicted for it at least twice in Livingston.[35] As mentioned, he went missing in the minds of the Hoppes sometime after June
of 1895 (for he recorded a mining conveyance then), but Maggie did not
look for him because she was divorced and romancing Frank Holem.

Maggie Williams—divorced from Bud for nearly nine years—became
Maggie Ann Holem on December 21, 1898, when she married Frank
Holem (1865–1940), who was seven years her junior, and she served as
the town's last postmaster from 1897 until Cinnabar's post office closed
on June 15, 1903. She ran the "M. A. Holem store" at Cinnabar until the
town died and then rented Bob Orem's shop in Gardiner. She and her
husband, Frank, moved to Gardiner in 1903, where she helped him operate his blacksmithing (later auto repair) business in partnership with Henry Pilger in the stone building that today is the Two Bit Saloon. She was

active in the Red Cross, her Episcopal Church, and social affairs for the rest of her life. The influenza epidemic of 1918 carried her away at the young age of sixty, along with her sister-in-law (Hughie Hoppe's wife) Millicent Hoppe.[36]

Maggie Hoppe was connected to little Ida and her mother in another way as well. Before he died, Hugo Hoppe promised Ida's mother that she and Ida could live in Maggie and Bud's old cabin on their homestead at Horr, and Ida says they moved into it in the summer of 1896. It was a lonesome place, near the foot of Devil's Slide where the railroad's proximity had made cattle raising impossible. Young Ida was walking around the house one day when, she says, "I fell into a hole and yelled bloody murder." Shaken but not deterred, she investigated further and found that the hole took her to a tunnel that led to an old cellar door that she pried open. She saw a human bone and then another and another. "When I had finished picking up bones," she wrote later, "I had a human skeleton." Terrified, she ran back upstairs to tell her mother. That evening a Mr. and Mrs. Allen from Horr came to see them, and Ida and her mother told the couple about the bones. Mr. Allen chuckled, said Ida, and proclaimed, "Everybody wondered what became of Bud Williams." Looking up at the ceiling at a dozen or more holes "that my mother often wondered how they came to be there," Mr. Allen said. "Those holes up there is where Bud used to shoot at Maggie when she was upstairs and he was down here . . . used to keep her dodging pretty fast to miss them." Had Maggie finally gotten fed up with Bud's drunken, violent ways, killed him, and left him in the cellar? Or had he somehow died while down there alone and she never found him?[37]

Believing they had found Bud's skeleton, little Ida and her mother, Geneva, wondered how he died, probably speculating as to whether Bud had an accident of some kind when alone at the house after he and Maggie split up. The two divorced in early 1890, and according to Bud's voter registration, he was living at Horr by 1894 in George Welcome's boardinghouse. Most likely Bud could not stand the thought of living by himself in his and Maggie's homestead at Horr, so he moved to the boardinghouse. As for his disappearance, Horr seemed to add to it because that town was a place where an unskilled laborer could get a job in the coal mines and become "lost" and anonymous by working underground. Perhaps Ida and her mother wondered whether Bud had gone to his empty house one day to check on it and somehow fell while in the cellar. Perhaps they wondered whether he was bitten by a rattlesnake while rummaging in the darkened cellar. Geneva Miller must have wondered about the most interesting possibility of all—that Maggie had her revenge upon Bud with no one knowing about it until little Ida Miller stumbled upon his bones.[38]

The finding of the bones was a fascinating story with an apparent resolution that Ida and her mother both believed, but the skeleton was not Bud's. Ida and her mother went to their graves convinced that Bud had been found; regardless, the evidence is compelling that his disappearance from Horr related to his merely moving away and not to his death. The *Livingston Enterprise* reported in August of 1897 that Morgan T. "Bud" Williams was alive and engaged in prospecting at Castle, Montana.[39] The mystery that remains is, of course: Who was the dead man (or woman) in the cellar?

At Hugo Hoppe's death in late 1895, the Hoppe siblings and their friends at Cinnabar were understandably overwhelmed. According to Ida Miller, Lee Hoppe told her what he experienced with the family's property in 1895 and 1896, at the time he was encouraging her and her mother to move to Maggie and Bud Williams's vacant house at Horr:

> Father told us all to let you live there and to help you if we could, but Maggie and Walter got everything [of their parents' resources]. Hughie has the Tom Miner Basin ranch and George is running the [Cinnabar] hotel for Walter, but Albert and I don't have a thing. I don't think George is making any more than expenses and Hughie is in debt [for his ranch], so Maggie and Walter are the only ones who really have anything.[40]

What Walter inherited was Hugo Hoppe's estate, assessed at $7,853.50. That included proceeds from Mary Hoppe's land at Livingston, and he apparently shared much of that with Maggie Williams.[41] This was not riches, but it was enough to keep the family businesses going.

Several if not all of the Hoppe brothers remained close to each other throughout their lives. Although George and Lee moved away, Lee returned to the Cinnabar property late in life and lived there with Albert. Those two brothers must have been a comfort to each other in their old ages, and it probably helped them emotionally that their brothers Walter and Hughie were nearby. It seems somehow appropriate that both the oldest brother, Walter, and the youngest brother, Albert, lived on their father's land for so many years.

CINNABAR LIVES ON THROUGH ITS PEOPLE

"So pass the little people into oblivion, but by their hands has the destiny of a state been fashioned."
—Doris Whithorn, historian of the Upper Yellowstone

Thus spoke a local historian who was an expert on Park County, Montana, and who probably also knew that from its earliest days, Cinnabar was a town of "kaleidoscopic travelers and customs." If nothing else, the town was colorful. Hugo Hoppe and his large family were forefront characters in the history of the Cinnabar flat beginning in 1882. Hoppe noted that one of the delightful features of Cinnabar was its cowboys who stayed in town "until they could see their way home and their money was gone," implying a few bouts with blind drunkenness. These temporary residents made about forty dollars a month for six months out of the year but never had to pay room or board, so the money went further (a bunkhouse situation that is somewhat similar today for concessioner employees of Yellowstone National Park). Hoppe noted that the cowboys sometimes made extra money by rustling stray cattle for their bosses at five dollars a head. "No matter how sleepy Cinnabar got," says Hoppe, "the cowboys racing in with a whoop and a yipee put elastic in its toes and when they raced in[to] town and jerked their ponies to a buck at the end of the street everybody was rearin' to go."[42] Thus we see how the colorful phrase "raring to go" came down to us from horse-drawn America—moving from "rearing" to "raring" at a time when horses "reared" onto their hind legs in anticipation of running.

Cowboys at Cinnabar did not always get along well with tourists. In Livingston, fifty miles to the north, cowboys sometimes instructed greenhorn tourists in "exhibition dancing" on the railroad platform. Cinnabar was no different. Comments made by tourists about the clothing worn by Westerners occasionally caused trouble. On more than one occasion cowboys' pistols frightened tourists, and mock trials were sometimes the result of those confrontations, with an order to leave town for added punctuation.[43]

Ida Miller says she watched one of those mock trials at the Cinnabar hotel one evening in 1894, shortly after she arrived in town. "I had just taken a piece of cake," she said, "when I dropped it because of horses galloping around the hotel and men shouting, 'Come on out arunnin' yew blame yahoos an' with your paws up!'" Ida saw her Uncle Hugo run out the door to see the show, followed by his five sons: "Leo, Walter, Hughie, Albert, and George." When she heard the cowboys loudly yell out a second command—"Throw 'em up an' claw the air!"—she threw up her own hands in fear. Aunt Mary grinned at her and observed, "Don't be afraid . . . it's just the cowboys having some fun with them tourists for calling their chaps funny pants . . . go out and watch the fun!" Walking out onto the town's boardwalk with her mother and Jessie Hoppe, Ida saw several cowboys—guns drawn and kerchiefs over their faces with looks of mock sternness—ordering the tourists to march down Cinnabar's Main Street. What was especially funny to her was the fact that the dude men wore red-flannel shirts and the dude women red-flannel nightgowns. When Ida asked her uncle Hugo what the cowboys did to them, he replied: "They gave them a mock trial for calling their angora chaps funny pants and gave them until daylight to get out of town." Hugo stated that he tried to tell the visitors that it was all in good fun but they insisted upon chartering a runt train for fifty dollars to take them back to Livingston![44]

Ida Miller loved to watch the tourists on the platform at Cinnabar's depot. She described an especially striking woman there as wearing

> a white silk shirt waist trimmed with pin tucks down the front, and a black-silk, accordion-pleated skirt; a black-and-white toque held down with a wide, long billowing light-blue chiffon scarf. She was sporting a light-blue belt fastened with a fancy buckle and carried a chatelaine bag on her wrist by a gold link chain. She wore sharp-pointed leather shoes that buttoned high above the ankle. They were the most sensible things she wore, except [for] the long scarf that wouldn't let her toque get away. All the tourists dressed very similar[ly] to that [during] the first decade of travel through Cinnabar to the Yellowstone Park, much to the disgust of the natives. Westerners used to say, "By their dress ye shall know 'em."

If the dress of tourists was fancy enough to offend Western tastes, the look of the locals was more pleasing to those who cared little for Easterners. Ida Miller described some of the local folks at Cinnabar too:

> Cinnabar's bartender with his white, halter-style apron rolled on his fat belly; the Chinaman cook with pigtail flying, sandals flopping and arms folded with hands in the sleeves of his black, sateen tunic; the railroad agent with leather cuffs and green visor; Billy Hall with pencil and paper; Walter Hoppe with a slab of wood from the saw mill; Albert, George, and Leo in overalls and blue denim shirts; the liveryman with pitchfork, and smelling like horse manure; the dish washer with a cake of soap and wearing a blue denim, halter-style apron; a cook wearing a white cook's apron and a white cap; the blacksmith wearing a leather apron and hammer in hand; gamblers wearing Prince Alberts and diamond stickpins shining like a locomotive headlight and Hugo Hoppe wearing a dark-blue, flannel suit with a three-button sack coat and a fedora.

Ida Miller identified other locals. Hugo Hoppe's Chinese cook was "Tung Loo," who was constantly teased by area cowboys. Mr. and Mrs. Will Schreiber lived on the north side of the river just "up the path" from Hoppe's ferry, and Ida described their ranch house in detail. And the A. W. Chadbourns lived at the west base of Chadbourn Hill, just southeast of Cinnabar, "about a mile and a half up the valley toward the park." They supplied the Hoppes' hotel with vegetables, chickens, and eggs, and little Ida played with their daughter Tudy. The year Ida arrived, future Yellowstone Park stagecoach robber George Reeb was living on the Chadbourn Ranch and probably working for the Chadbourns.[45]

Of course some of the biggest names in the history of Yellowstone Park traveled through Cinnabar at various times, and even some persons well known in the history of other parts of the American West occasionally spent time there. Frank Grouard, the government scout celebrated in Joe DeBarthe's *Life and Adventures of Frank Grouard*, visited Hugo Hoppe at Cinnabar in the summer of 1894. Ida Miller stated that Calamity Jane and Joe LeFors attended the grand Fourth of July celebration that year, too. Independence Day was often observed with a three-day gala in all of the upper Yellowstone towns, and according to little Ida, who saw her, Calamity Jane was there at Cinnabar. "Dressed in buckskin trousers, fringed buckskin jacket and a man's wide-brimmed hat," she was "in the height of her glory," proclaimed Ida, "because she was creating a sensation." (Sure enough, historian James McLaird confirmed this by using it in his reputable biography of Calamity Jane.)[46] Joe LeFors, the lawman later involved in the Tom Horn affair at Cheyenne, Wyoming, was working for the Murphy Cattle Company then. Ida also remembered seeing June Buzzell (the renowned Montana bronco rider and companion of "Pretty Dick" Randall), Tazewell Woody (Theodore Roosevelt's guide from North Dakota and longtime Yellowstone guide), John Dewing (Cinnabar's practical joker whose mistreatment of his ex-wife, G. L. Henderson's daughter Jennie, had resulted in some hard feelings toward him), "Pretty Dick" Randall (soon to be owner of the legendary OTO Dude Ranch and a Yellowstone wrangler for a decade), the numerous daughters of Selleck M. Fitzgerald (who became wives for so many area men), and other men like Wilbur Williams, Jimmy Parker, Dave Rhode, Hi Jehnsen, Al Brundage, and Billy North. In fact, those last two men plus "Pretty Dick" made up a small Cinnabar band for dancing purposes, with Dick on harmonica, Brundage on fiddle, and North on guitar. As late as 1900, Brundage and North were still performing for Cinnabar's dances.[47]

There is more on the irascible Calamity Jane's association with the area. Already mentioned is Jane's occasional collaboration with Specimen Schmidt to sell souvenirs to Yellowstone-bound tourists, but Jane lived at Horr and Livingston for several years during the period 1896–1902, so if she could not get a train ride to Cinnabar, she would walk it, and often it was just as easy for her to get drunk at Horr. It was probably in 1902, when five-year-old Judith Murphy either saw this happen personally or heard it from her father, J. B. Murphy, who was station agent at Horr. And it probably happened more than once:

> When I was quite young, but old enough to know what it was all about, Calamity Jane used to come up [to Horr] from Livingston to booze up at the saloon. After a day or two, when she became a nuisance, the proprietor or store manager would load her into the store wagon and send her to the depot. When the train was about to depart, my dad and a section man or train man, or perhaps a bystander, would get on each side of her and "heist" [hoist] her into the baggage car. There she would repose until she arrived in Livingston, where she had a cabin.[48]

Jane also visited Walter Hoppe's Cinnabar saloon on numerous occasions, and Mrs. Hoppe recalled one occasion when Calamity was too drunk to make it home to nearby Horr. Walter Hoppe felt that he should help Calamity get bedded down for the night, so he called his wife, Ella Hoppe, to help him. Said Mrs. Hoppe: "He had to pull off her boots; I undressed her. But I couldn't hardly stand it."[49] Apparently it had been awhile since Jane partook of bath water, for the smell nearly overpowered Walter's wife.

Ella Hoppe was not the only person to see Calamity Jane at Cinnabar. Kay Baker's father, Henry Pilger, saw her there one afternoon or evening in 1902, before he moved to Gardiner in 1904. Henry stated that as usual, "she was drunk."[50] It might have been on that drunken occasion, or the one mentioned by one of the local newspapers, that someone—probably Richard Lee—robbed Calamity Jane of a gold ring. As always, Calamity Jane was so well known that she would make the newspapers, especially when drunk. But in 1901, Calamity was hanging around Horr and Gardiner, helping her friends through illness in the way that earned her "heart of gold" reputation. To visit a sick friend, she would daily walk the road that connected Horr with Aldridge, Montana, traversing the low divide between those two towns that lay south of Cinnabar Mountain.[51]

The only US Census that we have for Cinnabar as an active town (because the 1890 census was accidentally destroyed) is from 1900, which shows that ninety-four people lived there at that time. Although Cinnabar lasted only twenty years as a town, it never lacked for color in its residents and in those who visited.

TRANSPORTATION OPERATORS

Stagecoach/transportation operators have been mentioned as playing an instant and ever-present role in the life of Cinnabar. All of their names will probably never be known, as many operated temporarily and some for very short terms, but many individuals are known.

A. W. Chadbourn was present as a transportation operator at Cinnabar from 1882 until he and George Wakefield swapped ranches in 1901 so that Wakefield could return to running stages in Yellowstone.[52]

Hugo Hoppe may have run some passenger transportation in the park, but we know little about it. He seems to have been more interested in transporting freight than in passengers in Yellowstone, and his sons continued that endeavor after his death.[53]

Al Brundage, previously mentioned as a musician, also ran his own transportation company ("Al Brundage and Company") from 1885 through at least 1893, for one of his business cards is in the park archives. He offered a four-horse team with driver for ten dollars per day (carrying five persons) and a two-horse surrey (carrying three persons) for eight dollars.[54]

Before he opened a store there, W. A. Hall ran a livery and saloon, and briefly the hotel at Cinnabar during the years 1890–1893. In late 1891, soldiers in the park arrested his customer Sam Brown at Mud Volcano for failing to pay Hall his horse-rental fee and instead riding up to join a park road crew (Hall subsequently sued Brown and won his money). In 1892, Hall was "well supplied with teams, vehicles and camping outfits . . . which are let at reasonable rates either with or without drivers." His livery business hit a snag in the summer of 1893, when acting park superintendent George Anderson temporarily restricted private livery operators from running in the park. Hall then became a storekeeper at Cinnabar, but he apparently continued to dabble in the livery business for a few more years.[55]

W. E. Knowles, better known for his ownership of Chico Hot Springs, Montana, is thought to have taken at least one party through the park in 1897 and was issued a park license in 1898. Likewise, Frank Slaughter ran two wagons during at least the season of 1902. Both of these men seem to have been residents of Cinnabar for an unknown period of time.[56]

Mentioned in the annual report of the superintendent for 1898 are G. W. Torbert, H. M. Gore, W. J. Kupper, Adam Gassert, Henry George, and George Reese, all Cinnabar men who held licenses "to conduct [a] camping business." Others known to have had licenses "to conduct and transport passengers" through the park were R. H. Menefee (1891, 1900), Nik Hoffmann (1897), J. A. Ennis (1897), and C. C. Chadbourn (1899).[57]

Charlie (or Charley) T. Smith ran a small transportation outfit (four or five wagons) from Cinnabar through the park in at least the years from 1898 to 1903. He was listed in the US Census for 1900 as a "park tourist guide" and was probably the Smith known to have been in partnership with blacksmith Frank Holem as "Smith and Holem." A promotional piece for them gave the following information in 1900:

> The Smith & Holem Stage and Transportation line for Yellowstone
> Park make[s] a specialty of catering to the desires of tourists in fur-

nishing local camps with hacks, carriages and saddle horses for their conveyances. Competent drivers and guides are provided, with head-quarters at Cinnabar, Montana. Their patronage are always delighted on a return trip through the Park, as they know that with these experienced pioneers they have certainly seen all there is to be seen, and not that they have merely passed through it in a hurried manner. Messrs. Smith & Holem are so well equipped with outfits that they can accommodate any number of tourists, who are ready to start for Wonderland, immediately after the arrival of trains. Cleanliness, courtesy and a jovial spirit are elements that are prominent throughout their trips. [58]

And George Wakefield, who ran the main stagecoach company in the park from 1883 to 1891, returned (this time to Cinnabar) in 1901 to again carry passengers when he and A. W. Chadbourn swapped ranches. Wakefield worked in partnership with Frank Moore and used eight wagons. He is known to have operated at least from 1901–1903, and he then moved back to Livingston, probably in 1904 after he sold his ranch at Cinnabar to L. H. Van Dyke. [59]

This listing of transportation operators includes only men known to have lived in Cinnabar. But the Cinnabar train depot was the pickup point for hundreds of transportation operators who lived in the nearby towns of Gardiner, Cooke City, Horr, Jardine, Aldridge, and occasionally Livingston, Bozeman, Butte, and other places as shown in the park archives. Their competition with the Yellowstone Park Transportation Company was well known and bordered on being cutthroat during the entire life of Cinnabar. In 1893, the park superintendent, whose allegiance to the Park Company was obvious, reported:

Several of them [independent stage/tour operators] have regular "runners" at Livingston and on the trains between there and Cinnabar who make false promises about what their own line will do for tourists and false statements about what the regular line does do. The result is their getting good business and providing poor service. [60]

Anderson stated this during the period when the Secretary of Interior was considering banning independents from transporting tourists, and the "poor service" was certainly not true in every case.

RELIGION

Religion occasionally reared its head in Cinnabar, but not too often. Nearby Gardiner, according to the *Livingston Enterprise*, had twenty-one saloons in 1883 but no churches, at least through 1885, and no churches are known to have ever been built in Cinnabar. In January of 1896, Robert Livingston, a "Minister of the Gospel," was living at Cinnabar and preaching there, as well as at Horr, Gardiner, and Ft. Yellowstone. He petitioned park superintendent George Anderson for permission to cut timber in the park to build churches at Cinnabar and Gardiner. If he ever completed such buildings, they are not known. Another hint of religion in 1896 was a mention by the newspapers of the Rev. J. W. Bennett "of Cinnabar, who as presiding elder of the Bozeman district" of some denomination, "was holding quarterly meetings at Cinnabar." No more is known, but whichever denomination Rev. Bennett represented apparently was having some influence that year, as the reverend was called upon to perform a wedding for John C. Allen and Susan McCullum at Mammoth. Occasionally a traveling preacher would deliver sermons at Cinnabar, as Reverend W. W. Edmondson of Pine Creek, Montana, did in May of 1900.[61]

Religion seems never to have been a large factor in the life of Cinnabar, although some of its residents probably traveled to Aldridge for services. In Gardiner's case, as late as 1903, the resident who authored the poem "Little Town of Gardiner" stated that the town had no churches while delivering an unmistakable slap at the snootiness of some of those establishments:

> They hain't no style in our town—hits little-like and small;
> They hain't no churches, neither—jes th' school house is all;
> They's no sidewalks to speak of but the highways all's free
> And the little town of Gardiner is wide enough for me.[62]

This writer saw the lack of churches as a state of affairs about which some locals boasted.

DUDE RANCHING

Dude ranching was another Cinnabar endeavor. By the turn of the century, James N. "Pretty Dick" Randall had established what he claimed was the first "dude" ranch in the nation, his "OTO" on Cedar Creek, across the river and some miles northeast of Cinnabar. Other area folks took that as their cue to get into the same business. The outfitting and guiding of hunters, fishermen, and leisurers had joined the transporting of tourists as yet another way to make a living in the Yellowstone country. [63]

One of the Cinnabar area persons who entered this business by 1900 was Robert McCune. Born in 1853, McCune went to sea at age fourteen, circumnavigating the globe twice. In 1879, he located in Gallatin Valley, Cooke City, and finally in Tom Miner Basin. In 1891, he married Mrs. Mary Pfohl (pronounced "pool"), who had located with her first husband on the upper Yellowstone in 1877. McCune and his new wife established "Robert McCune's Hunting and Fishing Resort." The local newspaper ran a photograph of the ranch in 1900 and stated of it:

> This resort is a typical one for this region and in close proximity to the National Park. It is situated in the midst of a paradise for hunting and fishing and for geological parties, the noted peaks of Electrical [sic] Dome and Emigrant presenting a distinct and interesting view. The ranch furnishes them all the fruits and vegetables that could be desired by any one, and is situated directly on the Park Branch railway. Owing to the fact that Mr. and Mrs. McCune are pioneers of this region for many miles around, they are certainly capable of waiting on the public in a satisfactory manner. [64]

CINNABAR TRAGEDIES

Like any other town, Cinnabar had its share of tragedies. Phillip Bassett, whose relative William Bassett has been mentioned in this book and whose family left their name on a stream north of the park, killed himself at Cinnabar on May 1, 1884, using an unspecified poison. We know nothing else about the incident.

Gus Nelson drowned at Cinnabar. Nelson, a Swede from Gardiner, fell into the Yellowstone River while fishing during the week of July 7–12, 1889. A stock tender for the Yellowstone Park Transportation Company saw Nelson go under, and his body was found floating near Emigrant a week later.

The runaway accident suffered by J. L. Sanborn at Cinnabar illustrates something that happened fairly often in horse-drawn America, and it happened on Hugo Hoppe's ranch at Cinnabar, which at that time was being leased by W. A. Hall. Sanborn, who resided for many years at Bozeman and who was described as "one of the pioneers of Montana," was mining at Cooke City with his wife and son in 1890. On August 12, during a visit to Hoppe's ranch, Sanborn got into a playful mood and, after loosening the picket rope from his saddle, attempted to lasso Joe Keeney's horse. That movement started both horses on the run, and in the excitement, Sanborn's horse rode him against the side of a building. Sanborn's head struck it with such force that his neck was instantly broken.

Whether or not Oliver Atkins's death was a swimming fatality is not certain, but probably it was. Atkins, twenty-six, disappeared from Gardiner, Montana, on March 20, 1905, and was missing for more than two months. His large family there merely thought he had gone somewhere else for employment. However in late May, Atkins's body was found floating in "Lake Cinnabar," probably one of the small lakes on Landslide Creek southeast of Cinnabar. An inquest determined that he had drowned there.

Sometimes these tragedies ended humorously. A rattlesnake at Cinnabar bit one "Red River Dick" on July 2, 1886. That the bite was not taken seriously, for whatever reason, is evident from this account of it:

> A couple of gallons of snake bite juice drove all the poison out of his system. The snake is dead. Speculation is now rife as to which received the most poison from the kiss, the snake or Dick. It is the general opinion there was a mutual exchange, as there is no proof the snake was killed from any other cause. [65]

AFTER HUGO HOPPE'S DEATH, 1896–1903

The five Hoppe brothers were a big part of the life of Cinnabar, and they were some of the most important of the people who made the town live on after Hugo Hoppe's death. All five brothers undoubtedly had their moments of wishing that they could find a way to make Cinnabar into a year-round business, but during this period it simply was not happening. The end of each summer would bring them reminders of this. "The Park season is over and Cinnabar is slowly dying," sneered the *Enterprise* in 1898, and "the interment will take place soon." Sarah Brooks, a St. Paul journalist who passed through in 1900, summed up something that the Hoppes had to have known:

> Cinnabar might just as appropriately be construed Slabtown, save for [its] lack of distinction from various other villages en route. But, whatever its name, no one gives it more than a passing glance, while scrambling for seats upon tally-ho or in surrey, in preparation for the eight-mile stage ride to Hot Springs, or Fort Yellowstone, and no one remembers it again until the circle and string of sight-seeing is completed.[66]

The town seemed unable to break out of its smallness, and that fact must have been frustrating to the five brothers and their sister, Maggie. It was this very smallness, combined with the fact that visitors were parsimoniously saving their camera film for Yellowstone, which resulted in today's shortage of historic photos of the town of Cinnabar.

However, the beginning of each new season brought fresh optimism to the Hoppes. They held parties at Cinnabar, such as this one where their description was all confidence:

> A very pleasant evening was spent in dancing on the splendid open air platform at Cinnabar Saturday evening July 29th. Most elegant music was secured for the occasion and an elaborate lunch was served at Hoppe hotel.

It was probably one of the Hoppe brothers, perhaps George, who wrote the following boosterish piece in his reporting for June of 1899:

> Cinnabar is a busy place these days, and especially this time of the year. Since the activity and progress of the Bear Gulch mines [has been occurring,] so much freight is landed at this station that it is almost impossible for two agents to accommodate the public. It looks like the Northern Pacific Railroad company will have to get a man to do nothing else but check out the freights. There has not been so much business in Cinnabar before as is shown now and to prove this one can look at the switch yard and any day see cars strung along for one-half mile in length. New ties have been put in and take the place of those which have been buried under the rails since 1883. It seems as though a split in the county will soon occur and the county seat will be Cinnabar.[67]

Whichever Hoppe was writing this, with regard to his final sentence he was dreaming in print if not coming close to hallucinating. But who can blame him? Just reading about Cinnabar today makes us root for the town, even from our vantage point of one hundred fifteen years later!

That youngest brother Albert Hoppe was still optimistic about Cinnabar as late as 1900 is evident from a newspaper column he wrote for the May 19 edition of the *Enterprise*, even as he was in the early stages of an affair with Mrs. Harry Bush. Undoubtedly he was the "Vincent" who gushed on in a column called "Cinnabar Observations" that "more life and stir is prevailing at the Terminus as the tourist season reaches its dawn." "Drummers [traveling salesmen] are coming in on every day's train," said Albert, and he noted that his brother-in-law, Frank Holem, would "soon commence work on the two story business house." Albert wrote another installment of the column a week later. In it he noted that the Riverside addition to Cinnabar was "building up rapidly," he mentioned Harry Child and S. S. Huntley arriving on the train escorting three Chinese cooks to feed their YPTC stagecoach drivers, and he stated that Frank Holem "has all he can do to attend to his blacksmith trade." In a parenthetical note, Albert sang the praises of the new mine owner at Jardine named Harry Bush. "Mr. Bush is a hustler," he wrote, "and just the man to push industries ahead to absolute success."[68] But as we have already seen, his dealings with the hustler would eventually become a huge disaster for Albert, if a slightly lesser one for Harry and Ada Bush.

Living in a touristic place, the people of Cinnabar were used to strange visitors, but Louis Sperling was too much in early 1901 even for the Hoppes. After he had lived at their hotel for a while, they complained about him and Undersheriff McDonald came up to Cinnabar and took him to jail in Livingston. Those were the days before sophisticated rules existed about mental illness and during a time when idleness was considered errant, so Mr. Sperling was "charged with lunacy" and scheduled for a hearing before two doctors and a judge:

> A number of witnesses testified to the man's character, saying that Sperling had boarded at Hoppes hotel for several months, [and] that he never tried to get work and seemed to be off his balance. Sperling told several people that he together with several persons residing in Jardine and Cinnabar were implicated in a bank robbery in Minnesota, and that his share of the plunder was to be $151,000, and acted altogether in such a peculiar way that Mr. Hoppe preferred a charge of insanity

against him. On being questioned by Judge Henry about the supposed bank robbery the fellow denied anything of the kind. The commission arrived at the conclusion that Sperling was simply an idle vagabond. His honor saying in discharging him that he thought six months on the rock pile would have been beneficial for his disease, which he thought was simply laziness.[69]

As one friend of the Hoppe family remembered, Walter Hoppe "saw his father's township dissolve practically overnight." The *Enterprise* reported that the train cars bringing visitors from Livingston to Gardiner for President Roosevelt's speech on April 24, 1903, also carried twenty-five carloads of freight—twenty-three for Gardiner but only two for Cinnabar. Those and other indicators must have been depressing for Walter Hoppe. He knew at least as early as 1902 that Cinnabar's life was coming to an end.[70]

10

"WAIL OF A CINNABARITE"

The Death of Cinnabar (1902–1903)

They're going to build a railroad,
And they're going to pass us by;
They'll never stop at Cinnabar;
I'll wager that's no lie.
—Sarah Gassert, Cinnabar resident, 1901

The ranch owner who wrote those lines saw the end of Cinnabar coming eighteen months before it arrived. In one way Cinnabar died during the summer of 1902, when the railroad extended its tracks to Gardiner after having been denied that opportunity for nearly twenty years. In another way, the town died in June of 1903, when its post office disappeared. Regardless, in Gardiner there was great rejoicing.

Simultaneously, Hugo Hoppe's sons and daughter and many other Cinnabar residents were devastated; indeed, the subtitle of Sarah Gassert's mournful poem was "The Wail of a Cinnabarite." The newspaper at Gardiner noted that the extension would "be a death blow to Cinnabar, as a town, for of necessity, its business houses will be forced to follow the [rail]road and its live business men are already making arrangements" to move to Gardiner. These changes marked the end of a happy way of life at Cinnabar, Montana, and the change must have been difficult for many residents—especially the Hoppes.[1]

But effectively it took a whole year to kill the town. The author of "Cinnabar Clippings," probably one of the Hoppes, proclaimed in February of 1902 that the "railroad talk has all died down," that real estate sales were "looking up," and that "in the spring we expect to see a great deal of building." Notwithstanding this optimism, the ominous rumors were true. The Northern Pacific Railway (which had officially changed its name in 1896 from "railroad" to "railway") announced on May 4 that it would indeed extend its rails from Cinnabar to Gardiner, the implication being that the Northern Pacific had finally obtained the necessary ownership of the land. By May 17, Gardiner was touting itself as the terminus and Northern Pacific's president Charles Mellen and other railroad officials were riding to Cinnabar to sign up laborers. One Livingston newspaper stated that the railroad extension would be a gain for Gardiner but "a loss to Cinnabar which will knock that town into a cocked hat." The Gardiner *Wonderland* newspaper referred to "authoritative and official notice" that the road would be completed to Gardiner "in time for all tourist travel for the year 1902."[2]

These announcements were premature. Although the first use of Gardiner as the temporary new passenger terminus occurred in July, store owner O. M. Hefferlin decided at the end of that month to defer removal of his store from Cinnabar to Gardiner "until later in the season, when the freight business of the road will be brought to Gardiner" (he finally moved it the following winter). A newspaper article at the end of July noted that business at Cinnabar "is still as good as it ever was," as illustrated by W. A. Hall's ability to keep five or six employees busy. Appropriately, at least from the point of view of many Cinnabar residents, the huge Independence Day festivities at Gardiner planned by the towns of Livingston and Gardiner to celebrate the railroad's extension were essentially rained out. As late as October, resident Louis Hartman stated that "the removal of the railway terminus from Cinnabar to Gardiner has not seriously affected the life of the former town and there seems to be more going on in a business way in Cinnabar now than at any time for years past."[3]

That was overly optimistic. People were beginning to move to Gardiner or to somewhere else. Although her husband, Frank, closed his blacksmith shop in November to conduct business at home, Maggie A. Holem continued to receive merchandise and to sell it at her store, advertising in each issue of the Gardiner newspaper as Cinnabar remained the freight terminus through the summer and fall. Gus Graef, who had already personally moved to Gardiner, waited until April of 1903 to remove his building from Cinnabar and set up his new barbershop in Gardiner. Even as late as April 24, 1903, when President Theodore Roosevelt came to Gardiner to dedicate the new north entrance arch, his train remained parked at a siding at Cinnabar because the "newly laid track to Gardiner was not [completely] ready for use." Thus real use of Gardiner as both passenger and freight terminus did not begin until the summer of 1903. Workmen completed the new Gardiner depot—a beautiful log structure designed by architect Robert Reamer—in early July, and the first travelers passed through the park's new "entrance" on or about July 10, 1903. The arch itself was completed August 15, 1903.[4]

Facing Cinnabar's approaching death, the town of Gardiner became more raucous itself—at least temporarily. Someone known as "Inquirer," who was probably the newspaper editor M. W. Pettigrew, noted that prostitutes and drunken rioting and shooting seemed to be present in Gardiner constantly.

> The people of Gardiner would like to enquire why the disorderly element are permitted to disturb the peace of the town, free from molestations. Nights are made hideous by drunken riots. Monday night there was almost continuous yelling and shooting from midnight to daylight. Women of ill-fame live in the central part of town and exhibit themselves daily on the streets in bedroom wrappers, and make a show of themselves at doors and windows on the arrival of the train, their houses being only a few yards from, and facing the station.[5]

It must have been quite a show. Another writer, who signed his letter "L.T.S." and who was probably Cinnabar landowner Lou Stoll, did not like Gardiner's whores and drunks and called for law and order there:

> The town is well represented with what are called secretary's [sic] of women that are occupying houses of ill fame. According to the state laws of Montana, the county officials should look after the latter, and they should also look after the drunks that stagger along the streets day and night, using vulgar and profane language in every way imaginable—language that is uncalled for—language that will provoke a moral man to anger and cause fights, which are often seen and heard of in Gardiner. Respectable women of this town will not stir upon the streets in the evenings for fear of being insulted by some of these characters.[6]

"L.T.S." desperately wanted a jail in town. Sure enough, workmen erected a stone structure a few months later—on the riverbank, and it still stands today under the highway bridge.[7] One suspects that Cinnabar's death contributed to Gardiner's problems, as Cinnabar's rowdier citizens moved three miles to the east.

Gardiner was certainly scurrying to cover these shadier parts of its fabric, because 1903 was quickly becoming the biggest year in its history. President Theodore Roosevelt was slated to vacation in the park beginning on April 8, and he had agreed to lay the cornerstone in town for the official entrance to Yellowstone—what would eventually be called the Roosevelt Arch. The Northern Pacific Railway was gearing up to build a fancy new depot designed by architect Robert Reamer. Anticipating growth because of the railroad's extension, town fathers had formed a company to improve and upgrade Gardiner's water system and electrical lighting system, and workmen were erecting several, fancy stone houses around town. Butchers Lewis Van Dyck and J. H. Deever were completing their new butcher shop at the corner of Second and Main on the site of today's K-Bar. In anticipation of its new depot, the railroad had completed its oval "loop-track" so that arriving trains could easily turn around, and crews were now "building a wagon road around the south side of the loop and past the depot site, in order that the travel[er] from Cinnabar may not be compelled to cross the track" (this wagon road was essentially a slight moving to the south of what today is still known as the "Old Yellowstone Trail"). Along with all of this, Yellowstone National Park announced that it would soon build a fence from the mouth of Gardner River along Park Street "to the steep mountain west of Gassert ranch" (Boundary Hill) to keep animals inside the park.[8] That was a plan that would never work very well, even when that fence was replaced with the present wrought-iron fence in 1913. All of this joy and bustle in Gardiner stood in stark contrast to the deepening gloom in Cinnabar.

Appropriately, if sadly, a couple of small tragedies occurred as Cinnabar was dying. In an event that must have seemed symbolic, W. A. Hall's house at Cinnabar and an adjoining building caught on fire May 1, 1902, at 10:00 a.m. and burned to the ground. The loss was about fifteen hundred dollars.[9] And a work train crashed into the rear of a special car of the regular passenger train, smashing the bumper car of the special and destroying a flat car in the process.[10]

On the heels of those events, persons who had lived and worked in Cinnabar for years made transitions, often in the form of plans to leave or commute to Gardiner. Walter Hoppe had already purchased the Fitzgerald Hotel in Gardiner, but continued to run his hotel at Cinnabar until it was officially closed a year later on May 27, 1903. As if to signal the town's end, longtime Hoppe employee Washington "Wash" Northrup died on June 30, 1902. Both O. M. Hefferlin and Frank Holem had already been in Gardiner looking for new locations. In November, Holem moved his blacksmith and wagon shop operations to Gardiner, and he moved another building in March (one of these buildings in Gardiner would soon become the headquarters for the Masons on the day of President Roosevelt's visit). Carl Wood, who had worked for W. A. Hall for so long at Cinnabar moved away to take up farming in Brooklyn, Michigan. W. A. Hall moved his store operations to Gardiner, erecting the large building in 1903–1904, which is the Yellowstone Association's visitor center today. Arthur Welton, an old Cinnabar resident, got married and moved to Gardiner. George Ferrell, whose family had been in Paradise Valley since the 1870s and for whom Ferrell Lake was named, moved from Cinnabar to Gardiner. And Sarah Gassert rented her ranch, southwest of Cinnabar, to someone else for the summer. [11]

Sarah Gassert, whose deceased husband, Harry, had purchased their ranch from Hugo Hoppe in 1887, [12] was the author of the earlier-mentioned poem titled "They're Going to Build a Railroad." She probably was moved to write the poem in mid-December of 1901, when the *Livingston Enterprise* announced that Gardiner residents were excited because it suddenly looked like the railroad would obtain the rights to extend tracks to Gardiner. [13] Sarah Gassert's poem had a lot to say about the upcoming death of Cinnabar and the role played by local Gardinerites. Here is the entire poem:

> They're going to build a railroad,
> And they're going to build it soon;
> It will start at Cinnabar village
> And go to Gardiner town;
> Gardiner is the gateway
> That leads to Wonderland;
> Its streets are strewn with boulders
> And its houses built on sand;
> But they say they'll go to Gardiner;

In spite of all the band.

They're going to build a railroad,
As sure as you're alive;
They'll start it in the springtime,
When the bees begin to hive;
They'll never stop for nothin'
When they once begin to build,
But they'll plow and scrape and shovel
'Till every sag is filled;
They'll lay a track to Gardiner,
For so the powers have willed.

They're going to build a railroad,
For the coin is all in sight;
Scott said he'd give five hundred,
And McCartney'll do what's right.
They've an option on the townsite,
They'll buy it for a song;
They'll corral all the business
That happens to come along;
For they swear they'll have a railroad
If they build it all alone.

They're going to build a railroad;
We're all afraid it's so;
Breck interviewed the Big Guns,
They said it was a go;
We're very glad he told them,
For they were unaware,
That every native was ready
To do his proper share;
So for this blooming railroad
The chances seem quite fair.
They're going to build a railroad,
Without any more ado;
Culver says it's straight goods,
They'll surely put it through;
It would please the Transportation,
And Capt. Chittenden as well;
Would cheapen their expenses,

As near as they can tell;
If the railroad went to Gardiner,
And this report's no sell.

They're going to build a railroad,
And they're going to pass us by;
They'll never stop at Cinnabar—
I'll wager that's no lie;
But we'll load our goods and houses,
And we'll put 'em in a car,
And we'll bill them through to Gardiner—
That's not so very far;
If they build that tarnal railroad
As they say they surely are.

In this poem we can clearly see C. B. Scott (Gardiner merchant), James McCartney (first Gardiner resident and "mayor"), George Breck (transportation manager for YPT Company), E. C. Culver (store owner, postmaster, justice of the peace, and transportation agent for YPT Company), and park road engineer Hiram Chittenden all apparently quite happy at the railroad's extension to Gardiner. And Sarah's "every native" at Gardiner who was "ready to do his proper share" included A. A. Spiker, George Mack, Maggie French, Thomas Casey, Joseph Brown, and others, all of whom were busily purchasing pieces of the Gardiner townsite from longtime owner Clara McCutcheon. [14]

What most of those people and others were not happy about, however, was a proposal that reared its head in early 1902, when it became apparent that Gardiner was to be the new terminus. The proposal might have originated with the local newspaper or with someone who suggested it to the editor. At any rate, the proposal suggested changing Gardiner's name to Cinnabar, "insomuch as the old Cinnabar would disappear and that people might not understand that Gardiner was simply an extension from Cinnabar. Besides the railroad maps and all publications speak of Cinnabar." Gardiner residents quickly rejected the idea, and the suggestion died within a few weeks after several discussions in the newspapers. [15]

Because of President Theodore Roosevelt, Cinnabar was not quite dead. In April of 1903, Roosevelt visited Yellowstone and dedicated the laying of the cornerstone for what would become the Roosevelt Arch at Gardiner—still standing at Yellowstone's north entrance today. Nearly everyone in the region attended those huge festivities on April 24, 1903, and the occasion was well documented with photographs and newspaper articles. Walter Hoppe must have been pleased for the rest of his life every time he looked at the photograph of "Mayor" James McCartney carrying his son—five-year-old Paul Hoppe—on the saddle while riding into town for the festivities with President Theodore Roosevelt and Major John Pitcher.[16] Roosevelt's special train car called the "Elysian" was parked at Cinnabar for sixteen days with his secretary William Loeb placed in charge there during the time TR was out riding in the park. Thus one of the last events in the life of Cinnabar was its becoming the "temporary capital of the United States" for those sixteen days, with the "Elysian" as its official office.

Much of President Roosevelt's visit was centered on his trip inside Yellowstone and his speech at "Gardiner's Big Day," and those stories have been well told elsewhere.[17] But the story of what Roosevelt's staff did at Cinnabar from April 8 through April 24 while the president was exploring the park has not been told until now. One journalist fortunately left us a full-page newspaper article about it plus photographs in a Washington, DC, newspaper. A second writer, known only as "A.N.B.," supplemented it with a shorter posting. He stated that there "isn't much at Cinnabar except a depot, a few houses, a store, a livery stable, two saloons, and, at present, a bunch of exceedingly bored gentlemen from Washington." This writer added that the town had only one hotel (Hoppe's), that a good number of the parties were ensconced there, and that these press people "find Cinnabar just about the dullest place they ever struck." "Now and then someone rides over to Gardiner," he wrote, "and looks at the edge of the guarded park, then returns and wonders why he went." This Mr. A.N.B. recorded a humorous event that happened to President Roosevelt's assistant at Hoppe's hotel just after the president arrived. Secretary William Loeb's experience in telephoning at Cinnabar "jarred his dignity fearfully":

> The only telephone in town was in the dining room of the hotel, reached only by way of the barroom. This instrument is on a party line extending from Livingston to Mammoth Hot Springs, each phone on the line having a separate signal call. There was much telephoning on Wednesday between the army post at the springs and Mr. Loeb. He had to stand in that dining room full of people and shout official messages into the phone, pausing every now and then as some subscriber up the line cut in to order a sack of potatoes, and then continu-

ing. It was not the most impressive manner that could be devised of transacting the president's business.[18]

This shouting scene must have been hilarious to just about everyone except Mr. Loeb.

The other writer, R. H. Hazard, gave us added details, but he wrote with even more big-city pretentiousness. He too griped about being stuck in the small town. Hazard whined about the president's staff being "condemned" to spend all that time "gazing up at the snow-crowned mountains that environed the collection of mud-covered hovels named Cinnabar." He feigned a look backward at Cinnabar's history, saying that in 1883 there was "perhaps an excuse for the village's existence" but certainly not now. He lamented that the train trip from Livingston to Cinnabar had once taken seven or eight hours, an untrue assertion because trains in 1883 could certainly travel more than eight miles per hour. He complained about how the locals charged visitors money for elk teeth, a reference to the philosophy of selling souvenirs that even then was being shared by every other touristic locality in the nation. He demeaned the railroad for continuing to stop at Cinnabar—which he described as "two or three saloons, a cattle corral, and a stretch of gray sagebrush." In that summary, he both portrayed the town as smaller than it was and ignored a fact that he well knew, namely that much of the formerly interesting town had already moved to Gardiner.

And he cheered the town's demise by denigrating Cinnabar's postmistress Maggie Ann Holem:

> The only person who regretted this action [of killing Cinnabar] was probably the postmistress. She is the sister-in-law of the man who conducts the general store, and, before the President's special came to Cinnabar, made an average of fifty cents a day out of her job. While [our] party lingered in Cinnabar the postmistress drew nearly $5 a day, her pay being governed by the amount of cancellations credited to her office. The coming of the President to Cinnabar, therefore, brought joy to at least one person in the doomed village.[19]

Hazard wrote this as if many other local residents had not been ecstatic to see President Roosevelt! Surely he knew that most locals were joyful at the president's visit, because Hazard had undoubtedly attended Roosevelt's speech at Gardiner three days earlier.

Once his pseudo-sophisticated griping about Cinnabar was over, Hazard admitted that he had actually had a good time in the dying town. He loved Cinnabar's "glorious atmosphere, as pure as the snow that glistened on Electric Peak." He praised the horses of the US Army that were always available for his party to ride into the hills. He loved the trout leaping in ice-cold streams and the four-horse stagecoaches that the company had put at the disposal of his party for gold prospecting or sightseeing. He applauded the level field next to the train that they used for baseball and the availability of revolvers and rifles for target shooting. And he showered affection upon the "dining car Gilsey" for the good food it provided to the staff of "White House officials, telegraph operators, newspaper men, and Secret Service operatives [who] killed time in Cinnabar" while President Roosevelt vacationed in Yellowstone.

For the benefit of posterity, Mr. Hazard provided a summary of how the affairs of state were conducted at Cinnabar, during a time when such affairs were infinitely fewer in number and far less complicated than today.

> Assistant Secretary Barnes was the nine members of the cabinet rolled into one. Every morning bright and early the Acting President and his Cabinet would get together in the Elysian and hold a consultation over the affairs of state. Letters would be dictated to the bureau chiefs in Washington, orders would be issued for the movement of men or offices, queries propounded by big personages about the country would be answered, and the hundred and one details of the Executive Department would be disposed of just as it is done in Washington when the President is in his stationary official home. [20]

When the morning's work was finished, Mr. Hazard recorded, the acting president and his cabinet would "seize their fishing tackle" and head for the river, and that was his segue into a story about what many individuals actually did with their time for those sixteen days. He pictured Mr. Loeb as not skilled with fishing tackle. Mr. Barnes, resplendent in a "blue shirt and lovely yellow leggings," was equally terrible at fishing in a river where locals routinely caught twenty-five fish in twenty minutes. Frank Hall, a White House messenger, was more proficient, catching at least six fish per trip. A second Mr. Hall was even better at both fishing and taking elk antlers and teeth (those latter activities are illegal today). However, Lindsay Denison of the New York *Sun* was not. He plotted to take dozens of elk teeth from a group of carcasses that he had discovered, but returned to his secret place to find all already stolen.

Meanwhile, drunks and baseball games became part of Hazard's story. Sergeant Durgin—assigned to protect the sidetracked train—argued with C. F. McCoy of the Pennsylvania Railroad over whether Durgin could lounge inside the comfortable train car, which resulted in McCoy throwing him out and Durgin proceeding to get drunk at Cinnabar. Baseball games were held nearly every day. The scores that piled up were enormous on both sides, and the collection of bruises and sprains after each game "would have gladdened the heart of a young man just released from medical college." The train's crew and its guests comprised the two teams, and the crew team "outbatted, outfielded, outran, and outeverythingelsed their opponents." Harry Colman, for example, "fanned out" whenever he went to bat.

Finally, the man in charge of the telegraph walked around each morning and evening to collect "copy" from the reporters. The supply was small, he said, because after the president left there was little to report. "Most of my business seems to be deadhead," he remarked. "I have sent about three lines of paid newspaper stuff and franked seventeen messages to loving wives and sorrowing mothers." Franking was a reference to officially stamping a letter to be mailed at government expense.

In many ways, this story represented the final moments of Cinnabar's life. "The saloon keepers of Cinnabar have all bought property in Gardiner," said Hazard, "and are now engaged in moving their bars to the more fortunate town. Every day the sound of ripping boards and falling timber in Cinnabar, and of the hammer and saw in Gardiner, proclaims the dissolution of the one village and the rejuvenation of the other." As Walter Hoppe heard those sounds, he must have paused on several occasions to mourn his parents and their town, and to be at least somewhat glad that Hugo and Mary were not alive to see Cinnabar die.

Appropriately, Hazard's article had begun with this: "The jumping-off place, which for sixteen days enjoyed the distinction of being the temporary capital of the United States, will cease to exist upon the first of May." That date was actually May 3, and another newspaper article got it right. Headlined "This Is a Sad Tale" and published on Saturday, May 9, 1903, it stated that Cinnabar "was officially wiped off the map Sunday." Few local persons shared the opinions of either our chronicler R. H. Hazard or Harry Colman, an Associated Press manager. Colman stated of

Cinnabar's death: "Well, thank goodness this blooming town will be wiped off the map when we leave. It's a mystery to me how it ever got on in the first place."[21] That careless and mean-spirited wisecrack would have broken Hugo Hoppe's heart.

The Northern Pacific Railroad discontinued the train station at Cinnabar on May 3. The Gardiner newspaper reported on May 28, 1903, that the town was "wiped off the railway map in the past few days," because the depot was "loaded bodily on flat cars on Sunday and moved" to Gardiner "to be used as a freight depot." And the US Postal Service and postmistress Maggie Holem—waiting for final letters to arrive—officially killed the post office on June 15, 1903.[22] The town of Cinnabar had lasted for eleven weeks short of twenty years.

It is ironic that the man whose mining claim blocked the railroad and thus started Cinnabar was still in the area when the town died and may have played a role in its demise. As discussed in the notes, we do not know when or exactly how Robert Cutler removed the mining claim that blocked the Northern Pacific's ultimate path from Cinnabar to Gardiner, but we do know that this removal was a factor that caused Cinnabar's death. In addition to the railroad, the town's life and origins had deep ties to mining. Robert Cutler's decision to sell or otherwise lift his mining claim that blocked the advancement of the railroad to Gardiner might have occurred because he needed money in connection with his divorce from Eva M. Cutler in 1902, and that divorce was bound up in mining as well. Fed up with years of his prospecting and constantly leaving her alone with the children rather than obtaining a real job, Eva filed for divorce and child custody in the summer of 1901, and the case came to trial in early 1902. The proceeding got racy, with the newspaper stating that "the evidence introduced was of such a nature that no paper would care to publish it."[23] The end result was that "Buckskin Jim" Cutler's divorce left him destitute, so it might have been a factor in the relinquishment of his mining claim.

Cutler's sad divorce is worth discussing further as a commentary on mining—whether it occurred in the town of Cinnabar, the county of Park, the state of Montana, or the American West as a whole. Eva Cutler was a woman who was "sweet" but otherwise fed up with mining and her husband's crude old ways as related to his work. Their mutual experiences reflected those of hundreds if not thousands of other miners. Mining, with its hopes of riches, was addicting for many people, and they could not give it up for more secure careers. Like gamblers always dreaming of striking it rich, they often wasted their lives in low-chance endeavors. Another example in Montana was that of a prospector named Poker Davis, who committed suicide at Helena in 1896. "He was once a miner," proclaimed the Helena *Independent*, "and eighteen years ago was employed at good wages on the famous Whitlatch Union at Unionville." Davis left that employment, said the newspaper, "to prospect for himself and wandered over the country in search of the fortune he did not find." Lamented the editor, "It was the fate of many a man similarly situated in the west; disappointed and embittered he became a drunkard." Eventually ex-miner Poker Davis killed himself by drinking rat poison. [24]

OCCUPIERS OF THE CINNABAR REGION, 1903–1918

In the face of the death of Cinnabar, the large Hoppe family held on in the region, but without George and Lee, who had moved away. During general sadness in November 1902 at the demise of Cinnabar, there were two bright notes. Walter and Hughie Hoppe rejoiced at the near-simultaneous births of their daughters, Marjorie Pearl and Mary L. Hoppe, and on November 27, Walter held a successful dance at his hotel in Gardiner. [25] Traveler Grace Hecox, who passed through Cinnabar on July 14, 1903, stated that she "found post office and everything else gone . . . could buy nothing at Cinnabar except flour, which we had." A 1905 traveler who passed through what had been the town stated that her party housed their horses "in Mr. Hoppe's stable," a reference to Walter's continuing occupation of his father's land that had once been in town. As mentioned, in 1900 four of the Hoppes (all the brothers except Albert) conveyed their interests to Walter Hoppe. Walter Hoppe gradually bought back his father's ranch and the entire Cinnabar townsite, took a first mortgage on the family land in 1909, and kept the family ranch until late 1925. [26]

According to Albert Hoppe, questions about the estate of Hugo Hoppe were not fully settled for many years, but they were largely *his* questions. Having previously owned the riverfront lots at Cinnabar, he had a sentimental attachment to that land, but Walter owned it now. In or about 1913, Albert Hoppe moved onto the family (Walter's) ranch, and that set the stage for a family misunderstanding that would have grave ramifications for Albert Hoppe. [27] One could summarize all of this by saying that disagreements among members of the large family, along with a general tendency to let legal arrangements slide, resulted in land-title problems later.

With the town of Cinnabar gone, the region quickly reverted to quiet ranch country, but occasionally more boisterous sounds broke the stillness. A 1911 shooting involved Cinnabar's "last" resident, the previously mentioned August "Specimen" Schmidt. Schmidt continued to live on the old Hoppe ranch at Cinnabar for years after the town disappeared in 1903, becoming known locally in jest as "the mayor of Cinnabar" and its only resident. On the evening of August 6, 1911, Andrew McCune (probably a relative of Robert McCune, who owned a nearby guest ranch) went to Schmidt's house to celebrate Schmidt's seventy-fourth birthday the following day. Schmidt sent him to Gardiner to get some whiskey, and McCune came back with "a liberal amount both inside and out." The two got "gloriously full," and when morning came on August 7, they were still "lit up like a church."

The men had a series of quarrels. After the first one, Schmidt put McCune in a nearby cabin to sleep it off, but in the morning Andy started another quarrel. Schmidt talked him out of it, but Andy drank some more and again began to "chew the rag." He struck Schmidt over the head with an iron cane. Schmidt got to his feet, and Andy hit him again and then again, beating him about the head and arms. Schmidt backed into his cabin with McCune following, picked up a shotgun sitting just inside the door, leveled it at McCune's chest, and pulled the trigger. McCune, shot in the heart, died instantly. Schmidt then started for Gardiner, but passed out drunkenly on the way. Picked up by a passing vehicle, he reported the killing to Deputy Sheriff Welcome. In a subsequent hearing, Schmidt was freed on grounds of self-defense.[28]

In thinking about the death of Cinnabar, one wonders whether Walter Hoppe ever nurtured the thought of trying to change the outcome by purchasing the land that had lain in the path of the railroad for so long. At any point did he wistfully wish that he had the money to obtain Robert Cutler's mining claim or the Gardiner townsite itself? Fleeting though it might have been, that thought must have passed through his mind at some point, whether in 1902 or later. We do not know whether he had prior knowledge of the relevant land sales, let alone the desire to stop them or the necessary money to cinch the deals, but a part of us vicariously loves the image of Walter Hoppe jubilantly waving his new land deeds at railroad officials with the townsfolk of Gardiner angrily shaking their fists at him! Cinnabar had grown perceptibly in its final six years, and if this imaginary (and admittedly unlikely) scenario had occurred, the entire valley's history—to say nothing of Cinnabar's—would have been indelibly changed.

11

OLD CINNABAR

The Struggle to Preserve It Forever (1919–1932)

> The critical factor that controls the life of the northern elk herd is winter range.
> —Yellowstone Superintendent Roger Toll, September 12, 1930

That fact was long known about elk in Yellowstone National Park. A massive slaughter of all park animals had occurred during the 1870s,[1] and although hunting was technically prohibited in Yellowstone in 1883, poaching remained a problem for park officials, especially at Gardiner and old Cinnabar. Many Yellowstone elk traditionally traveled north in the fall and winter to lower lands, seeking food. Additionally, legal hunting north of Yellowstone was killing more animals than some officials thought could be replaced.

Thus by the teens, park officials began to worry about the survival of Yellowstone's elk due to inadequate safe winter range, and that problem became one of park superintendent Horace Marden Albright's first priorities when he arrived in 1919. To preserve the elk, the park needed the land that had previously been occupied by the town of Cinnabar, land that had been the natural winter range of that animal for eons. Albright considered the three most worrisome factors to be poaching all over the park; the legal "firing line" east of Gardiner where elk were slaughtered each fall by hunters; and several, recent severe winters that killed large numbers of elk. "The time is coming," wrote Superintendent Albright, "when a terrible, long, cold winter is going to kill the Yellowstone elk herds if existing conditions outside the Park are maintained." He lamented the inordinately long hunting season in Montana that he called "unworthy of a civilized state" and told horror stories of unregulated elk slaughter by hunters. Scientists and historians today do not agree with all those claims, but those claims represented what the park was doing at that time.[2] Park officials also considered winter range for antelope and deer in their plans, but most of their attention was on elk. They believed that unless immediate steps were taken to round out the winter range for the elk, the prized northern herd faced virtual extermination.[3]

A government plan began to take shape. In 1917, a proclamation by President Woodrow Wilson withdrew certain federal lands north of the park from patentability "in aid of legislation." In 1919, another such proclamation closed all such federal lands to entry under the public lands law.[4] That same year park officials promulgated what was known as the Graves Nelson Report for the protection and perpetuation of the northern Yellowstone elk herd. This plan, the result of investigations by the US Forest Service and the US Biological Survey, contemplated and recommended the acquisition by the federal government of a great many small tracts of private land in the territory between Gardiner and Yankee Jim Canyon.[5] As might be expected, this land acquisition plan was to be depicted by some observers as a struggle between heroic, "powerless" private individuals and a large, powerful, "evil" government. However, seldom is anything that simple. Many of the private individuals involved were anything but powerless, and the government officials involved were often anything but powerful.

Park superintendent Horace Albright was powerful within Yellowstone but not always so powerful outside the park. Strangely, his annual park reports, his monthly park reports, his personal reminiscences, and the two books about his life all say little about this land acquisition program, which he seems to have inherited and then pushed to ultimate success. Nevertheless, the program was to occupy years of Albright's time and attention, and the archival records of the program make clear what occurred. It is the story that we tell here.

Albright seems to have been the key man in the courting of Thomas Cochran (of the J. P. Morgan Company) and George D. Pratt, two New York businessmen who became the founders of the main entity in Albright's land acquisition program—namely the Game Preservation Company. That private company of monied individuals, formed in 1922, eventually purchased and donated thousands of acres of land to Yellowstone National Park and Gallatin National Forest.[6]

From Albright's letters, it is clear that he was the main actor in this land acquisition program. In early 1926, he wrote at length to US senator Thomas Walsh (D-MT) as to what legislation needed to be introduced to make everything legal, even attaching a proposed bill for Walsh to introduce. Albright says he got support for the bill from Gardiner businessmen as well as the Park County Chamber of Commerce, two groups who would later become antagonistic. "Several of the ranchers are in very bad financial condition," wrote Albright in noting the decline of the cattle business and a corresponding drop in land prices: "the purchase of their properties will be a godsend to them." He noted that most of the acquired lands would go into the national forests rather than into the park and referred to the plan as "one of the outstanding conservation measures of the twentieth century."[7]

Congressional legislation passed in 1926 and 1928 was the cornerstone for the lands acquisition program. On May 26, 1926, President Calvin Coolidge signed Public Law No. 295 (44 Stat. 655) that gave the Secretary of the Interior the right to accept private funds donated for acquisition of lands north of Yellowstone to Yankee Jim Canyon and deposit them into a special account. In further legislation on May 18, 1928 (45 Stat. 603), Congress approved one hundred fifty thousand dollars to match private contributions for the program, which was then expected to cost a total of four hundred thousand dollars. The Game Preservation Company believed that if it were to advance half the money for parcels of land, then the government should pay the other half. The 1926 and 1928 legislation made this possible.[8]

The 1926 legislation stimulated land fights in the Gardiner, Montana, area, which were to last until the early 1940s. As might be expected, some locals favored the government acquisition program and some were against it. Some changed sides one or more times in the subsequent years, depending upon their personal interests. Many Park County residents outside of Gardiner favored the legislation, because it paid for improvement of the main road north of Gardiner with federal funds. That road did not extend through Yankee Jim Canyon into Paradise Valley until 1926, and travel prior to that time was via the dirt road—today called the "Old Yellowstone Trail"—on the west and south sides of the Yellowstone River.[9]

These fights were not generally the result of the federal government's taking of lands by eminent domain; most of the time, the feds purchased the lands without force. In many cases, local people sold their lands willingly, either because they needed the money during hard, Great Depression times or because they truly supported the government's drive to preserve animal habitat. For example, Thomas Sidebotham, one of many locals who willingly sold his land to the government, stated to Horace Albright in 1926, that he had decided "you are right for it won't be but a short time until the deer, antelope and elk will be extinct if you don't do something to stop it [animal slaughter]. So I am willing to sell my homestead for $7,500."[10] On the other hand, Albert Hoppe would eventually become embroiled in an "adverse possession" battle with the NPS.

THE CONFLICT WITH ALBERT HOPPE

It became immediately apparent to Horace Albright that Walter Hoppe's ranch (today's "Stephens Creek Ranch") was one of the most important parcels in park plans for winter elk range. From that ranch, Walter Hoppe, himself nearly as much a conservationist as a rancher, took great interest in the elk, deer, and pronghorn that came onto his ranch in fall and winter. "He protected elk, deer, and antelope," explained Albright, "when other residents of the neighborhood were interested only in killing them." The National Park Service had a long, friendly relationship with Walter Hoppe, which involved the leasing of his horses to the government for park work, the purchase of his oats for park horses, and the hiring of him and his brother Albert to work seasonally in the park. Officials appointed Walter to be a park buffalo herder in 1918. Moreover, Walter Hoppe and the park agreed during the winters of 1922–1923 and 1923–1924 that park rangers whom Hoppe allowed to live on his property would keep the elk out of his haystacks and that the park would reimburse him up to two hundred dollars for his damages by elk.[11]

Even with this help, Walter Hoppe was carrying a triple mortgage on his father's land in 1925. Land values and the cattle business in the Gardiner area, so high and profitable in the late teens, took a sharp decline by the mid-twenties. Walter was faced with having to take second and third mortgages on his property in 1919 and 1923. Albright stated that in the summer of 1925, Ella (Mrs. Walter) Hoppe came to see him and told him that her husband was in very poor health, that he had a crop he was not able to harvest, and that they must sell the ranch immediately if they were to avoid losing the crop. Albright told her that he could make no promises, but that he would try to interest some "game conservationists" in the land.[12]

Horace Albright spoke in a kindly manner about Walter Hoppe. He stated that from time to time Walter would "talk to me" about the possibility of selling his property "to someone who would be interested in using it for the conservation of wild life." In 1925, Albright succeeded in getting some New York conservationists who had visited Yellowstone interested in a plan to acquire several ranches north of the park to be kept as a perpetual game preserve. Wrote Albright:

> Mr. Hoppe's place was the first one that I considered. He was extremely anxious to sell it and it was purchased at . . . $22,500. . . . I might say that there were mortgages on the property amounting to a total of about $16,000 and if Mr. Hoppe had not sold the property it would most certainly have been sold to meet the outstanding encumbrances. Mr. Hoppe was in poor health and he was glad to sell his property and get a considerable sum in cash over and above his debts. Mr. Hoppe was entirely satisfied with the transaction. I promised to employ him from time to time on the place as long as he was strong enough to work. He was allowed to live on the property for a year or more. I recall that he did have charge of the property one summer but he was not able to conduct it according to our policies and in subsequent years he was replaced by another man.[13]

About the price of the ranch, Albright was to note later that it was "worth only $16,000 to $20,000" but that the Game Preservation Company paid more "because it was so heavily mortgaged that had this sum not been paid the Hoppe family would have received nothing for the property and the bank would have gotten it all."[14]

Although the Game Preservation Company obtained the Hoppe ranch consisting of nearly one thousand acres in late October of 1925, the federal government was not able to accept title until 1931 due to legal issues clouding the title. During that interim the ranch was placed at the disposal of the NPS for the care of elk, deer, and antelope in winter. The NPS operated it as a hay ranch for the feeding of game animals as well as government horses. At the time NPS obtained the property, two hundred twenty-five acres were cultivated and the rest was grassland, sagebrush, timber, or barren. The ranch was plowed, seeded, and irrigated into hay almost as soon as it was acquired, and it yielded one hundred forty-four tons of hay that first year. By 1931, the NPS had three hundred acres there in hay cultivation. [15]

In a written agreement, the NPS allowed Walter Hoppe to remain on the land until April 1, 1926, but even after that, because there was "no compelling need for the farmhouse and barn," Hoppe was allowed to remain. "Perhaps he can stay there all summer," wrote Albright, but he required Hoppe to remove all stock from the premises except his personal horse so that the NPS could cultivate hay and natural grasses could grow free from stock grazing. [16]

Although he felt sorry for Walter Hoppe regarding his health and financial problems, Albright was ecstatic to have gotten the Hoppe ranch. He wrote enthusiastically to George Pratt that the ranch extended all the way to the Yellowstone River and that the extensive land would allow the NPS to double its cultivation of hay for protection of the park elk. Albright noted that when the Walter Hill ranch, just east of the Hoppe place, and some railroad lands were acquired, only the Stoll ranch would remain between "our preserve and the north entrance arch." The Hoppe ranch could hold the park's "entire antelope herd" and also considerable elk. The sale was "happening at just the right time," wrote Albright, because the upcoming winter would probably otherwise kill many elk, as occurred in 1919, when so many died from starvation and from massive slaughter by hunters. Animals "are already being shot in the streets of Gardiner," lamented Albright, who noted that a large deer buck with the "finest head of horns I have ever seen on a mule deer" was shot down near the Northern Pacific depot. NPS rangers immediately posted "No Hunting" signs on the Hoppe ranch and began ranger patrols. Because of the NPS's acquiring of the ranch, noted Albright, "we have the antelope problem solved now." He wrote enthusiastically to Thomas Cochran about the ranch's importance:

> I will never be able to find the words to express how I feel about your aid in making this ranch property available to us. In my judgment, it is the most constructive thing that has been done in game protection around Yellowstone Park in the past twenty years or more. I only hope that when we are in a position to tell the story, you will let me tell the truth about your connection with this achievement. [17]

Later scientists and historians disagreed with Albright's claims of a big die-off and a slaughter, but Albright was very much in charge of Yellowstone during the period from 1919 through 1928.[18] At that time, his opinions carried the day.

As early as 1930, the Hoppe ranch was called the "Game Preservation Ranch," which was soon shortened to "Game Ranch." The name was applied because the ranch preserved game and was part of the park game preservation plan and also because the Game Preservation Company was its initial owner.[19]

The government did not take title to the Hoppe ranch until 1931, for two reasons: one was simply getting enough money to match the GPC funds, and the other was the "cloud on the title," namely Albert Hoppe's legal claim of adverse possession.

As previously noted, Walter's unmarried brother, Albert Hoppe, had lived on Walter's ranch since 1913. By verbal agreement with his brother Walter, Albert occupied a "shack" on the river north of the railroad right-of-way. Correspondence and conversations between Horace Albright and the Hoppe brothers make it clear that Albert thought Walter would at some point sell him the land he lived on or perhaps give it to him as part of his inheritance. But twelve years after Albert had settled there, Walter sold the land to the Game Preservation Company. Albert was concerned, but because the NPS continued to let both of them live there and because Walter had promised him the place (perhaps also because of his lack of understanding of legal matters), Albert did nothing for five years. Another possible reason for this forbearance might have been because he was employed seasonally by the NPS at the Buffalo Ranch and did not want to "make waves."

NPS relations with the Hoppes began to deteriorate, probably when the NPS did not rehire Walter as manager of the ranch in 1927.[20] Albert applied in 1929 for the position and was not given it. He then petitioned the NPS to sell the land to him, stating that Horace Albright had agreed to it. The NPS refused, and Albert tried a different tactic. Because he had lived on the land for twelve years prior to the sale, Albert believed he had a land claim under the legal doctrine known as "adverse possession." All states recognized that real estate doctrine, and in most of them the possession had to be open, continuous, exclusive, apparent, notorious, hostile, actual, and unequivocal to the actual landowner. Albert's claim fit most if not all of those criteria, and thus it soon became apparent to the NPS that transfer of the ranch title to them would be held up by Albert Hoppe's lawsuit. Another brother, Lee B. Hoppe, would soon be a party as well, for he had moved back to Gardiner in the 1920s and now lived at Cinnabar with Albert.

The decree by the NPS in 1928 that hunting would be prohibited on all lands not in private ownership in the Cinnabar triangle no doubt made relations with the Hoppes worse. It also added to the NPS's troubles with Gardiner residents and other local folk that would return to plague the Service at a later time. Albright wrote of the hunting situation on his hated Deckard Flats (outside the park to the north):

> We are not alarmists. We are not opposed to hunting, but we honestly feel that the time has come to call a halt on the slaughter [of elk occurring] about Gardiner . . . the shooting on the flats east of Gardiner where the elk come out of the park in bands is a disgrace and should be stopped.[21]

During 1930, relations between the NPS and the Hoppes further soured. Albert Hoppe began to write letters to the NPS, to the Department of the Interior, to the Game Preservation Company, and to his senators and representatives. He stated that Horace Albright had agreed to "fix this deed up" for him but that "nothing has been done." He also made claims that "the public" (meaning probably just him) was "sore" about the government pasturing its own horses on the ranch. Albright—having left his superintendency in Yellowstone to assume the directorship of the NPS in Washington—encouraged the new park superintendent to "give full consideration" to "the attitude of Hoppe when he next applies for employment in Yellowstone National Park." Nevertheless, this probably spelled the end of Albert's employment in Yellowstone, further angering him. When GPC members queried Albright about the matter, he responded in detail, stating that

> [w]e have let him live in a house on the property simply because he had been living there for a great many years and we had no particular use for the house. His charges about the use of the ranch are absolutely absurd.[22]

Albright noted that the NPS was using the ranch only to harvest hay and was not conducting "regular" ranch operations. And when Albert Hoppe wrote again to Albright claiming that Albright had "promised" to get him the land, the NPS director told him he had no recollection of such a promise. Albright declared to Albert Hoppe:

> If you have a quarrel with anybody about your opportunity to buy this property it is with your brother who had plenty of opportunity to sell it to you. He did not do so, neither did he withhold any right for you to buy it when he sold it to the Game Preservation Company.[23]

Further fuel was added to the dispute, when Paul Hoppe (son of Walter) leased the "Slaughter House Ranch" property to the east (property that the NPS badly wanted) and charged fifteen dollars to anyone who wanted to bring game across it. Additionally, the Hoppes alleged that the NPS had failed to return personal property of theirs, an old sled that had been loaned ten years earlier.[24]

By April of 1931, Albert Hoppe, still living on the land, was formally asserting his adverse possession claim. He refused to move and stated that he would sooner "take a lawsuit." Now Albert was also suddenly claiming that he had paid Walter three thousand dollars for the land. When the NPS went to Walter for confirmation, Walter denied that he ever sold the land to Albert and, strangely, denied that Albert even lived on the land for much time before he sold it to the GPC. It appears from the correspondence that the Hoppe brothers had begun to argue among themselves about matters that were rooted in family disagreements reaching back to their father Hugo's death in 1895. Because of Albert Hoppe, the NPS was faced with the prospect of getting the GPC to issue a new deed for the land so that matching funds could be more quickly forthcoming. Government monies could not be released with a cloud upon the land title. Thus the NPS, tired of a land deal that had dragged on for five years, told Walter to either quiet the title between himself and Albert or else to prepare for a lawsuit that the GPC would file against him for breach of warranty of title.[25]

After arguing with the Hoppes all summer, the NPS convinced the Game Preservation Company to file suit against Albert and Lee Hoppe.[26] The Hoppes hired a Livingston lawyer who immediately became ill, further delaying the case. The Hoppes began to represent themselves in the matter. Albert demanded ten acres for a dude ranch and ten thousand dollars. The NPS refused.[27]

As might be expected with a lawsuit pending, relations between the NPS and the Hoppes were strained during much of 1932. Albert Hoppe continued to write letters, denouncing the government for everything from his brother's financial troubles to the 1926 congressional legislation that he believed fed Albright's "land grabbing hobby."[28]

In an attempt to settle differences, Albright met with the Hoppes in late summer of 1932, and both sides seem to have compromised some. Walter Hoppe claimed that at the time he sold the land, he had in mind trying to make some arrangement whereby the GPC or the NPS might sell the land north of the railroad back to his brother Albert but that he did not get around to it because the deal was done before he could see Albright and bank officer Fitzgerald simultaneously. Walter Hoppe also stuck to his story that about a year later Albright told him "this might be arranged." Albright stated that he had no recollection of such a conversation but admitted that Walter Hoppe "might be right." Thus the stage was set for compromise. Albright remembered Hoppe asking him if he objected to his brother "continuing to live" there, and Albright thought *that* was the source of the miscommunication.

But because Albright could not be certain, the parties negotiated an agreement. "All his brother wants," wrote Albright about what Walter told him, "is the privilege of living on the property the rest of his life and. . . . [H]e was really not so much concerned about obtaining title to it." It seemed Albert felt not only that Walter owed him money from their father's estate and that Walter had promised to deed him the property, but also that the whole family owed him something for having borne more than his fair share of his father's medical care prior to 1895.[29]

Arguments with the Hoppes, which had dragged on for seven years past Walter's sale of the land, were finally concluded when the case was settled on September 2, 1932, the day before it was scheduled for trial. The following five structures were listed as being on the Hoppe ranch in or about 1932: 1) dwelling house of seven rooms (frame building of two stories); 2) granary (15 x 24); 3) combined chicken house and toilet (6 x 12); 4) hay house (a roofed structure with no sides, 14 x 16); and 5) two-story barn (45 x 18). Albert Hoppe signed a quitclaim deed relinquishing any claims on the land. In return the NPS gave him the right to live on the tract the remainder of his life—a "life estate" in legal parlance.[30]

Strangely, the NPS was to have one more round with Albert Hoppe. In 1934, Ranger Harry Trischman was given orders to clean up old fences on the property around the "shack" where Albert lived. According to the acting superintendent, Hoppe "contended yesterday that we had no authority to go in and that he still owned the land and that he intended to fix up his fences and plow this thirty-seven acres this spring." Trischman proceeded with the cleanup anyway, and the superintendent noted that "by that time Albert Hoppe had decided that we meant business and had ceased his bluffing." A comment of the superintendent's that "as he gave us a quitclaim deed . . . he has absolutely no rights down there" makes one wonder whether or not the NPS had forgotten its promise to let Albert Hoppe live there for the rest of his life. At any rate, Albert spent the remainder of his days on his father's land, effectively becoming the last living resident of old Cinnabar.[31] He died on May 24, 1936, and the NPS tore down his cabin.

With the Game Preservation Company's purchase of the Hoppe ranch in 1925, and Horace Albright's continuing attempts to obtain other lands in the region, the stage was set at Old Cinnabar for President Herbert Hoover to add (by executive order) a large, three-cornered piece of land to Yellowstone National Park. It was an area that is still shown on today's maps as just northwest of the town of Gardiner—a parcel that would later become known as the "Cinnabar triangle."

12

TUSSLES OVER THE TRIANGLE

President Hoover Adds the Cinnabar Triangle to Yellowstone National Park (1932 to Present Time)

I, Herbert Hoover . . . do proclaim that the area hereinafter described shall be . . . added to and made a part of the said park.
—President Herbert Hoover, October 20, 1932

President Herbert Hoover's Executive Order of October 20, 1932, added some 7,609 acres to Yellowstone National Park. Congress's 1926 act (44 Stat. 655) had already authorized the president to add land to the park in this manner. Most of Hoover's addition was land that had been gradually obtained by Horace Albright and the Game Preservation Company. It included the Hoppe ranch, part of the Armstrong ranch, and part of the Van Dyke/Hill ranch. But 1,163 acres of private land remained inside the park after the presidential proclamation.[1]

At least one newspaper article about the new park "addition"—which was not technically an addition yet because not all the land had been obtained by the government—went to great lengths to emphasize that politics were not behind the addition. Members of the Livingston Chamber of Commerce emphasized that one of the reasons for the town's support of the 1926 legislation was so that the road from Yankee Jim Canyon to Gardiner might be constructed (improved) "with one hundred per cent US Forest Service money."[2]

Although all of the land that was eventually to be included in Yellowstone Park was within the 1932 presidential proclamation, the federal government also continued through the 1930s to purchase private lands to be added to Gallatin National Forest.[3]

Following the 1932 addition of over seventy-six hundred acres to Yellowstone National Park, 1,163 acres remained within the proclaimed ("park") area that was privately owned. Roy N. Armstrong (165 acres) and Anton (Tony) Stermitz (one hundred acres) owned the largest of these tracts. Of these properties, nearly all of the Stermitz place—which was the same as the earlier "Rife Ranch"—and 41.7 acres of the Armstrong place were within the proclaimed park boundaries. Stermitz owned much of the old George Reese ranch, and Armstrong owned the premises just southwest of the most northerly point of the present Cinnabar triangle boundary (adjacent to the Rife/Stermitz ranch).[4]

Horace Albright noticed the Stermitz land in 1925. Albright approached the Stermitzes at that time, but they were not interested in selling. Albright summarized:

> It seems that Mr. Stermitz'[s] father bought the place for him, paying $8000 for it. The boy [Anton Stermitz] is to pay the old man [Joseph Stermitz, Sr.] back in certain installments. The boy married a girl whose family lives just a little farther north along the Yellowstone River and it is the desire of himself and his wife to make the Reese place their home. They are thrifty, hard-working people and believe that they have a good place that they can make a little money on. To get this place we would probably have to pay as much as $10,000.[5]

While this information probably reflected what the family told Albright, deed records lead one to believe that Joseph Stermitz, who "obtained" the land in 1924 from Ernest Rife, did not formally convey the premises to Anton Stermitz until August of 1932, just before the government proclaimed the land to be inside of Yellowstone Park. Because of the loose way the conveyance was handled from the Rifes, Stermitz's title was probably not completely marketable.[6] Regardless, Albright was forced to deal with Anton Stermitz, because Stermitz and his wife were occupying the land. The Stermitz and Armstrong lands were of much lower priority to the NPS than were those of Hoppe, Walter Hill, and others, so Albright kept them on the back burner for several years. Every so often he would approach Stermitz and Armstrong to no avail.

By 1930, with the other properties in government hands, it became apparent to the NPS that the Stermitz and Armstrong families would not sell their lands. Assistant Superintendent Guy Edwards put forth the possibility of a "taking" with "just compensation," as was allowed by the US Constitution. He wondered that year that "were the park extended to include these lands, [whether] condemnation proceedings could be instituted if necessary to purchase these properties, although it would hardly be advisable at the present time." But takings were a decade away.[7]

Due no doubt partly to the Great Depression and partly to the dogged obstinacy of the two families, nothing was resolved for ten years. The NPS, the Stermitzes, and Roy Armstrong went along tolerating each other if only barely. It became apparent to federal authorities in the mid-thirties that private funds could not be secured to match what remained in the appropriated land balance from the legislation of 1928. No money remained from the old Game Preservation Company. Money, in the 1930s, was tight for everyone.[8]

In the late thirties, harsher disagreements began to surface. The government, unable to get private matching funds, got legislation introduced (S. 1216) to remove the matching provision from the 1926 and 1928 acts so that the Stermitz and Armstrong lands could be purchased outright without help from the private sector. This legislation—misunderstood by local people in the Gardiner, Montana, area as a larger than it really was land-taking scheme and an attempt to prohibit hunting on national forest lands—galvanized anti-NPS sentiment in the area. It became a classic example of local paranoia coupled with the usual anti-governmentalism. The Stermitzes, Hoppes (Lee, Walter, and George were still living, along with many Hoppe descendants), and Roy Armstrong led this opposition and fed it by drumming up other local antagonism. The Park County Board of Commissioners and the Gardiner Commercial Club both passed resolutions condemning any further park extension, even though no such extension was contemplated. The NPS office at Washington attempted to explain that no further park extension was planned, that the project would further benefit Montana's wildlife management, and that being allowed to liquidate unprofitable holdings and relocate on nearby lands more suitable for agriculture would benefit several local landowners.[9]

But damage had been done to the NPS plan because locals were, as always, suspicious of the federal government. Roy Armstrong and others were convinced that the feds were attempting to extend the park north all the way to Yankee Jim Canyon, and he spread that incorrect information around the valley. Other locals feared that land would be removed from Park County tax rolls or that hunting would somehow be prohibited. The entire affair was a textbook example of local paranoia against the federal government. The rumors that the park was going to again extend its boundaries northward could not be squelched irrespective of what the NPS did. Part of that problem was being exacerbated by the fact that the Service was simultaneously entrenched in a battle with Wyoming interests to extend Yellowstone's southern boundaries to include the Grand Tetons. That proposal *did* contemplate park extension, which did not help Yellowstone's case. [10]

Spurred on by Armstrong and the Stermitzes, Park County locals began to inundate the NPS Washington office with "a flood of protests." Montana congressman James O'Connor misinterpreted the proposed legislation, asked the Livingston Chamber of Commerce to go on record opposing any further extension of the park, and himself went on record as opposing the proposed legislation. Also during 1938, the no-hunting policy, which the NPS was enforcing on the Stermitz and Armstrong lands because they were within the 1932 proclamation, became a focus of dissatisfaction among locals. The NPS went so far as to ask for a legal opinion as to what had been done with hunting in a similar inholding at California's Lassen National Park. [11]

Attempting to mend relations, the NPS held a meeting with the Gardiner Commercial Club that was composed of local businessmen. On January 3, 1939, Acting Superintendent J. W. Emmert, Special Assistant Joseph Joffe, Chief Ranger Francis LaNoue, and Assistant Chief Ranger Maynard Barrows met with Gardiner club members, including Armstrong and Stermitz. The Gardiner club presented its resolution against the "park extension bill." The NPS informed them there was no such extension planned and that the bill was only to allow the properties to be purchased with no private matching funds. Club members stated that if the NPS extended the boundaries in 1932, they could do it again anytime they wished. The NPS said no, that an act of Congress would be required for that. After discussion, the club stated that it would not oppose further land acquisition toward Yankee Jim Canyon as long as the area would remain open to hunting. The NPS agreed that hunting would continue in national forest lands and suggested the club contact its Montana senators and congressmen for confirmation of what the NPS had just said. Apparently from this meeting, the club decided not to distribute two hundred hand-bills against the "park extension."

Then Armstrong and Stermitz brought up hunting on their own lands. They objected to the NPS's enforcement of its no-hunting edict on their properties that were within the new park boundaries and stated that they believed the NPS was overstepping its authority. Ready for such an even-tuality, the NPS presented a legal opinion from the solicitor of the Depart-ment of the Interior that cited the 1891 ceding of exclusive jurisdiction by the state of Montana to the federal government of all lands within Yel-lowstone Park. That quieted the club although resentment lingered. Arm-strong and Stermitz, who had previously complained to congressman O'Connor that the park boundary was inadequately marked, now castigat-ed the NPS for "overstepping its authority" by marking the boundary. [12]

As soon as the meeting was over, club members who still did not believe the park was not going to be extended went back to work in opposition. In direct conflict with what he had heard at the meeting, Roy Armstrong told local landowners that the feds planned to extend the park north to Yankee Jim Canyon and circulated a petition among them oppos-ing it. Gardiner businessman George Welcome (son of the earlier man with this name) and three other members of the club called on Superin-tendent Emmert at his office to tell him they did not believe the park was not contemplating extension. Even a letter from the NPS Washington director to Senator Wheeler did not convince them, but Emmert got club members to agree to a proposition: if the NPS could get a majority of ranchers in the area to agree to sign a statement saying that they would be willing to talk about selling their lands to the government should monies become available, then the Gardiner club would push Congressman O'Connor to withdraw his objections to the private monies bill. From this it is apparent that not all area landowners opposed the NPS's land acqui-sition program. Many locals wanted to sell out because times were hard and they needed the money. [13]

But other opposition continued in the form of bills in both the Monta-na legislature and the US House of Representatives. Armstrong, Stermitz, George Welcome, and others appealed to their state representatives for help, using information they had gained from the NPS in the meeting at Gardiner. A son-in-law of George Welcome introduced a bill into the Montana legislature to repeal the 1891 state law ceding jurisdiction of state lands to the NPS. That bill eventually died, but Armstrong and Stermitz were not finished yet. They began trying to convince Montana Congressman O'Connor to introduce legislation into the US House to reconvey all of the new Yellowstone Park lands to the state of Montana. [14]

Smarting from this new opposition, the NPS decided to meet again with Gardiner Commercial Club members. On March 21, Acting Superintendent Emmert and his compatriots again encountered hostility. The club members "nearly all felt antagonistic towards the Park Service," wrote Emmert, "which is a carry-over from 1926 [*sic*], when the Park addition at the Game Ranch was added." Emmert stated that many Gardiner old-timers had been prejudiced against the land acquisition program since the mid-twenties. But Emmert saw divisions within the Gardiner Commercial Club. Predictably it voted against the NPS land program, but the vote was close, 15–11. Emmert noted that there were some sympathetic club members, who consisted

> mainly of businessmen of the town who feel that their whole future is tied up with that of Yellowstone and that they should be for us. However, the opposing votes were those of the old timers who still feel that anything the park wants is bad. [15]

It was an old story in the arena of government hating.

Stermitz and Armstrong continued to cause trouble for the NPS. They wrote letters to Montana senator Burton K. Wheeler and of course to Congressman O'Connor, who was already on their side in a way that was arguably devoted to the narrowest of local interests rather than dedicated to a more balanced view that fairly encompassed the national interests involved on federal lands. Now Stermitz and Armstrong concentrated on problems they had had with animal depredations and visitors for several years. Elk, antelope, deer, and coyotes ate their haystacks and killed their chickens, turkeys, and calves. They wanted the NPS to build game-proof fences. The park did not want to build such fences along the property lines "for that would be too expensive and it is not advisable also because funds will soon be available for the purchase of these lands." Additionally, because the main road from Livingston, Montana, to Gardiner passed directly through the Stermitz and Armstrong lands, [16] visitors knocked on their doors at all hours to ask questions about the required sealing of firearms. (The NPS had posted signs on park lands all around them prohibiting hunting and requiring all firearms to be sealed.) The Stermitzes and Roy Armstrong wanted money for their damages and did not believe the park had the authority to prohibit hunting on their lands nor to keep them from shooting depredating animals.

The NPS responded with a compromise. It allowed firearms to be carried without seals on the roadway "until such time as it is practicable to maintain an entrance station there." And it permitted the two families to shoot coyotes on their properties.[17]

The NPS attempted to explain these compromises to Montana senator Wheeler and to enlist his support for the private-monies legislation that would facilitate the acquisition of the Stermitz and Armstrong properties. Wrote NPS director Cammerer:

> If those tracts can be acquired, the present owners will be able to locate in a more suitable location. Every consideration will be given in allowing them time for readjustments. As long as private lands remain within the area actually frequented by the elk and other wild animals, whether within or outside the park area, the problem will remain insoluble. The owners will continually be faced with serious difficulties [from animals], notwithstanding anything [that] may be done to relieve them. It is only fair to them that they be given an opportunity to dispose of their holdings at a fair price.[18]

But such bad relations were not easily repaired even with fair words. In June, Congressman O'Connor introduced H.R. 6975 to reconvey all new parklands to the state of Montana. That bill eventually died, but not before the bill sent the NPS scurrying to defend against it.[19]

There is evidence that Stermitz considered selling to the NPS that summer of 1939 but became bogged down in title problems. Superintendent Edmund Rogers noted in July that "Stermitz has expressed a willingness to sell the property at about $9700." But Stermitz also knew that there was probably a flaw in his title because of the loose transfer from Rife, and he was afraid of clause five in the contract that empowered the government to quiet title at his expense if his title was not good.[20] "Quieting title" was and is a term used by lawyers to refer to the process of making certain that a land title is not only clear to someone who reads it but also able to withstand any kind of legal challenge to its authenticity.

Now the NPS began proceedings in earnest to acquire the Stermitz and Armstrong lands through condemnation. It prepared a "request for condemnation" and a "declaration of taking" for the signatures of officials.

Under the declaration of the taking, the NPS proposed to pay into court the estimated "just compensation" price of $11,690 for the lands of Armstrong and Stermitz and two other uncontested pieces that belonged to Harry Child and Lena Bassett.[21] Faced with this, Anton Stermitz accepted "options to sell" his land on July 17, 1939—T9S, R8E, S8: lots 3, 4, 5, 6, 7, and SE4 of SW4, for the amount of ninety-seven hundred dollars.[22]

Strangely the government was here placed in the unique position of paying for the Stermitz land twice: once in 1929 from the Rifes and once in 1939 from the Stermitzes. Legal research on the loose 1924 "conveyance" from Rife to Stermitz has not been completed, but it would seem that had the government's attorneys done better research, federal authorities could have paid for the land only once instead of twice. On the other hand, perhaps the solicitors were worried that Anton Stermitz could have made a strong adverse possession case, for he had been on the land for fifteen years. If that is the case, one can argue that the government should never have paid the Rifes for the land.

The legislation to erase the private matching monies (S. 1216) was never acted upon by Congress, because its congressional sponsor (Senator Wheeler) discovered that the Gardiner Commercial Club opposed it. The NPS still favored the legislation as late as 1943, but it was never passed. Of the one hundred fifty thousand dollars appropriated by Congress in 1926, only about fifty thousand dollars were spent. Congress never authorized release of the balance of the funds.[23]

Attorneys for the US government filed a condemnation proceeding titled *United States v. 228 Acres of Land Situated in Park County, Montana, Roy N. Armstrong, et al.* in 1939, and the Acting Assistant Secretary of the Interior signed a declaration of taking the same day, October 3, 1939. The taking declaration stated that the land was necessary

> for use in connection with a Public Works project which contemplates the conservation of natural resources, the prevention of soil erosion, forestation and reforestation, the preservation of scenic beauty, the building of foot trails, roadways, cabins, shelters, and other structures and improvements necessary and appropriate to provide public facilities for the preservation of wildlife and the protection and development of other land of the United States adjacent to and intermingled with the lands hereinafter described, and the aforesaid construction of useful public improvements thereon [which] will afford relief, work relief, and will reduce and relieve unemployment.

Title to the Stermitz land passed to the United States on or before March 13, 1940.[24]

Anton Stermitz, along with Harry Child's heirs and Lena Bassett, reached agreements with the NPS on the price of their lands prior to the US declaration of taking, and those monies were deposited with the court as "just compensation." But no easy agreement could be reached with Roy N. Armstrong, so his case continued.[25]

Stermitz was understandably miffed at the government when he had trouble getting his money for several years. The NPS and the Department of the Interior were required legally only to deposit the money into court. At that point, the law prevented their further involvement. When the court held up payout of the funds until a lawsuit could settle defects in Stermitz's title to the land, Stermitz perceived only that the government was not giving him his money. To him, a court was still part of the government. Solicitor C. W. Buntin noted:

> I went further in assisting Mr. Stermitz to obtain distribution of the compensation deposited in the Registry of the Court for his lands than I would ordinarily go. All people connected with the Government extended to Stermitz every consideration possible. It was difficult to make him understand matters. The Government was in no sense responsible for any of the defects in his title to the lands.[26]

One can hardly blame Anton and Agnes Stermitz for their frustration, but the court could not legally release money until the land title was quieted. Ironically, a second reason that the Stermitzes' money was held up was the fact that his neighbor and compatriot Roy Armstrong refused to accept the government's assessment of his own land damages and contested the entire transaction in a later court action. That too held up their money.[27]

The government was worried that any or all of ten or so surviving members of the Reese family might claim title to the Stermitz lands because of the loose way in which the lands had changed hands. Defendant Stermitz petitioned the court for release of his money, and that was finally done in an order dated December 3, 1941. The court gave Stermitz $9,392.07 but kept $307.93 to be given to Robert Reese (whose father had owned an undivided one-third interest in the land). That amount was apparently eventually given to Stermitz as well.[28]

The appraisal sheet for the Stermitz land described it as 101.61 acres. Fifty-one acres were under cultivation, 12.5 were uncultivated (formerly cultivated), five contained buildings, and 32.5 acres were brushland. Improvements consisted of one three-room house, one five-room house, ten other buildings (including a cow barn, garage, blacksmith shop, smokehouse, granary, chicken house, milk house, stock shed, root cellar, and one other shed), corrals, a lawn fence, haystack yards, orchard (twenty-six apple and cherry trees), and a domestic water system.[29]

A letter to Anton Stermitz outlined the government's position. He was to be given reasonable time to dispose of his crops and stock. The government preferred him to be off the property on or before February 1, 1940, but in case of problems he was given until May 1, 1940.[30]

Other letters summed up the personal situation of the Stermitzes and their real estate. They had lived on the land for fifteen years and had kept careful records. Their average annual income had been $1,508.91 from ranching and four hundred fifty dollars from rooming and boarding hunters in hunting season. The water rights from Reese Creek were eight hundred inches, or almost all of the stream's water, which had come down from George Reese. Maps in the file showed the land cultivated in wheat, oats, alfalfa, and potatoes.[31]

The NPS began cleanup of the Stermitz property in April of 1940. The plans for such cleanup recommended razing of nine of the ten buildings (one was to be used as a ranger station), sloping and leveling of ground where buildings were located, and removal of a dump and all fences. Irrigation ditches were to be improved and cottonwood trees and willows were to be planted along Reese Creek. Shrubs were to be planted on old building sites.[32]

As for Roy Armstrong's land, the government acquired it through condemnation also, because Armstrong had refused all offers to sell.[33] In 1935, the government offered $22,194.50 to Armstrong for his various lands in sections 5 and 8 of T9S, R8E, and sections 9, 10, and 12 of T9S, R7E. Armstrong refused, saying the lands were worth more to him personally than was offered.[34] As the Great Depression progressed, the government could no longer get that much money and was thus relegated to negotiating on Armstrong's small parcel of about forty acres within the 1932 park boundary. In August of 1939, Rangers Francis LaNoue and Maynard Barrows interviewed Armstrong about the small parcel. Armstrong stated that he would never sell the part of his land that was inside the 1932 park boundary because 1) the more private land between his property and the park that was placed in government ownership the more accessible his property would be to animal depredations, and 2) he considered the part of his land inside the park that straddled Reese Creek to be an important adjunct to his main property because of the water and shelter holdings there.

One can understand and perhaps sympathize with Armstrong's water-rights argument, but his argument about animal damage was specious. After all, he and other landowners had in fact "come to the park"—which was established many years before private owners were in proximity—and thus arguably had to take the land he had come to with all its limitations, including its animals.

Thus the government proceeded with condemnation actions for the 41.7 acres of Armstrong's ranch that were inside of the proclaimed park area, tendering two hundred fifty dollars as its estimate of damages to the remainder of his ranch by the taking of part of his land. Armstrong contested that offer, and the court appointed several Montana men to act as commissioners to review the assessment. They fixed Armstrong's damages at $1,750. The government appealed that decision and had the case tried before a jury at Helena. The jury gave Armstrong damages of $1,808.50. Apparently the jury sympathized heavily with Armstrong, for the judge stated that "in all his forty years experience as a lawyer and judge that he had not seen a verdict so out of line with the evidence given." Nevertheless, the court was bound by the verdict. Armstrong's attorney saw it as a victory for Armstrong regardless of the fact that some of Armstrong's land was taken.[35] The conflicts over these lands during the nation's Great Depression serve as a case study not only in government hating and paranoia by private citizens but also in how both sides often misunderstand each other.

The land taken from Armstrong had no improvements upon it, as all of his buildings were on his other land outside the 1932 boundary. Maps in the file showed the layout of Armstrong's cultivated crops. Moreover, detailed forage studies showed the types of grasses and other plants that grew on the parcels. The NPS work plans on the Armstrong property included removal of fences and general cleanup of the area.[36]

The march to add these lands in the Cinnabar triangle to Yellowstone National Park during the period 1920 to 1940 may seem to us today as if it were inexorable and somehow almost preordained. But it could not have seemed so to Horace Albright and an entire generation of Yellowstone officials. To them the process must have been spasmodic, arduous, knotty, and capable of being lost at any moment.

13

CONCLUSIONS

The Cinnabar triangle, or Game Ranch portion of Yellowstone National Park, is relatively quiet today, just as it was in the 1860s before most Euro-Americans arrived on the scene. But beginning in the 1870s, it became the site of ranches and small farms, initially the Henderson and Reese families, and eventually many more. There is much more to the story of the triangle—that three-sided extension of Yellowstone's boundary west of Gardiner—but it is complex and only peripherally related to Cinnabar, the community that stood within it.[1]

The town of Cinnabar rose there in 1883, on Hugo Hoppe's belief and knowledge that "they are going to build a railroad," and it lasted until 1903, when much of the dying town moved to Gardiner. During that period, the Northern Pacific Railroad's terminus was at Cinnabar, and passengers disembarked there for stagecoach tours of Yellowstone National Park. The town of Cinnabar was small but colorful during its twenty years of existence, and it was the center of much activity related to Yellowstone National Park. Hugo Hoppe labored valiantly to make Cinnabar into a genuine town but ultimately failed. He overestimated the strength of the area's gold and coal, overestimated the clout of terminal towns along the railroad, underestimated the influence of the town of Gardiner, and underestimated the power of Yellowstone National Park and its burgeoning tourism. In all of that he cannot be faulted. The powers of minerals, railroads, and terminal towns were known and proven forces while the power of a new park's tourism was not. No one knew whether Yellowstone would ever receive many visitors or whether tourism would even work in the American West, let alone that this park would become a worldwide touristic phenomenon. And too, he had no way of knowing that the desire to preserve Yellowstone for future generations would someday cause the American public (through the National Park Service) to reach out and absorb the townsite of Cinnabar itself, along with the rest of the Cinnabar triangle.

In all of this, Hugo Hoppe was typical of many Westerners who invested their dreams in businesses that became ghost towns and in homes, barns, and corrals erected on the prairie only to become empty, windblown skeletons. Cinnabar died, as it had lived, dependent upon the railroad and ceasing to exist when the railroad extended its tracks to Gardiner, especially with the nearby towns of Horr and Aldridge blooming. During the town's last three years, Cinnabar resident Sarah Gassert wrote the heartrending poem "They're Going to Build a Railroad," which decried the extension of the tracks to Gardiner.

Cinnabar is gone, but its story stands tall in the cultural history of Yellowstone National Park. Some of its residents are interred today in the Gardiner Cemetery, located only a mile to the east. In 2007–2008, archeologists from Montana State University excavated building sites on the townsite and found more than eighteen hundred artifacts. Today the site is temporarily fenced so that the National Park Service can begin procedures to restore the area—now informally known as "Gardiner Basin"—to the native grasses that once grew there and which were destroyed by years of agricultural planting.[2]

After Cinnabar died in 1903, the area reverted to quiet ranching activity until 1925. That year the National Park Service began a drive to purchase various private lands north of Yellowstone Park for winter range of elk and other animals. The National Park Service purchased lands owned by Walter Hoppe, Charles Stoll, Ernest Rife, Walter Hill, W. J. Moseley, Lena Bassett Ross, and Harry Child's heirs. Lands owned by Anton Stermitz and Roy Armstrong were forcibly taken and paid for through the government's constitutional power of eminent domain that requires "just compensation." A presidential proclamation in 1932 added 7,609 acres of the Cinnabar triangle to the park's north boundary, but not all of those lands belonged yet to the federal government. Following a 1941 court case and finally the 1972 conveyances of railroad lands to the United States,[3] the park boundary with regard to the Cinnabar triangle was officially completed as we know it today. The conflicts over these lands during the 1930s and early 1940s serve as continuing lessons for us today in the ways that government and private citizens often misunderstand each other.

Rail passenger service to Gardiner, Montana, ended officially in 1948, with "specials" to bring employees to the park occurring as late as 1957. Freight service continued through 1975. In 1976, workmen removed the tracks between Livingston and Gardiner. This author, then a twenty-six-year-old park bus driver and tour guide, remembers watching the tracks being removed all the way to Livingston while driving passenger buses along that stretch of US Highway 89. I shed a few personal tears that summer while witnessing the end of nearly a century of railroad-related history. Little did I know as I watched the tracks disappear that the historical saying "They're going to build a railroad!" had already become an exclamation relegated to a bygone era.

NOTES

INTRODUCTION

1. Important Yellowstone histories are Aubrey L. Haines, *Yellowstone National Park: Its Exploration and Establishment* (Washington: GPO, 1974); Haines, *The Yellowstone Story* (two volumes, Boulder: Colorado Associated University Press, 1977, 1996); Richard A. Bartlett, *Yellowstone: A Wilderness Besieged* (Tucson: University of Arizona Press, 1985); James A. Pritchard, *Preserving Yellowstone's Natural Conditions: Science and the Perception of Nature* (Lincoln: University of Nebraska Press, 1999); and Paul Schullery, *Searching for Yellowstone: Ecology and Wonder in the Last Wilderness* (Helena: Montana Historical Society Press, 2004). The original iteration of the present work was Lee H. Whittlesey, "'They're Going to Build a Railroad!': Cinnabar, Stephens Creek, and the Game Ranch Addition to Yellowstone National Park," unpublished manuscript, March 9, 1995, YNP Research Library. The present book is a reworking of that manuscript without its extensive real estate (land title) citations and with considerable new material about both Hugo Hoppe and Cinnabar itself. See also Mary Shivers Culpin, "Historical Information and Context," in Ann Mary Johnson, "Cultural Resource Inventory for the Bison Environmental Assessment in the Stephens Creek Area, Yellowstone National Park," unpublished National Park Service studies, September 12, 1989, and December 20, 1995.

2. The gold strike that started Cooke City occurred in 1870, and for ten years the place was known as the "Clark's Fork mines." A major event occurred on June 11, 1880, when about fifty miners held a meeting and "the new town was unanimously named Cooke City," for Jay Cooke of the Northern Pacific Railroad, whose favor they were hoping to court in the form of a railroad that would never be built. The men listed at that meeting included three of the site's four

discoverers (Adam Miller, James Gourley, and A. Bart Henderson) along with numerous other men whose names became well known in Montana and Yellowstone history. The most famous were Jack Baronett, P. W. Norris, John X. Beidler, Fellows D. Pease, J. V. Bogert, R. B. "George" Rowland, M. M. Black, Charles W. Hoffman, J. H. "Pike" Moore, and George Ash. See "The New Town at Clark's Fork Mines," Bozeman (MT) *Avant Courier*, June 24, 1880, p. 3. By late August, miners were deserting the place and heading for a new strike at Nye City ("Local Layout," *Livingston* (MT) *Enterprise*, August 20, 1887, p. 3) and in October, the newspaper noted that "not more than twenty-five people" would remain at Cooke during the coming winter. "Local Layout," *Livingston Enterprise*, October 29, 1887, p. 3. But Cooke City would survive and Nye City would not.

3. The rising fame of Yellowstone National Park during the 1870s because of newspapers and magazines is in Lee H. Whittlesey, "Yellowstone: From Last Place Discovered to International Fame," *Site Lines* 5 (Fall, 2009): 9–10 (University of Virginia, Foundation for Landscape Studies), while the park's grand opening in 1883 is covered in Haines, *Yellowstone Story*, I, pp. 272–291; and Whittlesey, "'Oh, Mammoth Structure!': Rufus Hatch, the National Hotel, and the Grand Opening of Yellowstone in 1883," *Annals of Wyoming* 83 (Spring, 2011): 2–20. For Yellowstone in early US tourism, see Earl S. Pomeroy, *In Search of the Golden West: The Tourist in Western America* (New York: Knopf, 1957); David M. Wrobel and Patrick T. Long, eds., *Seeing and Being Seen: Tourism in the American West* (Lawrence: University Press of Kansas, 2001); John F. Sears, *Sacred Places: American Tourist Attractions in the Nineteenth Century* (New York: Oxford University Press, 1989); and Lee H. Whittlesey, *Storytelling in Yellowstone: Horse and Buggy Tour Guides* (Albuquerque: University of New Mexico Press, 2007).

4. One hundred five years after Cinnabar died, archeologists excavated portions of the townsite. Their report is David Scott Dick, Douglas H. MacDonald, Steven Seriff, and Lester E. Maas, "Cinnabar: Archeology and History of Yellowstone's Lost Train Town," 2010, unpublished manuscript, University of Montana, Yellowstone National Park, and the Rocky Mountain Cooperative Ecosystem Study Cooperative Agreement, a PDF posted at http://etd.lib.umt.edu/theses/available/etd-06182010-004451/unrestricted/CINNABAR.pdf. Archeologists understandably often believe that their findings were previously "lost," but the location of Cinnabar has been continuously known in Yellowstone National Park since the town's demise. See also Scott McMillion, "Digging up Cinnabar," *Bozeman* (MT) *Chronicle*, August 27, 2008.

1. BEFORE CINNABAR

1. "Presidential Proclamation Declares 7,600 Acres Land Added to Yellowstone Park," *Livingston Enterprise*, November 3, 1932.

2. An entry in A. Bart Henderson's diary for October 7, 1872, states that he "remained at home working on house until the 14th" and that his brother James went to Bozeman. The brothers abandoned the toll road when James broke his leg, and James "Yankee Jim" George took it over. Haines, *Yellowstone Story*, I, 1977, p. 232. A. Bart Henderson remained a prospector until the day he died on August 4, 1889, at Nelson, British Columbia, as reported in "Local Layout," *Livingston Enterprise*, October 5, 1889, p. 3.

3. Stokeley Henderson (age forty-four), his wife Mary (thirty-nine), and his six sons Stirling, Phelix, Finas, Bartlett, George, and Edward appeared in the US Census for 1880, as living in the upper Yellowstone valley (via Ancestry.com, John Hughes Mulherin search). Whether these Hendersons lived at the ranch with James and A. Bart Henderson or somewhere else nearby is not known. Stirling Henderson was fresh from having served as a guide only twelve days earlier to the ill-fated Cowan party of 1877, along with George Huston. See Frank Carpenter (H. D. Guie and L. V. McWhorter, eds.), *Adventures in Geyserland* (Caldwell: Caxton Printers, Ltd., 1935), pp. 65, 85, 200.

4. Haines, *Yellowstone Story*, I, pp. 232–233; Haines, "The Burning of Henderson's Ranch," *Yellowstone Interpreter* 2 (July–August, 1964): 52–54; Hugh L. Scott, *Some Memories of a Soldier* (New York: Century Company, 1928), pp. 60–69; and Lee Whittlesey, "A History of Parcels 'L' and 'M' in the Northern Addition to Yellowstone National Park, Formerly Known as the Stermitz Ranch," unpublished manuscript, March to May, 2006, pp. 4–6, written for National Park Service, YNP Library. For a primary source on this skirmish, see "Judge McPherson," *Bozeman* (MT) *Times*, September 6, 1877, p. 2. For Lt. Doane, see Kim Allen Scott, *Yellowstone Denied: The Life of Gustavus Cheyney Doane* (Norman: University of Oklahoma Press, 2006).

5. The stream through the property, which was shown on the 1878 Hayden survey map as "Henderson Creek," became known as Stephens Creek sometime after the land transfer and during the period that Stephens owned the property (1879?–1882). Lee H. Whittlesey, "Wonderland Nomenclature" (Helena: Montana Historical Society microfiche, 1988), entry for Stephens Creek, pp. 1763–1764. Stephens's declaration of his unsurveyed ranch appeared in Gallatin County land records, Bozeman, Montana, 1 Misc. 179, December 16, 1882: "commencing at a stake standing on the southerly bank of said Yellowstone River thence south forty chains to a stake, thence west twenty chains, thence south twenty chains, thence west twenty chains, thence north forty chains, thence east twenty chains, thence south twenty chains, thence east twenty chains to the

place of beginning (W2 of SW4 of S16; NE4 of NE4 of S20; and the SE4 of the SE4 of S17, T9S, R8E)." Park County, Montana, did not come into existence by being carved from Gallatin County until 1887.

6. This was noted in Bozeman (MT) *Avant Courier*, April 19, 1883. See also Haines, *Yellowstone Story*, I, pp. 267, 278, 321, for more on E. J. Keeney. G. L. Henderson is in Lee H. Whittlesey, *Storytelling in Yellowstone*, Chapter 11.

7. "Local Layout," *Livingston Enterprise*, December 1, 1883, p. 3.

8. George W. Reese, "Homestead Proof—Testimony of Claimant," Homestead Entry No. 585, December 3, 1883, slugged "4-369," Gallatin County land records, Bozeman, Montana (copies placed in Box L-21, YNP Archives). Reese stated in this document that he was forty-six years old at signing and that he established actual residence on the land in April of 1875. Other documents in Box L-21 show that one John W. Clark owned Lot 5 (near George Reese) in Section 8, T9S, R8E, and recorded it in 1892. He cultivated six or seven acres of it for at least five seasons. "Homestead Proof—Testimony of Witness [James Jenkins for John W. Clark]," November 13, 1897.

9. William Ludlow, *Report of a Reconnaissance from Carroll, Montana Territory . . . Summer of 1875* (Washington: GPO, 1876), p. 18, quoted at the beginning of this chapter.

10. This 1878 court case is mentioned in vol. 21, Miscellaneous Records, p. 389, "Judgment on the Declaration of Taking," case of *U.S.A. v. 288 Acres of Land . . . Roy N. Armstrong, et al.* Reese's opponent in the case was Jacob H. Pisor, later a resident of Horr for many years.

11. Rolling I. Reeves, "Field Notes of the Survey of the First Sixty Miles of the Northern Boundary of Wyoming Territory Made in the Year A.D. 1879," typescript, p. 11, YNP Library. Existence of the ferry in 1884 (perhaps a later one) is corroborated by Hugo Hoppe in McPherren, *Imprints*, pp. 200, 232, who placed it "straight down the road from Main Street half a mile to the Yellowstone." According to McPherren, the ferry belonged to Hoppe, and a ferryman operated it. The ferry was also mentioned as being located downstream from the town of Gardiner and called "Philbrick's Ferry" (probably run by George Philbrick who appeared in the US Census of 1900 for Gardiner) in "What Became of Black Hawk and His Booty," *Livingston Enterprise*, September 23, 1884, p. 3. In a time of few bridges, there were ferries up and down the Yellowstone River quite early. A "Mr. Allen" ran one near Emigrant Gulch in 1877, per "An Unfortunate Shot," *Bozeman Times*, October 18, 1877, p. 3. The Horr brothers were building one in July of 1884 ("Local Layout," *Livingston Enterprise*, July 18, 1884, p. 3), and Judith Murphy remembered another one nearby that the Jones family operated after 1902 (*Park County* [MT] *News*, February 19, 1948). Still another ferry at Cinnabar, or perhaps a replacement of one of these, was put into service in 1892, per "Local Layout," *Livingston Enterprise*, July 23, 1892, p. 5.

12. Aubrey L. Haines, *Yellowstone National Park: Its Exploration and Establishment*, p. 34. Reese's initial claim record is at Gallatin County land records, 1 Miscellaneous Records 152, Nov. 20, 1882, Declaration of Ranche on unsurveyed land: "beginning at the mouth of Reese Creek upon its south side at its junction with the Yellowstone, thence running along the bank of said Yellowstone southerly half a mile, thence west half a mile, thence north half a mile to the south bank of said creek, thence easterly along said south bank of said creek to place of beginning, settlement made in 1875." After surveying was completed, Reese described his land as "SE4 of NW4 of E2 of SW4 of SE4 of S8 [T9S, R8E]. This land being that declared before by me by my declaration already of record under date of November 20, 1882." Gallatin County land records, 1 Miscellaneous Records 573. A third record, at Park County Deed book, vol. 3, p. 586 (Bozeman, vol. 10, p. 41), shows a grant from the USA to George W. Reese, August 18, 1885, for lots 3, 4, 6, and 7 [and the] SE4 of SW4, S8, T9S, R8E (157.88 acres).

13. George W. Reese, "Homestead Proof—Testimony of Claimant," Homestead Entry No. 585, December 3, 1883, slugged "4-369," Gallatin County land records, Bozeman, Montana (copies in Box L-21, YNP Archives).

14. Jack L. Reveal, "Geo. Washington Reese, Historical Information," vertical files, YNP Library. A photo of one of the Reese residences is F. J. Haynes H-4140, Montana Historical Society. The Reveal papers have the locations of cabins two and three. The location of the first one is uncertain. Photos of two different Reese cabins are in Whithorn, *Photo History of Aldridge* (Livingston: *Livingston Enterprise*, no date [1966]), p. 117. The 1881 map is in Philip H. Sheridan, *Report of Lieut. General P.H. Sheridan, dated September 20, 1881, of His Expedition Through the Big Horn Mountains, Yellowstone National Park, etc.* (Washington: GPO, 1882).

15. Items in Bozeman *Avant Courier*, June 30, 1881, p. 3; July 7, 1881, p. 3; and September 8, 1881, p. 3. An 1889 summary of George Reese's situation stated that "a few years ago" George moved about a mile farther up Reese Creek toward Electric Peak, built a "snug little home," but could get no title to the land. Charles Arnold, who did get title to the land, brought suit in ejectment, so on September 22, 1889, George Reese repurchased his old ranch and "will move back in a few days." "A Newsy Letter from Horr," *Livingston Enterprise*, September 28, 1889, p. 1.

16. The NPRR grant appeared in Gallatin County land records, Miscellaneous Records, vol. 1, p. 460, June 20, 1883. The grant was for land one hundred feet wide and through Reese's land hereinafter described "with such additional ground as may be necessary for a depot, engine house, switches, side tracks, machine shops, telegraph office, water tank and railroad houses, the said strip of land being the surveyed line of the said company on its line of railroad from

Livingston to National Park and through the following premises to wit: commencing on the north side of Reese Creek at the north west corner stake thence
south one half mile thence east to the Yellowstone River thence north one half
mile thence west to the place of beginning containing about one hundred and
sixty acres under the Homestead Act."

17. Like that of nearly any piece of land, the conveyance history for the Reese
homestead is complex, but the land was passed from George W. Reese to Ellen
G. Horr and apparently back to George. He or someone else appears to have
made a conveyance of "lot 2" to the east to Henry J. Pickering, who conveyed it
to S. S. Errett in 1893, who conveyed it to James O. Murphy in 1906. Murphy
conveyed part of lot 5 back to Reese's sons in 1916, those men having received
some of their father's original property in inheritance. Bert and James Reese then
conveyed lots 3–7 and SE4 of SW4 to Ernest A. Rife in 1923. Rife held the
property for less than a year, conveying it to Joseph Stermitz in February of
1924. In August of 1932, Joseph Stermitz conveyed it to Anton Stermitz, and
Anton Stermitz's land (some of but not the entire Reese ranch) was taken by the
federal government through eminent domain in 1939–1940. Conveyances mentioned here (date followed by volume number and page number) are recorded in
deeds on file at Park County Clerk's office, Livingston, Montana, as follows:
11/27/89—1/623; 4/21/84—5/26; 2/12/90—4/59; 5/12/93—21/72; 9/22/06—
37/62; 3/15/16—46/76; 8/17/23—55/509 and Sheriff's sale 56/25, also in 1923;
2/7/24—56/125; 8/12/32—62/262; and 22M/522. George Reese's obituary was
published in *Livingston Enterprise*, May 20, 1913. Cultural ramifications for the
old Reese ranch are intense. The railroad passed through the property, so there
are railroad bed considerations there. Numerous buildings stood on the land at
various times, and the grave of a cowboy, supposedly killed about 1905 by a
bucking horse, exists on the property. Lee H. Whittlesey, *Death in Yellowstone:
Accidents and Foolhardiness in the First National Park* (Boulder: Roberts Rine-
hart, 2014), p. 311. George Reese had three sons early in his life (Thomas, John,
and James) and two later sons (Bert and Ira).

2. CINNABAR

1. Julia Ada Jones, "After Weary Years," *Livingston Enterprise*, November
30, 1895, p. 1. For early and important looks at this subject, see Olin D. Wheeler,
"Mining in Montana," in *Wonderland 1902* (St. Paul: Northern Pacific Railway,
1902), pp. 17–53; and Albert L. Babcock, "History of Montana's Mines," in his
An Illustrated History of the Yellowstone Valley (Spokane: Western Historical
Publishing Company, [1907?]), pp. 71–93.

2. Unnamed Seattle newspaper, quoted in "The Rush to Alaska," *Livingston Enterprise*, March 5, 1898, p. 4.

3. "First 'City' in Yellowstone Valley at Emigrant Gulch," *Livingston Enterprise*, June 20, 1933, p. 4. It is noteworthy that these numerous, 1933 newspaper reporters interviewed dozens of area pioneers and old-timers to piece together this oral history of the region. See also Haines, *Yellowstone Story*, I, 1977, p. 341 n19. By way of partial confirmation for the Sowl brothers story, Aubrey Haines acknowledged in his "The Park Branch Railroad: Doorway to Yellowstone," mimeographed 1963 (YNP Library, p. 9) that the coal mines of Cinnabar "were known in the [eighteen] sixties."

4. "Last Living Discoverer of the Early Montana Placer Diggings Tells How One Quicksilver Mine Was Not Found," *Park County News* (Livingston, MT), February 24, 1922. See also "The Last of Park County's Pioneer Gold Prospectors," *Park County News*, November 29, 1918, p. 1; and David B. Weaver, "Early Days in Emigrant Gulch," *Contributions to the Historical Society of Montana*, vol. 7, 1910, pp. 73–96.

5. F. V. Hayden, *Preliminary Report of the United States Geological Survey of Montana and Portions of Adjacent Territories, being a Fifth Annual Report of Progress* (Washington: GPO, 1872), p. 60; Earl of Dunraven, *The Great Divide: Travels in the Upper Yellowstone in the Summer of 1874* (Lincoln: University of Nebraska Press, 1967), p. 181.

6. W. H. Dudley, *The National Park from the Hurricane Deck of a Cayuse or the Liederkranz Expedition to Geyserland* (Butte City, Montana: Free Press Publishing Company, 1886), p. 29. The death of Charles H. Sowl (spelling it "Sowle") with a brief biography of him is in "Local Layout," *Livingston Enterprise*, March 30, 1889, p. 3; and another mention is in "Local Layout," *Livingston Enterprise*, October 1, 1887, p. 3. A search of the US Census of 1860 for Argyle, Wisconsin (via ancestry.com), turns up a Charles Sowl (age twenty) and a James Sowl (age seventeen), sons of William and Frances Sowl. They would have been the right age to have been involved in the 1865 explorations in Montana. No other names have turned up using spellings of "Soule" and "Soul." Charley Sowl's property sale due to his death appeared in "District Court," *Livingston Enterprise*, November 1, 1890, p. 1.

7. T. S. Kenderdine, *California Revisited, 1858-1897* (Newtown, PA: no publisher, 1898), p. 276.

8. Pilgrim, "Pilgrim's Progress—A Somewhat Lucid Description of the Sights in Wonderland," *Great Falls* (MT) *Tribune*, September 11, 1886, p. 1. In the language of the time, a "pilgrim" was anyone who was new to a region, and in the American West that was a great number of people. Park tour guide G. L. Henderson in 1887 attributed this tale of the devil at Devil's Slide to the Bannock

Indians. Henderson, "The Big Geysers . . . The Devil's Slide and Its Legend," *Richmond* (VA) *Dispatch*, August 14, 1887, p. 2.

9. William Tod Helmuth, *The Yellowstone Park and How It Was Named* (No place: H. O. Shepard Company, no date [1892?]), YNP Library. A printed and dated version of this poem (August 7, 1892) was also pasted into G. L. Henderson, Ash Scrapbook, p. 14, YNP Archives; and it appeared at the rear of many editions of the *Haynes Guide to Yellowstone*, such as the one from 1912.

10. The most important railroad completion information is in *Livingston Enterprise*, September 3, 1883, several articles. The little-known 1882 survey is mentioned in "Northern Pacific Branches," Bozeman *Avant Courier*, April 27, 1882, p. 3, which says a line from Benson's Landing to Yellowstone National Park has been surveyed by the NPRR. For completion of the Park Branch of the NPRR generally, see Northern Pacific Railroad, *Report of the President to the Stockholders at Their Annual Meeting, September 20th, 1883* (New York: E. Wells Sackett & Rankin, 1883), p. 25. For the NPRR's early history, see Jay Cooke and Company, *The Northern Pacific Railroad: Its Route, Resources, Progress, and Business* (Philadelphia: Jay Cooke & Company [February 1871]); and Eugene V. Smalley, *History of the Northern Pacific Railroad* (New York: G. P. Putnam's Sons, 1883). Gary Tarbox of today's Northern Pacific Railway Historical Association tells us that in 1896, the company officially changed its name to Northern Pacific Railway: "The Northern Pacific went into bankruptcy in 1893 during the national financial crisis and emerged from it in 1896 with the help of J. P. Morgan and James J. Hill. Essentially . . . the new Northern Pacific Railway was created in 1896. The only thing that existed of the NPRR after that point was the paper records held at the NP's headquarters in St. Paul. The operating railroad was transferred to the new NP. Most people don't know about this name change, so even today you see the NP Railway referred to as the NP Railroad." Gary Tarbox, NPRHA, Kirkland, Washington, e-mail message to Lee Whittlesey, February 16, 2014.

11. "Montana Matters," Helena *Independent*, August 8, 1883, p. 7.

12. Haines, *Yellowstone Story*, I, p. 267, quoting Bozeman *Avant Courier*, October 19, 1882; May 17, 1883; and May 24, 1883. See also Babcock, *History of the Yellowstone Valley*, pp. 161–163; and Bill and Doris Whithorn, *Sixty Miles of Photo History, Upper Yellowstone Valley* (Livingston: *Livingston Enterprise*, no date [1965]), p. [34]. For a discussion of the complexity of Robert Cutler's blocking of NPRR's rails when coupled with the Gardiner townsite dispute, see the notes in chapter 10.

13. "Local Layout" [Cutler case to be heard], *Livingston Enterprise*, July 2, 1883, p. 3; "Court Business" [McCartney fails to appear against Cutler in court so case dismissed], *Livingston Enterprise*, July 4, 1883, p. 1; "Local Layout" [arrangements could not be made], *Livingston Enterprise*, August 20, 1883, p. 3.

14. "N.P. Celebrated Completion of Line in 1883," *Livingston Enterprise*, June 20, 1933; Haines, *Yellowstone Story*, I, 1977, p. 290; Richard A. Bartlett, *Yellowstone: A Wilderness Besieged* (Tucson: University of Arizona Press), 1985, p. 44; Margaret Andrews Cruikshank, "My Trip to Yellowstone Park in 1883," unpublished manuscript, YNP Library, August 30 entry. For two more accounts wherein visitors disembarked from the train at points north of Cinnabar prior to September 1, 1883, see Jules LeClercq (Janet Chapple and Suzanne Cane, eds.), *The Land of Wonders: Promenade in North America's National Park* (Lincoln: University of Nebraska Press, 2013), pp. 42–43; and E. G. D. [Elbridge Gerry Dunnell], "In the National Park," *New York Times*, September 10, 1883, p. 2.

15. "The Last Blast," *Anaconda* (MT) *Standard*, August 11, 1883, p. 7, which reprints "Local Layout," *Livingston Enterprise*, August 8, 1883, p. 3. For Mulherin Creek, see Lee H. Whittlesey, *Yellowstone Place Names* (Gardiner: Wonderland Publishing Company, 2006), p. 184.

16. Aubrey L. Haines, "The Park Branch Line: Doorway to Yellowstone," mimeographed manuscript, YNP Library, 1963, pp. 9–10, which utilizes information from "Local Layout," *Livingston Enterprise*, September 3, 1883, p. 3; and "The First Train on the Park Branch," *Livingston Enterprise*, September 4, 1883, p. 1. A recent treatment of President Arthur's trip is Frank H. Goodyear III, *A President in Yellowstone: The F. Jay Haynes Photographic Album of Chester Arthur's 1883 Expedition* (Norman: University of Oklahoma Press, 2013), especially p. 30.

17. Hoppe in McPherren, *Imprints*, pp. 196–197.

18. "Local Layout," *Livingston Enterprise*, September 3, 1883, p. 3.

19. *Livingston Enterprise*, September 3, 1883, p. 2, quoted in Haines, *Yellowstone Story*, I, 1977, p. 290.

20. "Montana Matters" [Cinnabar may not be the railroad terminal], *Helena* (MT) *Independent*, September 19, 1883, p. 7; "Rails Taken Up" [after being mistakenly extended toward Gardiner], *Livingston Enterprise*, January 10, 1885; "Gardiner," in [E. C. Henry], *Livingston Enterprise Souvenir Park County* (Livingston: Enterprise Publishing Company, reprinted 1976), p. 57. E. C. Henry's name as author and a discussion of the upcoming *Enterprise*'s "Souvenir Edition" is in the newspaper for June 24, 1899, p. 4, and this souvenir edition originally went on sale March 17, 1900. For the "sacrosanct" quote, I am indebted to master historian Aubrey L. Haines, who said those very words to me when he told me Buckskin Jim's story at the Cinnabar site on one specific day in 1996.

21. Bartlett, *Wilderness Besieged*, p. 234, says the tracks reached Gardiner in June 1902, and both the *Wonderland* and the *Enterprise* back that up. It is apparent that the rails laid between Cinnabar and Gardiner were a rough, tempo-

rary measure, for even though passengers were first brought to Gardiner in July of 1902, freight was not carried there until 1903, and even in April of 1903, President Theodore Roosevelt's train remained at Cinnabar because the "newly laid track to Gardiner was not ready for use," hence the discrepancies in the NPRR's arrival dates in various accounts. Haines, *Yellowstone Story*, II, p. 230.

22. The Gardiner newspaper editor noted in 1902 that Cinnabar's growth, like that of Gardiner, "has been retarded to a large extent by the uncertainty of railroad extension. Many who desired to build hesitated for fear the road would extend and carry with it the business that naturally would follow the terminus. In this way only such lines as were absolutely sure of a highly lucrative business have ever engaged in business here." "Our Towns and What They Are," *Gardiner* (MT) *Wonderland*, vol. 1 #1, May 17, 1902, p. 1.

3. DREAMS OF STRIKING IT RICH

1. Hoppe in McPherren, *Imprints*, pp. 17–20, 83. There is a conflict as to Hugo Hoppe's year of birth. Three of Hoppe's obituaries (*Livingston Enterprise*, September 14, 1895, p. 4; *Livingston* (MT) *Herald*, September 19, 1895, p. 3; and *Livingston Post*, September 18, 1895, p. 3) state that he was born in 1835. The *Post* additionally states that he was "age 60 last February," giving the impression that the reporter spoke to someone in the family who stated that to them. Moreover, Hugo Hoppe's brief biography related to a political convention and published in *Northwest Magazine* (vol. 12, March 1894, p. 16) gives Hoppe's birth year as 1835, and that writer probably talked to Hoppe. However, Hoppe's tombstone at Livingston, Montana, gives his date of birth as "February 4, 1836," and the census of 1870, taken at Bozeman on July 15, listed his age then as thirty-four, with his birthday having passed (thus claiming that his birth year was 1836). Finally, the census of 1880, taken at Glendale on June 10, listed his age then as forty-five, with his birthday having passed. This author therefore sides with the three obituaries plus the census of 1880 and *Northwest Magazine* and chooses 1835 as Hoppe's most likely year of birth.

2. Genealogical information on Hugo Hoppe is from Ida McPherren as well as from Robert Moore, Portland, Oregon (conversation July 6, 2001), and now of Livingston, Montana (numerous conversations in 2013). Moore's wife, Darnell Jean Hoppe Wills, is a descendant of Hugo Hoppe (her mother was Jean Elrose Hoppe, who is Wayne Hoppe's sister and Hugo Hoppe's great-great-granddaughter). Moore is compiling family genealogy and took his information from a nineteenth-century Hoppe Bible and other family sources. The *Enterprise* and *Post* obituaries say that Hugo Hoppe emigrated at age nine, first to Bellville, Illinois, but McPherren's book makes that date later and does not mention Illi-

nois. Hugo Hoppe's self-attested voter registration on August 21, 1889, at Gardiner-Horr stated that he was born in Dresden, Saxony, Germany. "Official [Voters'] Register, 1889–1896, Gardiner-Horr," Yellowstone Gateway Museum, Livingston, Montana. An article published in 1958 with family help claims that Hugo Hoppe was "scion of the proud German house of Hans Carl Leopold von der Gabelenz," that the family was banished from Germany for opposing Prussian militarism, and that they thus met in St. Louis, where they decided "for security reasons" to take the mother's maiden name of "Hoppe" (probably "Hoppy" at that time). See Marjorie C. Matross, "Time Erases All Traces of Early Day Montana Town near Yellowstone Park," *Billings* (MT) *Gazette*, September 7, 1958, second section, pp. 1, 11.

3. Hoppe served in Company A of the Second California Cavalry, enlisting in May of 1861 and mustering out in June of 1863. See "A Souvenir of the [G.A.R.] Encampment," *Livingston Enterprise*, April 19, 1890, p. 1; and Hugo Hoppe, military records at ancestry.com.

4. Hoppe's marriage to Mary James is in McPherren, *Imprints*, p. 112, and its location is given as Salt Lake City in her obituary in *Livingston Herald*, November 7, 1894, p. 3. McPherren gives the German name that Hugo Hoppe preferred (Hugo von der Gabelenz) on p. 89. I am indebted to Doris Whithorn for the "turbulent" quote, which she used for Buckskin Jim Cutler in her *Sixty Miles of Photo History*, p. 34. See also Bob Moore, "Buffalo Bill's Cinnabar Cowboys," *Montana Pioneer* (Livingston, MT), March 2008, pp. 12, 15, 17.

5. Ida McPherren, *Imprints on Pioneer Trails* (Boston: Christopher Publishing House, 1950), p. 207. This book recorded so much western history in which Hugo Hoppe actually participated that Merrill Mattes, one of the great historians of the Oregon Trail, cited it in his large tome *The Great Platte River Road*, referring to it parenthetically as "Adventures of Hugo Hoppe." Recently, historian James McLaird has cited it in his authoritative study, *Calamity Jane: The Woman and the Legend* (Norman: University of Oklahoma Press, 2005, pp. 144, 317n1). Because Ida McPherren used Albert Hoppe's manuscript about his father's life plus Hugo Hoppe's original memorandum book and her own experiences of growing up in the area, her book is important even though it is at times rambling, disjointed, and disorganized. She inserted into it stories by people other than Hugo Hoppe, so readers must watch carefully for those transitions. And we must corroborate facts and dates where possible with other sources. Those things aside, it is this historian's opinion that she did well with dates in many cases and gave us hundreds of valuable details that we otherwise would not have. Ida Geneva Miller McPherren (February 9, 1885–September 30, 1953) was born in St. Louis and came to Cinnabar, Montana, with her mother in 1894 when she was nine. Although her tombstone in Sheridan, Wyoming, seems to be dated one year too early for her birth, several census records agree with the age she

gave in her book (age nine in June of 1894), and all together those point to her birth year as 1885. As noted in the *Livingston Enterprise* and her book (p. 315), she graduated from Livingston High School on June 5, 1905, as valedictorian. By 1910, she had married the sheriff of Sheridan—William Shaw McPherren (1877–1921). When he was killed at forty-four in the line of duty, she raised their two children, Bud and Elizabeth; completed college; and spent much of the next thirty-two years reading and writing family and western history, producing five other books that can be found today on the Internet. See Ida McPherren in "Find a Grave Memorial," number 52922616, Sheridan, Wyoming, accessed February 19, 2013; and "Sheriff [McPherren] Killed in Battle with Moonshine Gang," *Anaconda* (MT) *Standard*, October 9, 1921, p. 1.

6. Hoppe in McPherren, *Imprints*, pp. 86, 115, 123. The date of the Plummer hanging is confirmed in Frederick Allen, *A Decent Orderly Lynching: The Montana Vigilantes* (Norman: University of Oklahoma Press, 2004), pp. 226–228; and some of the territorial setting is given in Ken Robison, *Montana Territory and the Civil War* (Charleston and London: The History Press, 2013). Carrie Adell Strahorn heard the story about Plummer having killed people before he came to Montana from California, per her book *Fifteen Thousand Miles by Stage* (New York: G. P. Putnam's Sons, 1911), p. 103. "Calamity Jane" Canary and her siblings were reported at Virginia City in "Provision for the Destitute Poor," *Montana Post* (Virginia City), December 31, 1864, p. 2; and in McPherren, *Imprints*, pp. 131–132.

7. George H. Wright, "The Candidates" [endorsing Hugo Hoppe for commissioner], *Livingston Enterprise*, November 3, 1888, p. 2. Population statistics are from the US Census Bureau as quoted in Wikipedia, "Montana—Historical Populations"; and from Michael P. Malone et al., *Montana: A History of Two Centuries* (Seattle: University of Washington Press, 1991), p. 68. These figures compare favorably with "Population of the Territories—Montana Still Ahead," Bozeman *Avant Courier*, February 10, 1881, p. 2. The woman's skeleton was in "Territorial News," *Livingston Enterprise*, July 30, 1883, p. 1; while the skull at Dillon was mentioned in "Montana News," *Livingston Enterprise*, April 14, 1900, p. 7.

8. McPherren, *Imprints*, p. 123, claimed Walter's birth was at Helena, but primary sources put it in Virginia City. Many of Hugo's Virginia City adventures listed above were restated in his son Walter's obituary in 1940—"Walter Hoppe Passes in City," *Park County* (MT) *News*, May 9, 1940, p. 1—which also stated that Walter was born in Virginia City. An obituary published at Helena—"First White Child Born in Montana Is Dead at Age of 75," *Helena Daily Independent*, May 4, 1940—agrees with Virginia City. More important, Walter himself stated in his self-attested voter registration on August 21, 1889, at Gardiner-Horr that he was born at Virginia City. Walter's mother was Mary Jane Gee James/Hoppe

(born November 15, 1836; died October 30, 1894), and his sister, Maggie, was Margaret Ann James Hoppe/Williams/Holem (1857–1918). Militating in favor of Walter Hoppe having indeed been the "first white child" born in Montana was the fact that before 1887, the US Military Academy offered him a spot in that school, ostensibly to reward him for having been so born, and the fact that the statement ("first white child") appeared in Babcock's *History of the Yellowstone Valley* (pp. 587–588) in 1907. The military academy offering was also mentioned in "Local Layout," *Livingston Enterprise*, May 14, 1887, p. 3; and in Matross, "Time Erases All Traces," as cited. McPherren, *Imprints*, p. 18, tells us that Hugo and Mary named their first son Walter for Hugo's nephew, a Captain Walter Hoppe, who was killed during the Civil War and memorialized at St. Louis.

9. Items, "Letter from Blackfoot," *Montana Post*, July 14, 1866, p. 3. The name "Hugo Hoppy" also appeared in "List of Letters," *Montana Post*, September 17, 1864, p. 3; and again in July 15, 1865, p. 2.

10. Faust, "Letter from Blackfoot," *Montana Post*, July 7, 1866, p. 2.

11. "Hugo and Mary Jane Hoppe," in Doris Whithorn, ed., *History of Park County, Montana 1984* (Dallas: Taylor Publishing Company, 1984), p. 255. Several other generations of Hoppes are also biographed in Whithorn's book.

12. R[obert] N. S[utherlin], "Cataract, Canyon, and Geyser—Wonderland with Its Busy, Dusty Multitude of Pleasure Seekers," *Rocky Mountain Husbandman* (White Sulphur Springs, MT), November 7, 1889.

13. An obituary—"Hugo B. Hoppe Passes Away at Emigrant," *Livingston Enterprise*, October 20, 1931, p. 8—stated that son Hughie was born at Fort Benton, but Hugh B. Hoppe's self-attested voting registration for August 24, 1889, at Gardiner-Horr disagreed with Fort Benton and stated that he was born in Blackfoot, Montana. "Official [Voters'] Register, 1889–1896, Gardiner-Horr," Yellowstone Gateway Museum. My thanks go to Paul Shea at Yellowstone Gateway Museum for leading me to these crucial voting records, cited throughout this book.

14. The steamboating men had tried unsuccessfully for years to coax their boats to reach that ultimate point on the Missouri—3,560 river miles from the ocean—but it did not technically happen until 1860, although the *Chippewa* reached a point fifteen miles downstream from Fort Benton on July 17, 1859. See Hiram Martin Chittenden, *History of Early Steamboat Navigation on the Missouri River: Life and Adventures of Joseph La Barge* (New York: Francis P. Harper, 1903), vol. 1, pp. 219–220; and John G. Lepley, *Packets to Paradise: Steamboating to Fort Benton* (Missoula: Pictorial Histories Publishing Company, 2001), p. 20. For complete context on Missouri River steamboating, see William E. Lass, *Navigating the Missouri: Steamboating on Nature's Highway, 1819-1935* (Norman: University of Oklahoma Press, 2009), especially p. 225.

15. Dunraven, *Great Divide*, 1967, p. 11.

16. Hoppe in McPherren, *Imprints*, pp. 124–126, 128, 133, 138–140. George Hoppe's middle name was apparently given either from Lincoln Gulch in Helena where his parents lived or else for the martyred President Lincoln. The Springfield Hotel story is in "The Fourth at Lincoln," *Helena Weekly Herald*, July 15, 1869, p. 7, which stated: "Let me recommend the Springfield Hotel, kept by Hugh Hoppy, as genial and obliging a landlord as there is in the country, and who affords the best of fare and sleeping accommodations possible to the traveling public." The place of George Hoppe's birth is noted in "George L. Hoppe," *Livingston Enterprise Souvenir Edition*, 1976, p. 57. Hugo and Mary's infant daughter's death is in "From the *Independent* of the 7th," *Helena Weekly Herald*, August 12, 1869, p. 8. The Utah and Northern Railroad story is in Merrill D. Beal, *The Utah and Northern Railroad: Narrow Gauge* (Pocatello: Idaho State University Press, 1980); and in Robert Athearn, "Railroad to a Far-off Country," *Montana the Magazine of Western History*, 18 #4 (Fall, 1968): 2–23. According to Bob Moore, family lore has it that with regard to the beer business, Hugo Hoppe often had difficulty carrying heavy beer kegs on his horse-drawn wagons, even with some experience in freighting.

17. Hoppe in McPherren, *Imprints*, p. 142; US Census of 1870 for Bozeman, Montana, taken on July 15, 1870, at ancestry.com. This census showed that Hugh and Mary Jane "Hoppy" had five children at that time: Margaret (twelve), Walter (five), Hugh (four), George (one), and Leander Black Hoppe, whose age was shown as "3/12" or more likely "5/12." Leander's 1942 obituaries, cited later in this book, incorrectly gave his age as seventy-three at death and one even wrongly stated that he was born in 1869, but the 1870 census record clearly makes his birth year to have been 1870. It is likely that Hugo and Mary Hoppe named their new son for the 1869 Indian agent at Fort Parker—Leander M. Black (1830–1881)—who shortly afterward became a prominent Bozeman businessman. Called "one of the wealthiest and most flamboyant men in all of Montana Territory," Leander Black founded Bozeman's First National Bank in 1872 and established the *Bozeman Times* newspaper in 1874. He bought the Northern Pacific Hotel in Bozeman that Hugo and Mary Hoppe eventually managed, and it is likely that Black was a family friend whom Hugo Hoppe met at Fort Parker. See Phyllis Smith, *Bozeman and the Gallatin Valley: A History* (Helena: Two Dot Books, 1996), pp. 90, 132, 137; and "Col. Black Built First Bank, Developed Early Bozeman," *Bozeman Daily Chronicle*, February 27, 2011, accessed at http://www.bozemandailychronicle.com/100/newsmakers/article_09edc572-4202-11e0-9fc8-001cc4c002e0.html. Family members claim that Leander Hoppe was named for a "Dr. Black" who delivered him, but if that is the case this Dr. Black either lived outside of Bozeman that year or else moved away almost as soon as he delivered Leander, because *no* Dr. Black appeared in the US Census

taken at Bozeman on June 1, 1870. Nor does this alleged (other) Leander Black appear in ancestry.com as a Bozeman resident.

18. Hoppe in McPherren, *Imprints*, pp. 142–143. Land records from the 1870s make it clear that Hoppe owned several homes at Bozeman and near what became Livingston. See for example Gallatin County land records, Vol. I, pp. 490, 738; vol. K, p. 24, Bozeman, Montana; and the mentions of his activities in "Death of Hugo J. Hoppe," *Livingston Enterprise*, September 14, 1895, p. 4; and "Death of H.J. Hoppe," *Livingston Post*, September 18, 1895, p. 3. "Bozeman Chief" is in "Silver Bow," *New North-West* (Deer Lodge, MT), June 17, 1870, p. 3. "Hoppy's saloon" in Bozeman in late 1871 was mentioned in Bozeman *Avant Courier*, October 26, 1871, p. 3.

19. Hoppe in McPherren, *Imprints*, p. 144; Hugo Hoppe obituaries, previously cited from *Post* and *Enterprise*. For Benson's Landing as the first settlement in Park County and place of "disfavor," see Mark H. Brown, *The Plainsmen of the Yellowstone* (Lincoln: University of Nebraska Press, 1969), pp. 336, 432–433. Per the USGS Atlas, Livingston Folio, Livingston Sheet, 1894, Benson's Landing was located about three miles east of present-day Livingston, behind what is now the Calvary Cemetery on the Old Clyde Park Road. My thanks go to Paul Shea, curator at today's Yellowstone Gateway Museum of Livingston, for this information.

20. Hoppe in McPherren, *Imprints*, pp. 145–171. For other summaries of this trip, see Addison Quivey, "The Yellowstone Expedition of 1874," *Contributions to the Historical Society of Montana*, vol. 1, 1876, pp. 268–284; Bozeman *Avant Courier*, January 24, 1874; and "The Yellowstone Expedition," *Daily Independent* (Helena, MT), May 10, 1874, p. 3.

21. Merrill G. Burlingame and Mark H. Brown, both quoted in Don L. Weibert, *The 1874 Invasion of Montana: A Prelude to the Custer Disaster* (Billings: Benchmark Printers, 1993), p. 134. Weibert's book adds to the case suggested by Burlingame and Brown that the expedition resulted indirectly (Weibert thinks *directly*) in the Custer debacle two years later because it stirred up the Sioux. Fascinatingly, Weibert included (p. 108) a photograph by Henry Bird Calfee that depicts a man at forefront right who strikingly resembles Hugo Hoppe, even though Calfee did not have his camera with him on that 1874 trip. Calfee apparently took the photo at a different time. Unfortunately, Weibert did not tell us where the original photo was housed, and a search of numerous repositories has failed to locate it. Thus the image can for now be seen only in Weibert's book.

22. The official report of the expedition is J. V. Bogert, "Yellowstone Expedition—Final Report," Bozeman *Avant Courier*, May 15, 1874, pp. 2–3. Hoppe's prized scalp is in his own report of the affair (H. J. Hoppy, "Down the Yellowstone—Reconnaissance in Eastern Montana," *Helena Weekly Herald*, May 14, 1874, p. 3); and also in James S. Hutchins, "Poison in the Pemmican: The

Yellowstone Wagon-Road and Prospecting Expedition of 1874," *Montana the Magazine of Western History*, 8 #3 (July 1958), p. 22. Hoppe's carving at Pompey's Pillar is in Weibert, *The 1874 Invasion*, p. 21. See also Carroll Van West, *Capitalism on the Frontier: Billings and the Yellowstone Valley in the Nineteenth Century* (Lincoln: University of Nebraska, 1993), pp. 35, 40; E. S. Topping (Robert A. Murray, ed.), *Chronicles of the Yellowstone: An Accurate Comprehensive History of the Country Drained by the Yellowstone River* (Minneapolis: Ross and Haines, 1968), pp. 104–122; and Weibert, *The 1874 Invasion*, pp. 86, 136–137. For Benson's Landing generally, see Thomas LeForge, *Memoirs of a White Crow Indian* (Lincoln: University of Nebraska Press, 1974), pp. 41–42; and Van West, *Capitalism*, pp. 34–40.

23. Author's e-mail communication from Bob Moore, Livingston, Montana, June 27, 2013. The steamboat is also mentioned in Weibert, *The 1874 Invasion*, p. 126 and endnote 5. So far nothing else has been found about this boat, which may have been somehow connected to Hoppe's friend Paul McCormick, who was a celebrated steamboat pilot on the Yellowstone River and much discussed in issues of *Bozeman Times* in early 1875.

24. H. J. Hoppy, "Down the Yellowstone," as cited.

25. For his attempt to recover the bodies of his comrades fifteen years later, see H. J. Hoppe, "A Move in the Right Direction," *Livingston Enterprise*, March 30, 1889, p. 1.

26. Earl of Dunraven, *The Great Divide*, 1967, p. 11.

27. Topping, *Chronicles of the Yellowstone*, pp. 124–125. Topping's book was published serially in the *Bozeman Weekly Chronicle* during the spring and summer of 1883 before being published independently in St. Paul that same year.

28. "Killed by Indians," Helena *Daily Independent*, July 30, 1874, p. 3.

29. "Postmasters in Park County" in Whithorn, ed., *History of Park County, Montana 1984*, p. 46. "Personal Items," in *Bozeman Times*, February 9, 1875, p. 2, stated that H. J. Hoppy, postmaster at "Benson's Crossing," "has received his commission."

30. "Territorial News" [quoting Bozeman *Courier* of July 31], Helena *Daily Independent*, August 1, 1874, p. 3; Hoppe in McPherren, *Imprints*, p. 171; James Wright quoted in Brown, *Plainsmen of the Yellowstone*, p. 432.

31. Hoppe in McPherren, *Imprints*, pp. 175–176, 186. So far, we do not have Bob's last name, although we know a little more about Hi Jehnsen. Historian Doris Whithorn has mentioned that Jehnsen's name was originally given to present-day Spring Creek at Horr, the stream that once had coal flumes on it. Whithorn, *Photo History of Aldridge*, p. 5. McPherren (pp. 175–176, 208, 271) has stated that Jehnsen was killed in a wagon accident in 1896 near Cooke City. That was also the first year that the crude road from Horr to Aldridge was open, but Jehnsen's death did not appear in the *Livingston Enterprise* or the *Herald*.

She also gave us the likely reason that Jehnsen's name was given to the stream—namely because he was the person who ran freight back and forth from Cinnabar to Horr and Aldridge. The smelter at Cooke City—called the New Galena Smelting Works—did eventually get built, for US troops chasing the Nez Perce Indians encountered it in 1877. See Jerome A. Greene, *Nez Perce Summer 1877: The U.S. Army and the Nee-Me-Poo Crisis* (Helena: Montana Historical Society, 2000), p. 200.

32. Brown, *Plainsmen of the Yellowstone*, pp. 337, 434; Clyde McLemore, "Fort Pease: The First Attempted Settlement in Yellowstone Valley," *Montana the Magazine of Western History*, 2#1 (January 1952), p. 28. The Crow Agency on Mission Creek was called Fort Parker and was located on the north side of the river about ten miles east of present-day Livingston. Thomas LeForge, who lived there in the early 1870s, stated that it was located twelve miles downriver (east) from Benson's Landing. LeForge, *Memoirs*, pp. 41–42. For more on Fort Parker, see Marsha Fulton, "The World of Fort Parker," *Livingston* (MT) *Current*, vol. 7, February 7, 2012, pp. 6–11.

33. Van West, *Capitalism*, p. 40.

34. "The Yellowstone," Bozeman *Avant Courier*, May 28, 1875, p. 3.

35. "Bozeman Items," *Bozeman Times*, June 1, 1875, p. 2. For the complete context of (and quotations from) the history of animals in the Greater Yellowstone Area, see Paul Schullery and Lee Whittlesey, "Greater Yellowstone Mammals, 1796–1881: An Interdisciplinary Analysis of Historical Observations," manuscript and computer database, written for the National Park Service, 1992–2014, in possession of authors and awaiting publication.

36. Hugo and Mary's land sale to Bud Williams is H. J. and M. J. Hoppy to M. T. Williams, December 6, 1875, in Miscellaneous Records, Vol. 1, p. 738, river-front land that measured half mile on a side, for $4,000. Yankee Jim at Benson's Landing is in *Bozeman Times*, May 18, 1876, p. 3; and the best general work about him is Doris Whithorn, *Yankee Jim's National Park Toll Road and the Yellowstone Trail* (No place [Livingston]: No publisher [*Livingston Enterprise*], April 1989). That Bud and Maggie Williams were married by October 30, 1876, is attested to in their conveyance of land at Benson's to Edward Everett, at Park County Deed Records, vol. 2, p. 7.

37. Hoppe's conducting of citizens to Fort Pease is in McLemore, "Fort Pease," as cited, pp. 30–31. The newspaper's comment is "The Fort Pease Affair," *Bozeman Times*, January 27, 1876, p. 2; and "Territorial News—From the Bozeman Times," *Rocky Mountain Husbandman* (White Sulphur Springs, MT), February 3, 1876, p. 3. Mary Hoppe's running of the hotel in Bozeman is mentioned in *Bozeman Times*, January 20, 1876, p. 3; and the advertisement for the hotel on p. 2. See also "Compliments from Gen. Brisbin to H.J. Hoppy and

Citizens of Bozeman," *Bozeman Times*, March 23, 1876, p. 2. The ranch purchase was mentioned in "Quinn's Ranch," *Bozeman Times*, April 13, 1876, p. 2.

38. Helena *Daily Independent*, July 17, 1876, and *Bozeman Times*, July 20, 1876, both quoted in Rita McDonald, "The Tall Tales and Rumors," *Montana the Magazine of Western History*, 2#3 (July 1952), p. 46. The group photo of Hoppe's five sons, no date, circa 1877, is in the possession of Bob Moore of Livingston, and the author has a copy. Sale of the "Half-Way Ranch" is in "For Sale or Rent," *Bozeman Times*, March 29, 1877, p. 3.

39. Hoppe in McPherren, *Imprints*, pp. 177–178, 181, 186. Richard Dietrich is detailed on pp. 178–181. See also Greene, *Nez Perce Summer*, pp. 192–193.

40. Hoppe's swearing in at Miles City was reported in "Custer County Organized," Helena *Daily Independent*, July 7, 1877, p. 3, while his sudden trip to Hart Mountain (in Wyoming Territory just north of what became Cody, Wyoming) was in the same newspaper, July 13, 1878, p. 3. "Yellowstone Journal" in *Livingston Herald*, September 19, 1895, p. 3, says Hoppe "came to Miles City" as sheriff in late 1877. "Death of H.J. Hoppe," *Livingston Post*, September 18, 1895, p. 3, says he moved to Bozeman in 1879, following his stint as sheriff.

41. Moore, "Buffalo Bill's Cinnabar Cowboys," as cited. The *Butte* (MT) *Daily Miner*, September 7, 1879, p. 3, stated: "H.J. Hoppy returned from Glendale on Tuesday. He is quite indisposed and contemplates a trip to Mammoth Hot Springs for the benefit of his health." For the story of hot-spring bathing at Mammoth Hot Springs, see Lee H. Whittlesey, "'This Modern Saratoga of the Wilderness!': A History of Mammoth Hot Springs and the Village of Mammoth in Yellowstone National Park," unpublished manuscript written for the NPS, 2010–2014, p. 68, YNP Library.

42. "Local News," *Rocky Mountain Husbandman* (Diamond City, MT), October 2, 1879, p. 3, col. 3.

43. "Hoppe Settled with Him," *Livingston Enterprise*, February 17, 1900, p. 1, which appeared first as "Got His Money, Quick," in Bozeman *Avant Courier*, February 10, 1900, p. 1. This "gambling house" was probably a saloon, and it may have been the bar in the Northern Pacific Hotel. Details of Lt. Jerome's problems are in Barry C. Johnson, "Solved: The 'Mystery' of Lt. Lovell Jerome," *Montana the Magazine of Western History* 19 (October, 1969): 90–91. My thanks go to Kim Allen Scott of Montana State University for these last two citations.

44. His presence in Bozeman in 1880 was documented by Bozeman *Avant Courier*, April 22, 1880, p. 3 (Rev. Comfort at "Hoppy's") and in Glendale by the US Census, June 10, 1880, taken at Glendale (Beaverhead), Montana, p. 13, via ancestry.com. His exuberance in 1881 about the railroad is in McPherren, *Imprints*, p. 193. The Bozeman *Avant Courier*, August 4, 1881, p. 3, stated that "H.J. Hoppy" was operating a Glendale brewery, and *Butte Daily Miner*, August

30, 1881, p. 1, mentioned Hoppe and Petritz. For the Northern Pacific Hotel at Bozeman, see Mackintosh, "In its Day it was One of Montana's Best Known Inns," *Anaconda Standard*, December 16, 1900, p. 14. We also know of Hoppe's time spent in Glendale, Montana (thirty miles northwest of Dillon), because of his son George's brief biography published later, stating that he (George) lived when quite young at Glendale, during the period 1879–1882. "George L. Hoppe," in *Livingston Enterprise Souvenir Park County*, 1976 reprint, p. 57.

45. Hoppe and the Butte Brewery are in *Butte* (MT) *Daily Miner*, June 4 (p. 4), July 23, and others from the summer of 1882.

46. "The Bozeman Homicide," *Butte Daily Miner*, March 6, 1883, p. 3. See also, "Local News," *Butte Daily Miner*, June 26, 1883, p. 4; "Montana Matters," *River Press* (Ft. Benton, MT), March 7, 1883, p. 4; and "From Bozeman—A Bar-Room Killing and $10,000 Grab," *New North-West* (Deer Lodge, MT), March 2, 1883, p. 3.

47. "Pistol Practice—Fight About a Faro Bet Results Fatally," Bozeman *Avant Courier*, March 1, 1883, p. 3. The *Billings Herald* for March 1, 1883, carried this same story, which ended as follows: "Walters [came to] Montana from the Black Hills [and has] been in towns along the line of [the] Northern Pacific from Fargo [to] here. He [is said by] those who knew him to have [been] peaceably disposed. Hoppy is well [known in] Montana. He has been in bus[iness at] Glendale and Butte, although [he calls] this place his home. He has a [wife] here for whom sympathy is felt [as she is] distressed."

48. "Court Chronicles" [charged with manslaughter], *Bozeman Weekly Chronicle*, June 13, 1883, p. 3. "Court Chronicles" in the issue of June 20 (p. 3) stated that Hoppe was being held on $5,000 bond to appear "next term of court."

49. "Local Miscellany" [Hoppe has been at Cinnabar for *the past few months*, emphasis added], Bozeman *Avant Courier*, October 4, 1883, p. 3.

50. Author's various conversations with Bob Moore, 2013. "District Court," *Livingston Enterprise*, October 19, 1883, p. 2, stated that "Hugh Hoppy" was being held in the county jail at Bozeman ahead of upcoming court appearances.

51. "The City Chronicled," *Bozeman Weekly Chronicle*, November 7, 1883, p. 3, stated that "Nolle Prosequi was entered in the case of Territory v. Hugh J. Hoppe." The literal translation of this Latin phrase is "to be unwilling to prosecute." See also "Territorial Items [Nolle Prosequi]," *New North-West* (Deer Lodge, MT), Nov 23, 1883, p. 2.

52. "Local Matters," *Butte Daily Miner*, October 7, 1883, p. 4. Quoting *Billings Herald* for November 10, 1883, David Scott Dick et al., "Cinnabar Archeology," pp. 17–19, agrees that charges against Hoppe were dropped in early November but also states that Hoppe was incarcerated for many months through the summer. If that was so, it occurred at Bozeman, for Hoppe was not at Montana Territorial Prison. His name does not appear in the records there for 1883. See

Montana State Prison Records, State Microfilm 36, 1871–1885, at Montana Historical Society, Helena, Montana; and my thanks go to archivist Molly Krucken-
berg for checking these records.

53. "Gold Galore—New Finds in the Vicinity of Gardiner Cause Lively Prospecting—New Coal Beds Also Discovered," *Bozeman Weekly Chronicle*, October 17, 1883, p. 1.

4. "WHAT A BONANZA FOR A FREIGHTER!"

1. Hoppe in McPherren, *Imprints*, pp. 186, 193. Although Hoppe through
McPherren stated that he purchased James Henderson's ranch in 1881, he apparently misremembered the year, for land records show it as 1882 and 1883. See
Gallatin County Land Records, vol. 3, p. 385, May 6, 1882; Miscellaneous
Records, vol. 1, p. 513, August 4, 1883; and deed book, vol. 1, p. 20, March 7,
1883. Hoppe located Wilson Springs as being in the northeast quarter of Section
20, T9S, R8E, which places it near the head of Spring Creek (the first stream
west of Stephens Creek) and just above the present National Park Service horse
barns in today's Stephens Creek developed area (for more, see Whittlesey, *Yellowstone Place Names*, 2006, pp. 236, 264). Through time, Hoppe added and
subtracted lands to and from his ranch, such as in June of 1885 when he purchased three more pieces from Matthias Mounts and wife (vol. 8, p. 102, June
30, 1885), the same lands that he had sold to Mounts in late 1883 (Hoppe to
Mounts and wife, recorded at vol. 8, p. 19, December 31, 1883). Apparently
there was a problem of some kind with the 1885 conveyance, because in late
1885 the US government conveyed to Hoppe these same three pieces (recorded
at Misc. 2, p. 275, December 29, 1885), probably to remove all questions about a
"cloud on the title." A mystery so far is for whom Hoppe named Wilson Springs.

At that time, Hoppe's land was outside of Yellowstone National Park. The
1880 census, shown at ancestry.com, makes it clear that he had five sons in the
spring of 1880, and (calculating the birthdays that had passed by that time) they
were Walter M. Hoppe (fifteen), Hugo B. Hoppe (fourteen), George L. Hoppe
(eleven), Leander B. Hoppe (ten), and Albert V. Hoppe (eight). See also "Death
of H.J. Hoppe," *Livingston Post*, September 18, 1895, p. 3; "Death of Hugo J.
Hoppe," *Livingston Enterprise*, September 14, 1895, p. 4; and "Walter Hoppe
Dies," *Livingston Enterprise*, May 4, 1940.

2. H. J. Hoppe, declaration of water rights on Stephens Creek, five hundred
inches, October 12, 1885, recorded at volume 1, p. 175. This recordation was
based on his "prior appropriation" of 1883 that used his ditch, which tapped the
stream on its north bank at a point three-quarters mile above its mouth, "my box
and [flood] gate being there established." For Wash Northrup (1847–1902), see

"Local Layout" [obituary], *Livingston Enterprise*, July 5, 1902, p. 2, which stated that "in 1883 he came to Cinnabar with . . . Hugo J. Hoppe."

   3. Beginning in 1864 with the *Montana Post* and in the 1870s with land
records, the spelling "Hoppy" appeared so often that one must believe Hugo
Hoppe was using that spelling himself at that time and wonders whether he
formally changed it later, perhaps to what he perceived was the original German.
The "Hoppy" spelling also appeared in the 1870 census record at Bozeman, so
the family must have told it as such to the census taker. The census of 1880 at
Glendale spelled the name "Hoppe." Family expert Bob Moore has acknowledged the possibility (even likelihood) that Hugo changed the spelling himself
from *Hoppy* to *Hoppe*, but says he does not know the answer for certain nor
when Hoppe did it.

   4. Area prospectors (probably George Huston) built the "Turkey Pen Cabin"
in the park apparently in 1867, and it was most famous for being the cabin to
which Truman C. Everts was taken for convalescence following his ordeal of
being lost in Yellowstone in 1870 (Haines, *Yellowstone Story*, I, pp. 132,
346n98). Hoppe's Turkey Pen Cabin coal claim was recorded in Gallatin County
land records, vol. 1, p. 34, March 14, 1884, and again at vol. 1, p. 69, February
16, 1885. In the first entry, Hoppe's partners in the venture were Morgan T.
Williams, Zadock H. Daniels, and George H. Budd, and Hoppe himself used the
existing cabin as a reference point. In the second entry, Hoppe again described
the property, but this time referred to the cabin as "the remains of an old log
cabin." This probably dates the destruction of the Turkey Pen Cabin as sometime
1884–1885. According to historian Aubrey Haines, this Turkey Pen Cabin was
located 1.8 miles east (and a little south) of the Roosevelt Arch. In a claim for
water rights on Turkey Pen Creek, Hoppe noted that his "prior appropriation" of
water was dated February 13, 1885, and that his ditch tapped Turkey Pen Creek
on its east bank at the mouth of "Turkey Pen Cañon." Gallatin County land
records, vol. 1, p. 68, February 16, 1885.

   5. Hoppe in McPherren, *Imprints*, pp. 193–194, 207. Family historian Bob
Moore says that Hoppe likely learned of the approaching railroad from his friend
Benjamin Potts. Author's conversation with Bob Moore of Livingston, Montana,
February 27, 2013. For Benson's Landing residents reacting to the coming rail-
road, see "Benson's Landing Town-Site," Bozeman *Avant Courier*, August 10,
1882, p. 2.

   6. For example, the *Bozeman Weekly Chronicle* reported ("The City Chronicled," June 20, 1883, p. 3) that H. J. Hoppe bought an elk calf from the Bannock
Indians and kept it in his front yard in Bozeman as a pet.

   7. "Pre-Emption Proof—Testimony of Claimant [Hugo J. Hoppe]," December 31, 1883, in Homestead Application No. 585, 4/137, October 25, 1883,
Gallatin County Land Records (copies also placed in Box L-21, YNP Archives);

Hoppe in McPherren, *Imprints*, p. 194. Hoppe probably knew Elias Joseph Keeney in Bozeman as early as 1877. Keeney appeared in "Personal," *Bozeman Times*, May 10, 1877, p. 3, and other newspaper snippets that year, and in his 1937 biography (cited later) he stated that he came to Montana in 1875. For a photo of Keeney in these early days, see Evalyn Batten Johnson, *Images of America: Virginia City* (Charleston: Arcadia Press, 2012), p. 27.

8. H. J. Hoppe to P. H. Conger, April 15, 1883 [Hoppe applies to run a dairy at mouth of Gardner River], in NA, RG 48, no. 62, roll 2 (hardcopy at YNP Library); Hoppe in McPherren, *Imprints*, pp. 193–196, 201; "The Next Yellowstone City" [Carroll Hobart will soon own Cinnabar], *Livingston Enterprise*, August 12, 1884, p. 3.

9. Haines, *Yellowstone Story*, I, p. 267. Keeney's declaration of his ranch is in Gallatin County land records, Misc. Records, vol. 1, p. 334, April 21, 1883. Copies of other land records for E. J. Keeney are in Box L-21, YNP Archives. These records show that Keeney recorded his homestead on October 6, 1883, having settled upon it in March of 1883, at the same time Hugo Hoppe was settling upon his. Keeney's place was located (immediately north of Hoppe's) as "Lot 2 and the SE4 of the NE4 of S17 and Lots 2 and 3 of S16, T9S, R8E." See also 20/110 and 26/439, Park County land records, Livingston, Montana. Keeney and Huston were partners in mining at Cooke City but also owned this Cinnabar ranch together, so they ran back and forth between the two places.

10. Hoppe in McPherren, *Imprints*, p. 201; "Cinnabar," with photos of Hugo J. Hoppe and Albert Hoppe in *Livingston Enterprise Souvenir Park County*, 1976 reprint, p. 57.

11. "Local Layout" [party of surveyors], *Livingston Enterprise*, August 17, 1883, p. 3; "Local Layout" [new town], *Livingston Enterprise*, August 20, 1883, p. 3; G. M. Von Rath, *Sitzungsberichte der Niederrheinischen Gesellschaft fur Natur-und Heilkunde* (Bonn: Max Cohen & Sohn [Fr.Cohen], 1886), p. 206. I am indebted to Dr. Judith Meyer of Missouri State University for translating portions of this booklet by Dr. Von Rath from its original German. For a surveyor whom Hobart treated shabbily, see "W.P. Lambdin," *Livingston Enterprise*, September 28, 1883, p. 2; and for another named Landon, see Haines, *Yellowstone Story*, I, p. 309. These two were probably the same man.

12. "Local Layout," *Livingston Enterprise*, December 28, 1883, p. 3.

13. Advertisement in *Livingston Enterprise*, January 4, 1884, and numerous other issues during the summer and fall of 1883.

14. Carroll T. Hobart to a reporter, undated and untitled newspaper clipping [probably winter or spring, 1883], in Hobart Papers, box 7, folder 62, Yale University Beinecke Library (microfilm copy given to YNP Library by this author and quoted in Whittlesey, "This Modern Saratoga," pp. 107–108); "The Trial of John H. Surratt," *Evening Star* (Washington, DC), June 21, 1867, p. 1;

"The Surratt Trial," *Dubuque* (IA) *Daily Herald*, June 20, 1867, p. 1; "Trial of Surratt," *Anglo American Times* (London, England), July 6, 1867, p. 13; "Personal" [Hobart resigns from superintendency of Minnesota Division of NPRR], *St. Albans* (VT) *Daily Messenger*, April 5, 1873, p. 5. Ancestry.com says that Hobart was born on October 14, 1837.

15. Said land was "lot number six" plus the west half of the southwest quarter of Section 16, T9S, R8E, per Gallatin County land records, Bozeman, Montana, Miscellaneous Records, vol. 2, p. 51, December 24, 1883. The United States had conveyed at least part of this land to Clarence Stephens in November of 1883 (Gallatin County Miscellaneous Records, vol. 2, p. 203, November 22, 1883), whereupon George Huston conveyed it to Hobart on the very same day. Huston to Hobart, November 22, 1883, Miscellaneous Records, vol. 6, p. 72. See also E. J. Keeney to Yellowstone National Park Improvement Co., November 22, 1883, vol. 6, p. 73. The description of Carroll Hobart is from F. B. P[limpton], "The Yellowstone—Western Associated Press Excursion," *Cincinnati* (OH) *Commercial Tribune*, August 19, 1883, p. 3.

16. Snippet in Bozeman *Weekly Avant Courier*, January 17, 1884, p. 4.

17. H. H. Hollidge and Carroll Hobart, "Plat of the Town of Cinnabar, Gallatin County, M.T.," in box 8, oversize broadside folder 86, Carroll Hobart Papers, Beinecke Library, Yale University. Hobart stated here: "Be it known that I, Carroll T. Hobart for the 'Yellowstone National Park Improvement Company,' proprietors of the 'Town of Cinnabar,' in said County and Territory, do hereby acknowledge and certify that I procured and caused to be made a survey of the Southwest quarter (SW¼) of Section Sixteen (16), Township Nine South (T9S), Range Eight East (R8E) to be platted as the 'Town of Cinnabar' of which the plan is a true plat for the purpose of record." C. T. Hobart, November 22, 1883. Interestingly, Hobart stated that he erected stone monuments at the northwest corner of block six, Main Street and Cinnabar Avenues, and also at the northwest corner of block 50. The Edward Dawson "spy" story is in Bartlett, *Wilderness Besieged*, pp. 159, 322n9.

18. What happened to Hobart and his YNPIC in 1883 has been told elsewhere (Whittlesey, "Oh, Mammoth Structure!" and Haines, *Yellowstone Story*, I, pp. 272–291). For their railroad scheme, see "The Yellowstone Park Railway," *Livingston Enterprise*, March 14, 1885, p. 3, which gives details of the failed "proposal by Rufus Hatch and C.T. Hobart to give the Cinnabar & Yellowstone Park Railway the right of way through the National Park to the Clarke's Fork mining country" and states that "Mr. Hobart was here [in Washington, DC] in person to explain the enterprise and get favorable action from congress."

19. "The Next Yellowstone City," *Livingston Enterprise*, August 12, 1884, p. 3. This text was later quoted in Babcock, *History of the Yellowstone Valley*, pp. 170–171, which also stated that a second survey of Cinnabar was made that

month by Sigmund Deutsch. No record of that plat is known to have survived, although it reportedly changed the direction of some of the town's streets.

20. McPherren, *Imprints*, pp. 175–176, 200.

21. "Bozeman Again Visited" [by fire], *Bozeman Weekly Chronicle*, December 10, 1884, p. 3; "Again the Fire Fiend," Bozeman *Avant Courier*, December 11, 1884, p. 3; "Destroyed by Fire," *River Press* (Ft. Benton, MT), December 17, 1884, p. 1. In reporting it later, other newspapers muddled the date of the fire. "Amalgam," *Butte Daily Miner*, December 27, 1884, p. 4, implied that it occurred on Tuesday, December 23, while "Neighborhood News," *New North-West* (Deer Lodge, MT), January 2, 1885, p. 3, indicated that it occurred on Tuesday, December 30.

22. For the cold weather, see "Local Miscellany," Bozeman *Avant Courier*, December 25, 1884, p. 3. Bud and Maggie Williams appeared in the US Census of 1880 at Bozeman as a married couple with Morgan listed as "farmer." Ancestry.com (Morgan T. and Margaret Williams). Photos of the Gee family taken later at Reese Creek school have been provided to the author by Bob Moore of Livingston. George H. and Mary Ann Gee were Mary Jane Gee Hoppe's parents, who were then living in Bozeman. For information on them, see Mary J. Hoppe to District Court, decree in the matter of Mary Ann Gee's estate, April 21, 1890, in Misc., vol. 4, p. 402, Gallatin County land records; and "Personal Points," *Livingston Enterprise*, March 22, 1890, p. 3.

23. New York Civil War Muster Roll, 1861–1865, p. 2825, and New York Report of Adjutant General, 1865 (for Morgan T. Williams, New York); Census of 1850, Aurora (Erie County), New York, p. 54 (Oliver H. and Menutable Williams and their five children including Morgan); US Census of 1880, Bozeman, Montana (Morgan T. and Margaret Williams), all accessed at ancestry.com, April 18, 2013. The "Official Register [of voters], 1889–1896, Gardiner-Horr [Montana]" at Yellowstone Gateway Museum has Morgan T. Williams's handwritten registration wherein on August 19, 1889, he stated that he was born in Hamburg, New York, and was forty-seven years old. The 1870 census at Bozeman showed Morgan T. Williams as "barkeeper."Ancestry.com (Morgan T. Williams found through James C. McCartney). For "Governor" Williams, see "Local Miscellany," Bozeman *Avant Courier*, December 25, 1884, p. 3. That Maggie and Bud were married by October 30, 1876, is apparent from Morgan T. Williams and Maggie Williams, conveyance of land at Benson's Landing to Edward Everett, recorded October 30, 1876, at Deed Records, vol. 2, p. 7, Park County Clerk's Office.

24. [G. L. Henderson], "Park Notes," *Livingston Enterprise*, January 10, 1885, p. 1; "Local Layout," *Livingston Enterprise*, February 14, 1885, p. 3. For Hoppe's hiring by Hobart and the hotel's new steam-heating system, see Whittlesey, "'This Modern Saratoga,'" 2010–2014, p. 193.

25. [G. L. Henderson], "Our Park Letter," *Livingston Enterprise*, January 17, 1885, p. 3; [G. L. Henderson], "Park Matters," *Livingston Enterprise*, March 28, 1885, p. 3.

26. "Local Layout," *Livingston Enterprise*, February 21, 1885, p. 3.

27. A note in the *Livingston Enterprise* ("Personal Points," February 21, 1885, p. 3) and several more mentions that winter by the newspaper made it clear that the editors were discussing W. T. Hall, not to be confused with W. A. Hall, who did not move to Cinnabar and Gardiner until 1890. A check of voting records confirms that these were two different men. W. T. Hall was from Kentucky and age forty-three when he registered to vote in Gardiner on October 13, 1896. W. A. Hall registered to vote in Cinnabar on October 9, 1894, and his registration showed that he was from Missouri and age thirty-three. See original Voting Registers at Yellowstone Gateway Museum of Park County, Livingston, Montana.

28. "That Horse," *Livingston Enterprise*, February 21, 1885, p. 3; "Coast and Interior—the National Park Stampede," *Daily Tribune* (Salt Lake City), March 4, 1885, p. 3. The *Enterprise* announced on January 31 that "the telephone line between Livingston and Gardiner will be in operation in a few days." "Local Layout," *Livingston Enterprise*, January 31, 1885, p. 3.

29. Secondary accounts of this Washington affair are in Haines, *Yellowstone Story*, I, pp. 315–317; Bartlett, *Wilderness Besieged*, pp. 243–244; Whittlesey, "This Modern Saratoga," pp. 191–192; and A. L. Haines, "Secure That Horse," *Yellowstone Interpreter* 2#3, May–June, 1964, pp. 29–32, YNP Library. This last item is the same as Aubrey L. Haines's "Tales from the Yellowstone," chapter 3, "Secure That Horse," unpublished 1994 manuscript in author's possession. Carpenter's friendly letters to Hobart about this affair and about their winter lobbying together are R. E. Carpenter to CTH, May 27, 1885; and July 19, 1885, both in box 2, folder 13, Carroll Hobart papers, Beinecke Library, Yale University, New Haven, CT.

30. "That Horse," *Livingston Enterprise*, February 21, 1885, p. 3.

31. Aubrey Haines stated (*Yellowstone Story*, I, p. 316; "Secure That Horse," p. 29) that this event occurred at "Hall's store" in Gardiner. This store owner was W. T. Hall, not to be confused with a later store owner named W. A. Hall. The "Local Layout" column (*Livingston Enterprise*, January 17, 1885, p. 3) printed the following: "R.A. Bell has disposed of his business at Gardiner to W.T. Hall who has long been connected with the store as a popular employee." The same column for February 21 (p. 3) stated that a new phone had just been installed at Gardiner in "R.A. Bell's store," for which the line ran south from the Western Union office at Livingston.

32. "National Park Legislation" [segregation bill passes the House], *Livingston Enterprise*, February 21, 1885, p. 3; Haines, *Yellowstone Story*, I, p. 316;

"That Horse," *Livingston Enterprise* as cited; "News from the Mountains," *Livingston Enterprise*, March 14, 1885, p. 2.

33. "The Park Bill" [segregation bill fails in the Senate], *Livingston Enterprise*, March 7, 1885, p. 3; "The Yellowstone Park Railway," *Livingston Enterprise*, March 14, 1885, p. 3.

34. "The Other Side of the Story," *Livingston Enterprise*, April 18, 1885, p. 3. In this article, Carpenter also denied being in contact "with anyone outside of Washington about the progress of the Vest [railroad] bill," thus denying contact with the "son" at Livingston.

35. "That Horse," *Livingston Enterprise* as cited; Haines, "Secure That Horse," as cited.

36. Steve Mishkin, lawyer and historian in Olympia, Washington, who is working on a long history of the law in Yellowstone during this period, found the ages of Carpenter's and Hobart's children in the US Census of 1880. Hobart's children were Carroll J. (or John Carroll), who died in May 1880, at the age of three, and James O. Hobart, born "around 1881," which would have made him about four years old in 1885. Robert Carpenter's first son, Cyrus Clay, was born on January 13, 1878, so he would have been only seven years old in early 1885. Steve Mishkin e-mail communication to Lee Whittlesey, February 27, 2013.

37. John N. Shoolbred to T. C. [*sic*] Hobart, January 10, 1885, in Carroll Hobart papers, box 2, folder 13, Yale Beinecke Library. My thanks go to researcher Tina Schlaile of Santa Rosa, California, for finding this letter and understanding its significance.

A little more is known about Shoolbred. He appears to have been an English "attorney in fact" who on May 23, 1883, signed Wills Company's Articles of Incorporation on behalf of owner Frank Wilcox, which articles were also signed by Duff F. Sherman and Phil S. Rountree. An 1883 newspaper article referred to him as "treasurer" of the Wills Company, and he also appeared in the 1891 England Census and the "England and Wales Death Index." A London newspaper article dated February 4, 1902, gave his death date as February 1, 1902, at the approximate age of eighty (probably seventy-nine). The 1891 census lists his middle initial as "H," while the Articles of Incorporation shows it as "L" and his own signature on the letter to Hobart in two places makes it appear to be "N." We use "N" here, because his signature seems the most reliable. My special thanks go to Steve Mishkin, who found all of the following documents. "An English Dude's Idea of Propriety," Helena *Independent*, October 28, 1883, quoting Bozeman *Courier*; Sherman, Rountree, Wilcox, and Shoolbred, "Certificate and Articles of Incorporation of the Wills Smelting and Mining Company," May 23, 1883, filed in the office of the Montana Secretary of State; *England Census*, 1891, p. 11, via ancestry.com; *England and Wales Free BMD Death Index, 1837-1915*, vol. 2a, p. 32, via ancestry.com; "Deaths" [John Shoolbred], *London*

Standard, February 4, 1902, p. 1. Additionally, there is a deed from John N. Shoolbred conveying a mining lode at Cooke City in Quartz Deeds, vol. 2, p. 314, recorded September 16, 1889.

38. "Local Layout" [townsite of Cinnabar for sale], *Livingston Enterprise*, January 31, 1885, p. 3.

39. Dabney Brothers, "Bill of Complaint," November 25, 1885, in D. H. Budlong and C. M. White, *Dabney, et al. vs. The Yellowstone National Park Improvement Company, a Corporation, George B. Hulme and Carroll T. Hobart*, filed in Wyoming State Archives, Uinta County Clerk of the District Court, Civil Case File 4-487, Cheyenne, Wyoming. My thanks go to Steve Mishkin for providing me with a copy of this document.

40. F. Jay Haynes, photo H-1573, "H.J. Hoppe's Ranch, Upper Yellowstone, Montana," October 8, 1885, at Montana Historical Society; "Park Affairs" [new syndicate takes over park company], *Livingston Enterprise*, October 31, 1885, p. 1; "Personal Points" [Hobart and wife leave on train], *Livingston Enterprise*, November 14, 1885, p. 3. As one might expect, Carroll Hobart gave Hugo Hoppe the go-ahead by November 7 to take over management of Mammoth Hotel in the event that YNPIC's affairs improved, but if that switch ever happened, it could not have lasted long because arrival of the new syndicate was imminent. "Notes from Mammoth Hot Springs," *Livingston Enterprise*, November 7, 1885, p. 3.

41. Dabney Brothers in Budlong and White, "Bill of Complaint," November 25, 1885, as cited; Diana Smith, finding aid to "Carroll T. Hobart Papers," February 2001, Yale Beinecke Library; Whittlesey, "'Oh, Mammoth Structure!': Rufus Hatch, the National Hotel, and the Grand Opening of Yellowstone in 1883," as cited, pp. 18–20.

42. CTH to "My dear Allie," December 27, 1885; H.J. Hoppe to NPRR, November 7, 1885, both in Hobart Papers, box 2, folder 15, Yale Beinecke Library. Hobart stated that he borrowed the money from Hoppe in CTH to Robert Harris, February 8, 1886, same file.

43. CTH to "My precious Allie," December 29, 1885, in Hobart Papers, box 2, folder 15, Yale Beinecke Library; Carroll Hobart, "Response," March 19, 1886, in Dabney Brothers/Budlong and White, as cited.

44. CTH to "my dear Allie, December 30, 1885, in Hobart Papers, box 2, folder 15, Yale Beinecke Library.

45. This advertisement ran continuously in the *Livingston Enterprise* from December 26, 1885, through June 12, 1886, sometimes on page one.

46. "Local Layout" [Hoppe is freighting to Cooke], *Livingston Enterprise*, February 6, 1886, p. 3.

47. CTH to Robert Harris, February 8, 1886; CTH to H.J. Hoppe, February 15, 1886, both in box 2, folder 15, Yale Beinecke Library.

48. "Territory vs. Hugh J. Hoppe" in "District Court" [grand jury indictment], *Livingston Enterprise*, April 3, 1886, p. 4; "Territory vs. E.J. Keeney" [verdict of guilty], in same story; "District Court" [twenty dollar fine for Keeney], *Livingston Enterprise*, April 10, 1886, p. 4; "Territory vs. H.J. Hoppe: assault, bond filed," in "District Court," *Livingston Enterprise*, April 17, 1886, p. 4; "Personal Points" [Hoppe "honorably acquitted"], *Livingston Enterprise*, April 17, 1886, p. 3. See also "District Court," *Bozeman Weekly Chronicle*, April 7, 1886, p. 2; and "Sentenced" [three hundred dollars], same paper, same issue, p. 3.

49. "Local Layout" [Hoppe ceases freighting], *Livingston Enterprise*, June 19, 1886, p. 3. See also the same column for June 12, wherein Hoppe's "lease of the [Keeney's] house" expired and E. J. Keeney "assumed proprietorship of the hotel and bar at Cinnabar."

50. "Local Layout" [Hoppe resumes freighting to Cooke and will build warehouse], *Livingston Enterprise*, July 24, 1886, p. 3; Hoppe's freighting advertisement for the "Cinnabar and Cooke Transportation and Forwarding Company" appeared in the issue of August 7, 1886, p. 3, which ran through autumn.

51. H.J. Hoppe to CTH, September 1, 1886, in box 2, folder 17, Yale Beinecke Library. The *Livingston Enterprise* carried Hoppe's freighting-only-and-no-hotel advertisements from August 7, 1886, through December 11, 1886, even though Keeney apparently gave the hotel back to Hoppe by September 1.

52. H.J. Hoppe to CTH, September 28, 1886; H.J. Hoppe to CTH, October 16, 1886, both in box 2, folder 17, Yale Beinecke Library.

53. "District Court," *Livingston Enterprise*, June 25, 1892, p. 1.

54. Hobart's 1898 venture is mentioned in Diana Smith, finding aid to "Carroll T. Hobart Papers," February 2001, Yale Beinecke Library. Hobart's letters at Yale after 1886 show his frustration at the NPRR and his South American venture. My thanks go to historian Steve Mishkin, who found an obituary, which is "C.T. Hobart Funeral Held at Lakewood [Cemetery, Minneapolis, MN]," *Minneapolis Morning Tribune*, November 23, 1915, p. 10.

55. H.J. Hoppe to CTH, September 1, 1886, in box 2, folder 17, Yale Beinecke Library. Hobart's failures have been discussed in Whittlesey, "Oh, Mammoth Structure!"; in Haines, *Yellowstone Story*, I, pp. 307–311; in Bartlett, *Wilderness Besieged*, pp. 148–151; and in Whittlesey, "This Modern Saratoga," pp. 143–150; 191–195.

5. FREIGHTING, FARMING, AND POLITICS

1. "Personal Points," *Livingston Enterprise*, December 11, 1886, p. 3.

2. Haines, *Yellowstone Story*, II, p. 6; G. L. Henderson, "Park Notes," *Livingston Enterprise*, February 5, 1887, p. 3; "Death from Exposure," "Buried

in a Snowslide," and "Local Layout" [old-timers say], all in *Livingston Enterprise*, January 15, 1887, p. 3.

3. "Local Layout" [J. H. Dean], *Livingston Enterprise*, March 5, 1887, p. 3.

4. "Personal Points" [goes to Livingston to purchase feed], *Livingston Enterprise*, February 12, 1887, p. 3; "Personal Points" [Hoppe spending time with legislature], *Livingston Enterprise*, February 26, 1887, p. 3; "Local Layout" [begins freighting for coal company], *Livingston Enterprise*, March 19, 1887, p. 3.

5. "Personal Points" [spring planting], *Livingston Enterprise*, April 30, 1887, p. 3; "Local Layout" [more teams needed], *Livingston Enterprise*, May 7, 1887, p. 3.

6. "Local Layout" [Walter Hoppe injured], *Livingston Enterprise*, May 14, 1887, p. 3; "Local Layout" [Walter Hoppe recovering], *Livingston Enterprise*, May 21, 1887, p. 3. The newspaper could not resist revealing the fact that the injured Walter Hoppe had been nominated to the US Military Academy a few years ago but had declined because he did not want the military life.

7. Acquisition of the saloon may have been the conveyance from Thomas Smith to H. J. Hoppe, January 3, 1887, in Park County Deed Records, vol. 9, p. 325. Regardless, the Hoppes' large property sale on September 23, 1887, included "one bar at Cinnabar station." "Hugo J. Hoppe et al. to Harry Gassert and Jacob Reding, Bill of Sale [for freighting outfit]," September 23, 1887, in Park County Clerk's Miscellaneous Records, vol. 1, p. 147, recorded and filed October 10, 1887.

8. "Local Layout" [Hoppe moves to Cinnabar for summer], *Livingston Enterprise*, June 18, 1887, p. 3.

9. "Personal Points," *Livingston Enterprise*, June 25, 1887, p. 3. W. M. Hoppe's advertisement, in *Livingston Enterprise*, July 2, 1887, p. 4, stated: "For sale—mules, horses, wagons, harness, and saddles." The park's correspondent noted later in July that "H.J. Hoppe is busy with his teams freighting into the Park, but in the line of freighting there is very little doing at present as compared with a year ago." [G. L. Henderson], "Our Park Visit," *Livingston Enterprise*, July 23, 1887, p. 3.

10. "United States to H.J. Hoppe" [per the Homestead Act], August 20, 1886, in Park County Clerk's Deed book, vol. 4, p. 311, recorded and filed September 29, 1890. It described the land as E2 of SE4 of Section 17; NE4 of NE4, S20; and NW4 of NW4 of S21, all in T9S, R8E. The vesting (ripening) of Hoppe's homestead was reported in "Real Estate and Mining Transfers," *Livingston Enterprise*, October 4, 1890, p. 1.

11. "Hugo J. Hoppe, Mary J. Hoppe, Walter M. Hoppe, and Hugh B. Hoppe to Harry Gassert and Jacob Reding, Warranty Deed," September 23, 1887, in Park County Clerk's Deed book, Vol. 1, p. 66, recorded and filed October 10, 1887; and "Gassert and Reding to Mary J. Hoppe, Bond for Deed," at Park

County Clerk's Miscellaneous Records, vol. 1, p. 148, recorded and filed October 10, 1887. This last instrument stated that Gassert and Reding were bound to the Hoppes for the sum of $5,742.15 and that the Hoppes would give them a warranty deed if they paid the entire amount by September 23, 1890. It appears that Gassert and Reding had the money for this land purchase because they had purchased the Morning Star mine at Cooke City from Joe Keeney in 1885 and, according to the newspaper, "struck it rich" there in 1887. "Local Layout," *Livingston Enterprise*, March 5, 1887, p. 3.

12. "Hugo J. Hoppe, et al. to Harry Gassert and Jacob Reding, Bill of Sale [for freighting outfit]," September 23, 1887, in Park County Clerk's Miscellaneous Records, vol. 1, p. 147, recorded and filed October 10, 1887. In this instrument, the Hoppes sold the following to Gassert and Reding and described them in detail: eleven mules, twelve horses, eighteen wagons, four sleighs, and "one bar [saloon] at Cinnabar station," otherwise known as "the entire Hoppe freighting outfit." The saloon seems to have been merely thrown into the mix because it certainly was not part of the Hoppe freighting outfit.

13. Gassert and Reding to Mary J. Hoppe et al., Lease," September 23, 1887, at Park County land records, Miscellaneous, vol. 1, p. 151, recorded and filed October 10, 1887. In this instrument, the Hoppes leased the ranch from Gassert and Reding for a period of three years at the cost of $689 per year as rent.

14. "Personal Points," *Livingston Enterprise*, November 12, 1887, p. 3.

15. Whithorn, *Photo History of Aldridge*, p. 5; Doris Whithorn, *Images of America: Paradise Valley on the Yellowstone* (Charleston: Arcadia Press, 2001), p. 29. The newspaper article that announced this was "Items from the Horr Coal Camp," *Livingston Enterprise*, April 14, 1888, p. 3. Acting Superintendent Moses Harris's complaint about Hoppe's sawmilling on Reese Creek was Harris to Department of Interior, December 29, 1887, in Letters Sent, vol. II, pp. 193, 196, YNP Archives. However, Captain Harris looked at dry firewood as a separate matter from building timber. In 1888, Harris—perhaps currying favor from the citizen who had so much influence at Cinnabar—decided to give Hugo Hoppe a permit to cut dead-and-down firewood from the park. Hoppe mentioned this in 1893 in a letter to Acting Superintendent George Anderson, wherein he stated that the written permit allowed him "to take whatever dry timber I wanted from the limits of the Park" and asked Anderson to "continue to accord me the privilege of getting my firewood from the park as I have always done here before." Hoppe to George Anderson, Archive Document 1036, January 14, 1893, YNP Archives. Hoppe wrote this letter on his business stationery, which was headed "H.J. Hoppe, Contractor and Freighter."

16. "Personal Points," *Livingston Enterprise*, May 12, 1888, p. 3. The same comment occurred again in "Personal Points" for June 2. Life expectancy in various periods of history is complex, but the calculation used here can be seen at

http://www.ancient-origins.net/news-evolution-human-origins/life-expectancy-
myth-and-why-many-ancient-humans-lived-long-077889. Regardless, many
Park County and other Montana obituaries that appeared in 1883–1903 in the
Livingston Enterprise make it clear that a good number of the subjects were sixty
to ninety years old, so as in any era, some people did manage to live long lives.

17. This context for the town of Gardiner, the land segregation bill, and
Hoppe's hope for his other homestead on Gardner River appeared in "Gardiner
Notes," *Livingston Enterprise*, May 12, 1888, p. 2.

18. "Republican County Convention," *Livingston Enterprise*, September 15,
1888, p. 3; "The Candidates," *Livingston Enterprise*, November 2, 1888, p. 2.

19. "Local Layout" [Keeney sells to French], *Livingston Enterprise*, December 8, 1888, p. 5.

20. "Synopsis of Proceedings" [of county commissioners], *Livingston Enterprise*, September 16, 1893, p. 1. A check of the Commissioners' Proceedings
record books at Park County reveals that Hoppe and his fellow commissioners
were generally paid from "Contingent Fees" and that the amounts varied depending upon how much work they did, how much work was needed, and the availability of tax revenues. Hoppe's pay seems to have been in at least the following
amounts: $590.50 for 1889; $446.00 for 1890; $296.00 for 1891; and $454.80 for
1892. See Commissioners, vol. 1, pp. 58, 91, 102, 111, 133, 146, 150, 162, 178,
198, 211, 224, 245, 265, 280, 284, 295, 298, 325, and 358.

21. For the town's naming, see "At the Gateway—Entering the Wonderland
through Livingston," St. Paul *Daily Globe*, September 1, 1883, p. 2. For its
population, see "Total Population of Montana," *Livingston Enterprise*, November 21, 1891, p. 2; "Local Layout" [county population by town], same issue p. 3;
and "Livingston's Population," *Livingston Enterprise*, December 22, 1900, p. 4.
For the two men involved in the town's naming, including Crawford Livingston's "laughing at his boom town before he sees it," see "A Surprised Scribe,"
Livingston Enterprise, September 15, 1883, p. 3; and "Johnston Livingston,"
Livingston Enterprise, July 16, 1884, p. 2.

22. These were the Bloom, Northrup, and Douty trials, all on page one of
Livingston Enterprise, January 28, 1893. For the hanging of Robert Anderson,
see "Death Penalty Pronounced," *Livingston Enterprise*, May 26, 1894, p. 1; and
"Anderson Hanged," *Livingston Enterprise*, July 14, 1894, p. 1.

23. "Opium Joint Raided," *Livingston Enterprise*, December 23, 1893, p. 1;
"[Two] Opium Joints Raided," *Livingston Enterprise*, March 24, 1894, p. 1.
Although the *Enterprise* editor sometimes joined the usual haranguers from other
parts of Montana in condemning Chinese (see for example, "A Righteous Decision" [against Chinese] in the edition of May 20, 1893, p. 4), an extended perusal
of the newspapers shows that Livingston was generally more tolerant of minorities and outsiders than many other in-state towns. One wonders whether the

constant arrival of Yellowstone tourists (of great diversity) liberalized this outlook.

24. These were the *Livingston Gazette* (1883); *Livingston Tribune*
(1883–1884); *Livingston Enterprise* (1883 to present); *National Park Pioneer*
(1883); *Livingston Post* (1889–1895, 1900–1902, 1908–1914); *Livingston Senti-
nel* (1888); *Livingston Herald* (1891–1898, but all that survive are 1896–1898);
Montana Agriculturist (1895); the *Silver Republican* (1898); *Park County Republican* (1899–1902); *Livingston Free Press* (1914); and *Park County News*
(1917–1960s). Some of these are unfortunately nonexistent today, because they
were not saved. The Montana Historical Society, the Yellowstone Gateway Museum of Livingston, and the Library of Congress possess the existing issues. See
Babcock, *History of the Yellowstone Valley*, pp. 655–659.

25. "Local Layout" [Cyprians], *Livingston Enterprise*, January 28, 1893, p. 5.
When "Lulu" St. Clair—"one of the habitués of the red light district"—died in
1898, her funeral was well attended and many nice things were said about her,
even though the *Herald* judged her as having led a "wasted life." See "Local
Items," *Livingston Herald*, February 17, 1898.

26. "Local Layout" [Mary Mason], *Livingston Enterprise*, October 29, 1892,
p. 5. The same went for "Tilly the Tramp," who was convicted of "disturbing the
peace" rather than her "real" crime, in the issues of February 7 and March 21,
1891, p. 3.

27. "Local Layout" [demi-monde], Livingston *Enterprise*, January 11, 1896,
p. 5. For more on prostitution, which the city council had made legal on B Street
in 1890, see "Bawdy Houses," *Livingston Post*, October 2, 1890, p. 3; and
"Lewdness on the Street," *Livingston Post*, December 18, 1890, p. 3.

28. "Tar and Feathers," *Livingston Enterprise*, March 28, 1891, p. 3; "Arrested for Robbery," April 4, 1891, p. 3. Seating capacity at the court hearing
"was found inadequate to accommodate the crowd in attendance."

29. "Another Rustler Killed," *Livingston Enterprise*, April 23, 1892, p. 3.
Referring to Park County, the local Stock Growers' Association proclaimed that
"a considerable portion of the range country is infested with cattle thieves and
horse thieves, commonly designated rustlers." See "The Stock Growers' Association," same issue, p. 1.

30. "Charged with Adultery," *Livingston Enterprise*, February 25, 1893, p. 1.

31. "A Terrible Tragedy," *Livingston Enterprise*, October 7, 1893, p. 1.

32. "Return of the Stranglers' Victim," *Livingston Enterprise*, June 2, 1894,
p. 4.

33. "Smallest Tramp on Earth," *Livingston Enterprise*, November 4, 1893, p.
1. In the midst of numerous niceties, the editor referred to the diminutive boy as a
"wandering pickaninny."

34. "Sunday Closing Don't Go," *Livingston Enterprise*, April 7, 1900, p. 1.

35. That Livingston's connection to live theater extended to the very beginnings of the town is apparent from mention of "Truax and Galloway's Gem
Opera House" in 1883, per "Twenty Years Ago," *Livingston Enterprise*, June 13,
1903, p. 4; and advertisement for the same in issue of July 5, 1883, p. 3, which
stated that the theater was "open every night the year round" and that "a change
of programme is made three times each week." One of the Hoppes was affected
by theater activities in 1891 when, in July, Mrs. Millicent J. Hoppe was forced to
move her confectionery store because the "new Hefferlin opera house" was
slated to take over the spot. "Local Layout," *Livingston Enterprise*, July 25,
1891, p. 3. See also "Planning for Hefferlin's Opera House," *Livingston Post*,
March 10, 1892, p. 3; and "Fowlie's Hall" [advertisement], *Livingston Enterprise*, March 28, 1891, p. 3. For examples of circuses, see *Livingston Enterprise*,
May 27, and July 22, 1893, p. 1.

36. "Personal Points" [Hoppes at Albemarle Hotel], *Livingston Enterprise*,
January 5, 1889, p. 3; "Personal Points" [Hoppes house-sit at home of J. H.
Elder], *Livingston Enterprise*, January 19, 1889, p. 5.

37. "Local Layout" [George Hoppe is clerk], *Livingston Enterprise*, April 27,
1889, p. 5; "Local Layout" [HJH will build house next fall], *Livingston Enterprise*, May 11, 1889, p. 5.

38. "Local Layout" [Hoppes move back to Cinnabar], *Livingston Enterprise*,
May 11, 1889, p. 5; "For Sale or Rent," *Livingston Enterprise*, May 25, 1889, p.
6. The ad, which ran all summer from "Hoppe and Company," described the
ranch as "100 acres under cultivation, crops all in consisting of timothy, oats,
peas, potatoes, and garden vegetables, best improved ranch on Yellowstone.
Horses, mares, cattle; one stallion thoroughbred Percheron 4 years old; weight
1700. Wagons of all description, harness[es], implements and household goods
of all description for sale at Cinnabar."

39. Hoppe bought the mining claim from Zed Daniels, and it was mentioned
in "Important Deeds Recorded" [Z. H. Daniels conveyance to H. J. Hoppe],
Livingston Enterprise, March 23, 1889, p. 1.

40. Probably to make extra money, Hoppe had sold an undivided one-half
interest in this coal claim in 1887 to Ed Zimmerman. Hugo Hoppe to Ed Zimmerman, February 23, 1887, Park County Deed records, vol. 8, p. 240. The land
was described as the NE4 of Section 14, T9S, and R7E, on upper Hoppe Creek.
The Cinnabar Mountain coal claim was probably the one he sold in 1890 to C. E.
Llewellyn, per "Local Layout," *Livingston Enterprise*, August 16, 1890, p. 3.

41. "H. J. Hoppe" [living at Horr], *Livingston Enterprise*, August 24, 1889, p.
2; "Local Layout" [constructing house], *Livingston Enterprise*, September 21,
1889, p. 5; "Local Layout" [Hoppe leases "his ranch at Horr" for two years to
Sylvester Cooke and moves to Livingston], *Livingston Enterprise*, November 16,
1889, p. 3. See also "Personal Points" in same issue, on same page. Hoppe's self-

attested voting records for August 21, 1889, and September 30, 1890, both stated that he was then living at Horr. "Official [Voters'] Register, 1889–1896, Gardiner-Horr," Yellowstone Gateway Museum.

42. Commissioner Hoppe's filing of his three thousand dollar bond with the city is in "Local Layout," *Livingston Enterprise*, November 16, 1889, p. 3. Details of county commissioners' election requirements and their terms are in "New County Commissioners," *Livingston Enterprise*, September 16, 1893, p. 4; "Synopsis of Proceedings," *Livingston Enterprise*, November 11, 1893, p. 1; and "With Wednesday's Session," p. 4.

43. "Local Matters" [Williams purchases Cinnabar hotel], *Livingston Post*, November 14, 1889, p. 3. For whatever reason (perhaps it was her money that was used to buy the hotel), Maggie's name appeared as the licensee for a "saloon and hotel" on the "List of Licenses Issued . . . ending Nov 30, 1889," *Livingston Enterprise*, December 7, 1889, p. 5.

44. "Local Layout" [Williams's renovation of Cinnabar hotel], *Livingston Enterprise*, February 15, 1890, p. 3. If the newspaper is to be believed, the money came from Bud's wife, for it stated: "Mrs. M. A. Williams has purchased the Cinnabar hotel" even though Bud Williams would manage it. "Local Layout," *Livingston Enterprise*, November 16, 1889, p. 3. However, in the December 7 edition of "Local Layout," the paper stated that Bud purchased the hotel.

45. "District Court—Sixth Day" [Williams divorce], *Livingston Enterprise*, January 18, 1890, p. 3. Bud's murder threat, his arrest, and the court case of *State v. Morgan T. Williams* are in "Local Layout," *Livingston Enterprise*, December 7, 1889, p. 5.

46. "Police Court News" [Williams pleads guilty to drunkenness following row in Albemarle Hotel], *Livingston Enterprise*, March 15, 1890, p. 3; "Local Layout" [Williams again convicted of drunkenness], *Livingston Enterprise*, April 19, 1890, p. 3. The civil lawsuit involving James McCartney was mentioned in "District Court," *Livingston Enterprise*, April 19, 1890, p. 1.

47. "An Enterprising Skunk," *Livingston Post*, April 30, 1891, p. 3. And of course with its "roses" comment, the *Post* could not resist getting in a "dig" at its rival, the *Enterprise*.

48. "Real Estate and Mining Transfers," *Livingston Enterprise*, April 26, 1890, p. 1. It is not known why Bud Williams sold the hotel to someone besides his father-in-law. Considering his divorce, perhaps he was angry at the entire Hoppe family. Or perhaps Hugo Hoppe did not yet have the money to buy it.

49. "Local Layout" [Hoppe's new house], *Livingston Enterprise*, March 8, 1890, p. 3; "Local Layout" [George will open confectionery store in Livingston], *Livingston Enterprise*, March 29, 1890, p. 3. George opened the store in early April, per *Livingston Enterprise*, "Personal Points," April 5, 1890, p. 3.

50. "Local Layout" [H. J. Hoppe will open butcher shop at Horr], *Livingston Enterprise*, May 31, 1890, p. 3. The "List of [business] Licenses Issued" by Park County published in the *Enterprise* for September 6, 1890, p. 4, stated that W[alter] M. Hoppe was the licensee for the butcher shop but it was Hughie who later partnered in it with Lewis Van Dyck. That partnership folded in August of 1893, when Hughie apparently decided that he was not cut out to be a butcher. Van Dyck continued the business for many years, eventually moving it to Gardiner. "Local Layout," *Livingston Enterprise*, August 19, 1893, p. 5.

51. "Personal Points" [lease to Hall], *Livingston Enterprise*, May 17, 1890, p. 3. Technically, Hoppe assigned his own lease of the ranch to Hall, because Hoppe himself was now leasing the ranch from its true owners, Gassert and Reding. Knowing that his lease would eventually end, Hall eventually made arrangements to purchase a house in Livingston. "Local Layout" [Hall purchases house], *Livingston Enterprise*, November 15, p. 3.

52. "Local Layout" [HJH obtains government freighting contract], *Livingston Enterprise*, July 5, 1890, p. 3; "Local Layout" [Hoppe sells to Llewellyn], *Livingston Enterprise*, August 16, 1890, p. 3. McCormick was mentioned at Fort Pease and as an early steamboat navigator on the Yellowstone River in "Local Miscellany," Bozeman *Avant Courier*, December 4, 1884, p. 3.

53. "Local Layout" [John Work sells hotel to Fairfax], *Livingston Enterprise*, November 8, 1890, p. 3. Background for Fairfax's purchase is "Destructive Blaze—The Town of Gardiner Wiped Out of Existence," *Livingston Enterprise*, September 7, 1889, p. 3. Fairfax was Elmour J. Fairfax, born at Fairfax Court House, Virginia, and age sixty-two in 1894 when he registered to vote at Horr. "Official Register—Voters—Horr," 1894 et al., Yellowstone Gateway Museum. He showed up later in the *Enterprise* as a miner at Emigrant.

54. "Personal Points" [contract with Camp Sheridan and travels to Bozeman], *Livingston Enterprise*, March 14, 1891, p. 3; "Local Layout" [HJH and McCormick get Camp Sheridan contract], *Livingston Enterprise*, May 23, 1891, p. 3; "Local Matters" [Camp Sheridan is rechristened Fort Yellowstone], *Livingston Post*, May 21, 1891, p. 4.

55. "Local Layout" [George sells Livingston store], *Livingston Enterprise*, February 14, 1891, p. 3; "Local Matters" [George sells], *Livingston Post*, February 12, 1891, p. 3; advertisement for "Williams and Hoppe Store," *Livingston Enterprise*, April 24, 1891, p. 4. Lee Hoppe did this for a short time and then apparently briefly left the store in Maggie's charge to work for an Eastern cigar manufacturer.

56. "Personal Points" [Lee Hoppe quits cigar job and goes to Cinnabar for freighting], *Livingston Enterprise*, May 23, 1891, p. 3; and his store advertisement in *Livingston Enterprise*, July 11, 1891, p. 3. Lee Hoppe was quite flighty this year. For whatever reason, he thought he wanted to again leave Cinnabar

after only one summer. He sold the Cinnabar store in October, with the idea of moving it to Big Timber, Montana. "Personal Points," *Livingston Enterprise*, October 24, 1891, p. 3. His Big Timber store lasted exactly one week, and he headed back to Cinnabar to again run the Cinnabar store in 1892 and 1893. "Big Timber Items," *Livingston Enterprise*, November 7, 1891, p. 4.

57. These switches are detailed in the *Livingston Enterprise* "Local Layout" columns of July 4, July 25, and August 22, 1891; and January 30 and February 6, 1892. Millicent Hoppe later bought her own millinery store in Livingston, for she was running it in 1901. "Local Layout" [Millicent Hoppe moves millinery shop], *Livingston Enterprise*, January 15, 1901, p. 5.

58. "Before the Courts" [Fairfax arrested], *Livingston Post*, January 29, 1891, p. 2; "Local Matters" [Baronett says cold], *Livingston Post*, March 5, 1891, p. 3.

6. A DREAM REALIZED

1. Hall's personal business card for the "Cinnabar Hotel and Saloon" (in the YNP Museum Collection) was hand dated, probably by him, as February 15, 1891. Business licenses issued by Park County and published in the newspaper showed Hall as obtaining a hotel license beginning in May and June 1891. Compare the "List of Licenses Issued [for period] . . . Ending May 31, 1891," in *Livingston Enterprise*, June 6, 1891, p. 1, with the previous list of county licenses in the *Enterprise* for March 7, 1891, p. 1. Additionally, the *Enterprise* reported W. A. Hall as the "proprietor of the Cinnabar hotel" in "Personal Points," edition of May 23, 1891, p. 3. Interestingly, Fairfax also sold in May his barn at Cinnabar (known as the "Wakefield building") to George Ash of the YPT Company, who undoubtedly began using it for company business. *Livingston Enterprise*, "Local Layout," May 23, 1891, p. 3.

2. "Local Matters" [freighting job at Manhattan], *Livingston Post*, May 12, 1892, p. 3.

3. "Personal Mention" [Hall opening a livery at Cinnabar], *Livingston Post*, April 23, 1891, p. 3; "List of [Park County] Licenses . . . Ending Dec 1, 1891," *Livingston Enterprise*, December 12, 1891, p. 1.

4. Assuming that Carroll Hobart paid him the money quickly, Hoppe could have been aided by the $1,138.97 civil verdict given him by a district court. "District Court" [verdict for Hoppe], *Livingston Enterprise*, June 25, 1892, p. 1. Hoppe was shown in the *Enterprise*'s "Licenses" for June 11, 1892, p. 8, as suddenly being the licensee of a saloon, while W. A. Hall, who had been licensed with a saloon on March 12 (p. 2), was suddenly shown as the licensee for a hotel and no saloon.

5. "Local Matters" [post office established at Cinnabar], *Livingston Post*,
June 30, 1892, p. 3; "Local Layout," *Livingston Enterprise*, August 13, 1892, p.
5. One historian has stated that Cinnabar was granted a post office on September
6, 1882, and Hugo Hoppe (through McPherren) said it was established in 1883,
but both of these years were much too early, because real postal records plus the
newspapers agree that Cinnabar's first actual post office appeared in 1892 with
Leander B. Hoppe as postmaster. Only one building was in place at Cinnabar
before August of 1883, that being Hugo Hoppe's warehouse, and thus the town
was too small for a post office until much later. Hoppe stated that he personally
chased local cowboys for their signatures to establish a post office in 1883–1884.
But the establishment happened much later, so his chasing escapade must have
occurred in 1891 or 1892. Postal information is from United States Post Office
Department, "Records of Appointments of Postmasters, State of Montana, 1864-
1929," in RG 29, National Archives, Microfilm 466, at Montana State University, Special Collections; and Dennis Lutz, *Montana Post Offices and Postmasters* (Minot, ND: Montana Chapter, National Association of Postmasters, 1986),
pp. 13, 126 (my thanks go to Kim Allen Scott of Montana State University for
these records). See also Whithorn, ed., *History of Park County Montana*, p. 43.
These three sources all give the postal establishment year as 1892. Hugo Hoppe's
version is in McPherren, *Imprints on Pioneer Trails*, pp. 194, 197–198. Aubrey
Haines's version (listing September 6, 1882) is in his "The Park Branch Line:
Doorway to the Yellowstone," unpublished manuscript, YNP Library, 1963, p. 9,
his information being taken from J. A. Martinek to Elmer J. Binker Jr., February
11, 1966, in box H-3, file "4.2.5 Post Office," YNP Archives. It was the best
information available in 1966, but since then primary source documents have
surfaced to confirm the 1892 post office.

6. "Local Matters" [ferry], *Livingston Post*, July 21, 1892, p. 3.

7. "List of Licenses [issued by Park County] . . . Ending Aug 31, 1892,"
Livingston Enterprise, September 17, 1892, p. 8. Listed in this enumeration was
"H. J. Hoppe, hotel and saloon." In the "List of Licenses" for the quarter ending
February 28, 1893 (*Enterprise*, March 11, 1893, p. 2), L. B. Hoppe was listed as
the store owner and Hall merely listed as being licensed for a "saloon and
livery."

8. Carrie Belle Spencer, "Journal of a Trip to Yellowstone National Park,
1892" (Keya Paha County, Nebraska), entry for August 17, 1892, original in
possession of descendants, posted athttp://www.usgennet.org/usa/ne/county/
keyapaha/Carrie%20Belle%20Spencer.html. At this time Secretary of Interior
John Noble had just taken away the transportation rights in Yellowstone Park
from nine-year operator George Wakefield and awarded them to Silas Huntley,
whose new company was now called Yellowstone National Park Transportation
Company (later YPT). Harassment of outside stage operators by the park super-

intendent lasted all summer, but one account is "Fired from Wonderland," *Livingston Post*, July 28, 1892, p. 3. Although a few six-horse tally-ho coaches had been present in the park since 1886, new operator Huntley purchased several more for 1892.

9. "Local Layout" [Hoppe leases house to sheriff], *Livingston Enterprise*, December 5, 1892, p. 5.

10. "Horr-Cinnabar-Tom Miner Voting Records," October 1892, Yellowstone Gateway Museum, Livingston.

11. "Local Layout" [Hoppe remodels hotel], *Livingston Enterprise*, April 22, 1893, p. 5. For the Chicago World's Fair in general, see Robert W. Rydell, *All the World's a Fair: Visions of Empire at American International Expositions* (Chicago: University of Chicago, 1987), p. 53 and others.

12. "Local Layout" [Chadbourn's stages], *Livingston Enterprise*, June 24, 1893, p. 5; "Real Estate and Mining Transfers," *Livingston Enterprise*, April 15, 1893, p. 1, W. Y. Northrup to Lewis H. Van Dyck, lots 3–4 and E2 of SW4 of S18, T9S, R8E.

13. "Local Layout" [huge trout mounted], *Livingston Enterprise*, April 29, 1893, p. 5; "Local Layout" [poking fun at Yankee Jim], *Livingston Enterprise*, May 13, 1893, p. 5. The freighting contract is in "Local Layout," *Livingston Enterprise*, May 20, 1893, p. 5.

14. "Real Estate and Mining Transfers," *Livingston Enterprise*, June 3, 1893, p. 2, US to E. J. Keeney, Lot 2 and SE4 of NE2 of S17; and lots 2–3 of S16; T9S, R8E. This was probably merely the vesting of Keeney's homestead or perhaps only a quiet-title conveyance, with Keeney previously owning it, but regardless it comprised a fair amount of Cinnabar.

15. The park's visitation statistics for those years are in Haines, *Yellowstone Story*, II, p. 478.

16. Doris Kearns Goodwin, *The Bully Pulpit: Theodore Roosevelt, William Howard Taft, and the Golden Age of Journalism* (New York: Simon & Schuster, 2013), p. 159.

17. "The Gallatin Valley Closes"; "Another Gone" [Great Falls]; "Temporarily Closed" [Livingston]; and "Helena's Troubles," all on page one of the *Livingston Enterprise*, July 29, 1893; "Think It Over," *Livingston Enterprise*, July 29, 1893, p. 4; "The Big Strike" [NP railroad company], *Livingston Enterprise*, June 30, 1894, p. 4.

18. "Park Bank Closed," *Livingston Enterprise*, August 5, 1893, p. 1; "Took a Tumble" [Chicago Board of Trade], p. 3; "The Milwaukee Cuts Salaries," p. 3.

19. "Pullman Boycott," *Livingston Enterprise*, June 30, 1894, p. 1; and David Whitten, "The Depression of 1893," edited by Robert Whaples, August 14, 2001, EH.Net Encyclopedia, http://eh.net/encyclopedia/article/whitten.panic.1893, accessed June 9, 2013. Another study is Charles Hoffman, *The Depression of the*

Nineties: An Economic History (Westport, CT: Greenwood Publishing, 1970). See also Eugene V. Debs, "The Pullman Strike, Chicago, 1894," at http://www.kansasheritage.org/pullman/, accessed June 12, 2013; and Richard White, *Railroaded: The Transcontinentals and the Making of Modern America* (New York: W.W. Norton Company, 2011), pp. 393–398, 423.

20. "Local Layout" [freighting contract renewed], *Livingston Enterprise*, July 1, 1893, p. 5; "Local Layout" [W. A. Hall appointed postmaster to replace Lee Hoppe; Lee decides to remain in Bozeman with wife], *Livingston Enterprise*, July 22, 1893, p. 5; "Local Layout" [Walter and Maggie to World's Fair], *Livingston Enterprise*, October 28, 1893, p. 5; "Out of the Park—W. A. Hall's Transportation Privilege Suspended and His Outfits Confiscated," *Livingston Enterprise*, August 12, 1893, p. 1. See also "Called Down and Escorted Out," *Livingston Enterprise*, August 19, 1893, p. 1.

21. "Local Layout" [HJH distributes provisions; HBH exits partnership], *Livingston Enterprise*, August 19, 1893, p. 5; "Local Layout" [Horr store closed; attachments begin], *Livingston Enterprise*, November 4, 1893, p. 5; "Synopsis of Proceedings" [of commissioners], *Livingston Enterprise*, November 11, 1893, p. 1; "With Wednesday's Session" [HJH's last day], *Livingston Enterprise*, November 11, 1893, p. 4; "Reduction in Wages" [by NPRR], *Livingston Enterprise*, December 2, 1893, p. 1; "Local Layout" [AVH begins classes], *Livingston Enterprise*, November 4, 1893, p. 5; "Local Layout" [HJH's grandson born], *Livingston Enterprise*, November 25, 1893, p. 5.

22. "Local Layout," *Livingston Enterprise*, January 13, 1894, p. 5, and advertisement on p. 7. This advertisement continued to run through the May 19 issue, but Hoppe had no buyers.

23. "Personal Points," *Livingston Enterprise*, May 5, 1894, p. 4.

24. "Local Layout," *Livingston Enterprise*, March 24, 1894, p. 5.

25. White, *Railroaded*, pp. 433, 435; "Pullman Boycott," *Livingston Enterprise*, June 30, 1894, p. 1; "The Big Strike," *Livingston Enterprise*, June 30, 1894, p. 4.

26. Most of these events are detailed in the many snippets of "Local Layout," *Livingston Enterprise*, July 21, 1894, p. 5. The Muir tunnel is in "Around Livingston," *Anaconda Standard*, July 9, 1894, p. 1. US troops at Livingston are in W. Thomas White, "Boycott: The Pullman Strike in Montana," *Montana the Magazine of Western History* 29 (Autumn, 1979): 2–13, especially pp. 9–10.

27. Dr. Liston H. Montgomery, "To the Editor" [distressed and stranded], *Livingston Enterprise*, July 21, 1894, p. 4.

28. Captain George S. Anderson in "Make Good Indians . . . The Year in Yellowstone Park," Helena *Independent*, December 1, 1894, p. 1; "Local Layout" [threshing], *Livingston Enterprise*, August 25, 1894, p. 5; "Personal Points" [Cinnabar is lively], *Livingston Enterprise*, August 25, 1894, p. 6. Shutdown of

the Park Branch Railroad was covered in the July 7, 14, and 21 editions; and in "Thanking the Soldiers," *Livingston Enterprise*, August 18, 1894, p. 1. Park visitation is in Haines, *Yellowstone Story*, II, p. 478; and in "Make Good Indians," as cited.

29. Beley and Lockwood quoted in White, "Pullman Strike in Montana," as cited, pp. 9–10; "Tried to Incite a Riot—A Drunken Military Blackguard's Dastardly Deed," *Livingston Post*, July 12, 1894, p. 2.

7. THE TOWN ITSELF

1. This icehouse could have been the same as Hoppe's "root cellar," which archeologists believe they found in 2007–2008 at the base of a hill on the northeast side of the Cinnabar landscape. David Scott Dick et al., "Cinnabar Archeology," figure 3, p. 42. Randy Ingersoll's and my field check of the spot on May 24, 2013, agreed with both the archeologists' finding of the site and two NPS photos (YELL-29997-1, 2), showing the root cellar before the NPS destroyed it in the late 1930s.

2. McPherren, *Imprints*, pp. 199–200. Hoppe's sawmill was not the same as the one sent by the railroad to Cinnabar in late 1882, for that one was quickly moved to Mammoth. Whittlesey, "This Modern Saratoga," as cited, 2010–2014, pp. 108, 112, 144; and Haines, *Yellowstone Story*, I, p. 310.

3. Bill and Doris Whithorn, *Photo History of Aldridge*, p. 9.

4. A. M. Ingersoll, "My Trip to the Yellowstone Park," in Chicago, Milwaukee, and St. Paul Railway, *Gems of the Northwest* (St. Paul: Chicago, Milwaukee, and St. Paul Railway, no date [1885?]), p. 73; F.B., "Roughing it in the National Park," *Forest and Stream* 24 (March 26, 1885): 164; F.F.F., "A Modern Pilgrimage to the Mecca of Sportsman and Tourist," *American Field* 24 (October 17, 1885): 373.

5. F. Jay Haynes photo H-1544, "Cinnabar City, M.T., 1884," Montana Historical Society. See also "St. Paul News—Westward Ho," *St. Paul* (MN) *Daily Globe*, June 18, 1884, p. 2.

6. Hoppe in McPherren, *Imprints*, pp. 194, 197, 199–200.

7. O. S. T. Drake, "A Lady's Trip to the Yellowstone Park," *Every Girl's Annual*, 1887 (London: Hatchard's, 1887), pp. 347–348. This account is reproduced with notes in Lee H. Whittlesey and Elizabeth A. Watry, *Ho! For Wonderland: Travelers' Accounts of Yellowstone, 1872-1914* (Albuquerque: University of New Mexico Press, 2009), pp. 105–113.

8. Dudley, *Hurricane Deck of a Cayuse*, p. 28.

9. "Montana" [Keeney and Huston sell to Reding and Gassert], *Butte Daily Miner*, January 30, 1885, p. 4. Keeney's mining partners at Cooke City had been

George Huston and John Curl. Per the newspapers, Harry Gassert and Jacob Reding were in Butte in 1883 and 1884. The Cinnabar townsite was again advertised for sale in late January and mentioned in "Local Layout," *Livingston Enterprise*, January 31, 1885, p. 3. There is another possible way that Keeney had made money and one that we offer here only for the record. The Helena *Independent*, January 22, 1884, p. 7 ("Montana Matters") announced that "J.E. Keeny [*sic*] has located a mineral spring between the Gallatin and Yellowstone rivers" whose waters "are flammable and will burn like petroleum." Did Keeney somehow make money from this? The proposition seems doubtful, because had it happened we would surely have more information about such a venture.

10. The 1883 traveler who stayed at Keeney's was partially quoted in Haines, *Yellowstone Story*, I, p. 278. For mention of the early saloon that Keeney and Huston ran together at their ranch in Cinnabar, see "Lambdin's Grievance," *Livingston Enterprise*, October 1, 1883, p. 2. Keeney's obituary and biography are in "Joe Keeney, One of Last of Northwest Pioneers, Dies at Local Hospital," *Livingston Enterprise*, September 27, 1938, p. 1; and "90-Year-Old Livingston Resident One of First to Discover Gold Ore Float in Cooke City Region," Bozeman *Courier*, undated clipping from the summer of 1937, in possession of author with copy at YNP Library. My thanks go to Steve Mishkin for finding these biographical articles about Keeney.

11. Owen Wister, "Diary—Notebook, British Columbia, Washington, Oregon, California, Wyoming, July–September, 1887," entry for September 1, 1887, Owen Wister Papers, collection 00290, Box 1, folder 2, American Heritage Center, University of Wyoming.

12. The bar fight is in Dick Pace, "W.W. Alderson—The Editor Who Told It Like It Was," *Montana the Magazine of Western History* 22 (Winter, 1972), pp. 87–89. A photo of Keeney with X. Beidler is in Evalyn Batten Johnson, *Images of America: Virginia City* (Arcadia Press, 2013), p. 27.

13. "Joe Keeney Shot," *Livingston Enterprise*, October 6, 1884, p. 3; "Another Account of the Gardiner Shooting," *Livingston Enterprise*, October 7, 1884, p. 3; "Keeney's Condition," *Livingston Enterprise*, October 8, 1884, p. 3. "Local Miscellany" in Bozeman *Avant Courier*, October 9, 1884, p. 3, says her name was "Ayrhart" and that the incident happened in the "Geyser Saloon." Keeney's Oregon roots and his age on August 26, 1889, are in "Official [Voters'] Register, 1889-1896, Gardiner-Horr," Yellowstone Gateway Museum. His age listed here was thirty-six, a discrepancy from his obituary and tombstone. Both gave his birth date as August 22, 1847.

14. "They Fought on Horseback," *Livingston Enterprise*, March 21, 1885, p. 3; and snippet in *Bozeman Weekly Chronicle*, March 25, 1885, p. 3. The "paragons" quote is in "Cooke City Locals," Bozeman *Avant Courier*, October 25, 1883, p. 3.

15. Calvin B. Swift stated that he was born in California and was forty-four and living at Yankee Jim Canyon when he registered to vote at Horr on October 10, 1894. Voting register at Yellowstone Gateway Museum, Livingston, Montana. For his Alaska exploits, see "Local Layout" [Swift leaves], *Livingston Enterprise*, November 20, 1897, p. 5; and S. S. Erret, "From the Frozen North" [Tommy Dolan allegedly murders Cal Swift], *Livingston Enterprise*, December 23, 1899, p. 1.

16. "Brained His Brother," *Livingston Enterprise*, December 9, 1893, p. 4; "Miller Acquitted," *Livingston Enterprise*, December 16, 1893, p. 1. Box E. Miller stated that he was born in Potosi, Wisconsin, and was twenty-nine and living at Tom Miner Basin when he registered to vote at Gardiner on August 31, 1889. Voting register at Yellowstone Gateway Museum, Livingston, Montana. The newspaper referred to him as "P.J. 'Box' Miller." See also "Killed His Brother," *Yellowstone Journal* (Miles City, MT), December 9, 1893, p. 1. Miller had a conviction for poaching in the park, which occurred in the fall of 1885. Haines, *Yellowstone Story*, I, p. 321.

17. "An Elopement and Marriage—Joe Keeney Furnishes Another Interesting News Item," *Livingston Enterprise*, August 1, 1885, p. 1; "The Keeney Elopement," *Bozeman Weekly Chronicle*, August 5, 1885, p. 3. Elias Joseph Keeney and Clara F. Parker were married on December 4, 1878, at Canaan, Maine, per Maine Marriage Records at ancestry.com.

18. Haines, *Yellowstone Story*, I, p. 321; "In Yellowstone Park," *Chicago Weekly News*, August 23, 1883, partially quoted in Haines, *Yellowstone Story*, I, p. 278; F.B., "Roughing it in the National Park," *Forest and Stream* 24 (March 26, 1885): 164; "New World Mining District" [Keeney is proprietor of a hotel at Cinnabar], Bozeman *Avant Courier*, June 24, 1886, p. 2; Owen Wister in Paul Schullery, *Old Yellowstone Days* (Albuquerque: University of New Mexico Press, 2010), p. 87. G. L. Henderson in "Our Park Visit," *Livingston Enterprise*, July 23, 1887, p. 3, stated that "E.J. Keeney is still mine host at the hotel at Cinnabar, in connection with which he is operating a livery and feed stable, and is doing a good business."

19. "Local Layout" [Mrs. Keeney arrested], *Livingston Enterprise*, September 5, 1891, p. 3; "Killed Trespassing Cattle" [Joe Keeney arrested], *Anaconda Standard*, August 1, 1889, p. 1; "Local Layout" [Keeney posts $500 bond], *Livingston Enterprise*, August 3, 1889, p. 3.

20. "Local Layout," *Livingston Enterprise*, June 12, 1886, p. 3. Hoppe's letter to Hobart on September 28, 1886, tells us that Hoppe was somehow back in the hotel business by that time, probably running Keeney's hotel. Keeney leaving for Boulder River is in "Personal Points," *Livingston Enterprise*, August 8, 1891, p. 3.

21. "Local Layout" [HJH ceases freighting and attends to his ranch], *Livingston Enterprise*, June 19, 1886, p. 3.

22. "Cinnabar and Gardiner," *Livingston Enterprise*, June 4, 1892, p. 2. Yellowstone collector Jack Davis of Bozeman, Montana, located an 1888 invoice of Joseph Keeney's indicating that Keeney's business was a hotel and livery tourist service at Cinnabar.

23. "Joe Keenney [*sic*]," *Big Timber* (MT) *Pioneer*, April 20, 1893, p. 3; *Big Timber Pioneer*, June 8, 1893, p. 7; "Local News" [Keeney has a road contract on Boulder River], *Livingston Post*, September 2, 1897, p. 3; "Local Layout" [Keeney to Alaska], *Livingston Enterprise*, January 1, 1898, p. 5; "Funeral Services for Pioneer Held in City Tuesday" [Keeney was once at Independence], *Livingston Enterprise*, September 28, 1938.

24. Hoppe in McPherren, *Imprints*, p. 197.

25. E. Catherine Bates, *A Year in the Great Republic* (London: Ward and Downey), II, 1887, p. 162; Edward Marston, *Frank's Ranche or My Holiday in the Rockies* (London: Sampson, Low, Marston, Searle and Rivington), 1886, p. 107; Owen Wister in Paul Schullery, *Old Yellowstone Days*, p. 87; W. J. Van Patten, "An Overland Journey April 28-June 18, 1887," bound typescript, no date [1887?], Yale Beinecke Library; Mrs. Paris, Junior, "To the Yellowstone Park in a Wagon," *American Field* 34 (August 23, 1890): 176; Anonymous [member of Ansiatic League of Westchester, Pennsylvania], "Fishing in the Yellowstone," 1889, handwritten journal owned by Randy Ingersoll, Gardiner, Montana, p. 3, of transcription sent to author. See also Frank Haynes photos H-3005 and H-3620, Montana Historical Society. Two other photos are in Burton Holmes, *Burton Holmes Travelogues* (Battle Creek, MI: Little Preston Company, 1901), pp. 11–12. The Gene Autry Museum of Los Angeles has what is perhaps the best photo of Cinnabar in its later life. Catherine Bates thought the depot so small in 1886, that she thanked fortune that her party had left their larger luggage at Livingston, because there was no room for storage.

26. McPherren, *Imprints*, p. 244, quoted in full on page 119 of this book.

27. F. E. Stratton, "The Yellowstone National Park, 1895," p. 10, original handwritten diary, MSC-034, box 1, YNP Archives.

28. "Local Layout" [depot at Gallatin City moved to Cinnabar], *Livingston Enterprise*, June 29, 1895, p. 5.

29. T. H. Thomas, "Yellowstone Park Illustrated," *The Graphic* (New York), August 11, 1888, p. 158.

30. J.H.H., "Conductors as Passengers," *St. Paul Daily Globe*, June 5, 1885, p. 3.

31. Charles W. Stoddard, "In Wonder-Land," *Ave Maria* 47 (August 13, 1898): 200–201. Stoddard did not date this trip account, but internal evidence requires it to have occurred in 1886. At Mammoth hotel, he stated that "Clara

Louise Kellogg had sung there in her time" (her only concert ever there, per the *Enterprise*, was in October of 1885). The US Army had not arrived in the park when Stoddard was present (troops arrived August 17, 1886), so these two mentioned events placed Stoddard's trip in 1886, before August 17.

32. Fred Slocum, *23rd Annual Enclave and A Royal Outing; Michigan State Press Association; A Story Written by the Editors Themselves* (Saginaw, MI: Seeman and Peters, 1891), p. 31. The "weather-beaten drivers" quote is from Myra Emmons, "From New York to Heaven," *Recreation* 15 (December, 1901): 432.

33. George H. Bockoven, *Travel and Adventure Experienced in Crossing the Continent* (Palmyra, NY: Press of F.G. Crandall, 1896), p. 28, copy at Yale Beinecke Library.

34. Amelia J. Lyle, *Reminiscences of Travel at Home and Abroad* (Burlington, IA: German Literary Board, 1907), pp. 57–58. Her mentions of troops recently being sent to the Boxer Rebellion in China and of the Golden Gate Bridge "being under repair" (pp. 70, 73) confirmed the year of her trip as 1900, the year her ballyhooed Senator Clark got into big trouble in Washington, DC, for corruption.

35. These three quotes are from McPherren, *Imprints*, pp. 212–214, 230, 246–247.

36. R. Livingston, "Wayside Gleanings," *Livingston Enterprise*, October 1, 1898, p. 7.

37. McPherren, *Imprints*, p. 214.

38. McPherren, *Imprints*, pp. 265–270. The Gardiner celebration appeared in "Local Layout," *Livingston Enterprise*, July 13, 1895, p. 5, while Fort Yellowstone's was in "Yellowstone National Park—Preparations Being Made," *Livingston Enterprise*, June 27, 1896, p. 1.

39. Albert V. Hoppe, "Preparations Being Made to Blow Up Cinnabar on July 4th," *Livingston Enterprise*, June 3, 1899, p. 2; "Cinnabar Celebrates," *Livingston Enterprise*, July 8, 1899, p. 1; "Glorious Fourth, Cinnabar Celebrates," *Livingston Post*, July 6, 1899; "It Was Rockinger," *Livingston Post*, July 13, 1899, p. 1; Whittlesey, *Death in Yellowstone*, 2014, pp. 237–238. An oral-history interviewee at Livingston's Yellowstone Gateway Museum remembered many years later that the Rockingers "were an outlaw family" who lived in Gardiner.

40. "Horr Items" [dancing], *Livingston Enterprise*, August 5, 1899, p. 1; "Local Layout" [grand ball planned], *Livingston Enterprise*, December 29, 1900, p. 5; "Personal Points" [grand ball held], *Livingston Enterprise*, January 5, 1901, p. 6.

41. A man named "Mulheron," probably the same, was at Chico in the summer of 1876 and keeping a "boarding house" there in 1877 per "Mr. Melin and Mulheron," *Bozeman Times*, August 17, 1876, p. 3; and "A Trip to Emigrant,"

Bozeman Times, June 28, 1877, p. 2. The US Census of 1880, p. 198 (at ancestry.com for John Hughes Mulherin) shows Mulherin with wife, Martha, and four children, all present as settlers in the "Upper Yellowstone valley" of (then) Gallatin County, Montana, along with his neighbors, some of the area's earliest pioneers: C. J. Baronett, W. D. Bassett, George W. Reese, Philip and Frederick Bottler, and a few others. For Mulherin's presence as proprietor of the saloon at Mulherin Creek, see "Local Layout," *Livingston Daily Enterprise*, August 21, 1883, p. 3; September 21, p. 3; and November 14, p. 3. By February 17, 1884, Mulherin had stationery that read "Cinnabar Saloon.—John Mulherin, Proprietor—Warm meals at all hours," for Charles Hobart wrote a letter from there on that date (quoted in Whittlesey, "This Modern Saratoga," as cited, p. 142n301). Mulherin sold his ranch to C. B. Scott in 1889 (per "Local Layout," *Livingston Enterprise*, March 16, 1889, p. 3) and moved to Absarokee, Montana. An obituary for Mulherin is "Old Timer Gone," Gardiner (MT) *Wonderland*, August 13, 1904, and there is another obituary on that same date in the *Livingston Enterprise*. John Mulherin stated in 1883 that he first arrived in the area fourteen years ago (1869). "Local Layout," *Livingston Enterprise*, September 17, 1883, p. 3.

42. John Cumberland, "A Night at Cinnabar," *Marion* (OH) *Daily Star*, June 10, 1886, p. 1.

43. James McCartney (1835–1908) was almost forty-eight years old at this time, and he recorded his age and New York origins when he registered to vote on August 31, 1889. "Official Register, 1889-1896, Gardiner-Horr," Yellowstone Gateway Museum, Livingston, Montana.

44. "Capture of Horse Thieves," *Livingston Enterprise*, August 24, 1883, p. 2. Some leopards never change their spots, for "Black Jack" Miller was still stealing horses in 1895 when soldiers at Fort Yellowstone arrested him in the park, while Archibald K. "Scotty" Crawford landed at Aldridge, where he continued getting into trouble. See "Additional Local," *Livingston Enterprise*, August 24, 1895, p. 4, and another mention on p. 6. Another possibility for horse thieves in 1883 was Press White and one of his five brothers, wanted as ringleaders for horse theft in Indiana, Kentucky, and Tennessee. See "Brief Items" [horse thief captured at Bozeman], Helena *Independent*, September 7, 1883, p. 5. That Gardiner had a jail by 1889, which escaped the fire of that year, was attested to by Babcock, in *History of the Yellowstone Valley*, p. 162.

45. John Cumberland, "A Night at Cinnabar," *Marion* (OH) *Daily Star*, June 10, 1886, p. 1. Jack Baronett did not join President Chester Arthur's expedition as guide until August 26–31, 1883, so he could have been present here. Robert E. Hartley, *Saving Yellowstone: The President Arthur Expedition of 1883* (Westminster: Sniktau Publications, 2007), pp. 31, 121–129.

46. Cumberland, "A Night at Cinnabar," as cited.

47. Marston, *Frank's Ranche*, p. 107; Aubrey L. Haines, audiotape interview with Mrs. Robert Cutler, December 13, 1961, YNP Archives; Van Patten, "Overland Journey," as cited; "Hugo J. Hoppe, et al. to Harry Gassert and Jacob Reding, Bill of Sale [for freighting outfit and saloon]," September 23, 1887, as cited; Mary Keeney declaration, October 25, 1887, in Misc. 1, p. 154, Park County Deed Records.

48. See the earlier citations under hotels chronology, and also compare the many quarterly announcements of county licenses issued to merchants and other business operators as published in the *Livingston Enterprise*. They are headlined as "List of Licenses Issued . . . ending" with dates at the end of February, May, August, and December, and they appeared up to four times per year before 1897.

49. "Local Layout" [Mary Keeney arrested], *Livingston Enterprise*, September 5, 1891, p. 3; "District Court" [Mary Keeney not guilty and Joe Keeney found guilty], *Livingston Enterprise*, November 14, 1891, p. 1.

50. John Muir, "Yellowstone Park," in his *Picturesque California: The Rocky Mountains and the Pacific Slope* (New York and San Francisco: J. Dewing Company), 1888, p. 424.

51. McPherren, *Imprints*, p. 213. For George L. Hoppe's name on the hotel's official stationery, see Archive Document 2895, Frank Rose to Captain W. E. Wilder, May 27, 1899, YNP Archives. This document also contains George's signature and those of W. A. Hall and Walter Hoppe.

52. "Cinnabar and Gardiner," *Livingston Enterprise*, June 4, 1892, p. 2; "Horr-Cinnabar-Tom Miner Voting Records," October 11, 14, 1892, pp. 41–42; and October 12, 1894, pp. 33–34, Yellowstone Gateway Museum.

53. "Local Layout," *Livingston Enterprise*, June 20, 1896, p. 5. According to J. E. Williams, the keeper of one of Cinnabar's saloons in 1888 was also the general tourist agent for the town, which may have indicated that he had a connection with the railroad. J. E. Williams, *Through the Yellowstone Park. Vacation Notes. Summer of 1888. Copied From the Amherst Record* (Amherst, MA: Amherst Record, no date), p. 7. Killings in Gardiner saloons are recorded in Whittlesey, *Death in Yellowstone*, 1995, 2014.

54. "For Highway Robbery," *Anaconda Standard*, January 16, 1900, p. 2; "Local Layout" [Mitchell], *Livingston Enterprise*, January 20, p. 5; "End of Mitchell's Trial at Livingston for Highway Robbery," Helena *Independent*, February 14, 1900, p. 7.

55. Robert D. McGonnigle, *When I Went West. From the Bad Lands to California* (Pittsburg, PA: no publisher, privately printed, 1901), pp. 64–72, 93, as reprinted in Whittlesey and Watry, *Ho! For Wonderland*, pp. 217–238, especially p. 219. This man was "Hellroaring Bill Jones," probably the same man who had been a confidant of Theodore Roosevelt in Medora and who was named

Patrick McKeone there. He died at Gardiner of freezing in 1910. Haines, *Yellowstone Story*, II, pp. 234–235; Whittlesey, *Death in Yellowstone*, 2014, p. 116.

56. "Shot to Miss but Hit—Gang of Rowdy Men Come to Grief Near Cinnabar," *Anaconda* (MT) *Standard*, September 14, 1900, p. 2; "Current Items," *Big Timber* (MT) *Pioneer*, September 20, 1900, p. 5.

57. William H. Walsh, "Tim Reagan's Ghost—A Frontier Tale Illustrating the Life of Montana Miners," *Bath* (ME) *Independent*, February 15, 1896, pp. 1, 5.

58. Haines, Lena Potter interview; Haines, Mrs. Robert Cutler interview, YNP Archives; Hoppe in McPherren, *Imprints*, p. 197; Jack Haynes's interview with Joe George, March 24, 1944, in Haynes collection 1504, file 108:23, Montana State University.

59. "Hundreds Attend W.A. Hall Funeral, Bozeman," *Park County News*, July 2, 1931, p. 1. There is an additional, very short obituary a few days earlier in the *Livingston Enterprise*. Hall died June 24, 1931.

60. "Personal Points" [Hall store], *Livingston Enterprise*, July 2, 1887, p. 3. An advertisement for W. A. Hall's store at Fridley appeared on page 1 of this same issue. Birth of Hall's son Arthur at Fridley was mentioned in "Upper Yellowstone Notes," *Livingston Enterprise*, February 4, 1888, p. 3. Mrs. Hall was noted as living at Fridley in "Upper Yellowstone Notes," *Livingston Enterprise*, July 21, 1888, p. 4. Hall's ranch at Tom Miner Basin was mentioned in "Brained His Brother," *Livingston Enterprise*, December 9, 1893, p. 4; and "Local Layout" [homestead], *Livingston Enterprise*, April 14, 1894, p. 5.

61. Doris Whithorn placed family papers relating to the W. A. Hall family in the Yellowstone Gateway Museum of Park County, Livingston, Montana, including photos, family-group sheets, and [Sons of W. A. Hall], "Hall Description #1." W. A. Hall's children were Arthur F. (1888–1936), Earl H. (1889–1950), Warren E. (1893–1962), Wilda (a daughter who lived for only six weeks in 1896), and James R. (1900–1951).

62. "W.A. Hall Dies after Illness," *Bozeman Daily Chronicle*, June 25, 1931, p. 4; "Pioneer Park Co. Merchant Is Dead," Bozeman *Courier*, June 26, 1931, pp. 1, 12. See also Tom Stout, *Montana: Its Story and Biography* (Chicago: American Historical Society, 1921, 3 vols.), vol. 1, pp. 278–279.

63. [Sons of W. A. Hall], Hall Description #1, Yellowstone Gateway Museum; advertisement for W. A. Hall and his store at Fridley in *Livingston Enterprise*, July 2, 1887, p. 1; "Upper Yellowstone Notes" [W. A. Hall has new son at Fridley], *Livingston Enterprise*, February 4, 1888, p. 3; "Personal Points" [Hall leases Hoppe's ranch at Cinnabar for one year], *Livingston Enterprise*, May 17, 1890, p. 3. Completeness requires that we report the *Livingston Enterprise*'s mention in November of 1889 of county commissioners there issuing a business license for a "Weaver & Hall" company for a livery stable, as well as a "hotel"

license to a "W. P. Hall," which could have been a typographical error for W. T. Hall, who had formerly resided in Gardiner (a different person from W. A. Hall). No location was given for these businesses, which may have been located in Livingston rather than Cinnabar, but if this "Hall" was in fact W. A. Hall, it indicates that he arrived in Cinnabar a few months earlier than 1890. See "List of Licenses Issued . . . ending Nov 30, 1889," *Livingston Enterprise*, December 7, 1889, p. 5. At present, we cannot be sure who this Weaver (first name unknown) even was, let alone whether he partnered with our W. A. Hall in Cinnabar or partnered with some other Hall in Livingston. So to be safe, he is mentioned only in this note. And too, W. A. Hall's own recollections stated that he arrived in Cinnabar in 1890 (rather than late 1889) and did not mention this Mr. Weaver at all.

64. Jack E. Haynes, interview with W. A. Hall, May 18, 1953, in Haynes collection 1504, files 112:10, 97:2, Montana State University; W. A. Hall store advertisement in Gardiner *Wonderland*, May 29, 1902. An example of W. A. Hall's advertising for his Cinnabar store is "Yellowstone Park," *Anaconda Standard*, July 26, 1898, p. 10.

65. "Personal Points" [Hall purchases hotel], *Livingston Enterprise*, May 23, 1891, p. 3; "Personal Mention" [Hall's new livery], *Livingston Post*, April 23, 1891, p. 3; "Licenses Issued . . . Ending May 31, 1891" [showing Hall's hotel], *Livingston Enterprise*, June 6, 1891, p. 1; printed business card "W. A. Hall, Cinnabar Hotel and Saloon," hand dated February 15, 1891, sent to Yellowstone National Park museum collection by descendant William J. Hall. In July, Hall was called the "popular manager of the Cinnabar hotel, per "Personal Points," *Livingston Enterprise*, July 4, 1891, p. 3. In addition to purchasing the Cinnabar hotel from E. J. Fairfax, Mr. Hall also purchased some additional lots at Cinnabar from John T. Work. This land transfer occurred April 23, 1891, and was described as two certain lots, each 25 × 50 feet and located in Lot 2, and the SE4 of NE4 of Section 17; and lots 2 and 3 of Section 16, T9S, R8E, "being the same lands and premises conveyed to the said William A. Hall by John T. Work and wife," April 23, 1891 (Park County Deed Records, Vol. 6, p. 442).

66. L. B. Hoppe, advertisement for "The Cinnabar Store, the only store in Cinnabar," *Livingston Enterprise*, July 11, 1891, p. 3; "Local Matters" [post office established at Cinnabar], *Livingston Post*, June 30, 1892, p. 3; "Local Layout" [L. B. Hoppe is postmaster], *Livingston Enterprise*, August 13, 1892, p. 5. Lee Hoppe closed his store, apparently only for the winter, in October per "Personal Points," *Livingston Enterprise*, October 24, 1891, p. 3.

67. "List of Licenses . . . ending Dec 1, 1891" [Hall's licenses for gambling], *Livingston Enterprise*, December 12, 1891, p. 1; "Local Matters," *Livingston Post*, February 11, 1892, p. 3; "Local Matters," *Livingston Post*, February 18, 1892, p. 3; "List of Licenses . . . ending February 28, 1892" [Keeneys doing

business without license], *Livingston Enterprise*, March 12, 1892, p. 2; "Local Layout" [Mrs. Keeney's gambling arrest], *Livingston Enterprise*, September 5, 1891, p. 3; and "District Court" [*State v. Mary and Joe Keeney* for "keeping a gambling house without a license"], *Livingston Enterprise*, October 24, 1891, p. 1. Conviction of Joe but not Mary is in "District Court," *Livingston Enterprise*, November 14, 1891, p. 1.

68. "Local Layout" [Maggie closes her Livingston store], *Livingston Enterprise*, February 6, 1892, p. 3; "Local Matters" [post office established at Cinnabar], *Livingston Post*, June 30, 1892, p. 3; "Local Layout" [W. A. Hall appointed postmaster at Cinnabar to replace Lee Hoppe, resigned; Lee Hoppe and wife will remain in Bozeman at the Monroe House], *Livingston Enterprise*, July 22, 1893, p. 5.

69. An 1893 letter documented Hall's presence at Cinnabar as a storekeeper that year, when it referred to the "storekeeper at Cinnabar Billie Hall." E. B. Rapley to George Anderson, August 19, 1893, archive document 1272, YNP Archives. Hall and Lee Hoppe might have seen this coming or even planned it, for they traveled together with their wives to Livingston in March and stayed together at the Albemarle Hotel. One wonders what they discussed. See "Personal Points," *Livingston Enterprise*, February 18, 1893, p. 4.

70. W. A. Hall ("merchant" listed twice), in "List of Licenses Collected for Quarter ending February 28, 1895," *Livingston Enterprise*, March 23, 1895, p. 2. A Christmas card from the W. A. Halls in the YNP museum collection stating that Hall's store was "established 1893" has to be referring to his Cinnabar store, but his first dual license was mentioned in the *Enterprise* of March 23, 1895, which cinches the establishment of his Gardiner store. Owning stores in Fridley, Cinnabar, Gardiner, and Aldridge must have made it difficult for him to recall exact years, but in his interview with Jack Haynes in 1953 (previously cited), Hall stated that he had established his Gardiner store in 1895. Additionally, his store stationery in 1942 stated that the W. A. Hall Company was "established 1895," and that date has to refer to Gardiner. See Earl H. Hall to National Park Service, October 16, 1942, in Series 02-E, box 16, "Public Utilities Correspondence, 1940-1948," YNP Archives.

71. "Real Estate and Mining Transfers," *Livingston Enterprise*, November 12, 1898, p. 5.

72. Bill and Doris Whithorn, *Photo History of Gardiner, Jardine, Crevasse* (Livingston: Park County News, no date [1968]), p. [8]; Whithorn, *Paradise Valley on the Yellowstone*, p. 15. Hall's store in Aldridge is in Whithorn, *Photo History of Aldridge*, p. 82; in "Local Layout" [Hall's Aldridge store burns], *Livingston Enterprise*, February 2, 1901, p. 5; and in "Additional Local" [Hall has moved into his new store at Aldridge], *Livingston Enterprise*, May 10, 1902, p. 6. Termination of his partnership with D. S. Terry at Fridley is in "Local

Layout," *Livingston Enterprise*, October 6, 1894, p. 5, and an advertisement in the October 13 issue. Hall's announcement of his abandoning his Cinnabar store and moving everything to his Gardiner store is "Hall Will Move," *Livingston Enterprise*, March 7, 1903, p. 1.

73. "Cinnabar and Gardiner," *Livingston Enterprise*, June 4, 1892, p. 2; advertisement for W. A. Hall, *Anaconda Standard*, July 7, 1898, p. 7, and many others that summer. That Mr. Hall made a big change in 1895 was attested to by the *Enterprise* of September 21, 1895 ("Local Layout," p. 5), which stated: "W. A. Hall of Cinnabar has bought the building of F. B. Tolhurst at that place and will remove it, together with his other buildings, to a new location on lots near the Northern Pacific Depot."

74. "M.A. Holem," *Livingston Enterprise Souvenir Park County*, 1976 reprint, p. 57.

75. "Our Faking Post," *Livingston Enterprise*, April 27, 1901, p. 4, stated that the Hefferlin Mercantile Company is building a large general store at Cinnabar. For its movement to Gardiner, see "Our Towns and What They Are," Gardiner *Wonderland*, vol. 1#1, p. 1, May 17, 1902, p. 1; "Local News," May 17, 1902; and "Local News," July 31, 1902. Movement of the Cinnabar store to Gardiner and the Hefferlins moving back to Livingston is in "Local Layout," *Livingston Enterprise*, December 6, 1902, p. 5. This date of 1902 is from those newspapers, but see Bill and Doris Whithorn, *Photo History of Gardiner*, p. [11], which shows a photo of the "O.K. Store" in Gardiner in what the book says was 1900, so perhaps Hefferlin had a store in Gardiner earlier. The O.K. Store may have received its name from the Hefferlin brothers or perhaps from Mr. and Mrs. Hefferlin—O.M. and K.—hence "O.K."

76. Haines, interview with Mrs. Robert Eugene Cutler, December 13, 1961, YNP Archives. The fact that there were three stores at Cinnabar was reported in "Gardiner News," *Livingston Enterprise*, September 28, 1901, p. 2.

77. Frances Lynn Turpin, "A Trip through Yellowstone Park, 1895," no date, unpublished manuscript at Montana State University, pp. 9–10.

78. [G. L. Henderson], "Our Park Visit," July, 1887, in Ash Scrapbook, p. 7a, YNP Library. This clipping was originally published in *Livingston Enterprise*, July 23, 1887, p. 3.

79. "Drowned in the Yellowstone," *Livingston Enterprise*, June 9, 1894, p. 1; "[W. H.] Davis' Body Recovered," *Livingston Enterprise*, July 21, 1894, p. 4.

80. Haines, *Yellowstone Story*, II, pp. 104–105. Jack Haynes apparently recalled this man's name incorrectly for he was "Specimen Schmidt," not Schultz. See Whittlesey, *Death in Yellowstone*, 2014, pp. 220–221.

81. The article stated: "An old hunter at Cinnabar, who has lived for fifteen years on the banks of the Yellowstone, and who is known as 'Old Specimen,' says he is satisfied with the park regulations." W. F. H[atfield], "Play With the

Bears," no date [probably 1894], in Scrapbook 4209, p. 56, YNP Library. Schmidt's hand-signed voting record is in "Horr-Cinnabar-Tom Miner Voting Records," October 9, 1894, pp. 67–68, Yellowstone Gateway Museum.

82. Bill and Doris Whithorn, *Calamity's in Town* (Livingston: *Livingston Enterprise*, no date [1977]), p. 45; Whithorn, *Photo History of Aldridge*, p. 171. The Schmidt–Calamity association probably occurred 1896–1902. Calamity Jane was often present in Livingston and the towns of the upper Yellowstone like Cinnabar during the period from 1896 to 1902. She is known to have been selling her booklet in 1897 at Yellowstone Lake, for traveler E. S. Kenderdine encountered her there and the local newspapers carried her exploits often. For examples, see T. S. Kenderdine, *California Revisited, 1858-1897*, pp. 299–300; and "A Distinguished Visitor" [Calamity Jane], *Livingston Post*, August 12, 1896, p. 3.

83. "'Specimen' Schmidt—A Unique Old Character that Livingston Delights to Honor," *Anaconda Standard*, August 13, 1892, p. 7. See also "Local Layout" [Schmidt comes to town], *Livingston Enterprise*, August 13, 1892, p. 5.

84. "Local Layout" [Lindstrom dies], *Livingston Enterprise*, June 18, 1892, p. 5; A[lbert] F. Zaum, "The Yellowstone Park" [in many parts], *Notre Dame Scholastic* 22 (January 19, 1889): 330–331.

85. McPherren, *Imprints*, p. 230; "'Geyser Jim' in More Trouble," *Livingston Enterprise*, May 9, 1885, p. 3.

86. William Davis in [G. L. Henderson], "Our Park Visit," *Livingston Enterprise*, July 23, 1887, p. 3 (this also appeared in G. L. Henderson, Ash Scrapbook, p. 7a, YNP Library); J. E. Williams, *Through the Yellowstone Park*, p. 7; Owen Wister, "Diary—Notebook, British Columbia, Washington, Oregon, California, Wyoming, July–September, 1887," entry for September 1, 1887, University of Wyoming, American Heritage Center.

87. "Local Layout," *Livingston Enterprise*, November 26, 1887, p. 3; "Local Layout," *Livingston Enterprise*, December 17, 1887, p. 3; "Local Layout" [sheep], *Livingston Enterprise*, January 3, 1891, p. 3.

88. F. B. Nash, "Vacation Notes," 1891, Scrapbook 4208, p. 20, YNP Library. A photo of the bear is YELL-13981, YNP photo archives.

89. "Butte Current Notes" [Gassert's zoo], *Anaconda Standard*, May 16, 1893, p. 4. Mrs. McNeil's photo, dated 1888–1891 and reproduced elsewhere in this book, shows elk at Gassert's ranch.

90. "Livingston Herald," in *Big Timber Pioneer*, June 8, 1893, p. 1. For an unusually environmental commentary by a Cinnabar resident on protection of the park's animals, see "Captain Goode is Good," *Livingston Enterprise*, December 15, 1900, p. 7.

91. William E. Curtis, "The Bear, the Cage, and the Mules," a *Chicago Record* story quoted in the *St. Louis* (MO) *Republic*, September 16, 1900, magazine section, p. 6. For more on Curtis, see "Sketch of William E. Curtis" in

pamphlet, "William E. Curtis of the Chicago Record-Herald, Lecture Tour," no date, University of Iowa digital collection. Curtis's trip to the West began on July 16, per "Curtis' Trip over Burlington," *Omaha* (NE) *World Herald*, July 14, 1900, p. 12. For Curtis as "most reliable" writer, see "Curtis on the Situation," *Goshen* (IN) *Democrat*, September 26, 1900, p. 2. Hofer spent many months in 1900 in Alaska trapping Kodiak bears but arrived back in Yellowstone a few days before July 29, 1900, per H[ofer], "Notes from the Yellowstone Park," *Forest and Stream* 55, August 11, 1900, p. 196. For Hofer trapping bears in Alaska, see "After the Biggest of Bears," *Springfield* (MA) *Republican*, May 29, 1900, p. 10. For Hofer, Theodore Roosevelt, and William E. Curtis, all three, see Curtis, "Wouldn't Throw up a Good Job," *Scranton* (PA) *Tribune*, October 11, 1900, p. 4.

92. McPherren, *Imprints*, p. 214; *Harper's Weekly* article in Scrapbook 4208, 1893, YNP Library, p. 6. The taxidermy shop at Livingston belonged to the Wittich brothers beginning in the early 1880s.

93. Hoppe in McPherren, *Imprints*, p. 201; McPherren in McPherren, *Imprints*, pp. 253–256.

94. Photo 2006.045.0589, Yellowstone Gateway Museum of Park County, Livingston, Montana. The 1887 date of this photo may be the reason that McPherren gave the origin of Buffalo Bill's Wild West show as "1887" when in fact it was 1883.

95. Hoppe in McPherren, *Imprints*, pp. 254–256.

96. Hoppe in McPherren, *Imprints*, pp. 256–257. McPherren's memory of seeing Canfield disembark from the train is on pp. 253–254.

97. McPherren, *Imprints*, pp. 269–270. A check with historians at the Buffalo Bill Historical Center, Cody, Wyoming, fails to confirm any of this information about Buffalo Bill holding tryouts at Cinnabar, but the name Sherman Canfield did turn up in their records. In a letter to the author dated February 26, 2013, Jeremy Johnston, managing editor of the papers of Buffalo Bill Cody, cautioned that a number of towns have claimed that Buffalo Bill held tryouts in their town and that some of those claims "do not hold water." While none of the Cinnabar cowboys' names in the portrait appears on the master list of Buffalo Bill's Wild West show at McCracken Library in Cody, Wyoming, it is apparent from the existence of the portrait at Yellowstone Gateway Museum and its attached caption that something happened at Cinnabar on July 4, 1887. We also have Ida Miller's claim that she personally saw Sherman Canfield disembark from the train in the summer of 1894, as well as Hugo Hoppe's long testimony—quoted above—to his relatives (chronicled by McPherren) about the event. On the other hand, there is no mention of these festivities in the *Livingston Enterprise* for July 9 and 13, 1887, as there arguably should have been had such "big doings" been happening at Cinnabar.

98. McPherren, *Imprints*, pp. 201, 249–250.

99. "Cinnabar and Gardiner," *Livingston Enterprise*, June 4, 1892, p. 2.

100. Park visitation statistics are in Haines, *Yellowstone Story*, II, p. 478.

101. "News of the Week," Bozeman *Avant Courier*, August 30, 1883, p. 2. The *River Press* (Ft. Benton, MT) for August 29, 1883, p. 5 ("Local Notes") also reported this.

102. M. Harris to Secretary of Interior, October 29, 1886, in Letters Sent volume, p. 58, YNP Archives; Archive Documents 2859, 2865, YNP Archives. The extension of this telegraph line from Cinnabar to Mammoth was announced in "Our Exchange Table," *Daily Yellowstone Journal* (Miles City, MT), May 19, 1886, p. 1.

103. "Exit Telephone Pete," *Livingston Herald*, March 26, 1896, p. 3; "Local Matters," *Livingston Post*, February 12, 1896, p. 3. See generally Ellen Arguimbau, "From Party Lines and Barbed Wire—A History of Telephones in Montana," *Montana the Magazine of Western History* 63 (Autumn, 2013): 34–45.

104. Whithorn, *Photo History of Aldridge*, pp. 5, 111. Whithorn's reference here was probably to "Cinnabar News," *Livingston Enterprise*, October 8, 1884, p. 1. For 1901, see "Local Layout" [school divided from Horr], *Livingston Enterprise*, November 9, 1901, p. 5.

105. Chester and Irene Allen, brown family scrapbook beginning "Georgia Allen," 11 Strawberry Creek, Livingston, Montana, p. 25; "Local Layout" [school trustees select Pearl Fitzgerald], *Livingston Enterprise*, December 7, 1901, p. 5; "School Apportionment," *Livingston Enterprise*, December 13, 1902, p. 1; "Things They Are Doing" [Cinnabar school], *Livingston Enterprise*, February 14, 1903, p. 1; "Local Layout" [Nellie Mahoney], *Livingston Enterprise*, March 21, 1903, p. 5.

106. "Local Layout," *Livingston Enterprise*, June 20, 1896, p. 4.

107. G. L. Henderson, "Park Mention," *Livingston Enterprise*, January 28, 1888, p. 3.

108. There has been great confusion in both the land records and the documentary literature between Harry R. Horr and Henry R. Horr, because both men were H. R. Horr. But now there is proof that "Harry" Horr and "Henry" Horr were one and the same person. See letter dated May 15, 1896, in 54th Cong., 1st Sess., House Report 1846, SN-3464 (Washington: GPO, 1896), pp. 11–12. Per the US Census of 1870 at Bozeman, Montana, Henry Horr was born in or about 1842 in New York. His sons and brothers lived in Horr (later Electric), Montana, for decades, and they appeared in area land records into the 1930s.

109. "Local Layout," *Livingston Enterprise*, March 14, 1885, p. 3, and "Personal Points," March 28, 1885, p. 3, have Harry Horr as a resident of Cinnabar interested in the coal at Horr. Whithorn, *Photo History of Aldridge*, p. 22, mentions that Harry Horr was a notary public at Cinnabar that same year. The

Livingston Enterprise announced on October 29, 1887 ("Local Layout," p. 3) that "a town is to be established at Horr coal mines to be known as Horr." "Park Branch Notes," *Livingston Enterprise*, February 18, 1888, stated that the town of Horr recently "sprang up" and was named for the "irrepressible Harry." Old-timer Joe George remembered him as "Harry Horr" and stated that he early called the place "Horr Coal Mines." Jack Haynes's interview with Joe George, March 24, 1944, in Haynes collection 1504, file 108:23, Montana State University, Bozeman, Montana.

110. "The Cinnabar Coal Mines to Be Opened," *Livingston Enterprise*, October 1, 1887; "Local Layout" [new town of Horr], *Livingston Enterprise*, October 15, 1887, p. 3; "Montana News" [coke ovens], *Great Falls Tribune*, November 17, 1887, p. 3; Gallatin County Land Records, vol. 1, p. 32, Henry R. Horr, May 24, 1884, Declaration of water rights on Reese Creek: 400 inches of Reese Creek for irrigation of his homestead to wit: E2 of NE4 and the E2 of SE4, S6, T9S, R8E; Park County Land Records, vol. 31, p. 35, USA to Henry R. Horr, March 29, 1904; vol. 13, p. 104, August 22, 1895. Historian Doris Whithorn isolated the very beginnings of the town of Aldridge in her *Photo History of Aldridge*, p. 27, which discussed the "tapping of the number seven vein." See also Aubrey L. Haines, audiotape interview with Lena Spiker Potter, April 20, 1962, YNP Archives. For general history of Horr, see Culpin, "Historical Information and Context, as cited, p. [1].

111. "Horr" [Aldridge not named yet but growing and road is proposed], *Livingston Enterprise*, July 8, 1893, p. 4; "Pinching Poachers" [possible road to Aldridge being discussed], *Anaconda Standard*, June 24, 1896, p. 9. Initially residents referred to Aldridge as "the new mines at Mulherin Lake," "New Horr," and "Lake Camp."

112. "Synopsis of Proceedings" [of county commissioners], *Livingston Enterprise*, August 15, 1896, p. 1. See also same story for July 18.

113. Culpin, "Historical Information and Context," as previously cited, p. [1].

114. "Mrs. Gassert's Farm," *Livingston Post*, August 19, 1896, p. 3. For Jacob Reding and the long-running court case, see "Got His Own and Died," *Butte Weekly Miner*, February 11, 1897, p. 2; "Park's Real Estate . . . Jacob Reding's Will," *Anaconda Standard*, February 22, 1897, p. 10; "The Reding Will Case," *Livingston Herald*, March 18, 1897; and "The Will Stands," Helena *Independent,* January 28, 1899, p. 1. According to an obituary, Harry Gassert (1841–1896) and Jacob Reding discovered the first silver mine at Butte. See "The Funeral of Mr. Gassert," *Anaconda Standard*, February 21, 1896, p. 1; and "Death of Harry Gassert," *Big Timber Pioneer*, February 20, 1896, p. 4.

115. Moses Harris to T. F. Oakes, February 22, 1887, in Letters Received volume, YNP Archives; Harris, *Annual Report of Superintendent of Yellowstone . . . 1887* (Washington: GPO, 1887), p. 4; 1888, p. 5.

116. Moses Harris, *Annual Report of Superintendent of Yellowstone . . . 1888* (Washington: GPO, 1888), p. 12; "Yellowstone Park," newspaper clipping, 1895, in Scrapbook 4209, p. 58; Archive Document 2029, YNP Archives.

117. George S. Anderson, *Annual Report of the Superintendent of Yellowstone . . .1891* (Washington: GPO, 1891), p. 6.

118. "Railroad Wreck—A Passenger Train on the Park Branch Rushes Down an Embankment," *Livingston Enterprise*, September 6, 1883, p. 1.

119. LeClercq in Chapple and Cane, eds., *Yellowstone Land of Wonders*, pp. 37–38.

120. Henry T. Finck, "A Week in Yellowstone Park," *The Nation* 45 (September 11, 1887): 167.

121. "Local Layout," *Livingston Enterprise*, August 22, 1891, p. 3. For another mention of Dago Joe, see Whithorn, *Photo History of Aldridge*, p. 96.

122. "Railroad Rumblings," *Livingston Post*, January 28, 1892, p. 3; "A Perilous Ride," *Livingston Enterprise*, January 23, 1892, p. 3.

123. "Wreck on the Park Branch," *Livingston Enterprise*, June 18, 1892, p. 1.

124. "Crushed to Death—A Wreck on the Park Branch," *Livingston Enterprise*, May 13, 1893, p. 1. The *Post* had recently discontinued, so no comparable story from it exists. The *Republican* did not yet exist, and no copies are known of the *Herald* from 1893.

125. *Chicago News-Record*, "How It Feels to Be in a Railway Wreck," quoted in *Livingston Enterprise*, January 14, 1893, p. 6.

8. "THE ONLY LITTLE GIRL IN CINNABAR"

1. McPherren, *Imprints*, p. 205.

2. McPherren, *Imprints*, pp. 208–209.

3. McPherren, *Imprints*, pp. 209–210.

4. McPherren, *Imprints*, p. 216.

5. McPherren, *Imprints*, pp. 244–245.

6. McPherren, *Imprints*, pp. 215–216. The voting record pages for 1892 show that Hugo and his sons (excluding Albert) all lived there then. The 1894 pages show that by that time, both Albert Hoppe and Frank Holem were living there too, and this was probably where Maggie Williams met Frank Holem. The 1896 list shows that all five of Hoppe's sons were living at Cinnabar that year but does not specify where, although it was probably still at their hotel. "Horr-Cinnabar-Tom Miner Voting Records," October 1, 3, 7, and 11, 1892, pp. 31–32; and October 12, 1894, pp. 33–34, Yellowstone Gateway Museum.

7. McPherren, *Imprints*, pp. 229–230.

8. Page numbers for the mentioned items in McPherren, *Imprints* are Marcus
Daly, 220–221, 361; Geyser Jim, 230; Mrs. Schreiber, 232–233; Bill Price,
257–261; Fourth of July, 265–267; Calamity Jane, 273; F. Jay Haynes, 312; and
Hugo J. and Mary Hoppe, throughout. For mention of Ida Miller's visiting Aldridge in 1901, see "Aldridge Notes," *Livingston Enterprise*, August 3, 1901, p.
1. For Montana's election in 1894, see Brian Leech, "Hired Hands from Abroad:
The Populist Producers Ethic, Immigrant Workers, and Nativism in Montana's
1894 State Capital Election," University of Wisconsin, January 12, 2008, pp.
220–222, posted at http://digitalcommons.unl.edu/historyrawleyconference/21/
and accessed March 13, 2013. F. Jay Haynes's picture-taking stops throughout
the West were generally announced in local newspapers, but there was no such
notice in the *Enterprise* in 1894 and the location of that portrait of Ida Miller
today is unknown.

9. Dates of birth and death of Hugo Hoppe's children and ages calculated
from those dates are taken from ancestry.com; from the gravestones of many of
the family at Mountain View Cemetery in Livingston, Montana; and from other
sources as cited in this book. The vital dates were as follows: Margaret "Maggie"
Ann James Hoppe/Williams/Holem (born February 16, 1857; died November 29,
1918), Walter Monroe Hoppe (born August 6, 1864; died May 3, 1940), Hugo
"Hughie" Benton Hoppe (born September 25, 1865; died October 19, 1931),
George Lincoln Hoppe (born December 12, 1868; died November 20, 1951),
Leander "Lee" Black Hoppe (born February 19, 1870; died February 27, 1942);
and Albert Vincent Hoppe (born February 4, 1872; died May 24, 1936). Obituar-
ies are cited under each person's biography in this book.

10. McPherren, *Imprints*, p. 213, indicates that Bud Williams had disappeared
by 1894, but that was in the minds of the Hoppes, and Ida was apparently
remembering something she heard about a couple years later. McPherren, pp.
219–220, discusses Maggie's meanness according to little Ida. The *Enterprise*
last mentioned Bud in its issues of June 15, 1895 ("Mining Locations," p. 4), and
August 7, 1897 ("Castle Cullings," p. 2). Maggie was originally Margaret Ann
James. Hugo Hoppe adopted her, and thus she took the name Maggie Hoppe
until she married Bud Williams in Bozeman. They appeared in the US Census of
1880 there as a married couple, ages "38 and 22." Bud's age in 1880 squares
with his age of twenty-eight in the Census of 1870, also taken at Bozeman, where
he was listed as a "barkeeper." Therefore his birth year was in or about 1842.
Interestingly, a "boarder" who lived with them in 1880 was listed by the census
as "Mathew McGuirk," age fifty. He was one of the three men who founded
Mammoth Hot Springs in Yellowstone National Park in 1871. Bud and Maggie
Williams were shown sitting at far left in the F. Jay Haynes "porch" photo, H-
1573, dated October 8, 1885, Montana Historical Society.

11. Advertisement for "Williams and Hoppe" store in Livingston, *Livingston Enterprise*, March 21, 1891, p. 4; "Local Layout" [Lee Hoppe becomes postmaster], *Livingston Enterprise*, August 13, 1892, p. 5; "Local Layout" [Lee Hoppe marries Jessie Boomer], *Livingston Enterprise*, December 24, 1892, p. 5; "Local Layout" [Lee Hoppe resigns as postmaster; Lee and wife will remain in Bozeman for now], *Livingston Enterprise*, July 22, 1893, p. 5; "Local Layout" [funeral of Jessie Hoppe], *Livingston Enterprise*, August 11, 1900, p. 5; McPherren, *Imprints*, p. 200.

12. "Local Matters" [Hugh's marriage], *Livingston Post*, October 2, 1895, p. 3. Hugh's marriage occurred either in late September or on October 1, 1895. The end of his butcher-shop partnership is in "Local Layout," *Livingston Enterprise*, August 19, 1893, p. 5; and his ranch claim is in "Local Layout," *Livingston Enterprise*, May 5, 1894, p. 5.

13. McPherren, *Imprints*, p. 215.

14. McPherren, *Imprints*, pp. 233–234, 239–240; "Cinnabar and Gardiner," *Livingston Enterprise*, June 4, 1892, p. 2. George Hoppe's clerk job in Livingston is in "Local Layout," *Livingston Enterprise*, April 27, 1889, p. 5; and his store in Livingston is in "Local Layout," *Livingston Enterprise*, March 29, 1890, p. 3; and "Personal Points," April 5, 1890, p. 3. He sold the store to siblings Leander and Maggie in 1891, per "Local Layout," February 14, 1891, p. 3. His mining is at "Mining Locations," October 28, 1893, p. 1; and "Mining Locations," June 29, 1895, p. 6.

15. A. J. Campbell conveyance to Albert V. Hoppe, February 20, 1893, in deed records, vol. 21, p. 8; and Albert V. Hoppe conveyance to Hugo J. Hoppe, January 3, 1895, in deed records, vol. 21, p. 412. This latter conveyance was described as lots 2, 3, and 6 and the W2 of SW4 of S16, T9S, R8E. It was also reported in "Real Estate and Mining Transfers," *Livingston Enterprise*, January 19, 1895, p. 4, and the price was five thousand dollars.

16. Bob Moore, e-mail communication to Lee Whittlesey, August 8, 2008. Moore included a photo of Hugh and Albert Hoppe's freight line, probably showing the brothers and others on a freight wagon being pulled by at least eight horses or mules. See also "Commissioners' Proceedings" [Albert appointed election judge at Tom Miner], *Livingston Enterprise*, September 15, 1900, p. 8; "Personal Points" [Albert leaves "for his ranch in Tom Miner"], *Livingston Enterprise*, October 15, 1900, p. 3; and "Local Layout" [Albert appointed Republican chairman at Tom Miner], *Livingston Enterprise*, June 7, 1902, p. 5; "Additional Local" [Albert sues H. B. Hoppe to enjoin him from disposing of their jointly owned ranch], *Livingston Enterprise*, May 30, 1903, p. 6; and Maud Bond Strong to A. V. Hoppe, bill of sale for ranch property and personal property on the land in Tom Miner Basin, at Miscellaneous Records, vol. 8, p. 457, recorded February 2, 1904. See also vol. 33, p. 26.

17. McPherren, *Imprints*, p. 253.

18. McPherren, *Imprints*, p. 249. A "lorgnette" was a pair of glasses mounted on a stick for holding by the wearer.

19. McPherren, *Imprints*, pp. 250–251.

20. McPherren, *Imprints*, p. 252.

21. McPherren, *Imprints*, pp. 239, 253. Her "years of disillusionment and heartache" probably referred to the murder of her husband in 1921 in Sheridan, Wyoming, and her subsequent raising of their children. See the earlier footnote about her life.

9. HOPPE PLATS THE TOWNSITE, REORGANIZES HIS COMPANY, AND DIES, BUT CINNABAR LIVES ON (1895–1903)

1. Hoppe in McPherren, *Imprints*, p. 201; Babcock, *History of the Yellowstone Valley*, p. 171; "No Site Yet" [Hoppe incorporates], *Anaconda Standard*, June 6, 1895, p. 1; "Local Layout" [stock issuance], *Livingston Enterprise*, June 8, 1898, p. 5; "Local Layout" [Hoppe's property for sale], advertisement in *Livingston Enterprise*, January 13, 1894, p. 3; Whithorn, *Photo History of Aldridge*, pp. 14, 26. The *Livingston Post* obituary, September 18, 1895, p. 3, mentioned Hoppe as a county commissioner, and he appeared constantly in the newspapers during his period of service. The *Standard* spelled Campbell's name as "Chambelido."

2. "Plat of the Town of Cinnabar, Park County, Montana," scale one hundred twenty feet to an inch, June 20, 1895 (filed June 29), in "Restored Plats" drawer, Park County Clerk's Office. The *Enterprise* reported Hoppe's incorporation in "Local Layout," June 8, 1895, p. 5; and reported his filing of the plat in "Local Layout," July 6, 1895, p. 5. It reported his proposed road in "Local Layout," June 15, 1895, p. 5. The note in *Livingston Enterprise Souvenir Park County*, 1976 reprint, p. 57, which says "in the spring of 1895, H. J. Hoppe became superintendent of the enterprises of the town, he having purchased his partners' shares in the townsite at this time," seems to refer to this capitalistic venture.

3. "Rich Gold Mines," *Livingston Enterprise*, June 22, 1895, p. 1. Hoppe's two advertisements appeared in the *Livingston Enterprise*, June 22, 1895, p. 7.

4. Mary Hoppe's death is in "Local Matters," *Livingston Post*, November 1, 1893, p. 3; "Local Items," *Livingston Herald*, November 7, 1894, p. 3; "Death of Mrs. Hoppe," *Livingston Enterprise*, November 3, 1894, p. 5; and Allan R. Joy, "Tribute Rendered to the Memory of the Late Mrs. H. J. Hoppe At the [Her] Funeral Services November 2nd, 1894, at Livingston, Montana," Item number YELL-7934, Cabinet 13, Box M-2, YNP Museum Collection. The *Post*, the

Herald, and the *Enterprise* all gave her death date as Wednesday, October 31, but her tombstone shows the date as October 30.

5. Elva R. Howard, "Interview with Mrs. Walter M. Hoppe, Livingston," November 22–29, 1941, and second interview December 1–7, 1941, in WPA records, Montana State University, Bozeman, copy at YNP Library; Hugo Hoppe in McPherren, *Imprints*, pp. 112–113, 123, 127; marriage certificate for Richard William James and Mary Jane Gee, June 2, 1854, New Salem, Ohio (Richard shown as having been born in 1834 in Kentucky), via ancestry.com. Ella Fitzgerald, who married Walter Hoppe, remembered forty-seven years later that Hugo and Mary's marriage was "a romance similar to that of Tennyson's 'Enoch Arden.'" A historian of literature says that while the poem may seem "stilted and mawkishly romantic" to us today, it was written at a time when "unrequited love and unselfish devotion to one's family" were favorite subjects of English and American readers. See "Enoch Arden" commentary at http://www.enotes.com/enoch-arden-salem/enoch-arden-9560000228, accessed April 17, 2013. For the announced publication of "Enoch Arden," see "Tennyson's New Volume" ["will publish . . . tomorrow"], *Daily National Republican* (Washington, DC), July 29, 1864, p. 2; and "Literary," *Cleveland* (OH) *Morning Leader*, November 28, 1864, p. 1.

6. McPherren, *Imprints*, p. 312.

7. McPherren, *Imprints*, pp. 317–318.

8. Hoppe in McPherren, *Imprints*, p. 318.

9. "Local Layout" [Hoppe disposes of his business to Walter], *Livingston Enterprise*, December 29, 1894, p. 5. Or perhaps Hugo Hoppe felt that he was going to beat the disease and thus truly sold the entire business to Walter with the idea of retiring, because Ella Hoppe stated in her 1941 interview that Walter bought out his father's business just before she and Walter were married a few months later, including hotel, livery barn, blacksmith shop, post office, and store. Elva R. Howard, "Interview with Mrs. Walter Hoppe," as cited.

10. "Local Layout," *Livingston Enterprise*, January 19, 1895, p. 5, says Hugo and Maggie left for California on January 12, while "Livingston Notes," included in "A Perilous Journey," *Anaconda Standard*, July 25, 1895, p. 8, states that they came back in July and were soon leaving for Portland. Maggie Williams wrote the *Enterprise* ("Local Layout," August 10, 1895, p. 5) that Hugo was briefly confined to his bed in Portland but got better, so they headed south. The California announcement of Hugo Hoppe's death appeared in "Death of H. J. Hoppe," *San Diego* (CA) *Union*, September 14, 1895, p. 5, stating that Hoppe died at Ninth and Beech Streets, that he was an old friend of C. H. Stuart of Chula Vista, and that he died "yesterday," September 13 (incorrect). See also, "Death of Hugo J. Hoppe," *Livingston Enterprise*, September 14, 1895, p. 4; "Death of H. J. Hoppe," *Livingston Post*, September 18, 1895, p. 3; "H. J.

Hoppe—One of the State's Old Timers Passes from Earth," *Livingston Herald*, September 19, 1895, p. 3; "Funeral of Hugo J. Hoppe," *Anaconda Standard*, September 23, 1895, p. 8; "Two Pioneers Dead," *Anaconda Standard*, September 14, 1895, p. 7; and "Cinnabar," *Livingston Enterprise Souvenir Edition*, 1976, p. 57 (this article included a photo of Hugo Hoppe). The *Enterprise* obituary stated that Hoppe's funeral was to be held on September 17, "when the remains are expected to reach [Livingston] from California."

11. "[Body] Found in the Yellowstone," *Minneapolis* (MN) *Journal*, October 25, 1895, p. 3; "Popejoy His Name," *Anaconda Standard*, October 28, 1895, p. 9; and "His Identity Disclosed," *Livingston Enterprise*, November 2, 1895, p. 1. For the bridge, see Archive Documents 2551, 2552 [Hoppes building bridge], 1896, YNP Archives; "Local Layout" [CTC erecting bridge], *Livingston Enterprise*, April 25, 1896, p. 5; "A Road Session" [citizens erect bridge], *Livingston Post*, May 20, 1896, p. 1; and "Bridge Swept Away," *Livingston Post*, June 10, 1896, p. 2, stating that the bridge was built by the Cinnabar Townsite Company.

12. The *Enterprise* noted on September 21, 1895 ("Local Layout," p. 5) that "W. A. Hall of Cinnabar has bought the building of F. B. Tolhurst at that place and will remove it, together with his other buildings, to a new location on lots near the Northern Pacific Depot." See also "Upper Yellowstone Notes" [new construction at Cinnabar], *Livingston Enterprise*, May 9, 1896, p. 1; and "Local Matters" [boosterism], *Livingston Post*, August 19, 1896, p. 3. For the low park travel, see "Local Matters" [E. C. Waters comments], *Livingston Post*, October 21, 1896, p. 3; and Haines, *Yellowstone Story*, II, p. 478.

13. Per the land records, Leander Hoppe sold his interests in his father's land to his brother Hugh B. Hoppe on June 26, 1899 (vol. 22, p. 337). Walter bought out the interests of his brothers, Hughie, George, and Albert, and his sister, Maggie, on March 24, 1900 (vol. 26, pp. 98–101). He purchased the interests of Millicent Hoppe and Georgetta Hoppe (by then divorced from George) on October 5, 1907 (vol. 26, pp. 411–412); and that of Frank and Maggie A. Holem on March 31, 1908 (vol. 26, pp. 438–439). Walter also owned a piece of land on the east side of Yellowstone River and just north of Cedar Creek, which bordered Robert Cutler's land to the south. In late March of 1897, he contracted with Cutler for a half interest in the water rights of Cedar Creek. See "Local Layout" [Cedar Creek], *Livingston Enterprise*, April 3, 1897, p. 5.

14. "Local Items" [Walter marries], *Livingston Herald*, May 7, 1896, p. 3; "Local Matters" [Walter marries], *Livingston Post*, May 6, 1896, p. 3; "Local Layout" [Walter marries on May 4 at brother Lee's residence in Livingston], *Livingston Enterprise*, May 9, 1896, p. 5. "In Livingston," *Anaconda Standard*, May 10, 1896, p. 12, inconsistently says the date was May 7. Ella Fitzgerald Hoppe was "Edda E. Fitzgerald, age 5," in the US Census of 1880, but that spelling was corrected or changed later to Ella. She was from one of Gardiner's

most important families, her father, Selleck M. Fitzgerald, having been the park's assistant superintendent (1840–1932). As stated by Selleck Fitzgerald and his wife, Mary, they had thirteen children by 1900, with nine of them living at that time. At least eight of these children were girls, and that was grist for a joke that Mr. and Mrs. Fitzgerald provided marriage partners "for everyone in the county." See "City News" [Fitzgerald], *Bozeman Weekly Chronicle*, April 7, 1886, p. 3; and "S. M. Fitzgerald Passes Away at Fishtail, Mont.," *Livingston Enterprise*, March 23, 1932. Per the 1880 and 1900 US Censuses, the known Fitzgerald children and their birth years were Henry B. (1863); Ambrose (1864); Ransom (1865); Louisa (Eliza J.?) (1868); Mary M. (1869); Susan E. (Eva S.?) (1871); Selleck M. (1873); Ida B. (1874); Edda E. (Ella E.?) (1875); Emma M. (1876 or 1877); Jessie M. (1878); Etta P. (Pearl E.?) (1881); and Babe (1883). Compare these census records to Selleck Fitzgerald's biography in Babcock, *History of the Yellowstone Valley*, pp. 505–506.

15. W. Paul Hoppe, grave stone at Mountain View Cemetery, Livingston, Montana; Whithorn, *Twice Told*, vol. 3, p. 3; Whithorn, *Photo History of Gardiner*, p. [41]. Walter's obtaining and working of this contract was announced in "Cinnabar and Surroundings," *Livingston Enterprise*, October 8, 1898, p. 7; "Local Layout," *Livingston Enterprise*, October 29, 1898, p. 5; "Notes from Bear Gulch," *Livingston Enterprise*, November 26, 1898, p. 1; and "Local Layout" [Walter buys equipment], *Livingston Enterprise*, May 6, 1899, p. 5.

16. "Local Layout" [George takes over Cinnabar hotel], *Livingston Enterprise*, March 25, 1899, p. 5; "George L. Hoppe," *Livingston Enterprise Souvenir Edition*, 1976, p. 57; Whithorn, *Twice Told*, vol. 3, pp. 2–3. Whithorn, *Photo History of Gardiner*, p. [41] says Walter's hotel at Jardine—showing a photo of it in 1905—burned in or about 1942.

17. Ancestry.com (Walter Hoppe), including Empey Family Tree references and the US Censuses of 1900 and 1920 for Gardiner. Walter's purchase of the Fitzgerald Hotel was announced in "Local Layout," *Livingston Enterprise*, June 14, 1902, p. 5. Walter's purchase of additional buildings in Jardine was reported in "Local Layout," *Livingston Enterprise*, August 1, 1903, p. 5.

18. "Local Layout" [Walter and Frank Holem purchase Gassert's ranch of 320 acres], *Livingston Enterprise*, December 12, 1903, p. 5. See also Harry Gassert conveyance by administratrix to W. M. Hoppe; and Harry Gassert by administratrix to Frank Holem, both on November 25, 1904, in Park County deed records, vol. 33, p. 550, the NE4 of S20; NW4 of NW4 of S21; and E2 of SW4 of S17, T9S, R8E. Frank Holem's conveyances to W. M. Hoppe occurred December 26, 1906, recorded at vol. 37, p. 147; and January 14, 1907, recorded at vol. 37, p. 159.

19. "Walter Hoppe Passes in City," *Park County News*, May 9, 1940, p. 1; "Walter Hoppe Dies," *Livingston Enterprise*, May 4, 1940; "First White Child

Born in Montana [Walter Hoppe] Died at Livingston," *Kalispell* (MT) *Daily
Inter Lake*, May 4, 1940, p. 5; US Census of 1910 for Gardiner and US Census of
1920 for Gardiner, both in ancestry.com (Walter Monroe Hoppe). McPherren,
Imprints, p. 241, says that Walter bought out some of the interests of his brothers
and Maggie, but he also sold $3,650 worth of property to brother Hughie in 1897
(per February 27, p. 5). For Walter's elk trapping, see "Sending Elk to New
Pastures," *Anaconda Standard*, March 16, 1913, p. 20; and "Twenty-Eight Head
of Elk Are Loosed," *Anaconda Standard*, April 1, 1914, p. 6. For Paul Hoppe,
see Whithorn, *Photo History of Gardiner*, p. 18; and Whithorn, *Photo History
from Yellowstone Park* (Livingston: *Park County News*, no date [1970]), p. 43. In
two 1941 interviews conducted by Elva R. Howard and reposited at Montana
State University, Mrs. Ella Hoppe recalled that Walter also owned a thousand
acres of property along the river and "ranched" it with about one thousand head
of cattle, using the brand "Lazy H," but eventually was forced to sell because of
the destructiveness of elk upon his hay and fences.

20. Author's telephone conversation with Bob Moore of Livingston, Montana, March 1, 2013. That a "Bozeman College" of some sort existed in Bozeman
in 1887 is evident from "Bozeman College," *Avant Courier*, September 15,
1887, p. 3. Albert at the Helena College is in "Local Layout," *Livingston Enterprise*, October 18, 1890, p. 3. Establishment of Montana State University and
Peter Koch's influence is discussed in Kim Allen Scott, ed., *Splendid on a Large
Scale: The Writings of Hans Peter Gyllembourg Koch, Montana Territory, 1869-
1874* (Helena: Bedrock Editions and Drumlummon Institute, 2010), pp.
337–339.

21. "Mining Men Fall Out—Albert Hoppe, Well Known in Butte, in Jail in
Spokane," *Anaconda Standard*, October 23, 1901, p. 9; "Local Layout" [case in
Spokane against Albert Hoppe dismissed], *Livingston Enterprise*, October 26,
1901, p. 5; "Local Layout" [Albert files lawsuit in Butte], *Livingston Enterprise*,
September 5, 1903, p. 5; "Local Layout" [Albert's lawsuit], *Livingston Enterprise*, September 24, 1904, p. 3. Photos of Harry Bush and Ada Miller Bush are
in Whithorn, *Photo History of Gardiner*, p. [35]. Background for the mining and
Mrs. Bush are in "Adverse Claimants Restrained" [Harry Bush arrives at Bear
Gulch], *Livingston Enterprise*, August 13, 1898, p. 1; and Whithorn, *Twice Told
on the Upper Yellowstone*, vol. 3, pp. 1–8. The US Census for 1900 at Gardiner
showed Albert Hoppe working as an "assayer." See also "Local Affairs" [Albert
moves to Spokane], *Park County Republican*, April 20, 1901, p. 3; and "Personal
Points" [Harry and Ada Bush move to Spokane], *Livingston Enterprise*, February 2, 1901, p. 6. A website titled "More Montana Ghost Towns," http://
www.legendsofamerica.com/mt-ghosttownsummaries4.html, has Harry Bush's
misfortunes. Lena Spiker Potter, who lived in Gardiner much of her life, believed

that Harry Bush "ran the company into the ground." Haines interview with Lena Potter, April 20, 1962, as cited.

22. "It's a Racy Story—H. Bush and Albert Hoppe Air Their Troubles in Police Court," *Livingston Post*, October 31, 1901, p. 1.

23. Bob Moore, e-mail to Lee H. Whittlesey, March 5, 2010, regarding his interview with Jack Monroe Hoppe (who discussed Ella Fitzgerald Hoppe). Albert was living in Cinnabar in April of 1900, and in May he resigned a job as census taker for Park County. See "Personal Points" [Albert "of Cinnabar"], *Livingston Enterprise*, April 7, 1900, p. 7; and "Local Layout" [Albert resigning], *Livingston Enterprise*, May 19, 1900, p. 5.

24. Ada Bush conveyance to Albert V. Hoppe, July 6, 1901, in Park County deed records, vol. 30, p. 231; Harry Bush conveyance to Albert V. Hoppe, July 6, 1901, in deed records, vol. 30, p. 233; Harry Bush *et uxor*, conveyance to Albert V. Hoppe, July 8, 1901, in deed records, vol. 30, p. 234. These conveyances were also reported in "Local Layout," *Livingston Enterprise*, July 13, 1901, p. 5. Albert paid what in those days was the usual one dollar consideration for the contract.

25. "Wants a Divorce," *Livingston Post*, April 17, 1902, p. 1.

26. "Albert V. Hoppe Dies from Tick Infection," *Park County News*, May 28, 1936, magazine section, p. 5; "Three Deaths Occur in Park County from Dread Spotted Fever," *Livingston Enterprise*, May 26, 1936, p. 2; "Rites for Spotted Fever Victim Held in City Yesterday," *Livingston Enterprise*, May 27, 1936, p. 6; "Spotted Fever Claims Resident of Gardiner [Albert Hoppe]," *Billings Gazette*, May 26, 1936, p. 3. The US Census of 1910 at Gardiner recorded that Albert Hoppe at that time lived on Walter's land as a "boarder."

27. "Local Layout" [two stories: wedding license and wedding ceremony at church], *Livingston Enterprise*, March 6, 1897, p. 5; "Local Matters" [wedding at Albemarle Hotel], *Livingston Post*, March 4, 1897, p. 3; "From Livingston" [wedding of George Hoppe], *Anaconda Standard*, March 11, 1897, p. 9; "Farmers Will Meet" [serenade of George and Georgetta Hoppe], *Anaconda Standard*, March 16, 1897, p. 10; "Local Layout" [George moves to Cooke], *Livingston Enterprise*, May 22, 1897, p. 5; "Local Layout" [Schreiber opens beer hall in Livingston], *Livingston Enterprise*, June 5, 1897, p. 5; "Local News" [George moves back to Gardiner], *Livingston Post*, September 30, 1897, p. 3; "Local Layout" [George returns to Gardiner and leases the Fitzgerald Hotel], *Livingston Enterprise*, October 16, 1897, p. 5; "All Over Montana" [social event], Helena *Independent*, January 4, 1898, p. 6. Ancestry.com (George L. Hoppe and Washington Death Records for Georgetta) says that Georgetta Schreiber was originally Georgetta Williamson, born May 1864 in Ohio, who died April 2 [or 12], 1915, at Seattle. Ida McPherren called Georgetta's first husband "Will Schreiber" (p. 237), and Horr's voting registration, pp. 63–64, 67–68, shows him as

W. H. Schreiber who was living at Horr in a "frame house Grand Avenue" in 1892 and in a "log house" in October of 1894. "Personal Points," *Livingston Enterprise*, March 24, 1894, p. 6, says that Schreiber was then justice of the peace at Horr, while "Local Layout," *Livingston Enterprise*, November 17, 1894, p. 5, says he was formerly manager for George Welcome at Horr but now will go to Bear Gulch to open a store. In 1897, Schreiber moved to Livingston to open a beer hall, per "Local Layout," *Livingston Enterprise*, June 5, 1897, p. 5. For bits of George Hoppe's mining, see "Mining Locations" [at Crevasse], *Livingston Enterprise*, June 29, 1895, p. 6; and "Heard at the Hotels," *Anaconda Standard*, November 12, 1900, p. 7.

28. "Local Layout" [George leases Park Hotel for another year], *Livingston Enterprise*, March 5, 1898, p. 5; "Park Hotel" advertisement for "Geo. L. Hoppe," in *Livingston Enterprise*, June 4, 1898, p. 6; "Local Layout" [George secures Cinnabar hotel and begins there on April 1], *Livingston Enterprise*, March 25, 1899, p. 5; "Local Affairs" [George now lives in Butte], *Park County Republican*, December 8, 1900, p. 3; "Personal Points" [George is visiting from Butte], *Livingston Enterprise*, December 8, 1900, p. 6; "In Livingston" [Mrs. George Hoppe will move to Butte], *Anaconda Standard*, January 6, 1901, p. 18; "Local Affairs" [George moving to Spokane], *Park County Republican*, January 19, 1901, p. 3; "Personal Points" [George now located in Seattle], *Livingston Enterprise*, September 21, 1901, p. 6; "Additional Local" [George and partner are opening a saloon and billiard parlor in Seattle], *Livingston Enterprise*, December 28, 1901, p. 6. See also US Census of 1900, June 1, 1900, at Cinnabar, in ancestry.com (George Lincoln Hoppe). An example of George's official stationery for the Cinnabar hotel is Frank Rose to Captain W. E. Wilder, May 27, 1899, Archive Document 2895, YNP Archives.

29. "Local Affairs" [George now lives in Butte], *Park County Republican*, December 8, 1900, p. 3; "Local Affairs" [George moving to Spokane], *Park County Republican*, January 19, 1901, p. 3. The Census of 1910 at Seattle showed that he was then married to Anna Hoppe and was a hotel proprietor. The Census of 1920 at Seattle showed that George L. Hoppe, fifty-one, was then married to Agnes L. Hoppe, age forty-five from Pennsylvania, and was a traveling salesman. Ancestry.com (George Lincoln Hoppe). Sale of his Leopold Hotel is in "Brief Local News," *Bellingham* (WA) *Herald*, December 2, 1922. Family member Bob Moore says that George was later a podiatrist, and both Maggie's and Albert's obituaries referred to him as "Dr. George Hoppe" of Seattle.

30. McPherren, *Imprints*, pp. 200, 253; "Personal Points" [Lee manages Laclede Hotel], *Livingston Enterprise*, October 11, 1890, p. 3; "Local Layout" [Lee marries Jessie Boomer], *Livingston Enterprise*, December 24, 1892, p. 5; "Local Matters" [Lee marries], *Livingston Post*, December 29, 1892, p. 3; "Local Layout" [Lee follows wife to Bozeman], *Livingston Enterprise*, July 22, 1893, p. 5;

"Local Layout" [Lee considering leasing a ranch in Bozeman], *Livingston Enterprise*, September 1, 1894, p. 5; "Local Matters" [Lee living in Livingston], *Livingston Post*, January 22, 1896, p. 3; "Aldridge Notes" [Lee opens store in Aldridge], *Livingston Enterprise*, April 10, 1897, p. 2; "Personal Points" [Lee is traveling salesman for a Philadelphia company], *Livingston Enterprise*, February 11, 1899, p. 6 (also the same column in the February 4 and 25 editions, showing that he lives in Bozeman); "Death of Jesse Hoppe," Bozeman *Avant Courier*, August 11, 1900, p. 3; "Livingston" [death of Jessie Boomer Hoppe on August 6], Helena (MT) *Independent*, August 13, 1900, p. 2; "Local Layout" [Lee gets smallpox and is taken to pest house], *Livingston Enterprise*, March 2, 1901, p. 5; "Additional Local" [Lee discharged from pest house], *Livingston Enterprise*, April 6, 1901, p. 6; "Committed Suicide" [Lee was night bartender for a while at Albemarle], *Livingston Enterprise*, April 13, 1901, p. 1; "Local News" [Lee moves to Pony, MT, for business], *Livingston Post*, November 14, 1901, p. 5; "Aldridge Notes" [Lee is visiting and soliciting orders for clothing], *Livingston Enterprise*, April 26, 1902, p. 8; "Delegates Chosen" [Lee selected to be Gardiner voting official], *Livingston Enterprise*, September 20, 1902, p. 1; "Aldridge Notes" [Lee represents the Helena Liquor Company], *Livingston Enterprise*, November 29, 1902, p. 2; "Lee Hoppe Very Ill," *Anaconda Standard*, July 26, 1905, p. 8; "Lee B. Hoppe Dies, Funeral Here," *Park County News*, March 5, 1942, p. 5. Jessie Boomer Hoppe's obituary in the *Courier* stated that she was born on August 18, 1876, in Nova Scotia. Ida McPherren says that Leander and Jessie split up in 1892 but apparently that was a temporary separation for they were involved in a lawsuit together in 1897 and still married when Jessie died in 1900. See "Local News," *Livingston Post*, October 21, 1897, p. 3 (Lee and Jessie Hoppe lawsuit) and the above obituaries for Jessie Hoppe. The document "Appointments of U.S. Postmasters" for Park County, Montana, vol. 59, at ancestry.com (under Leander Hoppe) shows that Leander B. Hoppe served as postmaster at Cinnabar from June 20, 1892, through July 5, 1893, and was replaced the following day by William A. Hall, who served through July 20, 1897, and was replaced the following day by Margaret Ann "Maggie" Williams. According to the 1941 interview with Ella Fitzgerald Hoppe, Jessie Boomer was half Indian. Because of that fact, Ella—a product of her era—referred to Jessie disparagingly. But descendant Jackie Lingle of Bourbonnais, Illinois, who is tracing Boomer genealogy, says that Jessie was not Indian. Photos of Jessie support Lingle's statement. Author's telephone conversation with Jackie Lingle, June 25, 2013.

31. "Lee B. Hoppe Dies Friday; Funeral Services to Be Held Sunday," *Livingston Enterprise*, February 28, 1942, p. 8; "Lee B. Hoppe Dies, Funeral Here," *Park County News*, March 5, 1942, p. 5; US City Directories for Helena and Miles City, 1904, 1909, 1916, at ancestry.com; US Census of 1930 for Gardiner, Montana, at ancestry.com. Leander Hoppe's marriage to Coda Belle Lyle is in

Western States Marriage Record Index, vol. 1, p. 297, at ancestry.com. See also the many citations in chapter eight about Albert Hoppe's later years, wherein Lee Hoppe lived with him at old Cinnabar.

32. McPherren, *Imprints*, p. 241. Hughie's marriage was published in "Local Matters," *Livingston Post*, October 2, 1895, p. 3, and it occurred either in late September or on October 1, 1895. His ranch claim is in "Local Layout," *Livingston Enterprise*, May 5, 1894, p. 5. The Livingston City Directory for 1904 (ancestry.com) shows that Hughie Hoppe was ranching at Tom Miner at that time. For Hughie's ranch in 1900, see Doris Whithorn, *Twice Told on the Upper Yellowstone* (Livingston: D. Whithorn, 2000), vol. 3, p. 24. For mention of Millicent Hoppe's "millinery shop" in Livingston, see "Local Affairs," *Park County Republican* (Livingston, MT), June 8, 1901, p. 3. Nothing is known of Hughie's short residence in Arkansas except for what the deed stated when he conveyed his half of the water rights on Reese Creek to his brother Albert in April of 1893. Hugh B. Hoppe "of Hot Springs, Arkansas" to Albert V. Hoppe, April 22, 1893, in Park County deed records, vol. 21, p. 61. Hughie Hoppe probably moved to Arkansas to make money for the family's Cinnabar dreams, because he returned home just after he purchased land at Cinnabar from a long-time family employee, Wash Northrup. See W. Y. "Wash" Northrup to H. B. Hoppe, et al., April 12, 1893, in deed records, vol. 21, p. 44, described as town lots in E2 of SW4 of S18, T9S, and R8E.

33. "Local Items" [assault charge], *Livingston Herald*, July 23, 1896, p. 3; "Picnic and Sports," [assault of laundress Katherine Kersey], *Anaconda Standard*, August 21, 1896, p. 9; "Gold in the River—From Horr to Aldridge" [Hugh Hoppe is a reviewer for the proposed new road], *Anaconda Standard*, May 18, 1896, p. 9; "Hugo B. Hoppe Passes Away at Emigrant," *Livingston Enterprise*, October 20, 1931, p. 8; "Last Rites for H. Hoppe to Be Held Thursday," *Livingston Enterprise*, October 21, 1931, p. 6; "Hugo B. Hoppe Dies at Emigrant Home Monday," *Park County News*, October 22, 1931, p. 1; McPherren, *Imprints*, pp. 241–242. Hugh's request for a park transportation license in 1897 is in Archive Document 2529, YNP Archives.

34. US Census of 1920 at Emigrant, Montana, in ancestry.com (Hugh B. Hoppe); "Emigrant [Dorothy Hoppe's wedding to Harry Busby]," *Park County News*, October 22, 1931, p. 4. See also [Dorothy Hoppe wedding], *Livingston Enterprise*, October 22, 1931, p. 3. For a photo of all five of the Hoppe sons in their old age (about 1930), see Whithorn, *Sixty Miles of Photo History*, p. [43].

35. The divorce of Bud and Maggie Williams was announced in "District Court—Sixth Day," *Livingston Enterprise*, January 18, 1890, p. 3. Bud's convictions for drunkenness were in *Livingston Enterprise*, March 15, "Police Court News," p. 3; and April 19, "Local Layout," p. 3.

36. "Local Layout" [marriage of Margaret A. Williams and Frank Holem],
Livingston Enterprise, December 24, 1898, p. 5; "Around the State" [marriage of
Williams/Holem], *Butte Weekly Miner*, December 29, 1898, p. 15; "Margaret
Holem Is Dead at Gardiner," *Anaconda Standard*, December 5, 1918, p. 8;
"Death Ends Life of Mrs. M. Holem," *Livingston Enterprise*, November 30,
1918, p. 5; "Mrs. Margaret A. Holem," *Park County News*, December 6, 1918, p.
6. "Appointments of U.S. Postmasters" for Park County, Montana, vol. 59, at
ancestry.com [under Leander Hoppe] shows that Maggie Williams, who later
called herself M. A. Holem, served as postmaster at Cinnabar from July 21,
1897, to May 23, 1903, but the Lutz book gives the closure date as June 15,
1903. Her rental of Bob Orem's shop in Gardiner is in "Local News," Gardiner
Wonderland, May 17, 1902, p. 3.

37. McPherren, *Imprints*, pp. 318, 347, 351, 353; Whittlesey, *Death in Yellowstone*, 2014, pp. 154–155. Ida stated that this "Mr. Allen" was "the shoe
cobbler" at Horr who fixed their shoes (probably G. W. Allen).

38. Bud Williams's voter registration is in "Horr-Cinnabar-Tom Miner Voting Records," October 23, 1894, pp. 75–76, Yellowstone Gateway Museum. See
also a mention of him in "Mining Locations," *Livingston Enterprise*, June 15,
1895, p. 4. If the family reported the finding of this skeleton, there is no mention
of it in the newspapers.

39. "Castle Cullings" [Morgan T. Williams at Castle], *Livingston Enterprise*,
August 7, 1897, p. 2.

40. McPherren, *Imprints*, p. 339.

41. "Local Layout" [value of Hugo's estate], *Livingston Enterprise*, April 11,
1896, p. 5. Mary Hoppe's estate, including sale of her land, was in "District
Court," *Livingston Enterprise*, June 22, 1895, p. 1; and the classified advertisement was on p. 7. See also June 29, 1895, p. 1; and January 25, 1896, p. 4.

42. McPherren, *Imprints*, pp. 196, 200–201. The kaleidoscopic quote is from
p. 205.

43. McPherren, *Imprints*, p. 226. Haines, *Yellowstone Story*, II, p. 102, mentioned cowboys instructing dudes in the art of "exhibition dancing" in Livingston, and he probably got that information from "Local Layout," *Livingston
Enterprise*, June 21, 1883, p. 3. See also the "frolicsome cowboys" of "Twenty
Years Ago," *Livingston Enterprise*, July 11, 1903, p. 4.

44. McPherren, *Imprints*, pp. 225–226. Ida mentioned another instance where
a rich tourist at Cinnabar paid the standard fifty dollars for a train from Livingston to bring up a case of champagne because Cinnabar did not have any.

45. The quotes are from McPherren, *Imprints*, pp. 209–210, 220–221, 229,
233, 247–249, 284. Chadbourn is in "Ranch Home of A. W. Chadbourn," photo
and article in *Livingston Enterprise Souvenir Park County*, 1976 reprint, p. 52;
and in "A. W. Chadbourn, Park County's Oldest Pioneer, Relates Some Thrilling

Details of Early Life," *Livingston Enterprise*, February 15, 1942. Chadbourn's first name in both land records and the census was *Allen*, but he went by "A.W." George Reeb would later show up in the newspapers as residing at Horr.

46. McPherren, *Imprints*, p. 273, acknowledged and cited in McLaird, *Calamity Jane*, p. 144.

47. McPherren, *Imprints*, pp. 264, 270, 285; "Horr-Cinnabar-Tom Miner, Voting Records," October 29, 1894, pp. 61–62; "Local Layout" [Brundage and North], *Livingston Enterprise*, December 29, 1900, p. 5.

48. Ed L. Nowels and Judith Murphy Belshaw, "Cinnabar Story Recalls Memories of Early Life of Coal Camp Area," *Park County News*, February 19, 1948, second section, p. 1.

49. Bill and Doris Whithorn, *Calamity's in Town*, p. 45, quoting their interview with Bill Darroch, Livingston, Montana, Spring 1962.

50. Author's conversation with Kathryn "Kay" Pilger Baker, at Town Café, Gardiner, Montana, April 14, 2008. Kay's parents were Henry J. Pilger and Elizabeth M. Pilger, previously of Cinnabar, who moved to Gardiner when Cinnabar died. Kay Baker was born in 1922.

51. "Local Affairs," *Park County Republican* (Livingston, MT), May 31, 1902, p. 3. Calamity's walks in 1901 are discussed in Whithorn, *Calamity's in Town*, p. 31, quoting "Calamity Jane Dies," *Livingston Post*, August 6, 1903, p. 1. There are numerous histories of Calamity Jane's life, but many are filled with malarkey. The most reliable one (previously cited) is by James D. McLaird, who sorted through the malarkey and produced a dependable history of Martha Jane Canary. He has stated that she never returned to Montana after she left on the train for South Dakota in December of 1902.

52. A. W. Chadbourn to George W. Wakefield, November 19, 1901, in Park County land records, vol. 22, p. 610. Wakefield sold this land three years later to L. H. Van Dyck, March 23, 1904, in vol. 32, p. 615.

53. Whittlesey, *Death in Yellowstone*, 2014, p. 209.

54. Archive document 672, YNP Archives.

55. "Cinnabar and Gardiner," *Livingston Enterprise*, June 4, 1892, p. 2; "Out of the Park—W. A. Hall's Transportation Privilege Suspended and His Outfits Confiscated," *Livingston Enterprise*, August 12, 1893, p. 1; "Called Down and Escorted Out," *Livingston Enterprise*, August 19, 1893, p. 1. The lawsuit against Sam Brown is in "Local Layout," *Livingston Enterprise*, November 7, 1891, p. 3, and "Personal Points" on the same page.

56. Archive documents 2665, telegram, July 1897; 3413, June 2, 1898; 5188, September 11, 1902, YNP Archives.

57. Archive documents 3382, 3384, 3406, 3407, 3408, 3409, 3415, 3863, 3871, and 3879 (years 1891–1900), YNP Archives.

58. *Livingston Enterprise Souvenir*, 1976 reprint, p. 57; Archive documents 3407, 3861, 5167, 5186, 5189, 5352 (years 1898–1899 and 1902–1903), YNP Archives. Licenses were sometimes reported in newpapers; for example, see "Park Privileges," *St. Paul Daily Globe*, June 13, 1893, p. 1.

59. Archive documents 5171, 5181, YNP Archives; "Local News," *Livingston Post*, March 21, 1901; "Additional Local" [Wakefield and Chadbourn] *Livingston Enterprise*, March 23, 1901, p. 6; "George W. Wakefield, Pioneer of Montana, Dead," *Livingston Enterprise*, June 5, 1917, p. 3.

60. George S. Anderson, *Annual Report of the Superintendent of Yellowstone . . . 1893* (Washington: GPO, 1893), p. 5.

61. Archive document 2690, January 20, 1896, YNP Archives; Whithorn, *Photo History of Aldridge*, p. 9; "Local Layout" [preaching], *Livingston Enterprise*, January 25, 1896, p. 5; "In Livingston," *Anaconda Standard*, August 9, 1896, p. 13; "Cinnabar Observations" [Rev. Edmondson], *Livingston Enterprise*, May 19, 1900, p. 7.

62. "Little Town of Gardiner," poem by "Twin Sister" in "Gardiner News," *Livingston Enterprise*, October 17, 1903, p. 7.

63. See generally Roberta Carkeek Cheney and Clyde Erskine, *Music, Saddles and Flapjacks: Dudes at the OTO Ranch* (Missoula: Mountain Press, 1978; second edition, 2000); Dick Randall, *Ah, Yellowstone* (Washington, DC: Defenders of Wildlife, 1978); Babcock, *History of the Yellowstone Valley*, pp. 504–505 (James "Pretty Dick" Randall); and the George Perkins collection of OTO materials, YNP Library.

64. *Livingston Enterprise Souvenir Edition*, 1976 reprint, pp. 57–58, including a photo of the ranch. McCune was probably a relative of the Andrew McCune whose shooting in a disagreement with "Specimen Schmidt" is chronicled in Whittlesey, *Death in Yellowstone*, 2014, p. 221. For Mary McCune, see Babcock, *History of the Yellowstone Valley*, pp. 581–582.

65. All of these incidents appear with citations in Whittlesey, *Death in Yellowstone*, 1995, 2014.

66. Sarah A. Brooks, "Through the Yellowstone Park with the Dispatch Excursionist," *St. Paul* (MN) *Dispatch*, August 25, 1900, p. 11. The interment quote is from "Cinnabar and Surroundings," *Livingston Enterprise*, October 8, 1898, p. 7.

67. Observer, "Cinnabar Items," *Livingston Enterprise*, July 1, 1899, p. 1. The platform-dancing quote appeared in "Horr Items," *Livingston Enterprise*, August 5, 1899, p. 1.

68. Vincent, "Cinnabar Observations," *Livingston Enterprise*, May 26, 1900, p. 7; Vincent, "Cinnabar Observations," *Livingston Enterprise*, May 19, 1900, p. 7.

69. "Feigned Insanity," *Livingston Enterprise*, May 4, 1901, p. 1.

70. "Local Layout" [amount of freight for Gardiner and Cinnabar], *Livingston Enterprise*, April 25, 1903, p. 5; Frank Roberts in Gerald L. Bateson, *Growing Up in Yellowstone* (Gardiner: Pumice Point Publishing, 2011), p. 132.

10. "WAIL OF A CINNABARITE"

1. "Gardiner the Terminus," Gardiner *Wonderland*, May 17, 1902, p. 1; Sarah Gassert, "They're Going to Build a Railroad, or the Wail of a Cinnabarite," *Livingston Enterprise*, December 21, 1901, p. 2.

2. "Cinnabar Clippings," *Livingston Enterprise*, February 22, 1902, p. 1; "To Extend to Gardiner," *Anaconda Standard*, May 5, 1902, p. 2; "Will Be Extended," *Park County Republican* (Livingston, MT), May 10, 1902, p. 1; "Road to Gardiner—Northern Pacific Will Build from Cinnabar to Park Line," *Livingston Enterprise*, May 10, 1902, p. 1; "Gardiner the Terminus," Gardiner *Wonderland*, May 17, 1902, p. 1; "Local Layout" [NP railroad officials traveling to Cinnabar], *Livingston Enterprise*, May 17, 1902, p. 5. The Robert Cutler affair is complex and there is some mystery in it. A search in the Park County clerk's office of the grantor/grantee indexes (under "Cutler," "McCartney," "Stone," and even "Northern Pacific Railroad" as grantee) in warranty deeds, mining claims, and miscellaneous actions (leases, contracts, assignments, and even mortgages) has failed to turn up either a conveyance to or from Cutler of a piece of land between Cinnabar and Gardiner, or a mining claim or other action about such a claim on any land between Cinnabar and Gardiner owned by Cutler during the period 1879 to 1905. Any of these could have blocked the railroad's right-of-way to Gardiner. If Cutler indeed "jumped a claim," perhaps that fact has figured into why this author cannot locate such a relevant conveyance, mining claim, or other action in the land records of Park County (although one would think that the jumped claim was most likely to have been Ed Stone's).

That Cutler had such a claim is apparent from snippets in the Bozeman *Avant Courier*. These snippets make it appear that Cutler had disposed of his leaseholders and that Stone had gotten rid of the Cutler problem by May of 1883. The *Courier* stated in May that McCartney's land transfer to Ed Stone had occurred and so had "Buckskin Jim's subsequent disposal of lease-holds." Embracing the recent Chinese exclusionary law as a metaphor, it stated that Ed Stone took legal measures to have Buckskin Jim "fired" from Stone's new premises in Gardiner and "Buckskin Jim must [now] take the course of the Chinese, whom it is decided shall go." See "House Building in the Park," Bozeman *Avant Courier*, May 17, 1883, p. 3; and "Local Miscellany" [Cutler excluded from Stone-McCartney land conveyance], *Avant Courier*, May 24, 1883, p. 3. For the earlier transactions between McCartney and Stone, see "Visit of the NP Magnates,"

Avant Courier, October 19, 1883, p. 3; and "Jelly-Cake" [McCartney sells land to a Northern Pacific official for $1,500], same issue, same page.

Despite these claims in May, the *Enterprise* noted on August 20 that "arrangements could not be made by which Buckskin Jim's claim upon the Gardiner townsite could be transferred to the Northern Pacific and hence the new location at Cinnabar." "Local Layout," *Livingston Enterprise*, August 20, 1883, p. 3. So apparently Cutler's relinquishment of his mining claim came later.

Regardless of however and whenever Cutler was ultimately excluded from the process, the blockage then became a matter of who owned the Gardiner townsite. But it is strange that there are no 1901–1902 discussions in either the *Livingston Enterprise* or the *Livingston Post* about how Cutler had blocked access for so long. Instead, those newspapers concentrated on the role of the owners of the Gardiner townsite in blocking the NP railroad. Discussions in the *Enterprise* about realistically extending the rails to Gardiner began in its edition of December 14, 1901 ("Gardiner Gatherings," p. 6) when the newspaper announced that "an option has been secured on the townsite for ninety days." Thus we know that ownership of the Gardiner townsite (in section 23) was tied into the blockage. But the railroad's needed right-of-way from Cinnabar to Gardiner was in sections 16 and 22, and exactly how this needed land strip in those sections was released remains murky. The *Enterprise* made another announcement in its issue of March 15, 1902 ("Local Layout," p. 5). There the paper announced that Mrs. Clara McCutcheon of California sold the Gardiner townsite to Gardiner businessman C. B. Scott for thirty five hundred dollars, and Scott transferred one-third interest in those lands to James McCartney and Larry Link, and then all three men sold them to the Northern Pacific. (Scott apparently spent the ninety days gathering the money from these two business owners and from his own devices). While the railroad certainly needed lands in Gardiner for its buildings and ultimately its oval turnaround, it is the right-of-way to Cinnabar involving Cutler that remains somewhat mysterious. Clara McCutcheon's massive townsite conveyance to C. B. Scott is in Deed book, vol. 30, p. 390, recorded March 19, 1902; and the *Post* reported it in "Deeds in Gardiner Realty," *Livingston Post*, March 13, 1902, p. 3. Conveyance of the land for the railroad's oval turnaround ("loop track") is Harry W. Child to Northern Pacific, Deed book, vol. 30, p. 614, recorded November 21, 1902. See also "Local Layout" ["Mayor" McCartney explains resolution of Gardiner townsite], *Livingston Enterprise*, November 22, 1902, p. 5.

The *Post*'s explanation of the twenty-year delay in extending the rails centered on Ed Stone and did not mention R. E. Cutler. We quote their complete story here as follows: "It seems that one Ed. Stone had been employed by the Northern Pacific [in 1883] as a locator of townsites along the line of the road and that as soon as title had been acquired [to lands along the railroad's route generally] Stone transferred his rights to the company. He kept the faith for a long time [regarding the Gardiner land] but apparently thought that in the Gardiner townsite he had something the company must have, so he tried the hold-up game. When he delivered his ultimatum the grading was [already] done to within a mile of the town [Gardiner] and three miles beyond Cinnabar but it stopped short. His price was too high, and the company did not need the townsite so badly as the festive Stone imagined. After some years of waiting he sold his interest in the townsite to a Helena lawyer named McCutcheon. McCutcheon had afterward some domestic trouble and in the division of the property Mrs. McCutcheon acquired the Gardiner townsite, and some time afterward sold it to Messrs. Scott, Link, and McCartney, who are the present owners." "Going to Gardiner—Park Branch Will Be Extended," *Livingston Post*, May 8, 1902, p. 1.

Ed Stone sold some of his Gardiner land to Isaac McCutcheon of Helena on May 16, 1884. Two years later the Northern Pacific attempted to obtain the Gardiner townsite, or much of it, by filing a "Lis Pendens" (pending lawsuit) against those two townsite owners in an attempt to force the two men to convey the townsite to the railroad by claiming that they were trustees of the land for the railroad. See Northern Pacific, Lis Pendens against Stone and McCutcheon, October 11, 1886, at Miscellaneous 2, p. 379; "Local Layout" [Northern Pacific sues Stone and McCutcheon], *Livingston Enterprise*, October 16, 1886, p. 3; and Edwin Stone conveyance to Isaac McCutcheon at Deed Records, vol. 3, p. 304, sold May 16, 1884, and recorded April 30, 1885. That attempt failed, because subsequent deed records show that Stone and McCutcheon remained the owners of the townsite and Mrs. McCutcheon did the selling to C. B. Scott in 1902, who of course sold pieces to McCartney and Link before all three of them sold all to the NP railroad.

3. "Local News" [Hartman], *Livingston Post*, October 9, 1902, p. 5.

4. Haines, *Yellowstone Story*, II, pp. 51, 230. The chronology of the railroad's extension to Gardiner can be followed in "Passengers Transferred [for first time] at Gardiner," Gardiner *Wonderland*, July 3, 1902; "The Yellowstone Park Terminus," July 3, 1902; "Local News," July 31, 1902; "Local News," November 20, 1902; "Local News," March 5, 1903; and "Local News," April 2, 1903. The new Reamer depot was announced as being planned in "Local Layout," *Livingston Enterprise*, March 28, 1903, p. 5. It was nearly completed by July 2, 1903, per "The New Depot," Gardiner *Wonderland*, July 2, 1903, p. 1; and its completion and the arch's first travelers were reported in "Local Layout," *Livingston Enterprise*, July 11, 1903, p. 5. Actual completion of the arch is described in Lee H. Whittlesey and Paul Schullery, "The Roosevelt Arch: A Centennial History of an American Icon," *Yellowstone Science* 11 (Summer, 2003): 8. Demolition of Cinnabar is in "Local and Personal" [Cinnabar will soon be a memory], *Billings Gazette*, April 10, 1903, p. 5.

5. Inquirer, "Wants to Know," Gardiner *Wonderland*, June 18, 1903, p. 2. Pettigrew's biography—printed because he was running for state representative—was published in "The Legislative Ticket," *Livingston Enterprise*, October 11, 1902, p. 4.

6. L.T.S., "Wants Some Law and Order," Gardiner *Wonderland*, June 18, 1903, p. 1. Mr. Stoll was the only person bearing the initials "L.S." who appeared in the 1900 US Census for Gardiner.

7. "Our New Jail" [planning for it], Gardiner *Wonderland*, June 4, 1903, p. 1; August 6, 1903 [jail almost finished].

8. The town's new water and electrical systems were announced in "Getting Lively—Gardiner Will Be an Active Little City This Summer," *Livingston Enterprise*, March 28, 1903, p. 1; and "It's Little But It's Right Up to Date," *Anaconda Standard*, October 20, 1901, p. 6. Both the railroad's new wagon road past the loop track and the ground-breaking for Van Dyck and Deever appeared in "Hall Will Move," *Livingston Enterprise*, March 7, 1903, p. 1. Plans for the park's new fence appeared in "Fire at Jardine," *Livingston Enterprise*, April 4, 1903, p. 1; and the fact that Billy Torbert built it was reported in "Ordered to Manila—People of Gardiner," *Livingston Enterprise*, May 2, 1903, p. 1. Some background for Gardiner's response to Cinnabar's death is in Jared L. Infanger, "Gardiner's Historic Resources: Gardiner Historic Resource Survey," unpublished draft manuscript being reviewed by author, May 2013, pp. 18–19. See also "Town of Gardiner Experiencing a Boom," *Anaconda Standard*, June 2, 1903, p. 3.

9. "Blaze at Cinnabar," Gardiner *Wonderland*, May 17, 1902.

10. "A Wreck at Cinnabar," Gardiner *Wonderland*, June 12, 1902.

11. "'Wash' Northrup Dead," *Anaconda Standard*, July 2, 1902, p. 3; Gardiner *Wonderland*, May 17, June 12, November 27, July 3, 1902; January 8 and May 28, 1903; "Getting Lively—Gardiner Will Be an Active Little City This Summer" [Holem has contracted moving his "store" to Gardiner], *Livingston Enterprise*, March 28, 1903, p. 1; "Was a Great Day" [Holem's building used by Masons], *Livingston Enterprise*, April 25, 1903, p. 1. Prior to 1893, Wash Northrup and his wife owned the southeast quarter of section 18, high up on Reese Creek above Sawmill Creek, but sold it to Hugh B. Hoppe on April 12, 1893 (vol. 21, p. 44).

12. Park County Deed Records, vol. 1, p. 66, Hoppe et al. to Gassert and Redding, October 10, 1887. Land records spell Jacob Redding's name in that manner, but the newspapers often made it "Reding." Edith Ritchie remembered in a 1961 interview that Harry Gassert "rented teams" to visitors for many years. Aubrey Haines interview with Edith Ritchie, November 7, 1961, audiotape 61-3, side two, YNP Library.

13. "Gardiner Gatherings" [an option to purchase Gardiner townsite secured for ninety days with no mention of Robert Cutler], *Livingston Enterprise*, December 14, 1901, p. 6.

14. Gassert, "They're Going to Build a Railroad," *Livingston Enterprise*, December 21, 1901, p. 2. Clara McCutcheon's land sales to the named Gardiner residents are in Deed records, vol. 22, pp. 318, 357, 366, 398, 424, 492, and others in that volume.

15. "Gardiner or Cinnabar?" Gardiner *Wonderland*, June 5, 1902; "The Yellowstone Park Terminus," Gardiner *Wonderland*, July 3, 1902.

16. The photo appeared in Bill and Doris Whithorn, *Photo History of Gardiner*, p. [2]; in Doris Whithorn, *Twice Told on the Upper Yellowstone*, vol. 1, p. 17; and in Lee H. Whittlesey and Paul Schullery, "The Roosevelt Arch: A Centennial History of an American Icon," *Yellowstone Science* 11 (Summer, 2003): 11.

17. President Roosevelt's dedication of the arch at Gardiner is in Whittlesey and Schullery, "The Roosevelt Arch," pp. 2–24; and in all of volume one of Doris Whithorn, *Twice Told on the Upper Yellowstone*. For TR and Yellowstone generally, see Paul Schullery, "A Partnership in Conservation—Theodore Roosevelt and Yellowstone," *Montana the Magazine of Western History* 28(3): 2–15, Summer, 1978; Theodore Roosevelt, *Outdoor Pastimes of an American Hunter* (New York: Charles Scribner's Sons, 1920), pp. 320–351; and John Burroughs, *Camping and Tramping with Roosevelt* (Boston: Houghton Mifflin, copyright 1907). TR's local itinerary was published in "A Ten Minute Stop," *Livingston Enterprise*, April 4, 1903, p. 1.

18. A.N.B., "With the President," *Butte* (MT) *Inter Mountain*, April 10, 1903, pp. 4, 6.

19. R. H. Hazard, "Sidetracked for Sixteen Days at Cinnabar," *Washington* (DC) *Times*, April 26, 1903, magazine section, p. 2. Hazard mischaracterized Maggie Holem's relationship to any or all of Cinnabar's store owners. A shorter and less satisfying version of Hazard's article is "This Is a Sad Tale," *Livingston Enterprise*, May 9, 1903, p. 1.

20. Ibid.

21. "This Is a Sad Tale," *Livingston Enterprise*, May 9, 1903, p. 1.

22. "Local News," Gardiner *Wonderland*, May 28, 1903; "Local Layout" [Cinnabar depot moved to Gardiner for freight depot], *Livingston Enterprise*, May 30, 1903, p. 5; Craig Reese, "The Gardiner Gateway to Yellowstone," *The Mainstreeter* (Northern Pacific Railway Historical Association) 15 (Spring, 1996): 6. Postal information is from Dennis Lutz, *Montana Post Offices and Postmasters*. Whithorn, *Paradise Valley on the Yellowstone*, p. 27, gives the post office closure date as May 23, 1903, but Maggie Holem waited for the final letters. The park photo collection contains the following photos of the town of

Cinnabar and its immediate vicinity: YELL 298, 20153, 20154, 20155, 33305, 33370, 37112, 39016.

23. "Additional Local" [Eva Cutler files for divorce], *Livingston Enterprise*, June 15, 1901, p. 6; "Livingston and Park" [Cutler divorce], *Anaconda Standard*, February 10, 1902, p. 8; "District Court" [Cutler divorce], *Livingston Enterprise*, January 25, 1902, p. 2; "Additional Local" [Cutler divorce], *Livingston Enterprise*, February 8, 1902, p. 6; Haines interview with Mrs. Robert (Harriette) Cutler, December 13, 1961, YNP Archives. For a biography of Robert E. "Buckskin Jim" Cutler, see Babcock, *History of the Yellowstone Valley*, p. 519.

24. Helena *Independent* quoted in "Montana News," *Livingston Enterprise*, July 18, 1896, p. 7; Aubrey Haines, interview with Lena Spiker Potter, April 20, 1962, Gardiner, Montana, YNP Archives. Lena Potter knew Robert and Eva Cutler and stated that Eva was "sweet" but that Robert "was naturally a mean man" who seemed to reform a bit after he married Harriette E. Ball of Horr. They obtained a marriage license in late December of 1902, per "Additional Local," *Livingston Enterprise*, December 27, 1902, p. 6.

25. Gardiner *Wonderland*, November 20, 1902, p. 1; December 4, 1902, p. 1.

26. Grace E. Hecox, "Trip Thro' Yellowstone Park," in Doris Whithorn, ed., unpublished "Women's Stories of Early Trips Through Yellowstone Park," no date [1990s], YNP Library, p. 3; Archive document #4138, YNP Archives; "Our Towns," Gardiner *Wonderland*, vol. 1#1, May 17, 1900, p. 1; "George L. Hoppe," *Livingston Enterprise Souvenir Park County*, 1976 reprint, p. 57; Violet Sievert, "Diary of Trip through Yellowstone August 1905," p. 11, YNP library. The conveyances are in the Park County Clerk's office as follows: 3/24/00—26/98-101 and 3/31/08—35/502.

27. Horace Albright, "Memorandum for Judge Miller" (about his meeting with Walter and Albert Hoppe), August 16, 1932, Whithorn microfilm, YNP Archives. Albert Hoppe had purchased lots 2 and 3 in section 16 and lot 2 in section 17 (all riverfront property at Cinnabar) in 1893 (Smith and Wyman to Albert V. Hoppe, May 5, 1893, in vol. 6, p. 531) but sold it all back to his father Hugo in 1895 (Albert Hoppe to Hugo J. Hoppe, January 3, 1895, in vol. 21, p. 412). Hoppe family historian Bob Moore says that the Whithorn microfilm came to exist through the efforts of Wayne and Pat Hoppe. Wayne was the son of Paul Hoppe and grandson of Walter Hoppe.

28. The story is documented in Whittlesey, *Death in Yellowstone*, 2014, pp. 220–221.

I I. OLD CINNABAR

1. Paul Schullery and Lee H. Whittlesey, "Documentary Record of Wolves and Related Wildlife Species in the Yellowstone National Park Area Prior to 1882," in *Wolves for Yellowstone: A Report to the United States Congress*, John Varley and Wayne Brewster, eds. (YNP: Yellowstone Research Division, July 1992), pp. 96, 159. I used primary sources in this chapter to determine what was actually going on at that time, but this period in Yellowstone's history—when the elk population and its issues and supposed "extermination" were first coming to full national attention and controversy—has also been studied by both ecologists and historians, and they have provided in more recent years additional context and backdrop against which the Cinnabar land transfers were played out. Perhaps the most important sources are Doug Houston, *The Northern Yellowstone Elk: Ecology and Management* (New York: Macmillan, 1982); James A. Pritchard, *Preserving Yellowstone's Natural Conditions: Science and the Perception of Nature* (Lincoln: University of Nebraska Press, 1999); and Norman A. Bishop, Paul Schullery, Francis J. Singer, and John D. Varley, *Yellowstone's Northern Range: Complexity and Change in a Wildland Ecosystem* (Yellowstone National Park: National Park Service, 1997).

2. Horace Albright, "Annual Report of Superintendent . . . 1919" (Mammoth: mimeographed, 1919), p. 54; 1920, pp. 92–93. Douglas Houston's 1982 book has pointed out numerous errors in Albright's thinking here. Houston believes that Albright had it really wrong about the scale of the winterkills, and he cited on-the-ground counts by park and forest staff that simply got lost in the confusion of public statements by Albright and others. Houston stated that the alleged big winterkill of 1919 that seems to have actually worked its way into some wildlife management textbooks was likely to have been an overstated account. Houston, *The Northern Yellowstone Elk*, pp. 12–14, and Appendix III.

3. "Offered Lands" (Hoppe Ranch), no date, about 1931; Roger Toll to George D. Pratt, September 12, 1930, both on Whithorn microfilm.

4. Woodrow Wilson, Executive Order 2599, "Land Withdrawal [in Montana] for Classification and Pending Legislation for Game Preserve," April 16, 1917; Woodrow Wilson, Executive Order 3053, "Montana, Temporary Withdrawal of Certain Described Lands Pending Legislation," February 28, 1919. See also "Executive Order, Montana," April 16, 1917; and "Memorandum," no date, but cites Cochran's telegram of October 24, 1928, both on Whithorn microfilm.

5. H. S. Graves and E. W. Nelson, *Our National Elk Herds: A Program for Conserving the Elk on National Forests about the Yellowstone National Park*, US Department of Agriculture Circular 51 (Washington, DC: US Government Printing Office, 1919). See also "Offered Lands" (Hoppe Ranch), no date, about

1931, Whithorn microfilm; and Arno B. Cammerer to Burton K. Wheeler, January 3, 1938, in box L-10, file 602, YNP Archives.

6. Albright, "Annual Report of Superintendent . . . 1926," p. 39; Albright and W. M. Rush, "Memo for Mr. Thomas Cochran Re: winter feeding grounds for elk, antelope, and deer," no date [about 1928], Whithorn microfilm.

7. HMA to Senator Walsh (Montana), February 26, 1926 and HMA to George D. Pratt, November 19, 1925, both in Whithorn microfilm.

8. Toll to Kelley, August 12, 1929; Albright and W. M. Rush, "Memo for Mr. Thomas Cochran Re: winter feeding grounds for elk, antelope, and deer," no date, about 1929, both in Whithorn microfilm.

9. "More Range Provided for Yellowstone Herds," *Billings Gazette*, June 1, 1926, p. 10; "Finds State Roads in Fair Condition" [resurfacing on road through Yankee Jim Canyon to begin on June 21], *Billings Gazette*, June 17, 1926, p. 7.

10. Thomas Sidebotham to HMA, November 15, 1926, Whithorn microfilm.

11. Albright, "Memorandum for Secretary [of Interior] Dixon," January 27, 1932; Albright, "Copy," November 2, 1923, Whithorn microfilm; "Monthly Report of Superintendent," May, 1918, p. 5.

12. Plaintiff's reply to defendant's answer in *Game Preservation Company v. Albert V. Hoppe and Lee V. Hoppe*, January 9, 1932; HMA to Thomas Cochran, July 16, 1925, Whithorn microfilm.

13. Albright, "Memorandum for Secretary [of Interior] Dixon," January 27, 1932; "Interrogatories" with Horace M. Albright in court case of *Game Conservation Company v. Albert V. Hoppe*, June 2, 1932, Whithorn microfilm.

14. Albright to Senator Walsh (Montana), February 26, 1926, Whithorn microfilm. In a letter dated November 2, 1925, D. J. Fitzgerald (bank official) stated he had received the signed deed from the Hoppes and asked Albright to sign the attached contract allowing them to remain on the land until April 1, 1926. The Hoppe ranch was described in a solicitor's opinion as 972.21 acres on T9S, R8E: Lots 2, 3, & 6, and the W2 of SW4 of S16; lot 2, and the SE4 of NE4, the W2 of the NE4, the SE4, and the W2 of S17; NE4 of S20, NW4 of NW4 of S21, save and excepting the right-of-way of the Northern Pacific, together with 300 inches of the waters of Reese Creek as decreed on May 26, 1905, and all water rights from Stephens Creek and Wilson Springs appurtenant to the land. Solicitor's opinion (E. C. Finney), #M26413, March 20, 1931, Whithorn microfilm. The ranch's ten buildings are described and a map shown in "Offered Lands," no date [1931?], Whithorn microfilm.

15. M. F. Daum to Director of NPS, April 5, 1928; George D. Baggley, "Memorandum for Mr. [Guy] Edwards," no date, probably 1930 or 1931, Whithorn microfilm. The NPS took over management of the ranch in the spring of 1926, Chief Ranger Sam Woodring becoming its active manager who supervised its operations and the production of hay and feeding of game animals. Woodring

ran the ranch until May 1929, when he left and B. A. Hundley took over the duties of chief ranger and the ranch. The NPS stationed a laborer on the ranch each summer (including 1926) to irrigate the fields, repair fences, and keep trespassing stock from overrunning the premises. B. A. Hundley (Acting Superintendent), "Memorandum for the Director," April 2, 1930, Whithorn microfilm.

Hay operations on the Hoppe ranch were reported each year from 1927–1931 in the annual reports of the superintendent. Haying operations appear to have ceased in or about 1936, for a note by Jack Haynes says no haying has been done on Game Ranch for the "past couple of years" and that "none will be done this year (1938)." Haynes collection 1504, file 108:17, Montana State University.

16. HMA to Walter Hoppe, March 20, 1926, Whithorn microfilm.

17. HMA to George D. Pratt, November 19, 1925; Pratt to HMA, "Form of letter," no date [1925]; HMA to Thomas Cochran, November 6, 1925, Whithorn microfilm. It is apparent from this and other letters that there was considerable concern about the park's antelope that lived mostly on these private lands and that were thought to go to no other place in the winter.

18. This was the way that Superintendent Albright portrayed the elk and pronghorn situation, but subsequent studies by scientists and historians (cited in chapter 11, endnote 1) produced the opinion that Albright's assertions of a big die-off and slaughter in 1919 were terribly overblown. Douglas Houston, for one, reevaluated those claims in the early 1980s and decided that they were "patently incorrect." "Frankly," stated historian Paul Schullery recently, "I think Albright, whatever his thought processes or sincerity might have been, had complicated reasons for trumpeting this only partly real mortality." Confirmation for that statement awaits an extended study of Horace Albright, but as Schullery correctly points out, "It should be enough indication of how off-base Albright probably was about the elk that he could imagine that they somehow had the 'antelope problem solved now.' Pronghorn in this area have been in trouble ever since." Meanwhile Douglas Houston's interpretation about elk numbers historically remains the one that the National Park Service subscribes to today. Paul Schullery, e-mail communication to Lee Whittlesey, February 3, 2014; Houston, *The Northern Yellowstone Elk*, pp. 14–15 and Appendix III.

19. Guy Edwards to Regional Forester (Missoula), October 21, 1930, Whithorn microfilm.

20. See the quote of several pages ago about Walter Hoppe's having charge of the property one summer and being replaced because "he was not able to conduct it according to our policies." HMA, "Memorandum for Secretary Dixon," January 27, 1932, Whithorn microfilm.

21. HMA to Montana Fish and Game Commission, September 27, 1928, Whithorn microfilm.

22. HMA to Walter L. Linton (Secretary of Thomas Cochran), March 3, 1930; A. Hoppe to George Jordan, February 19, 1930; HMA to Toll, March 3, 1930; HMA to Albert Hoppe, March 11, 1930; A. V. Hoppe to Game Preservation Company, January 3, 1929, Whithorn microfilm.

23. HMA to A. V. Hoppe, May 10, 1930, Whithorn microfilm.

24. Miller and Miller, attorneys, to Guy Edwards, May 9, 1931; Comptroller General of US to W. M. Hoppe, March 20, 1931, Whithorn microfilm.

25. M. H. Wolff to Guy Edwards, April 6, 1931; Guy Edwards to Roger Toll, April 17, 1931; A. E. Demaray to park superintendent, June 26, 1931, Whithorn microfilm.

26. *Game Preservation Company v. Albert V. Hoppe and Lee B. Hoppe*, amended complaint, no date [1931], in suit to quiet title: "plaintiff avers that the said defendants claim and assert an interest [in the Game Ranch/Hoppe ranch] and that the claims . . . are without any right whatever." The complaint asked for defendants to set forth their claims clearly, that it be adjudged they have none, and that defendants be forever barred from so asserting said claim. See also Guy Edwards to Director of NPS, October 17, 1931, Whithorn microfilm.

27. Miller and Miller, attorneys, to Guy Edwards, November 3, 1931, Whithorn microfilm.

28. A. V. Hoppe to Secretary of Interior Joseph Dixon, January 3, 1932, Whithorn microfilm.

29. HMA, "Memorandum for Judge Miller" (on his meeting with Walter and Albert Hoppe), August 16, 1932; "Interrogatories" with HMA in Hoppe court case, June 2, 1932; Miller and Miller, attorneys, to park superintendent, May 29, 1931, Whithorn microfilm.

30. Guy Edwards to Director, September 9, 1932; Arno Cammerer to Walter L. Linton (secretary to Thomas Cochran), September 17, 1932; Joseph Joffe to HMA, September 3, 1932, Whithorn microfilm. Albert Hoppe's quitclaim (in vol. 62, p. 301, September 2, 1932) is attached to the Joffe telegram and gives the description of the disputed, adverse-possession parcels as lot 2 of S17, and lots 2, 3, and 6 of S16, all mostly north of the Northern Pacific and south of the river, in T9S, R8E. Chester Lindsley, "Chronology of Yellowstone," (typescript, YNP Library), p. 298, states that the land occupied by Albert and Lee Hoppe consisted of 38.2 acres. A "life estate," in legal parlance, is a "future interest" that allows a grantee to live on his land (or on the land of another) for the duration of his life but does not allow him to pass that land on to any heirs. At the time of the holder's death, the land reverts to the legal owner (who generally was the grantor that gave the "life estate" to the deceased). For the buildings, see "Description of Buildings to Be Disposed of in New Addition," no date, file 116.31, box L-10, YNP Archives. See also "Offered Lands," no date, for Hoppe ranch, Whithorn microfilm, which states that there were ten buildings on the Hoppe premises.

Perhaps five buildings had been removed by the time of this "Description" report.

31. Guy Edwards to Toll, January 25, 1934, Whithorn microfilm. At Albert Hoppe's death in 1936, Lee B. Hoppe was forced to move from the Cinnabar land. He lived for six more years, and he or Albert may have been the source of continuing stories within the family that the government had taken their land, when in fact Walter Hoppe had sold it.

12. TUSSLES OVER THE TRIANGLE

1. Herbert Hoover, "A Proclamation," no. 2013, at 47 Stat. 2537; "Privately Owned Lands," in box L-4, file 112.5, YNP Archives; Emmert to Toll, February 6, 1935, Whithorn microfilm. The incorrect figure of 1,288 acres left "inside" the park mistakenly included 125 acres of Roy Armstrong's land that were outside of the proclaimed park boundary. See also box L-10, file 116.31, YNP Archives; "Presidential Proclamation Declares 7,600 Acres Land Added to Yellowstone Park," *Livingston Enterprise*, November 2, 1932; Arno B. Cammerer to Burton K. Wheeler, January 3, 1938, in box L-10, file 602; Haines, *Yellowstone Story*, II, pp. 331–332. A recent map (no date, probably 1970s) of the entire Cinnabar triangle, showing ditches, diversions, and property statuses is in box L-21, manila envelope, YNP Archives. The private lands remaining in the park after the presidential order were as follows: NP Railroad 998 acres, Lena Bassett 20 acres (part of the "slaughter house ranch"), Roy N. Armstrong 39.7 acres, Anton Stermitz 100 acres, and W. M. Nichols 5 acres.

2. "No Politics in Territory Added to Yellowstone," *Livingston Enterprise*, November 4, 1932. See also "Park Area Order Result of Law Enacted Six Years Ago," *Park County News*, November 3, 1932.

3. A sample letter used in this campaign that was sent to landowners is C. B. Swim to W. T. McMurran, April 12, 1935, in file "W. T. McMurran," box L-13, YNP Archives. There are massive records for lands north of Yellowstone Park in the various L boxes.

4. "Privately Owned Lands," box L-4, file 112.5, YNP archives; J. Emmert to Roger Toll, February 6, 1935, Whithorn microfilm; "Presidential Proclamation Declares 7,600 Acres Land Added to Yellowstone Park," *Livingston Enterprise*, November 2, 1932. Roy Armstrong's links to the Cinnabar "triangle" extended to at least 1884, when his forebear William H. Armstrong purchased lot 6 and the W2 of SW4 of S16, T9S, R8E, from C. T. Hobart (deed at 6/210-—9/17/84, Park County deed books). Indeed, the Owen T. Armstrong who recorded a water right with Stirling Henderson on October 1, 1878, may have been a forebear of Roy Armstrong, vol. K, p. 546, Gallatin County land records; and Bill

and Doris Whithorn, *Sixty Miles of Photo History Upper Yellowstone Valley*, p. (9). Walter Hoppe also sold land in Section 12 to a "Ray" [Roy?] N. Armstrong in April of 1903, per "Real Estate Transfers," *Livingston Enterprise*, April 18, 1903, p. 1.

5. HMA to Thomas Cochran, September 17, 1925, Whithorn microfilm.

6. See deeds at 56/125—2/7/24 and 62/262—8/12/32, Park County Clerk's Office, Livingston, Montana. A copy of the warranty deed from Joseph and Kunigunde Stermitz to Anton Stermitz, dated June 27, 1932, is in file 610-01.1 "Purchase of Lands from Anton Stermitz," box L-15, YNP Archives.

7. Guy Edwards to NPS Director, October 27, 1930, Whithorn microfilm.

8. Emmert to Nichols, March 8, 1939, box L-4, file 610-01, YNP Archives.

9. Arno B. Cammerer to Senator Burton K. Wheeler, January 3, 1938, and resolution of Gardiner Commercial Club, December 20, 1938, both in box L-10, file 602; Cammerer to Wheeler, May 3, 1939, box L-4, file 610, YNP Archives.

10. Emmert to Supt. Rogers, February 21, 1939, in box L-4, file 610, YNP Archives. Some of the Grand Teton correspondence is in box L-10, file 602.

11. Joffe to Rogers, December 22, 1938, box L-10, file 602; Acting Solicitor to Secretary of Interior, July 22, 1938, box L-4, file 610, YNP Archives.

12. J. W. Emmert to Director of NPS, January 6, 1939, box L-10, file 602, YNP Archives.

13. Emmert to (Supt.) Edmund Rogers, February 25, 1939, box L-10, file 602; Emmert to Supt. Rogers, February 21, 1939, citing conversations with Paul Ross, in box L-4, file 610, YNP Archives.

14. Emmert to Supt. Rogers, January 30, 1939; G. A. Moskey to Conrad Wirth, July 5, 1939, both in box L-10, file 602, YNP Archives; "Bill to Oppose Adding Lands to Park Is Slated," *Billings Gazette*, January 27, 1939. See also "More Land for Park Is Fought," *Park County News*, February 4, 1939, and two other 1939 newspaper articles: "Loss of Taxable Land" editorial and "Government May Acquire More Land in Southern Park County," both in box L-4, file 610-01, YNP Archives.

15. Emmert to Director of NPS, March 25, 1939, box L-4, file 610, YNP Archives.

16. At that time there was no US highway 89 on the east side of the Yellowstone River, so all travel was on the west side of the river on the county dirt road, today called the "Old Yellowstone Trail." Stermitz's house and ranch buildings were located inside the park while Armstrong's buildings were outside the park. All visitors entering the area from the north passed through Armstrong and Stermitz properties to reach Gardiner.

17. J. W. Emmert to Director, April 14, 1939; Arno Cammerer to Senator Burton K. Wheeler, May 3, 1939, both in box L-4, file 610; Emmert to Director, January 6, 1939, box L-10, file 602, YNP Archives.

18. Arno Cammerer to Senator Burton K. Wheeler, May 3, 1939, box L-4, file 610, YNP Archives.

19. G. A. Moskey to Conrad Wirth, July 5, 1939; copy of H.R. 6975, introduced by O'Connor, June 23, 1939, in 76th Cong. 1st Sess., both in box L-10, file 602, YNP Archives. The federal court case of *Yellowstone Park Transportation Company v. Gallatin County, et al.*, 31 F.2d 644 (9th Cir. 1929), and other relevant legal cases and statutes are discussed in Arno Cammerer to Senator Wheeler, May 3, 1939, box L-4, file 610, YNP Archives. My thanks go to Steve Mishkin for providing me with information on both this court case and Congressman O'Connor's bill.

20. Edmund B. Rogers Memorandum for the Director, July 11, 1939, in file 610-01.1 "Purchase of Lands under Public Works Allotment," box L-15, YNP Archives.

21. Memorandum for Mr. Strasser from D. E. Lee, September 19, 1939, in box L-4, file 610, "Private Holdings (General)," YNP Archives. Both Bassett and the Child heirs agreed to sell their land to the NPS. For this story, see Whittlesey, "They're Going to Build a Railroad," as cited.

22. Maynard Barrows memorandum, October 26, 1939, box L-4, file 601, "Lands (General)"; "Option to Sell Real Estate to the United States Government," in box L-15, file 610-01.1 "Purchase of Lands from Anton Stermitz," YNP Archives. Strangely, some of this land seems to have been the same as that acquired by the NPS in 1930 from Ernest A. Rife. There was apparently a problem in quieting titles, for Rife had sold some of the old Reese property to the Stermitz family. A map of the triangular Stermitz property is included with the "Declaration of Taking" in file 610.01.1 "Purchase of Lands under Public Works Allotment, Part I," box L-15, YNP Archives. The Armstrong court case (copy at 21M/389, Park County land records) gives the price of the Stermitz land.

23. Hilory A. Tolson to H. L. Schantz, July 8, 1943; Edmund B. Rogers to Miles J. O'Connor, March 20, 1941, box L-4, file 610-01, "Purchasing of Lands," part two, 1940-43, YNP Archives.

24. "Declaration of Taking" in *U.S.A. v. 228 Acres of Land*, October 3, 1939, in file 610-01.1 "Purchase of Lands under Public Works Allotment (2)," box L-15, YNP Archives. See also J. W. Emmert to Anton Stermitz, January 25, 1941, file 610-01.1 "Purchase of Lands from Anton Stermitz"; Donald E. Lee (Acting Chief Counsel) to park superintendent, October 9, 1939, file 610-01.1 "Purchase of Lands Under Public Works Allotment (2)," both in box L-15, YNP Archives. The newspaper publication of the case statement is in *Livingston Enterprise*, May 4, 1940.

25. "Order Amending Final Judgment in Condemnation, *U.S.A. v. Roy N. Armstrong, et al.*, June 16, 1941, filed June 26, 1941; Hilory A. Tolson to YNP

supt., 5/21/41, both in box L-15, file 610-01.1, "Purchase of Lands Under Public Works Allotment (1)," YNP Archives.

26. Buntin to J. W. Emmert, January 21, 1943, in box L-15, file 610-01.1 "Purchase of Lands from Anton Stermitz under Public Works Allotment (1)," YNP Archives.

27. Edmund B. Rogers Memorandum for Director, December 7, 1940, in file 610-01.1 "Purchase of Lands from Roy N. Armstrong," box L-15, YNP Archives.

28. *U.S.A. v. Roy N. Armstrong, et al.*, At Law No. 74, "Order for Distribution," December 3, 1941; C. W. Buntin to Edmund B. Rogers, December 20, 1941, both in box L-15, file 610-01.1 "Purchase of Lands from Anton Stermitz," YNP Archives.

29. "Appraisal Sheet," in file 610-01.1 "Purchase of Lands from Anton Stermitz," box L-15, YNP Archives.

30. Edmund B. Rogers to Anton Stermitz, July 17, 1939, in file 610-01.1 "Purchase of Lands from Anton Stermitz," YNP Archives.

31. Fred B. Williams to Edmund B. Rogers, June 27, 1939; C. B. Swim to Anton Stermitz, April 11, 1935; "Tract Map—Surveyed Areas," February 20, 1935, all in box L-15, file 610-01.1 "Purchase of Lands from Anton Stermitz," YNP Archives.

32. "Proposed Work Plan," April 6, 1940, in file 610.01.1 "Purchase of Lands Under Public Works Allotment (1)," box L-15; "Topographic Map [of] Old Stermitz Place," no date (about 1940), NP-YEL 5554, YNP Archives. This author has been unable to find a large colored map that was apparently drawn of the Stermitz, Rife, Armstrong, Ross, Child, and other acquired properties about 1943. This map was striped and crosshatched in brown, blue, green, and red to indicate ownership with the various dates of deeds shown. The key/legend to this map is "Land Ownership Status of Additions to Yellowstone National Park, December 1, 1943," in file "Maps Showing Parcels," box L-11, YNP Archives.

33. The Armstrong land was described as "Parcel No. 4" in the court case: NW4 of SW4 [almost all] and the SW4 of NW4 [just a tiny portion] of Section 8 (T9S, R8E) "as lie within the boundaries of the Yellowstone National Park, containing 50 acres, more or less, of land." *U.S.A. v. Roy N. Armstrong, et al.*, "Judgment in Condemnation as to Tracts Numbered 1, 2, and 3," June 16, 1941, in file 610-01.1 "Purchase of Lands from Roy N. Armstrong," box L-15, YNP Archives. A warranty deed/indenture in the same file (copy) dated December 15, 1911, shows that Armstrong acquired the land on that date (along with a number of other parcels) from W. A. Hall and Larry Link, two Gardiner businessmen. For the original, see deed book, vol. 51, p. 338, Park County Clerk's Office, Livingston, Montana. A map of the Armstrong property is in the "Declaration of

Taking," October 3, 1939, in file 610-01.1 "Purchase of Lands under Public Works Allotment (2)," box L-15, YNP Archives.

34. C. B. Swim to Roy N. Armstrong, April 30, 1935, in file 610-01.1 "Purchase of Lands from Roy N. Armstrong," in box L-15, YNP Archives. Included in the file is a fold-up map of Armstrong's properties in the old townsite of Evandale, which he purchased from W. A. Hall and Larry Link in 1911.

35. Francis LaNoue to Superintendent Rogers, August 2, 1939; LaNoue to "The Files," January 20, 1942, both in file 610.01.1 "Purchase of Lands from Roy N. Armstrong Under Public Works Allotment (1)," box L-15, YNP Archives; "New Trial Denied by Federal Court in Armstrong Case," *Livingston Enterprise*, March 19, 1942.

36. Hand-drawn maps and "Forage Studies," in file 610-01.1 "Purchase of Lands from Roy N. Armstrong"; "Proposed Work Plan," April 6, 1940, file 610-01.1 "Purchase of Lands under Public Works Allotment (1)," both in box L-15, YNP Archives.

13. CONCLUSIONS

1. Some of this complex history, with its research and citations into the area's extensive land-title records, is available in Whittlesey, "They're Going to Build a Railroad," unpublished manuscript, 1995, YNP Library.

2. David Scott Dick et al., "Cinnabar Archeology," as cited. The restoration of vegetation discussion of today's Gardiner Basin is complicated and beyond the scope of this book, but it is worth remembering that physical changes in the land's vegetation occurred through long years and were arguably not the fault of individual landowners by themselves or of the NPS by itself, because both entities contributed. It is arguably not fair to judge agricultural settlers on the land in the same way that we look at a national park today, because those settlers were on the land before it was added to the park. (And too, historians caution against judging the past using rules of the present, because the past was a different time with different rules.) On the other side, valley residents today have sometimes blamed the NPS for "messing up the land," when it planted nonnative food crops on some parcels in an attempt to improve the land's forage value, and that blame is not fair either. Both sides need to remember the land's complicated history, and each side must shoulder a share of the blame for changing the vegetation. For current restoration measures, see E. William Hamilton III and C. Eric Hellquist, "Yellowstone's Most Invaded Landscape—Vegetation Restoration in Gardiner Basin," *Yellowstone Science* 20#1, 2012, pp. 25–31; and C. E. Hellquist, D. Frank, K. W. Ryan, and E. W. Hamilton III, "CO_2 Exchange of Native and Exotic Plant Communities in Gardiner Basin, Yellowstone National Park," in

*Proceedings of the Tenth Biennial Conference on the Greater Yellowstone Eco-
system* (C. Andersen, ed.), October 11–13, 2010, Mammoth Hot Springs Hotel,
Yellowstone National Park, pp. 105–113. See also Gardiner Basin Restoration
Workshop Steering Committee (including Yellowstone National Park, Gallatin
National Forest, and the Center for Invasive Plant Management), "Results of the
Gardiner Basin Restoration Workshop, April 19–21, 2005," unpublished PDF
available from Yellowstone Center for Resources, Yellowstone National Park,
Wyoming; and its briefing book (on CD) by same authors.

3. Burlington Northern Railroad to United States of America, two warranty
deeds dated April 28, 1972, for an equal value of national forestland, at microfilm roll 1, p. 547, Park County Land Office, Livingston, Montana.

INDEX

Ahart, Mrs. "Jumbo," 79
Alaska, 7, 8, 80, 82
Albany, Oregon, 79
Albemarle Hotel (Livingston, MT), 60, 137
Albright, Horace Marden (superintendent of YNP): elk issue, 171–172; land acquisition program, 172–181; Walter Hoppe's ranch: acquisition and conflicts, 174–181
Al Brundage and Company. *See* Brundage, Al
Aldridge, Montana, 15, 98, 108, 120; coal and coking operations, 109, 127; cornet band, 136; expansion, 109, 128, 196; Horr/Aldridge road, 109, 138, 145; religious services, 148; store of Leander B. Hoppe, 137; transportation operators in, 147
Allen, Chet and Irene, 108
Allen, Clarence Bradley, 108
Allen, John C., 148
Allen, Mr., 139
Allen, Mr. and Mrs., 139
Allen, W.H., Dr., 114
Anaconda, Montana, 20, 120
Anaconda (MT) *Standard* (newspaper), 98
A.N.B. (journalist), 162
Anderson, George S. (acting superintendent of YNP), 71, 72, 73, 98, 100, 111, 146, 147, 148

Anderson, James, 25
Anderson, Ole (specimen seller), 101
Apollinaris Spring (YNP), 124
Argentine republic, 51
Arkansas, Hot Springs, 138
Armstrong, Roy N., 184, 185–189, 190, 191, 192–193, 196
Armstrong ranch, acquisition, 184–193
Army, U.S., xiii, 24, 25, 104, 164; arrives in Yellowstone Park, 26
Arthur, Chester A. (President of U.S.), xiii, 12, 107
Atkins, Oliver, 150
Avant Courier (Bozeman, MT) (newspaper), 1, 13, 26, 29, 30, 38
Ayrhart, Mrs. "Jumbo". *See* Ahart, Mrs. "Jumbo"

Baker, Katherine "Kay" Pilger, 145
Ball, Harriette E. *See* Cutler, Mrs. Robert E. "Harriette"
Bank Saloon (Livingston, MT), 93
Barnes (assistant secretary), 164
Baronett, Collins John "Jack," 50–51, 65, 90
Barrows, Maynard, 186, 192
Bassett, Lena, 190, 191, 196
Bassett, Phillip, 149
Bassett, William, 90–91, 149
Bassett Creek, 91
Bates, Catharine (YNP traveler), 82

ABOUT THE AUTHOR

Lee H. Whittlesey is a professional historian for the National Park Service at Yellowstone National Park, Wyoming–Montana–Idaho. He is the author of ten published books. His most well-known book is *Death in Yellowstone: Accidents and Foolhardiness in the First National Park.* He lives and works in Yellowstone.